THE CONSERVATION
OF ANTIQUITIES AND
WORKS OF ART

DECORATED IVORY PLAQUE FROM NIMRÛD (9TH CENT. B.C.)

After treatment

For conditions before treatment see Plate 13

THE CONSERVATION
OF ANTIQUITIES AND
WORKS OF ART

Treatment, Repair, and Restoration

═══

SECOND EDITION

═══

H. J. PLENDERLEITH

DIRECTOR EMERITUS OF THE INTERNATIONAL CENTRE FOR
THE STUDY OF THE PRESERVATION AND
RESTORATION OF CULTURAL PROPERTY, ROME
(CREATED BY UNESCO)
PREVIOUSLY KEEPER OF THE RESEARCH LABORATORY
BRITISH MUSEUM

AND

A. E. A. WERNER

KEEPER OF THE RESEARCH LABORATORY
BRITISH MUSEUM

LONDON
OXFORD UNIVERSITY PRESS
NEW YORK   TORONTO
1971

Oxford University Press, Ely House, London W. 1

GLASGOW NEW YORK TORONTO MELBOURNE WELLINGTON
CAPE TOWN IBADAN NAIROBI DAR ES SALAAM LUSAKA ADDIS ABABA
DELHI BOMBAY CALCUTTA MADRAS KARACHI LAHORE DACCA
KUALA LUMPUR SINGAPORE HONG KONG TOKYO

SBN 19 212960 0

© OXFORD UNIVERSITY PRESS 1962, 1971

First published 1956
Reprinted (with revisions) 1962
Second edition 1971

The permanent paper on which this book is printed has
been made from specially refined chemical wood pulp
and contains a calcium carbonate filling to resist acidity.
It is sized with a neutral sizing agent, and has an esti-
mated theoretical useful life of about 500 years

PRINTED IN GREAT BRITAIN
AT THE UNIVERSITY PRESS OXFORD
BY VIVIAN RIDLER
PRINTER TO THE UNIVERSITY

TO OUR WIVES

ELIZABETH

AND

MARION

PREFACE TO THE FIRST EDITION

THIS book is concerned with the broad field relating to the restoration of antiquities and works of art, and with their subsequent preservation. It is intended as a handbook for the collector, the archaeologist, and the museum curator, and as a workshop guide for the technician.

As collectors know only too well, the acquisition of objects is but the first step towards their incorporation in the collection. In order to be able to appreciate and study the objects, it is usually necessary to clean, restore, and repair them, and *always* necessary to maintain a suitable environment which will ensure their stability whether in storage or on exhibition. In the following chapters simple instructions are given for cleaning and preservation, and the collector with a practical turn of mind who desires to carry out for himself the methods described can do so without any special technical training.

The archaeologist will find interest in the methods that science has to offer for the restoration of antiquities fresh from excavation and for revealing evidence of value to him in his researches. Many examples are given throughout the work, showing how unsuspected facts are brought to light during the normal course of laboratory investigation and treatment.

The requirements of the museum curator, who is not always in a position to call in the museum scientist, have been particularly considered, and it is hoped that this publication, which deals with the numerous causes of deterioration in museum objects and their treatment, will enable him to detect and arrest decay in its early stages, and also to carry out the simple cleaning operations that so often add interest and value to the material in a collection.

The subject-matter is necessarily very varied, based as it is upon the day-to-day problems that are presented in the Research Laboratory of the British Museum—problems relating to books, prints, drawings, manuscripts, textiles, coins, *objets d'art*, ethnographical specimens, and antiquities of all kinds. From this wide range of material examples have been selected that illustrate common types of deterioration, and an attempt has been made to recommend from among the various methods of treatment available those that have proved most effective and are at the same time relatively easy to apply. In order to preserve the balance, however, detailed descriptions are included of some of the major tasks of restoration that have been carried out. This has been done partly for the sake of interest, and partly to emphasize that it is impossible to prescribe for all contingencies; each specimen that is submitted for treatment presents its own individual problems, and standard methods of treatment may have to be adapted or new methods devised before a satisfactory restoration can be achieved. Whichever method of treatment is chosen, it should be applied so as to yield results that lie between the extremes of over- and under-cleaning, the aim being to realize the golden mean which will satisfy at the same time the requirements of science, art, and archaeology.

The special problems of the picture gallery have not been overlooked. In common with the museum, the picture gallery is vitally concerned with the stability of materials and methods of conservation, but the restoration of easel paintings is a highly specialized undertaking, and while instructions are given for carrying out some of the simpler studio processes, it is not the intention of the author to encourage the amateur to attempt intricate operations on valuable material. Such work is for the professional artist technician—one who has practical experience based upon a knowledge of the methods used by the Old Masters in the different schools of painting. It is important nevertheless that the collector or curator of paintings should himself be familiar with all aspects of picture conservation. He will then be able to discuss his problems in a knowledgeable way with the restorer, and take a personal interest in any treatment that may be required.

All the processes described herein have been tested, most of them at first hand, by the author. Many are standard methods that have been handed down through several generations, but some are offered for the first time. While the methods recommended are all based upon scientific investigation, the book is not written for the scientist. On the contrary, a conscious effort has been made to write for the non-scientist who has the responsibility of caring for art treasures. By presenting the material in this way it is hoped that the work will be of service to a wide range of readers not only in the museum world, but also in the home, where, indeed, many of our greatest treasures are still to be found.

I am greatly indebted to the members of my staff who have put their specialized knowledge at my service. In particular, my thanks are due to Dr. A. E. Werner for reading the manuscript and making many valuable suggestions; to Mr. R. M. Organ (metals); to Miss Mavis Bimson (stone, ceramics, and glass); to Miss Sylvia Schweppe for her help in collecting and collating the material; and to Mr. L. H. Bell for his help with photography.

H. J. P.

1956

PREFACE TO THE SECOND EDITION

THE phenomenal growth of interest in cultural property within recent years and the intensification of laboratory studies devoted to its conservation have provided the stimulus for a reappraisal of this book, which has now been brought up to date in many respects and partly rewritten.

While the general character of the work has been retained, the book now appears in a new guise under joint authorship, thus maintaining the valuable connection with the Research Laboratory of the British Museum where so much of the fundamental work on the development of scientific methods in the conservation of antiquities was first carried out.

The authors would like to express their sincere appreciation to their colleagues in the British Museum Research Laboratory for the co-operation that they have received from them in the preparation of this new edition. In particular thanks are due to Mr. A. D. Baynes-Cope (skin products and paper); to Miss Mavis Bimson (stone, ceramics, and glass); to Mr. W. A. Oddy and Mrs. H. Lane (metals); and to Mr. L. H. Bell for his help with photography. Thanks are also due to Mr. C. St-G. Pope, late of the National Parks Service, U.S.A., for his assistance in compiling the index.

H. J. P.

A. E. A. W.

1971

CONTENTS

PART III. SILICEOUS AND RELATED MATERIALS

APPENDIXES

LIST OF ILLUSTRATIONS

PLATES

FIGURES

ACKNOWLEDGEMENTS

Plate 7 is reproduced by gracious permission of Her Majesty The Queen.

Acknowledgements are due to the *Illustrated London News* for contributing the frontispiece; the British Leather Manufacturers' Research Association for permission to reproduce Pl. 1; the Dean and Chapter of York Minster for Pl. 18; the University of Aberdeen for Pl. 26; Walter Hege for Pls. 40 A and B; R. M. Organ for Fig. 7; for permission to reproduce all other illustrations the authors are indebted to the Trustees of the British Museum. The drawings were contributed by Mr. C. O. Waterhouse, M.B.E., of the British Museum.

INTRODUCTION
THE INFLUENCE OF ENVIRONMENT

THE condition of an antiquity or a work of art depends on two main factors—the materials of which it is composed, which vary enormously, and the conditions to which it has been subjected in the course of its life history. The materials in question may be divided, broadly, into two groups according as they are organic or inorganic in origin. The organic materials are generally considered to be the more susceptible to deterioration, but no single type of matter is stable under all conditions. It is equally true that when changes take place, these may be preponderantly chemical, physical, or biological in character, but they generally result from various types of deterioration being in operation at one and the same time.

Whatever may be the mechanism of change, the environmental conditions have an important influence upon the intensity of the action and a common factor here is the presence of air and moisture. The relative humidity[1] and temperature of the atmosphere have a profound effect on stability.

With the atmosphere in the museum under control (conditioned) it is possible to hold in check the major causes of decay. But it is natural for objects out of doors to be subject not only to widely varying hygrometric conditions but to sudden changes of climate and these changes can be just as damaging. The extreme example is found among antiquities which have been freshly excavated and suddenly forced to adapt themselves to the new environment above ground.

[1] Relative Humidity (R.H.): the relative humidity of a sample of air is the ratio of the amount of moisture actually present (m) in any volume to the amount needed for saturation (M) at the same temperature, i.e. R.H. $= (m/M \times 100)$ per cent. Air is said to be saturated when it is unable to take up any more water in the form of vapour. On cooling saturated air, water is at once deposited in the form of dew, because the air is unable to carry the same amount of water at the lower temperature.

HUMIDITY AND TEMPERATURE CHANGES ON EXCAVATION

Before archaeologists were aware of the damage that might result from sudden changes of relative humidity, it was not an unusual experience for them to open up a tomb in which the contents were in perfect condition, only to see them shrink and warp and sometimes even turn to dust when exposed to a change of atmosphere.

The principle behind this is that when objects are buried for a long time under conditions that are reasonably constant, they tend to attain a state of equilibrium with their surroundings. When excavated, the materials are submitted to an entirely new environment, the equilibrium is upset, and some objects suffer profoundly. When a tomb is opened, the access of cold air increases the relative humidity, even to the extent of causing deposition of moisture, while the entrance of hot dry air causes a reduction in the relative humidity. Such variations give rise to dimensional changes in organic material—due either to the absorption of moisture or to the loss of moisture—and such dimensional changes manifest themselves in swelling or in shrinking and warping.

A similar kind of problem arises when objects that have been excavated from damp soil are dried quickly instead of being allowed to adapt themselves gradually to the new environment above ground. In the case of organic materials, the sudden loss of moisture may cause shrinkage and severe distortion, and in the case of stone and pottery, crumbling. In order to prevent such deterioration, it is essential, on excavation, to keep objects in a cool place out of the sun, where they can give up their moisture slowly.

When objects having a cellular structure, such as wood, bone, and ivory, have become waterlogged, the problem, on excavation, is accentuated. It is essential to keep such objects immersed in water until such time as they can be packed in wet cloths, put into polythene bags and transported to the laboratory where they can receive suitable preservative treatment. If allowed to dry too quickly, the weakened cellular structure may collapse, and in the event of this happening no amount of resoaking in water will restore the original shape. An extreme case is that of damp organic material having an impervious covering that must be preserved, e.g. Chinese lacquer. With objects of this kind, the most careful treatment is not always a guarantee of success as the following example will show. In 1949 four trays made of very thin lacquered wood were excavated at Chang Sha in a waterlogged condition. They were immediately packed in zinc-lined boxes containing damp wool and sent by air for treatment in the Research Laboratory of the British Museum. There, in a series of closed vessels containing air of successively decreasing relative humidity,[1] they were allowed to dry out slowly for twelve months. Although all four objects received exactly the same treatment, only three of the trays could be dried out successfully; the fourth contracted, warped, and finally fell to pieces. The reason for this anomalous behaviour may have been the nature, quality, or direction of cut of the wood used in making this particular tray; on the other hand, the tray may have had a more chequered history than the others, in that it may have been subjected to periods of intermittent drying while still in the ground or even to partial drying when it was excavated.

Objects buried in salty ground are exposed not only to moisture but also to the action of salts dissolved in the ground water. When damp materials containing soluble salts are excavated, the water evaporates and the salts crystallize; in so doing they weaken the object and often disrupt the surface. In this case, it is essential to wash such objects in salt-free water to remove the absorbed soluble salts so as to prevent further crystallization on the surface.

Metallic objects also become contaminated in salty ground. Although they corrode in the ground there may come a time when they attain a state of equilibrium with their surroundings and the process of corrosion is brought, virtually, to a standstill. On being excavated and exposed to a new moist environment, corrosion may

---

[1] At a temperature of 70 °F. (21 °C.) the R.H. of the air within a closed space containing saturated aqueous solutions of the following salts is as follows: potassium nitrate 94 per cent, potassium chloride 86 per cent, sodium chloride 76 per cent, sodium nitrite 66 per cent, magnesium nitrate 53 per cent.

break out afresh as they proceed to adapt themselves to the new conditions.

HUMIDITY CHANGES IN THE MUSEUM

While antiquities may suffer deterioration through exposure to the sudden change in temperature and humidity consequent upon excavation, certain works of art may suffer as severely by exposure to ordinary everyday atmospheric changes. Easel paintings, for example, whether on panel or canvas, are very sensitive to changes in the atmosphere, and in particular to varying relative humidity. When a painted panel is subjected to variations in relative humidity, the wood undergoes sympathetic dimensional changes which impose rhythmical strains on the painting ground (*gesso*) and the paint layer. As a result of this movement, cracks and blisters may develop, and the paint may flake off. Before the Second World War a technician was employed for eight months in the year to deal with such defects in pictures at the National Gallery where the atmosphere was not conditioned. On the other hand, in the repository which housed the same pictures during the war and where the air was conditioned to 58 per cent R.H. at 63 °F. (17 °C.) the work of the technician was reduced to approximately one month during the first year, progressively less in the following years, and finally after five years his visits became a mere formality as there was no longer anything for him to do. The significance of the relative humidity factor in the conservation of pictures was further emphasized by the fact that, when the pictures were returned to London, they behaved in the same way as before the war, the paint flaking off as badly as ever in rooms that were not air-conditioned.[1]

Similarly, in a large repository used during the war to house the British Museum and Victoria and Albert Museum collections (antiquities, books, textiles, prints, drawings, manuscripts, furniture, etc.), the air was controlled at the constant figures 60 per cent R.H. at 60 °F. (16 °C.), and not a single case of deterioration was recorded in this repository.

[1] Keeley, T. R., and Rawlins, F. I. G., *Museum*, 1951, **7**, p. 194.

No more striking evidence could be brought forward to illustrate the paramount importance of maintaining temperature and atmospheric relative humidity constant at an appropriate level in museums and picture galleries. Where there exists an air-conditioning plant incorporating a dust extractor, as is customary in modern installations, conditions are ideal. Under such circumstances there is no longer any risk of damage by atmospheric pollution; soot particles are absent and it is safe to remove glasses from frames so that pictures may be enjoyed without the complication of specular reflections.

While such strict atmospheric control as 60 per cent R.H. at 60 °F. (16 °C.) is not essential for the majority of collections, there is everything to be gained by fixing an upper and lower limit of relative humidity and temperature and ensuring as far as possible that conditions are maintained within these predetermined limits. This involves keeping records (see Appendix IX), having the means of controlling heating and ventilation, and even adding moisture to the air if conditions should become excessively dry.

A graphic representation of the relationship between temperature and relative humidity is shown in Fig. 1, from which it will be seen that if at 70 °F. the reading is 50 per cent R.H. (point A)—conditions that might well be recorded by day—it only requires a fall in temperature of 10 °F. for the relative humidity to rise to 70 per cent (point B). This relative humidity is within the danger limit for the storage of material that is subject to attack by mould growth and, if allowed to persist, damage would be unavoidable. Incidentally, this diagram may be used in conjunction with the sling hygrometer to give an approximate figure for the relative humidity instead of using tables. Thus, when the dry-bulb thermometer reads 70 °F. and the wet-bulb reads 60 °F., the relative humidity will be seen to lie between the curved lines 50 per cent and 60 per cent and may be judged to be about 54 per cent.

It is interesting to compare continuous records of relative humidity and temperature that have been taken out of doors (where the instrument was screened under standardized conditions) with records taken at the same time indoors, and these, in turn, with the continuous

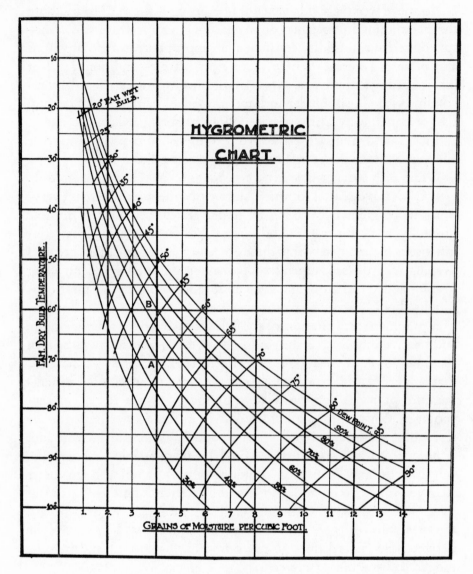

FIG. I

recording from an instrument placed within a closed exhibition case. The daily extremes of relative humidity out-of-doors in London during June–September were found to be approximately 30–90 per cent, and these were observed to be reduced in a museum gallery to 40–70 per cent, the mean temperature of the room being 67 °F., whereas, within the case, changes in relative humidity were so far reduced as to be almost imperceptible. The comparative results are shown diagrammatically in Fig. 2. The particular exhibition case used for this test had a capacity of 5 cub. metres, and a glass area of 8,000 sq. cm. The effect of the closed case was to slow down atmospheric changes until conditions were almost static within the case. The function of a glazed case or frame in excluding dirt may be more spectacular, but its usefulness in minimizing atmospheric changes is no less important when it is a question of long-term conservation. This comparative test demonstrates the value of keeping objects that are susceptible to moisture changes inside a closed case or frame.

In a private house, temperature may assume an importance as great as that of relative humidity, because collections are usually kept in small rooms where the air movement tends to be intensified by the opening of doors and windows and by the presence of heating appliances. In such circumstances there is usually a greater variation of temperature than in the larger rooms of a museum, and the use of a glass case or frame for susceptible material has undoubted advantages.

THE MUSEUM CLIMATE

Temperature and relative humidity have been shown to be interdependent. In a museum gallery the choice of temperature will be pre-determined to suit the comfort of visitors,[1] say within the limits of 60–75 °F. (16–25 °C.), and for the collections it will be a question

---

[1] Comfort is of course as much a matter of relative humidity as of temperature. In a discussion on the effects of the water-vapour content of the atmosphere (MacIntyre, J., *Journal of the Inst. of Heating and Ventilating Engineers*, 1937, **4**, No. 48, p. 570) it was claimed that for mental activity a relative humidity of under 55 per cent was ideal, while for rest and recuperation something above 55 per cent and possibly in the region of 70 per cent was desirable.

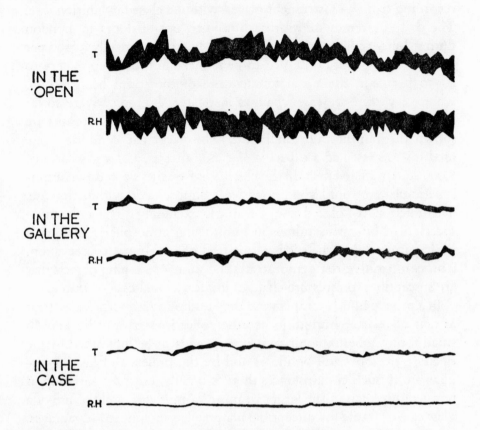

IN THE
·OPEN

IN THE
GALLERY

IN THE
CASE

FIG. 2. Summary of records taken concurrently over a period of four months in London (June–September). The variations of temperature and relative humidity in the open (broad bands) are to be compared with the less extreme conditions in the museum gallery, and variations are still further reduced in an exhibition case where the record of relative humidity is shown to be practically constant.

of establishing limits of relative humidity that can be considered safe within this range of temperature. The limits are determined by observing how the most susceptible materials are affected by exposure to extreme conditions and to variations of relative humidity.

A. The lower permissible limit of relative humidity

Hygroscopic materials are the most sensitive to over-drying because they normally contain moisture. Timber that is dried until it is in equilibrium with its surroundings is said to be 'seasoned' but it still contains some 12–15 per cent of its weight of moisture, and if dried below this moisture content it will warp. Seasoned timber continues to adjust itself in sympathy with changes in the relative humidity of the atmosphere, and the amount of adjustment will depend on the nature and dimensions of the wood, and the variations to which it is exposed. Small variations of relative humidity within the range 55–65 per cent are only of significance in the case of thin painted panels where the recurrent adjustments may in time cause cleavage between the surface of the wood and the ground or paint layer. In the case of heavier structures of wood, significant effects are only produced if the variations in relative humidity are large and persist over a long period of time.

The materials other than wood that suffer damage if dried below a certain point are paper, parchment, leather, and notably the adhesives used in making furniture and in bookbinding. Furniture that is decorated with marquetry or inlays is particularly liable to be damaged through desiccation of the glue, and over-drying has also much to do with the physical deterioration of bookbindings. Bindings soon become dilapidated if they are kept near a radiator or on a mantelpiece, or even if exposed for long periods to direct sunlight.

Taking into consideration the susceptibility of all organic materials to damage by desiccation, the lower safety limit should be fixed at 50 per cent R.H. This means that we choose to regard 50 per cent R.H. as the arbitrary limit of dryness within the agreed temperature range. If, on taking observations, the figure is observed to fall, say, to 45 per cent, no great harm would be likely to result, but if such a figure *persisted* over a period, this might well be dangerous, and it would be necessary to counter the tendency to over-dryness by reducing the heating, or by increasing ventilation. With books or papers either or both methods may be used, but with painted panels cracking may be caused by sudden draughts of air. In this case it would be safer to increase the relative humidity by cutting down the heating, or preferably by installing a humidifier.

B. The upper permissible limit of relative humidity

The greatest danger that can arise from an excessively high relative humidity is the tendency for moulds to grow on any material that can provide nutriment, such as glue, leather, paper. The presence of mould growths is a warning that the atmospheric relative humidity is above the limit of safety. When conditions are favourable to mould growth, for example in a library, a grey dusty bloom is observed in the first instance on the darker bindings, and it soon becomes fluffy with a tendency to be organized in circular patches. The words mould and mildew are used indiscriminately in a popular way to describe growths of minute fungi of which there are many different species, though superficially they are all very much alike. They consist of very tiny threads called hyphae. The hyphae felt together forming a mycelium which throws up fruiting bodies containing spores, and these are present in enormous numbers. Fungi thrive under conditions of damp, warmth, and darkness, and the materials upon which they grow may be stained by contact with the mycelium or with coloured matter formed during growth. The growth of moulds can be prevented by keeping the relative humidity of the atmosphere below 68 per cent,[1] and this figure is therefore to be regarded as the absolute danger limit at temperatures between 60 and 75 °F. (16 and 25 °C.). In actual practice 65 per cent R.H. is preferable for the upper limit of humidity, as this takes account of the fact that papers vary widely in hygroscopic nature according to the sizing, filling, etc.

[1] Groom, P., and Panisset, Th., *Ann. appl. Biol.* **20,** p. 633.

Closed island cases afford considerable protection from excessive humidity.[1] This was demonstrated by a war-time observation. In a flooded basement containing ethnographical material mould growths spread apace, whereas in the same basement a closed cupboard containing some of the same class of material was found, when opened, to be free from mould. As we have already seen, a closed case can slow down atmospheric changes, and in this instance although the cupboard was by no means air-tight, the air inside had remained sufficiently dry to preserve the contents. Conversely, it has been noticed that when parchment and paper have been packed on a wet day, or in a damp locality, there may be a subsequent growth of mildew, arising no doubt from the moist air included in the package.

The limits of atmospheric relative humidity are thus defined as lying between 50 per cent R.H. and 65 per cent R.H. at temperatures 60–75 °F. (16–25 °C.) and these conditions are not difficult to maintain in temperate climates. Such conditions are satisfactory for museums, libraries, and muniment rooms. Picture galleries are, however, in a special category because of the highly sensitive nature of the collections they contain, and in this case a constant relative humidity of 58 per cent at about 63 °F. (17 °C.) is the ideal to be aimed at.

ATMOSPHERIC POLLUTION

Reference must now be made to the problems that arise from various impurities present in the atmosphere. These are regional in character.

In the first place, there are difficulties peculiar to the preservation of museum materials near the seaside. Sea air, damp with salt spray, may blow well inland, give up its moisture, and become charged with a fine dispersion of minute salt crystals; these in turn may serve as nuclei for the deposition of moisture, resulting in the formation of mists and fogs. In one or other condition, sea air finds its way

---

[1] Discussed at length in Stolow, N., 'Fundamental Case Design for Humidity-Sensitive Museum Collections', *Museum News Technical Supplement*, 11 (1966).

indoors and deposits salt in minute amounts. The salt is hygroscopic and maintains a local relative humidity which will support the growth of micro-organisms, even in surroundings that are apparently quite dry. This may be a serious matter where there are collections of books and papers and, as it is difficult to prevent such contamination, it would seem advisable in such localities to keep things covered as far as possible, and to store susceptible material in cupboards or glazed cases rather than on open shelves.

In the second place, there is the problem of damage arising from the serious forms of atmospheric pollution in the neighbourhood of towns and industrial areas. This is indeed a menace to collections of all kinds and one that is substantially beyond control, for, while soot and grit may be excluded, there is no ready means of preventing access of sulphurous gases save by the installation of expensive air-conditioning plant. Sulphurous gases are the cause of widespread deterioration. Hydrogen sulphide reacts with all the metals of antiquity (except gold) to form dark-coloured sulphides, and is particularly damaging to paint films containing white lead (p. 87). Sulphur dioxide is even more damaging as it is eventually converted into sulphuric acid which attacks a wide variety of materials. The corrosive effects are obvious in specimens exposed to the weather—building stones, or metals—but a more subtle and equally damaging form of deterioration due, in the first instance, to sulphur dioxide is to be observed in organic materials which have been exposed to traces of the resulting acid over a long period of time. The rotting of paper (p. 56) and textiles (p. 118) can often be traced to the action of sulphuric acid, and it is this acid, generated perhaps by a local coke stove, that is so often responsible for the powdery and decayed condition of old leather bookbindings (p. 37).

All the sulphur in the atmosphere comes from the burning of fuel—coal, coke, or oil—and as the sulphur content of these materials is known, as well as the annual amount of fuel consumed, it was possible to calculate, with what is claimed to be a reasonable degree of accuracy, that the annual total of sulphur compounds polluting the atmosphere in the United Kingdom in 1953 corresponded to the

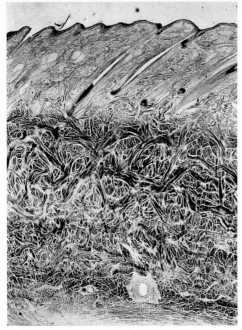

1. SECTION THROUGH A PIECE OF OX-
HIDE (×15) SHOWING GRAIN WITH HAIR
FOLLICLES AND FIBRE BUNDLES IN THE
CORIUM

*(Courtesy of British Leather Manufacturers' Research
Association)*

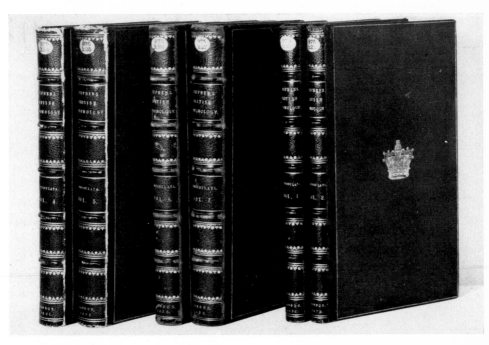

2. SIX LEATHER BINDINGS OF 1828–35

(1) Physical Decay—(*Left Pair*)—Hinges dry and cracked
(2) Chemical Decay—(*Centre Pair*)—General deterioration to powdery red surface
(3) Use of B.M. Leather Dressing—(*Right Pair*)—Books were in the condition of (1)
   before treatment

3. CHEMICAL DECAY OF LEATHER BOOKBINDINGS (ADVANCED STAGE)
(Hinges broken—covers detached—leather scruffed—headbands torn)

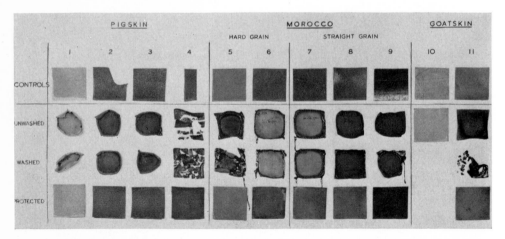

4. THE PEROXIDE TEST FOR ASSESSING THE DURABILITY OF VEGETABLE-TANNED LEATHER
Only protected leathers (bottom series and No. 10) have been able to withstand this accelerated ageing test. (See Appendixes XII and XIV)

equivalent of 9 million tons of sulphuric acid—a quantity more than five times the then annual commercial production of this acid![1] Such figures serve to emphasize the magnitude of the problem which is almost beyond comprehension, but the tragic effects are to be seen everywhere.

For industrial areas as for seaside districts the only protection is exclusion, as far as possible, of the agencies of decay and this means using glazed frames and closed cabinets whether the collections be exhibited in a museum or maintained in the more intimate surroundings of the home. An excellent account of air pollution from the point of view of conservation is given by Thomson,[2] who emphasizes the fact that adequate control of air pollution in museums is useless without adequate monitoring of the atmospheric pollutants.

Such are the main features of the environment as they affect antiquities and works of art. Specific references will be made in later chapters when discussing particular materials.

Of the many extrinsic factors that contribute to deterioration (Fig. 3), it will be seen that apart from accident or mechanical damage, all derive from the environment, which must therefore merit very close study on the part of the curator whose main responsibility is the conservation of the collections under his care.

MUSEUM LIGHTING

Even when precautions are taken to protect museum objects from atmospheric pollution, adverse climatic conditions, and biological attack, there still remains the very real dangers that may arise from exposure to light. Many materials, particularly those of an organic nature, are susceptible to damage by light; among the most sensitive are textiles, water-colours, paintings, and illuminated manuscripts. While daylight or a near equivalent is essential for the study and enjoyment of works of art, exposure to uncontrolled conditions of illumination will cause the photochemical degradation of susceptible

[1] *The Times*, London, 20 April 1953.
[2] Thomson, G., *Studies in Conservation*, 1965, **10**, p. 147

pigments and dyestuffs and the tendering of textiles. In studying the damaging effect of light two factors have to be taken into consideration: the quality of the light source and the actual level of illumination. The ultra-violet component in light is most potent in causing degradation, and clearly the higher the level of illumination, the greater will be the damage caused. Therefore exclusion of ultra-violet radiation and control of illumination at a reasonable level are the prime considerations.

Ultra-violet radiation can be excluded by the use of plastic sheeting that contains ultra-violet absorbing compounds; these sheets are cheaper and in general more effective than certain colourless glasses previously used. Such sheets are marketed under the trade names Oroglas UF3 (Plexiglas UF3 in the U.S.A.) and Perspex VE. Concerning the question of ultra-violet radiation emitted by fluorescent lamps, there is evidence that certain types on the market, such as Philips 37 and 27, emit considerably less ultra-violet radiation than other types. If necessary, special plastic sleeving containing ultra-violet absorbing compounds can be used to reduce the amount of ultra-violet radiation. The proportion of ultra-violet radiation in museums and art galleries can be measured with a special monitoring instrument—the Elsec UV Monitor Type 678.[1]

As regards the levels of light intensity, this problem has been studied in considerable detail by Thomson,[2] who has recommended the following specifications: 300 lux for objects not particularly sensitive to light, 150 lux for objects of medium susceptibility, and 50 lux for objects that are extremely sensitive to possible damage by light. The lux is the international unit for measuring luminous energy and is given in lumens/sq. metre; an alternative unit used in Great Britain and America is the foot-candle, which is expressed in lumens/sq. foot, and is approximately equal to 10 lux. Light intensity can be measured with a suitable light meter; one in which a selenium photocell is enclosed in an airtight Perspex hemisphere has been found serviceable for taking readings in museum galleries.

---

[1] Littlemore Scientific Engineering Co., Railway Lane, Littlemore, Oxford.
[2] Thomson, G., *Studies in Conservation*, 1961, **6,** p. 46.

Once the dangers inherent in lighting are realized, much can be done to mitigate them. Due consideration should be given to the following points:

(i) Storage rooms and galleries should normally be kept unlighted when not open to the public.

(ii) Direct sunlight should always be rigorously excluded by the use of blinds, louvres, or curtains.

(iii) Sensitive material should, if possible, not be kept on permanent exhibition unless conditions are strictly controlled.

(iv) Preference should be given, where possible, to methods of illumination in which the lighting is not direct but reflected and diffuse.

(v) Care should be taken to choose a type of fluorescent lamp that does not emit an undue amount of ultra-violet radiation.

(vi) Ultra-violet absorbing filters should be used where appropriate.

To sum up, it is clear that considerable progress has been made in recent years on the subject of museum lighting, and there is general agreement on the basic principles and the practical methods to be adopted.[1] Every effort must be made to eliminate unnecessary ultra-violet radiation and to reduce the illumination value to a suitable level, particularly where valuable susceptible objects such as textiles, water-colours, and illuminated manuscripts are exhibited.

SAFEGUARDING EVIDENCE

It may be assumed that the curator has recognized the dangers inherent in the environment and has countered these by establishing the best possible museum climate for his collections. He is now free to study the condition of individual specimens.

In the case of antiquities or ethnographical objects his attention will be arrested by those in the worst condition whether actively

[1] See *Conservation and Museum Lighting* by G. Thomson. Museums Association Information Sheet obtainable from Museums Association, 87 Charlotte Street, London, WIP 2BX.

deteriorating or whose interest is concealed by irrelevant incrustations. An antiquity, under the influence of its environment, may acquire certain features that are of significance in making an assessment of its age, authenticity, or provenance. These relate mostly to surface effects such as incrustations or weathering. In the preliminary examination the structure of the object should be studied and care taken to plan a method of conservation that will not cause the loss of any essential characteristics, such as technical features relating to the method of manufacture.

1. *Incrustation.* Before undertaking any wholesale cleaning of an encrusted object it is as well to remember that the incrustation may, itself, be of value. It may be a key to the exact find spot; it may contain pollen grains that are of potential value for dating purposes, or, if the object is a food-vessel, the incrustation may provide interesting information regarding dietary habits if the contents can be identified. Records should be kept of any details of texture found on muddy incrustations that may be evidence of contact with rush mats, basketry, textiles, etc. If a number of the same type of objects are excavated, some should be set aside with their surface deposits uncleaned, as a record of the condition of the objects as found—always provided that they can be relied upon to remain stable under museum conditions. Incrustations that are germane to an object and that do not conceal inscriptions or ornament should, as a general rule, only be removed if they are unstable, or constitute a serious disfigurement, and if the object is strong enough to withstand treatment. If an object is in fragments, it is usually easier to tell (from the surface staining) which pieces fit together before rather than after cleaning.

2. *Structure.* Examination of the microcrystalline structure of a metal can supply information regarding ancient metal-working techniques. It is possible, for example, by a metallographic examination to determine whether a metal object has been cast or wrought or what heat treatment it has been given in antiquity. To heat the object would vitiate the results of any such inquiry, and methods are restricted, for preference, to those that can be applied without the risk of changing the micro-structure. This is not always possible, how-

ever, and certainly not in the case of brittle silver objects which can only be toughened by a course of heat treatment.

3. *Decoration and technique*. Any material that has been fashioned by man is liable to bear decoration applied to or imposed upon its surface. This may be concealed under incrustations and the greatest care is necessary when cleaning an object by mechanical or chemical means to avoid removing evidence of decoration, and to avoid marking the object in such a manner as to lead to possible confusion or misinterpretation of evidence. For the same reason preference should be given to the use of modern materials in certain classes of repair work. This is important in repairing old textiles or embroideries where, unless a synthetic fibre is used, it might be impossible to distinguish old threads from new.

It must be clear that laboratory treatment of antiquities and works of art carries with it a great responsibility. The excitement of discovery and the urge to reveal hidden interests must be held in check and kept subservient to the duty of maintaining full laboratory records of the work *as it proceeds*, illustrated, where necessary, with sketches and photographs for incorporation in a permanent archive. This work calls not only for knowledge, foresight, ingenuity, and dexterity but for infinite patience. It should never be hurried.

FURTHER READING

FELLER, R. L., 'Control of Deteriorating Effect of Light upon Museum Objects', *Museum*, xvii, 1964, **2,** pp. 57–98.

PLENDERLEITH, H. J., and PHILIPPOT, P., 'Climatology and Conservation in Museums', *Museum*, xiii, 1960, **4,** pp. 203–89.

STOLOW, N., *Controlled Environment for Works of Art in Transit*. Butterworth London, 1966.

THOMSON, G. (Editor), *Museum Climatology*. Proceedings of Conference of International Institute of Conservation of Historic and Artistic Works. London, 1967.

CAUSES OF DAMAGE TO MUSEUM OBJECTS

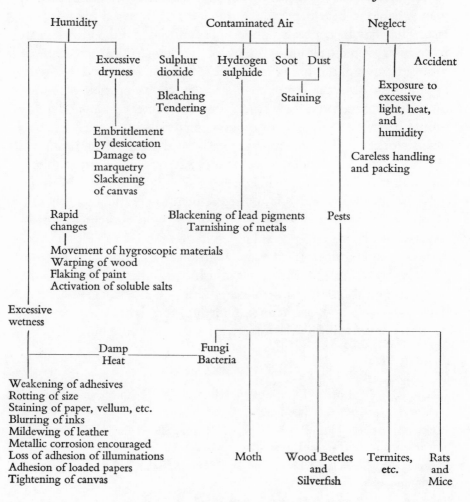

FIG. 3

PART I

ORGANIC MATERIALS

I

ANIMAL SKIN AND SKIN PRODUCTS

IN 1843 Michael Faraday,[1] when lecturing at the Royal Institution in London, exhibited leather-bound volumes belonging to the Athenaeum Club that were in a shocking state of decay. This condition he attributed to the products of combustion of coal gas, and he proceeded to demonstrate that the moisture from a gas flame, condensed on cold metal, contained sulphuric acid. The Athenaeum ventilating pipes were, in fact, thickly coated with green vitriol (iron sulphate), from the action upon iron of the acid fumes evolved on combustion and these same acid fumes were responsible for the decay of the leather bookbindings and upholstery.

Faraday's observations seem to be the earliest on record concerning the decay of leather by sulphuric acid, but nothing appears to have been done at the time to carry his contribution further. About the turn of the century a committee was appointed by the Royal Society of Arts to investigate the cause of the deterioration of leather, again relating to bookbindings: a report was published, and certain recommendations were made, but actually no concentrated attack was made on the many practical aspects of the problem until the British Leather Manufacturers' Research Association took up the matter in 1920. The Association has made an intensive study of the whole problem of the decay and preservation of skin and skin products, and the results of twenty-five years' research have been published in *Progress in Leather Science*.[2] This comprehensive review has been freely used in compiling the present chapter.

[1] Faraday, Michael, *On the Ventilation of Gas Burners*, Royal Institution Lecture, 7 April 1843.
[2] *Progress in Leather Science, 1920–1945*, British Leather Manufacturers' Research Association, Milton Park, Egham, Surrey.

Museum collections contain skin products of all kinds, in all stages of deterioration, from every part of the globe, and often dating back to remote periods. The skins may be plain or ornamented with tooling or with colour; they may be in the raw condition, or dressed by various processes, but whatever their nature it is the task of the museum laboratory to take measures for their preservation. Before considering what may be done to restore and conserve such objects, some attention must be given to the variety of material that is presented, and to the methods that have been adopted through the ages in preparing animal skins.

SKIN IN PRIMITIVE CULTURES

In the earliest times skin had to serve many purposes for which it has long since been superseded, and we can gain some idea of its wide application by studying ethnographical collections. The entire skin of an animal was sometimes sewn up and used as a water-carrier, or filled with air and used as a float or buoy; skin was used to cover primitive canoes or coracles; it was used for sails, tents, domestic utensils, hunting gear, harness, and accoutrements of every kind. The internal organs of animals were also utilized. Vases and waterproof clothing were made from the intestines of the cow and walrus, floats from bladders, and utensils from the stomach of the camel. Masks were made by moulding moist skins or bladders over a suitably modelled shape and allowing them to dry in position; the shape of the mould was retained by the tissue, which could then be stabilized by waterproofing with fat or oil.

Untanned skins and skin products are, however, not permanent materials; they are liable to attack by micro-organisms, and are very sensitive to moisture. These weaknesses can be overcome to a certain degree by methods of curing and dressing, and there is no doubt that such methods were employed in primitive times to protect the skins. Even at a time as remote as the last interglacial period[1] there is evidence

[1] Schwerz, F., *CIBA Review*, 1938, **8**, pp. 242–63. Gannser, A., *ibid*. 1950, *81*.

to suggest that simple methods of skin-dressing (smoking and treatment with oil) may have been practised with the object of preventing putrefaction and enhancing flexibility. However, skin does not last long in damp earth, and no actual examples from this age are still extant.

It is otherwise in the dry and sterile tombs of Egypt where many specimens of ancient skin have survived from Predynastic times. These have become rigid and brittle as a result of desiccation, and it is, therefore, not an easy matter to determine whether they may have been cured or processed. There is ample evidence that skin was exploited in ancient Egypt for utilitarian as well as for decorative purposes. In Tutankhamun's tomb it was used embedded in *gesso* to form a resilient backing for gold leaf that was later ornamented with tooling, and it was even used by the Egyptian scribes in the form of a scroll for writing upon. This latter use need occasion no surprise, as the flesh side when scraped and cleaned yields a smooth surface of pleasant colour which 'takes' ink satisfactorily. In this respect, however, it falls far short of parchment, both as regards its suitability for the purpose and its lasting properties.

In the fourth to third century B.C. thick leather was commonly used by Siberian nomads for making flat ornamental bas-reliefs of animals, and by gluing skins together it was even possible to sculpture animal heads in the round. The leather was sometimes coloured and employed as a covering for wooden statuary or for horse trappings. Splendid specimens from the Altai steppes are to be seen in the Hermitage Museum, Leningrad.

Parchment did not appear until the second century B.C., and then not in Egypt but in Pergamon (Asia Minor), from which its name is derived. The material is made from the tough, white corium, or inner layer of animal skin, by a process that relaxes and flattens the capillaries so that they are unable to reabsorb moisture. Though it is easily stained, and deformed by heat and damp, it is not subject to chemical deterioration, and has proved to be extraordinarily durable as a material for fine writing. Parchment is dealt with in detail on pp. 47 sqq.

PHYSICAL FEATURES AND MICRO-STRUCTURE

The word 'skin' is used as a general term for all classes of material, whether raw, cured, or processed, and skin from the larger animals, such as horse and cow, is known specifically as 'hide'. 'Curing' refers to a first-aid or field treatment to prevent putrefaction, and 'processing' to any more permanent treatment, including the manufacture of leather.

The science of the preservation of leather begins with the study of the untanned skin—the raw material before it is processed—and it may contribute to an understanding of the problem if we consider briefly the micro-structure of animal skin, and its main physical features.

When an animal is skinned the pelt is seen to take the form of a continuous membrane of fibrous tissue, having a hair side and a flesh side, the hair side being patterned with sweat glands and hair follicles (grain), and the flesh side lined with fat, muscles, and blood-vessels (Pl. 1). Skins from the different animal species exhibit great variations in physical structure, and this is most pronounced as between warm-blooded and cold-blooded animals. Even in the same species, however, where the pattern or grain tends to be constant, variation in micro-structure may be observed, and is caused by such factors as the age of the animal and quality of feeding. Some skins are valued primarily for their surface covering of hair, fur, or wool, some for the skin itself (rather than for the surface covering), whereas others, notably in the arctic regions, serve both purposes, the skin being impervious to the elements, and the fur acting as an insulator and a conserver of heat.

In the micro-structure of animal skin the true skin tissue or corium is composed of a reticulated network of protein fibres, the main constituent being the protein known as collagen—'the glue producer'. (If skin is boiled in water for a sufficient time, it undergoes hydrolysis and is converted into glue.) Recent chemical research has shown that collagen has a chain structure, i.e. it consists essentially of long molecules composed of many atoms attached together like links in a chain, with smaller side chains branching from the main backbone. These complicated molecules of collagen tend to orient themselves in the same direction, to associate in bundles, and to retain water pertinaciously in a loose form of chemical combination.

PROCESSING

In the normal course of events, the skin of a slaughtered animal is speedily a prey to the growth of moulds and bacteria, but the mechanical removal of associated fats, muscles, and blood-vessels eliminates much nutrient material, and the drying of the skin goes a long way towards rendering the tissue proof against putrefaction. In this condition, however, the skin is of little practical value; when the collagen fibres have been deprived of their water, the skin becomes horny and brittle, and flexibility can only be restored by relaxing the fibrous bundles so that they slide freely over each other again, as they did before the skin was dried. This relaxing of the skin may be accomplished in several ways, notably by some form of prolonged manipulation, or by the incorporation of lubricants, or, usually, by a combination of both methods.

The tramping of skins in tubs has been a traditional method of preparation in some parts of the world for many years. The Eskimos soften skins by chewing, a process which doubtless is enzymatic in action as well as being mechanical. Manipulative processes may, in themselves, be sufficient, but generally improved results are obtained by the use of dressings, such as castor oil, or sulphonated neat's-foot oil. These are often applied in emulsified form, and they penetrate and lubricate the tissue, partially replacing moisture as the skin dries.

Fur skins

An animal skin 'in the hair' (or wool) prepared for the taxidermist may have been softened by oil dressing, or merely worked mechanically to a condition of relative flexibility. Equally suitable as a method of preparing soft-dressed fur skins is the following process. The fresh skin is stretched out fur downwards and pinned to a board; the flesh side is scraped with a knife having a convex blade, until the surface of the skin is approximately uniform, and then the skin is allowed to dry. It is wetted again, and the process repeated. There seems to be a positive advantage in alternate drying and wetting, but as it is important in the preparation of fur skins to prevent putre-faction, the sequence of operations must not be interrupted; a little carbolic acid may be used if required to keep the skin sweet, or alternatively some salt and alum. Finally, the skin may be pulled over a beam-knife or stake. In the hands of an expert this yields a very soft and flexible product.

Alum dressing

The mention of alum suggests a process of skin dressing called tawing, which dates back to remote antiquity. This consists in treating the skin, after preliminary cleaning, with excess of alum, the resulting product being a substance light in colour, and having the properties of leather so long as the alum is present. The action is reversible, how-ever, and if the alum is removed by washing, as is easily possible, the skin is ruined. Water must not be used, therefore, with tawed skins. Tawing is still practised today in the manufacture of wool skins; tawed leather is used for making gloves, and to a limited extent for bookbinding.

Oil dressing

Oil tannage is employed today in the preparation of chamois leather. For this purpose the skin is split on a band-knife machine, the grain-split or surface side of the skin (skiver) being worked up as leather for bookbinding, while the flesh side is drummed with cod oil and thus converted into chamois. In chamois leather the fibres are protected with oxidized oil, and the skin absorbs water readily as there are comparatively wide capillaries between the fibres. Alter-natively, the flesh side may be converted into parchment (p. 47).

Tanning

Leather is animal skin which has been dehaired, defatted, neutral-ized, and rendered non-putrescent by a form of treatment that makes the skin impervious to water, while preserving the natural pliability.

This treatment is carried out with a tanning agent which may be of vegetable or mineral origin.

Vegetable-tanned leather. One of the earliest materials used for tanning leather in northern countries was an infusion of oak bark—the Breton word *tann* is the equivalent of oak. This infusion contains tannins which are chemical substances that have the property of combining with the collagen and other protein fibres of the skin, replacing the loosely bound water, and reinforcing the side-chains or cross links of the protein molecules. The result is a material having qualities greatly superior to those of raw hide, particularly as regards water resistivity, durability, and what is known as 'feel'—an elusive quality, but one that is perhaps sufficiently self-explanatory.

In ancient Egypt it is probable that tanning was first carried out using acacia pods rather than oak bark, and Lucas[1] mentions that articles of leather are common in Tasian, Badarian, and Predynastic tombs. The Egyptian tomb paintings provide some interesting illustrations of contemporary methods of leather-working, notably in a mural at Gurnah (seventeenth dynasty), and also in the tomb of Aba (No. 36) in the Asasif at Thebes (twenty-sixth dynasty). Some of the processes seem to differ little from the methods employed at the present day.

Besides oak bark and acacia pods there are many other plant products widely distributed in nature that have the property of stabilizing the protein structure of skin, and giving it the properties of leather. These vegetable tannins may be classified in two chemical groups, the catechol group and the pyrogallol group, though certain of them—and oak bark is an example—belong to both categories. These chemical groups are of significance in studying the permanence of leathers used in bookbinding and upholstery and will be referred to later.

Mineral-tanned leather. Alum tawing may be regarded as a form of mineral tanning, but this description is generally reserved for the modern process carried out by treating the skin with a salt of

[1] Lucas, A., *Ancient Egyptian Materials and Industries*, 4th edition, revised and enlarged by J. R. Harris, London, Arnold, 1962.

chromium which reinforces the side-chains of the collagen fibres as efficiently as the vegetable-tanning agents and produces leather of a distinctive quality. Chrome leather is practically non-wettable and very durable both physically and chemically, since it is not so vulnerable to attack by sulphuric acid as vegetable-tanned leather.

If the two types are compared as potential bookbinding leathers, the main difference lies in the fact that vegetable-tanned leathers can be relaxed and manipulated in the damp condition, and moulded to the shape of the book, whereas chrome leathers are intractable and difficult to relax and to mould permanently to any required shape. Vegetable-tanned leathers take gold leaf and stamped decoration or tooling well; chrome leathers badly, or not at all, but on the other hand, they are pre-eminent in their resistance to attack by moulds and chemicals. One day, perhaps, by some form of combined vegetable and mineral tanning, it may be possible to produce a new kind of bookbinding leather of improved quality and durability, in which the characteristic weaknesses of the chrome and vegetable-tanned leathers are suppressed, and the virtues of both preserved. Meantime, we are faced with the problem of preserving objects of skin and leather that differ widely in stability.

ACTION OF MOISTURE AND FUNGAL GROWTHS ON SKIN PRODUCTS

Moisture. In extreme cases the degradation of leather by moisture during burial in the ground may proceed to the limit, and nothing may remain in an excavation to indicate that leather was once present, save, perhaps, indefinite traces in the sand, such as were found in the Sutton Hoo ship burial between the various pieces of the purse complex. Gold coins were lying loose in the sand beneath the metal ornaments of the purse flap, and these no doubt were originally in a leather bag. Belt fasteners were also found in the sand with only a stain to mark where the leather belt had once been lying. That bacterial action contributes to such degradation is beyond question, and vestiges of leather sometimes remain as recognizable tissue where

5A. SIX ROLLS OF EGYPTIAN PAPYRI WRAPPED IN LINEN AS FOUND

5B. UNROLLING PAPYRI. IN THE FOREGROUND FRAGMENTS AWAITING
REPAIR

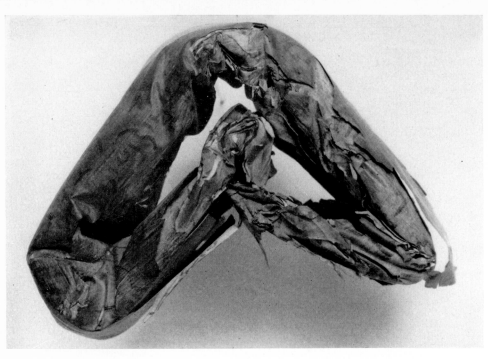

The tight roll of birch bark $(\times 1\frac{1}{2})$ as removed from the inside of a Buddhist image

Eleven thin birch bark sheets, inscribed in doggerel Sanskrit, recovered from the roll. $(\times \frac{1}{4})$

6. INDIAN BIRCH BARK WRITINGS (18TH CENT.)

they have been stained green with the products of corroded copper which have acted as a sterilizing agent. Peaty waters and very salt waters also have a protective effect. Exposure to the prolonged action of a low humidity, as in some Egyptian tombs, has converted skin into a black syrup of bitumastic appearance, which is sometimes found to be still tacky, but sometimes has run into a hard black solid with a superficial resemblance to ebonite. Both the syrup and the solid material are soluble in water. Leather manuscripts have been found that are only converted in part to this black material and there is then the problem of salvaging what remains before the writing is obliterated due to staining by the syrupy decomposition products.

Fungus. In ethnographical collections and in libraries, and, indeed, wherever skin and skin products are stored, humidity control is most important, because moulds grow readily on these materials when the relative humidity of the atmosphere is above 68 per cent at ordinary temperatures. The mould growths cause staining, and erosion may take place as well. Dyed leathers may change colour as a result of fungal attack, and leather bindings are thus particularly prone to damage. The use of fungicides to prevent the growth of mould is merely palliative, and is not as a rule advocated. The real cause of the trouble is a condition of dampness in the collection, known to be deleterious to all organic materials, and it is of first importance to take steps to restore dry conditions. Good ventilation is also essential and will help to arrest the spread of mould growths. In countries where there is persistent high relative humidity, and, in general, where leather has been allowed to become very damp, the use of fungicides may be considered a necessity.

A fungicide suitable for application to leather should not cause staining or rotting, and should be of low volatility. *Para*-nitrophenol, even in moderate concentrations, causes a yellow stain, but it has been proved to be a reliable fungicide for leather when employed in exceedingly dilute aqueous or alcoholic solution, strength 0·35 per cent; and pentachlorophenol is effective at 0·25 per cent strength. When these two fungicides are mixed in equal parts by weight, it has been found by the National Bureau of Standards, U.S.A.,[1] that they can be incorporated in combined concentrations as low as 0·2 per cent and still be effective for the preservation of leather against fungal attack. Such a mixture was an official issue to the American Army in the tropics towards the close of the Second World War, and proved to be highly satisfactory. When it is desired to afford protection over a prolonged period, greater concentrations of fungicide are, in general, necessary, and it is no longer possible to use *para*-nitrophenol on account of its staining properties. Preference may then be given to derivatives of pentachlorophenol or preferably *ortho*-phenylphenol. Thus the sodium salts known commercially as Santobrite and Topane WS or Dowicide A can be dissolved either in alcohol or in water to make a two per cent solution that is useful for impregnation; if a spraying technique is preferred, the lauryl ester of pentachlorophenol may be selected, a convenient preparation being the paraffin solution available commercially as Mystox L.P.

These methods of treatment have proved to be reliable for most types of ethnographical objects that include skin or leather in their composition. Wider issues are raised, however, where a variety of nutrient materials are present as in the case of leather-bound books, because these are susceptible to possible damage by discoloration. To deal with such problems special methods have been devised that will arrest mould growth and minimize the risk of staining (see p. 42).

INSECT ATTACK ON SKIN PRODUCTS

It is necessary to take special measures to protect skin products from attack by insects, and even under the best conditions skins should be inspected regularly and cleaned from time to time. Furs are especially prone to attack by moth larvae. Leather bindings are also liable to be damaged by moth, as well as by several other insect pests in northern countries, notably those of the order *Coleoptera*.

In a museum provided with special equipment, the usual first-aid treatment for an infestation on a large scale is to fumigate with hydro-

[1] *Microbiological Deterioration of Organic Materials* (Mis. Pub. 188), 1948, p. 36. U.S. National Bureau of Standards, Govt. Printing Office, Washington 25, D.C.

gen cyanide or methyl bromide. Where no special equipment is available and the infestation is on a smaller scale it may be possible to use carbon disulphide as a fumigant by constructing a gas-tight box, provided the necessary precautions are taken (see p. 132). Each of these chemicals is effective, but none confers lasting protection, and it is essential to examine the storeroom, and, if necessary, to treat the room also by some form of fumigation in order to ensure that infestation will not recur.

To deal with small outbreaks, spraying with liquid insecticidal solutions is generally adopted, using a good hand-operated atomizer or spray-gun. The insecticide should be highly atomized and brought into contact with the material. Packages must therefore be opened and folded leather and furs unwrapped, otherwise the labour will be expended in vain. The spray deposits a very fine film that retains its insecticidal properties for some considerable time, and, from this point of view, spraying has an advantage over fumigation. Where spraying has to be done regularly on a large scale, a power spray may be regarded as a necessity, and this generally employed at a pressure of about 30 lb. per sq. in. (2 kg. per sq. cm.).

An insecticide for the control of moth is usually dissolved in an odourless paraffin distillate that can be guaranteed not to cause staining, and the spray may act on the pests either as a stomach poison, or a contact poison, or both. It is a good idea to vary the insecticide occasionally, as insects have been found to build up a resistance to a particular poison. This has been observed in the case of DDT. Though slow in action DDT is a very effective insecticide, particularly when used with pyrethrum, which is immediately lethal to moth, and is said to have a high 'knock-down' value. Many effective commercial preparations are available, but if a fair quantity is required it is cheaper in the end and more satisfactory to prepare the solutions oneself than to use preparations of unknown composition.

The following formulae can be recommended.

1. *Pyrethrum/DDT spray solution.* Dissolve 50 gm. of pyrethrum concentrate (Pyefly) and 50 gm. of DDT powder in 1 litre of odourless distillate.

2. *Lethane spray solution*. Dissolve 50 gm. of deodorized Lethane 384 in 1 litre of odourless distillate.

Fur skins used to be prepared as a routine by rubbing with arsenical soap, but this has given place more recently to treatment with boric acid, or with borax, which is claimed to afford just as effective protection against insect attack as the arsenical compound, without the danger to the human subject attendant on the use of arsenic.

Where skin specimens are known to be free from insects, it is a wise precaution to shut them away or isolate them in tissue paper or in cellophane. This keeps the objects free from dust and may prevent pests getting at them. A cellophane hanging wardrobe as used for textiles may sometimes be brought into service for skins, and the polythene bags provided with zip-fasteners are also very useful. These may be charged with a handful of *para*-dichlorobenzene crystals. This also applies in the case of susceptible material kept in drawers, cases, etc. The insecticide is effective so long as some crystals remain unvolatilized.

Preservation of skin products other than bookbindings

For the preservation of skin and leather in museum collection it is fortunately not essential to be able to identify the method of processing. Raw uncured skin, when damp, putrefies. If kept in a reasonably dry atmosphere, skins, whether raw or cured, even if they have been flexible, tend in time to revert to the condition described as horny. Leathers are affected to a less degree and vary according to type, but there is generally a cumulative hardening.

It is no uncommon occurrence to find skins neatly folded in parcels where they have become rigid owing to years of neglect. To attempt to unwrap the brittle skin without some form of preliminary treatment would be to court disaster. If cracking has not already taken place, such specimens can usually be recovered in an undamaged condition by going over the skin, and particularly the folds, with a damp sponge, following this with a leather dressing. The moisture helps the dressing to spread easily. It should be given a little time to penetrate, and then it will be possible to work the skin gradually back into its original shape with the fingers. Skin clothing of all kinds should preferably be kept on coat-hangers, where it is less likely to suffer than if wrapped up and put away in drawers.

When skins are damaged by water, there are invariably complications due to the inevitable fluffy growths of moulds that cover the affected specimens, concealing ornament and disguising colour. A case in point was provided by a skin cloak (carossa) from Angola, which emitted an unbearable odour of putrescence, and was usually hidden under a covering of green mould. Preliminary cleaning was done in the open, using a soft dry brush. This removed the mould and revealed the clammy skin, which was purplish-red in colour, due to the use of the primitive dye-stuff, cam-wood. The cloak was then pinned out in a shallow case for exhibition purposes, and the relative humidity in the case was gradually reduced by means of silica gel (Appendix XI). After changing the silica gel several times, a paper hygrometer that had been placed in the case recorded a figure of 60 per cent relative humidity, and as this is a perfectly satisfactory figure for the preservation of organic materials susceptible to mould attack, it was unnecessary to treat the cloak with fungicides. The specimen has since given no further trouble.

Leather objects are occasionally found in bogs or damp ground, and these require special treatment. Though greatly weakened and distorted, the leather may retain a certain flexibility in the wet condition, which it would lose permanently if allowed to dry. In no circumstances should formalin be used on specimens of this kind as it makes the leather rigid. The object should first be photographed and measured, and the surface then washed with water, using a fine brush. It may then be rubbed over with a 2 per cent solution of phenol in alcohol; the leather should be immersed immediately afterwards in molten vaseline at a temperature of about 80–100 °C. and kept there for a day, or longer if necessary. This improves the appearance, and in favourable circumstances softens the leather still further so that it may be moulded back to shape. But there is usually a fair amount of shrinkage, and as the vaseline leaves a sticky surface, it is generally desirable, having recovered the shape, to replace the vaseline with paraffin wax. This is done by immersion for half an hour in molten wax at 110 °C. The leather is then removed, and may be stuffed with soft paper to maintain the shape as it cools. A very little bitumen powder may be added to the wax to darken it, so that it will not show as a light film on the leather.

The problem of treating waterlogged leather objects has been studied in the laboratory of the Swiss National Museum in Zurich,[1] and a satisfactory procedure has been developed in which the excess of water is removed by washing in several changes of methyl ethyl ketone followed by immersion in carbon tetrachloride containing a fungicide (the oxide or naphthenate of tributyl tin). This process enables the leather to be dried out in a flexible condition without undue shrinkage, and the object can be easily worked into shape afterwards.

A problem of a different kind arises when leather objects have been recovered from an excessively dry environment. In this case they will have become so desiccated that they are extremely hard and brittle, and it will be necessary to restore them to a flexible condition. This can be done by impregnation with one of the hydrophilic polyethylene glycol waxes (see p. 144).[2] The particular wax used for this purpose is the grade 1500 which is a blend of equal parts of the solid wax 1540 and liquid polyethylene glycol 300. The object to be treated is left immersed in the molten wax at 50 °C. until the leather has become flexible—usually a matter of a few days, but this will depend upon the thickness of the leather. It is then removed, washed with toluene to remove any excess of wax on the surface, and allowed to dry. It should be noted that the wax of grade 1500 is slightly hygroscopic, so that under humid conditions the treated leather may become moist, but this should not occur under normal museum conditions. However, to guard against this the object may be treated with the microcrystalline wax preparation described in Appendix XV.

[1] Mühlethaler, B., *Urschweiz*, 1964, **28**, p. 44.
[2] Werner, A. E., *Museums Journal*, 1957, **57**, p. 3.

REPAIRING OLD LEATHER

When leather has to be repaired this is best done with a paste mixture or a suitable emulsion adhesive *before* the application of leather dressing, because, once the leather has been lubricated with an oil dressing, the adhesive cannot be made to adhere. When degreasing is necessary prior to repair, this can be accomplished by trichloro-ethane, but it should be applied sparingly to the parts that have to be stuck together. Leather dressing may be applied, of course, after the repair has been carried out.

When leather has become so rotten that it has lost its fibrous structure, it is impossible to put new life into it, but even if the surface is cracked or broken it may be possible to strengthen it by sticking a strong material to the back. Such restorations are carried out in the case of flat leathers—screens, leather wall-coverings, and the flat parts of leather upholstery, especially when of light colour liable to be stained by dressings. If the surface of the leather is very dirty, it should first be cleaned by sponging it over with a little size water.[1] The leather is then removed (if necessary) from the object to which it is attached, and laid face downwards on a table covered with glass or linoleum, and if it is wrinkled, an attempt should be made to flatten the skin by damping, allowing time for the moisture to penetrate, and then gradually lowering a piece of plate glass upon it. When the leather is well relaxed, pressure may be applied by placing suitable weights on the glass and the pressure should be retained until the skin is dry. A piece of raw cloth canvas of suitable size and weight is now pasted to the back of the leather, the canvas is covered with newspaper, and pressed overnight. Next day the leather will be found to be considerably strengthened.

This will be all that is required in the case of a wall-covering. A screen panel would be remounted, possibly after applying webbing to the framework to prevent the leather being damaged if the screen

---

[1] On no account should commercial detergent powders be used for cleaning leather as they are liable to extract the tanning materials and ruin leather and chamois. Castile soap, soft soap, and saddle soap are harmless to leather provided they are used in strict moderation, but they may affect dye-stuffs.

were to be carelessly handled. The side of a leather chair is sometimes backed with thin tough millboard prior to remounting the leather.

It does not follow that because an object is of skin or leather it should necessarily be treated with leather dressing. It may be desirable to keep rigid leather stiff, rather than to make it pliable, and caution is required in dealing with tooled leather, as the sharpness of the pattern might be impaired were the leather to be softened. These remarks apply to such things as wooden chests covered with hide, and to accoutrements, scabbards, etc. Circumstances must determine what is the best treatment, whether it is better to consolidate by using some form of thin lacquer or microcrystalline wax (see Appendix XV), and so restore the appearance, or whether to aim at restoring flexibility.

PRESERVATION OF LEATHER BOOKBINDINGS

Vegetable-tanned leather is still virtually the only kind of leather that is used for binding books. It is subject to two forms of deterioration, physical and chemical, and these should be distinguished, though both may be present together in one and the same binding. Physical deterioration is due to normal wear and tear, and commonly takes the form of a breakdown of the surface, exposing the tough fibrous underlayers of the skin which are not easily scuffed with the fingernail. Chemical deterioration is accompanied by cracking and often by change of colour, and sooner or later it involves a complete breakdown of structure. Leather in this condition may be reduced to a fine powder by scuffing. Chemical decay takes place more quickly than physical decay, and its effects are more profound. Pl. 2 shows a series of leather bindings in which the hinges have suffered decay, partly physical and partly chemical in nature, since the period 1828–35.

Physical deterioration. Physical deterioration is determined in no small degree by bindery practice, and can be controlled to a large extent by the selection of suitable leathers for different sizes and weights of books, as well as by handling. Sharp corners on metal shelving are an obvious cause of fraying. When books are too tightly packed on the shelf the bindings become deformed, and the effort to pull a book out may result in the top edge of the back being torn. The evil practice of building shelving over radiators results in the speedy deterioration of books kept thereon; heat causes leather to harden and glue to become desiccated; and, if the shelving is open, a dust problem is added to the others.

Chemical deterioration. When leather volumes are standing together on a book-shelf the sides are protected, but the backs are exposed, as well as the top headbands, and (especially if in an industrial area) the exposed parts absorb sulphur dioxide from the atmosphere. Leather bindings invariably contain traces of iron compounds; these act as a catalyst in the conversion of sulphur dioxide to sulphur trioxide which, in turn, unites with water to form sulphuric acid. The sulphuric acid attacks the leather tissue in presence of oxygen, causing it to become very brittle. The opening of the books cracks the joints at the top, and this is usually the first visible sign of chemical deterioration. It is only the beginning, however; the hinges eventually become so weak that the covers split off, and the back may eventually fall to pieces (see Pl. 3).

In studying the deterioration of leather in a long series of dated bindings, such as the heavy volumes of *The Times* newspaper, bound in pigskin at the British Museum, certain anomalies can be observed. Some of the original bindings are still in use today after a hundred years' service—they are worn and frayed round the edges, as is only to be expected, but they show no signs of the powdery chemical decay that occurs on similar volumes later in the series. The younger leathers have decayed, while the older ones have survived. The second example is that of the *General Catalogue of Printed Books* ('G.K. 1'), in the British Museum Library. It contains serviceable though badly worn volumes of about fifty years of age in their original bindings of green straight-grained morocco, whereas others in the same series of only about fifteen years of age have had to be repaired, and some of the volumes have actually had to be rebound.

As a result of investigations initiated by the British Leather Manufacturers' Research Association, and carried out by R. Faraday Innes,[1]
it has been found that it is the presence of certain water-soluble substances in the old leathers that has protected them from chemical
attack. In the past, leathers used to be coloured by surface-staining,
but modern processes involve immersion of the leather in a dye-bath.
No doubt colour-matching has been facilitated by the modern
methods, but immersion of the leather means that the protective
water-soluble substances have been extracted, and the lasting quality
of the leather has thereby been impaired. Innes carried his researches
farther, and showed that if the water-soluble substances (so-called
'non-tans') have been removed from freshly manufactured leather,
it is possible to introduce certain simple salts which will confer protection (Appendix XII). He also devised an accelerated form of test
called the 'Peroxide' or 'P.I.R.A.' test (Appendix XIV) that might
indicate whether a given sample of leather is likely to be permanent,
i.e. whether the leather will resist deterioration when it is exposed to
oxidation in the presence of sulphuric acid.

The results of applying the peroxide test to a series of bookbinding
leathers are shown in Pl. 4. The first row contains 'controls' set
aside for comparative purposes—they all seem to be sound leathers.
The second row shows the result of applying the peroxide test to
other samples of the same leathers—only No. 10 has survived. The
third row gives results similar to the second; in this case the specimens
were washed before applying the test, but as the leathers had already
been deprived of their 'non-tans' during manufacture, the washing
made no difference. In the fourth row the leathers were protected,
before testing, by potassium lactate in accordance with the method
described in Appendix XII. The photographs show that the treatment recommended makes it possible for the leathers to survive intensive oxidation in the presence of sulphuric acid and it is thus
possible to ensure the life of vegetable-tanned leather by lactate
treatment.

'Real leather' can only be reliable for bookbinding if it is ade-

[1] British Leather Mfrs.' Res. Assoc., *Laboratory Reports, 1933*, **12**, 228.

quately protected by the presence of non-tans or salts. To ascribe any virtue to 'acid free leather' is purely illusory, as leather will absorb sulphur dioxide in any case in polluted atmospheres.

It should be added that protective salts are only of value when applied to freshly tanned leather: they have an insignificant protective action on old leather that has already absorbed some acid and is suffering chemical decay.

The problem of protecting leather against chemical deterioration is still receiving attention. There is prospect that it may be solved by the application of reagents to deprive the iron in the leather of its power to catalyse the formation of sulphuric acid. This has been shown to be possible by using a water-soluble oxalate,[1] and also by sequestering the iron (see p. 289) with potassium pyrophosphate.[2] The efficacy of these methods can only be determined by the test of time, however, as in this case the peroxide test is not applicable. This idea of sequestering the iron is still only of laboratory interest; so far as is known no commercial book-binding leathers are yet available that are claimed to be protected in this way.

A long-term test. In order to test the various factors that might be supposed to have a bearing on the permanence of vegetable-tanned leather, two identical series of bindings have been prepared, one series being kept in the clean atmosphere of the National Library of Wales, Aberystwyth, and the other set in the Department of Printed Books at the British Museum. The bindings have been done in leather from different animals, various tannages are represented (sumac, gambier, oak bark, etc.), and the leathers are either unprotected or else protected in different ways by impregnating with a variety of salts. Some leathers have been degreased, some treated with leather dressings, etc., the aim being to make the series as representative of all the variants as possible.

Each series contains over 600 volumes. These are examined every few years and, although the scheme has only been in operation for

---

[1] Cheshire, A., *Journal of the International Society of Leather Trades Chemists*, 1946, **30**, 134.

[2] Innes recommends the use of a 1 per cent aqueous solution.

forty years, some interesting information has already been accumulated.[1] Some of the main conclusions may be enumerated:

1. The volumes at the British Museum show considerably more
deterioration than those at Aberystwyth, where the atmosphere is
practically free from sulphur dioxide.

2. Salt-free tannages of the pyrogallol type are more resistant than
those of the catechol type, and it is beginning to be possible to distinguish which actual tannages are best and which are least durable;
thus, sumac and Nigerian acacia pod tannages are the best of the
pyrogallol type, and gambier the least durable of the catechol type.

3. Removal of soluble non-tans facilitates decay. Addition of
certain salts increases the resistance even of catechol-tanned leather.

4. The peroxide test appears to be rather unreliable as a guide to
the durability of vegetable-tanned leathers in polluted atmospheres.[2]

5. The following are *not* major factors in the resistance of bindings
to chemical decay: type of skin, type of cure, presence or absence of
grease, method of liming and pickling.

This short account of the scientific work that is being done on
vegetable-tanned leather brings to notice three matters of practical
importance in the preservation of bookbindings and of leather upholstery. In the first place, these leathers will be inclined to deteriorate
most quickly in rooms where the air is polluted by the fumes of
combustion of gas, coal, and especially of coke. Secondly, washing
the leather may be equally bad, in that it will tend to remove soluble
non-tans, and predispose the tissue to attack. Thirdly, leather dressings have little effect in protecting leather from chemical decay, however useful they are in the physical sense in lubricating the tissue and
thus keeping the leather supple.

On the basis of these considerations it is possible to evolve a practical treatment of vegetable-tanned bindings that are still in a reasonably

---

[1] British Leather Mfrs.' Res. Assoc. 1932, ii. 276. Long-term test commenced. 1945,
24, 104. 1st Interim Report. 1952, **31**, 380. 2nd Interim Report. 1954, **33**, 208. 3rd
Interim Report. 1962, **41**, 157. 4th Interim Report. 1968, **57**, 37. 5th Interim Report.
[2] Private communication from B.L.M.R.A. (1971).

sound condition with a view to prolonging the life of the leather. The treatment is not applicable to bindings that have suffered chemical deterioration to such an extent that the spine is no longer intact, or the spine and hinges have become partly detached.

The treatment is carried out in three stages as follows:

1. *Cleaning.* The surface of the binding is rubbed over with a damp sponge to remove surface dirt. If necessary the sponge can first be rubbed over a cake of high-quality toilet soap to assist the removal of the dirt, but all traces of soap must be removed afterwards with a clean damp sponge. It is important that an excessive amount of water should not be used so as to avoid the risk of causing localized staining.

2. *Chemical stabilization.* Since protective salts may be removed in cleaning, these must be replaced in order to stabilize the leather against chemical decay. For this purpose the bindings are treated with the solution of potassium lactate prepared as described in Appendix XII. This is applied with a sponge, care being taken to avoid excessive wetting at any one point with the risk of consequent staining, and the books are left standing on end in a warm place to dry.

3. *Consolidation.* British Museum Leather Dressing (Appendix XIII) is used in the final stage of the treatment to keep the leather flexible and thus lessen the mechanical wear. The smallest possible quantity of the dressing is applied (either with the finger-tips or with cotton wool dipped into the liquid and squeezed almost dry) and rubbed well into the leather, particular attention being paid to the hinges. It is important to avoid leaving any surplus of the dressing on the leather, which should feel only slightly greasy to the touch at this stage. After standing on end for a few days to allow the hexane to evaporate, and the lanolin to penetrate the leather, the book should be polished with a soft cloth. If necessary, a second application of the dressing can be made, but on no account should large amounts of the leather dressing be applied at any time as it is difficult to remove any excess, and the binding will be left sticky and greasy.

MOULDS AND INSECTS IN BOOKS

All books contain nutrients for moulds and are susceptible to attack by insects, and insect attack is often associated with mould growth (see below), which is likely to occur under warm damp conditions. If an outbreak of mould growth occurs, increased ventilation without heating should be adopted as a first measure. To heat a damp room without adequate ventilation would merely stimulate mould growth before the books could be adequately dried.

Books suffering from mould growth may be sterilized by being exposed in a closed container to the action of formaldehyde vapour using 500 ml. of formalin (40 per cent formaldehyde) per cubic metre of air space. However, care is necessary in the use of formalin, because it is possible that the colours of the bindings may be affected, and also it is not recommended for the treatment of parchment or vellum. An alternative method of sterilization is to interleave the book with tissue freshly impregnated with Santobrite or Topane WS (see p. 63) at the rate of one sheet of tissue for every ten pages. The tissue should be left in the books for two to six months depending upon the extent of the mould growth.

There are several varieties of insect that live on books, the most common in this country being booklice (*Psocoptera*), silverfish (*Thysanura*) and firebrat, and the woodworm (*Anobium domesticum*). Booklice appear to live on mildew and fungi which can grow on damp books. Silverfish and firebrats are able to digest cellulose from paper and can eat glue, paste, leather, etc. The woodworm is not a pest specifically of books, but it can easily invade books from infected wooden shelves, and it is the most damaging pest.

The best way to prevent infestation of books is by good housekeeping. Books should be kept dry (relative humidity from 50 to 65 per cent) so that moulds and fungi cannot grow and break down the paper or leather, thus providing ample food for booklice and silverfish. By reasonably frequent dusting of the books and shelves, edible dirt and dust is removed and incipient attack by insects detected and treated. Books obtained from places where infestation is suspected should be dusted very carefully, particular attention being paid to crevices and spines, and kept apart from other books for over a year with monthly inspection to ensure that they are free of any infestation. If the infestation is confined to a limited number of books, these may be treated as follows:

1. Brush the books in the open air to remove all dust, dirt, etc.
2. Place the books, opened fanwise, in a container in which is placed a dish of crystals of *para*-dichlorobenzene (1 kg. per cubic metre of air space) or a dish of chloroform (500 ml. per cubic metre of air space). Then seal the container, leave for at least a fortnight, and open it out of doors.
3. Thoroughly clean the drawers, cupboards, or shelving and brush them with a 0·5 per cent solution of DDT in white spirit (turpentine substitute), the solution being well worked into all crevices.

It should be noted that one treatment may not be sufficient to eliminate all the insects, as the eggs and pupae of the insects are resistant to insecticides. The treated books should, therefore, be kept under observation for at least a year; if insects reappear, fumigation should be repeated.

If a large-scale infestation has occurred, the only remedy is a thorough fumigation of the books under vacuum. Since this is an elaborate procedure requiring special equipment, it is best carried out by a firm of specialists. A satisfactory fumigant is ethylene oxide as this has both fungicidal and insecticidal properties. This was used for treating many thousands of books and innumerable manuscripts that were damaged in the floods of Florence in 1966.[1] Incidentally, books that have suffered flood damage should never be dried quickly, but set up on edge and exposed to a uniform current of cool air, the positions being changed daily to prevent the serious deformation that may result from the irregular loss of moisture.

[1] Horton, C., 'Saving the Libraries of Florence', *Wilson Library Bulletin*, 1967, p. 1035.

II

PAPYRUS, PARCHMENT, AND PAPER

ALL of the materials that have been worked by man have at some time or other been used for writing upon—metals, stones, clay, wood, ivory, leather—and yet history has been recorded for us, primarily, on three that might be considered to be the most ephemeral—papyrus, parchment, and paper. These three are completely destroyed by fire and water, easily stained, and subject to attack by moulds and insects, and yet, when kept dry, they have shown remarkable powers of survival.

While differing in chemical composition and physical properties, they have this in common, that they become brittle when desiccated, but when moistened they regain their flexibility to such an extent that they may be safely handled, flattened, and mounted in permanent form. The presence of carbon ink does not complicate treatment, and even the more fugitive iron inks, when decomposed in the tissue, leave a tracing of rust that is unaffected by the slight degree of moisture required for relaxation and manipulation. Parchment is a protein substance whereas papyrus and paper are composed of cellulose. However, the techniques of conservation, though differing to a certain extent in the three materials, are sufficiently related to justify their inclusion together within the present chapter.

PAPYRUS

The 'paper reed' of Egypt, *Cyperus papyrus* (Linn.), was grown in the delta of the Nile and exploited from earliest times to make ropes, sails, boats, matting, cloth, and later to make the paper-like material used for writing purposes. Lucas[1] describes how he succeeded in

[1] Lucas, A., op. cit., p. 138.

making papyrus sheets. The process he used is as follows. Longitudinal strips of the pith of the papyrus plant are laid parallel and slightly overlapping, a second series of strips is placed at right angles over the first, and welded to it by beating with a light mallet, the only cementing material being the natural sap, which, in the fresh reed, is sufficiently adhesive to effect a permanent join; it acts at the same time as a sizing material and prevents ink from spreading when writing on the sheet. Pliny refers to flour paste being used to join such sheets together to form a long roll.

Papyrus was used for writings in Egypt from about 3000 B.C. until about the ninth century A.D., when the advent of paper-making supplanted the manufacture of papyrus as an essential industry. While the majority of documents written on papyrus have come from Egyptian tombs, it is known that a form of papyrus was also cultivated in Sicily, and fragmentary remains of charred papyrus rolls have been recovered from excavations at Herculaneum. In Egypt papyrus writings are not only excavated from tombs, but sometimes taken from the mummies themselves. Sir Flinders Petrie found old papyrus manuscripts used as layers in the construction of the cartonnage of certain mummies of the late Ptolemaic period at Gurob. Some of these writings have been salvaged, but from the nature of the material and its contamination with plaster, it is not surprising that, as documents, they are incomplete and largely indecipherable.

Papyri can always be relied upon to arouse the interest of collectors, especially when they appear for sale in the form of tight rolls, tied and sealed, it may be, with the clay impression of a cartouche, perhaps of an eighteenth-dynasty king. It is not unusual to find, however, on opening such rolls, that the more attractive the parcel the less the interest of the contents. When the roll does contain fragments of documents, and this is by no means always the case, they may be merely the oft-repeated texts of the Book of the Dead, but where they are of literary texts interest is revived, as Egyptologists have at times been successful in discovering the parent document to which the missing fragments could be restored.

Method of unwrapping papyrus rolls

Papyrus is recovered from the tombs of Egypt in the form of tight rolls, the diameter being determined by the length of the document, and the width varying from a few inches to a foot or more in the larger specimens. Such rolls are often parcelled up in strips of linen. The linen may easily be removed, as the flexibility of the textile is unaffected by age, but the papyrus is always very brittle in the dry state, and must be relaxed by moisture before any attempt is made to unroll it, otherwise it would break into many pieces. The relaxing is done by wrapping the roll loosely in several layers of damp white blotting-paper and setting it aside for an hour or so on a sheet of glass. By this time the external convolutions will have become sufficiently limp to be manipulated without cracking, and unrolling can then be commenced.

Pl. 5A shows a number of papyri in the dry brittle condition as received for unwrapping, and Pl. 5B shows a stage in the course of the work. The damp blotting-paper has been removed from the relaxed papyrus and is under the bell-jar to the operator's right; the papyrus placed against a sheet of dry blotting-paper is lying on plate glass, and is gradually being unrolled, a little at a time against the paper. When a short length has been exposed, this is covered with dry blotting-paper, and flattened under glass. After a few inches of the roll have been unwrapped the operation is stopped and the unrolled portion covered with the wet blotting-paper to make a fresh piece flexible. This is repeated as often as may be necessary, until the whole of the papyrus has been unrolled and laid flat.

Once the papyrus is flat it must be dried without delay, by changing the blotting-paper several times in the course of a few hours. As a protection against moulds it is usual to sterilize the document by pressing it for several days in contact with thymol-impregnated blotting-paper (p. 62), after which it may be mounted passe-partout between two sheets of glass.

Complications arise when a papyrus is already broken or where it is incomplete, and it may then be necessary to get the fragments into register by studying peculiarities of grain, colour, thickness, and, of course, the writing. Cracks are reinforced with narrow strips of gold-beater's skin; for major repair work either flour paste or a good photographic mountant can be used—but it is more usual to fix detached fragments in position with gold-beater's skin. Smaller papyri may be enclosed in silk gauze and bound up in a guard-book, such as is supplied for newspaper cuttings; this is convenient for study as well as for storage purposes.

Birch bark provides the same problems as papyrus. It is as brittle as tinder in the dry condition, but it can be relaxed by moisture. A tightly wrapped wad of writings on birch bark (Pl. 6) was found inside a Buddhist image of the eighteenth century. It was possible to unwrap it, and to recover eleven legible documents from the wad. These documents are copies of sets of Northern Buddhist charms in doggerel Sanskrit, adorations of the Buddha, requests for purification, success, etc., in a series of imperatives fortified by magic syllables.

PARCHMENT

Parchment originated in Pergamon, Asia Minor, in the pre-Christian era. It is a stronger material than either papyrus or paper, and is able to withstand much harder usage, as one would expect, since it is derived from animal skin. Although parchment may be prepared from the skin of many animals, the commonest source is sheepskin, and this has provided the finest grades for the scribe and illuminator. It is, however, almost impossible by examining an old parchment to determine with any degree of certainty from which animal it has been derived. Exceptionally fine qualities are sometimes attributed to the deer, antelope, or smaller animals. In general, the younger the skin, the thinner the parchment made from it, and the less likely is it to be blemished. Calf parchment is known by the manufacturers today as vellum. It is usually harder than sheep parchment, and on this account of more interest to the binder than to the scribe, but the word vellum has lost its definitive character, and one often hears the finer grades of medieval parchment described as 'uterine vellum', a description which can seldom be justified.

Manufacture and qualities of parchment

The manufacture of parchment involves operations depending for their success on the experience and dexterity of the craftsman. Occasionally one comes across a *tour de force*, an old liturgical manuscript, perhaps, which in fineness and quality is a match for the best that can be made today, even with the modern abrasive and skin-splitting processes. Fineness is not the only criterion of a good parchment— flexibility, perfection of surface, and strength all contribute to the excellence of the material as a ground for fine writing and illumination.

The technique of parchment-making has changed little through the ages, except for the introduction of the splitting process. Parchment was formerly made from the entire skin; in modern practice it is made from the flesh side of a split skin. The whole skin is limed, dehaired, and very thoroughly defleshed, and a splitting-machine separates the skiver from the flesh side. The parchment split is then stretched on a frame and scraped down on both sides with a crescent-shaped knife. As it dries the skin tightens considerably, and scraping is continued with a knife of the same shape but having a blade with a burred edge. The parchment is then treated with hot water, scraped again, and, while still wet, rubbed on both sides with a pumice block. It is then dried on the stretcher frame.

The type of finish varies in accordance with requirements. In the case of writing material which must be white and flawless, it is bleached and any remains of grease are removed by lime wash. On the other hand parchment that is to serve as a ground for decorative illumination must be opaque, and the surface is sometimes finished by coating with talc. One of the chief aims of the manufacturer is to suppress the grain, but there is usually no difficulty in deciding by inspection which side of the material was originally the flesh side, and which the grain side; these correspond respectively to the rough side and smooth side of the sheet. In good-quality parchment the smooth or grain side is usually velvety to the touch, and as it provides a very agreeable surface for writing upon, it is preferred for this purpose to the flesh side. It is delicate, in the sense that it is easily damaged by erasures or staining, and tends in the coarser qualities of parchment to be yellowish and horny in character. In a bound manuscript both sides are used for writing and, in this case, like sides face each other, grain to grain, and flesh side to flesh side, so that when the book is open, there is less chance of disparity in the appearance of adjoining sheets.

Parchment may have a transparent quality resulting from less intensive stretching, or transparency may be obtained by chemical means. In 1790 Edwards of Halifax took out a patent for making parchment transparent by treating the flesh side with potash. In the King's Library at the British Museum there is a sample of Edwards's 'transparent vellum', as it was called, which takes the form of a binding for a 'Book of Common Prayer'. This transparent vellum is painted on the inner side and the colours show through the transparent membrane to the front. It has kept its appearance surprisingly well, showing no sign of cockling although it has been on exhibition for many years.

Alkalinity of parchment

A feature of parchment of all types is that it is alkaline. Liming of the skins is carried out in the early stages of fellmongering, prior to degreasing, and no subsequent acid treatment is applied to neutralize the alkali. A trace of lime remains, therefore, and this is firmly held by the collagen fibres of which the parchment is composed. This alkalinity confers a certain measure of protection against the action of moulds and micro-organisms, which prefer a substratum of slightly acid character. It may also provide a clue to the chemical stability of the material, as parchment is not affected by acidic atmospheres, and in this sense is a much more durable material than leather. One disadvantage of alkalinity, however, is the tendency to yellowing, so noticeable when parchment is much handled or exposed to dirt and grease. The main cause is probably the widespread distribution of iron as an ingredient of dust, yielding the coloured hydroxide. This staining action is intensified by damp, and protection from excessive humidity is of great importance in the preservation of parchment.

Moisture sensitivity

Parchment is a hygroscopic substance and under normal conditions it tends to adsorb and give up moisture in sympathy with the rise and fall in the relative humidity of the atmosphere. A test applied to a representative sample of parchment showed that it contained 10 per cent of its weight of water when in equilibrium with an atmosphere at 40 per cent R.H.; when, without changing the temperature, the atmosphere was suddenly raised to 80 per cent R.H., the parchment adsorbed moisture until, *in the course of three days*, it attained equilibrium with its new surroundings and the water content was then found to amount to no less than 30 per cent of its dry weight. This test shows how responsive the material is to changes in relative humidity; it also indicates that there is a time lag. If parchment is exposed to over-dry or moist conditions for a short period no harm will result, but if extreme conditions persist for a time, then deterioration will follow.

As an example, if parchment is exposed to excess of water for a lengthy period of time, a complete breakdown of structure will take place by the chemical action known as hydrolysis: the proteins are degraded, the organized structures disappear, and a form of gelatine known as parchment size is formed.

When kept in an atmosphere that is too dry, say at 40 per cent R.H. or less, parchment tends to become rigid and to cockle. This condition is reversible, however, as flexibility can always be restored by exposing the membrane to moisture, but permanent damage may have been caused to inks and colours through desiccation. Certain inks tend to flake from the surface of over-dry parchment and illuminations are liable to suffer in the same way. On the other hand, the damage resulting from exposure to high relative humidity is even more severe, especially if the manuscripts are illuminated or decorated with painted miniatures. The adsorption of moisture and its subsequent loss on drying causes deformation of the membranes which may result in loss of paint. Under humid conditions miniatures in colour may actually become off-set against adjacent leaves. When a bound manuscript is exposed for some time in damp surroundings (e.g. in a safe or deed box in a damp basement), the edges of the pages pick up moisture and become cockled. This type of damage is accelerated if the binding is too tight, or if a book has lost its clasp. The book tends to gape along the fore-edge, exposing a larger surface area to damp so that the wrinkling spreads until, in the end, it is no longer possible to close the book. Such distortion cannot be cured by drying or by putting the book in a press. The only satisfactory mode of treatment is to 'pull the book'—a task requiring special training and experience—and to deal patiently with the sheets one at a time.

Although so sensitive to moisture changes, parchment retains its strength and resiliency and is very durable, provided it is not exposed to extreme conditions for long periods. The great codices that have come down to us from the early centuries of the Christian era are surprisingly fresh in appearance, although they may have been cleaned, flattened, and rebound; this in itself is a testimony to the stability of the material.

Parchment documents that are in a hard and shrunken condition, and with individual pages adhering together, are sometimes brought in for treatment. In such cases no attempt must be made to separate the membranes until they have been relaxed. The relaxing process is very similar to that adopted in the case of desiccated papyri (p. 46), except that humidification should be less intense, and it should be given more time to take effect. The horny tissue of parchment takes about twenty times longer to relax than papyrus, and premature efforts to separate the leaves would certainly cause damage. In some cases it may prove to be impossible to restore the sheets to their original size. Even when the membranes are badly shrunken the writing may still be quite readable, and it is better to leave well alone rather than risk destroying the legibility of the writing.

Belaya[1] of the Leningrad Laboratory for the Restoration and Conservation of Documents has recently described a method for the softening of dry deformed parchment by treating it with a 10 per cent solution of urea in ethyl alcohol followed by the application of

[1] Belaya, I. K., *Restaurator*, 1969, **1**, p. 20.

a 2 per cent ethyl alcohol/benzene emulsion of spermaceti; the latter increases the strength and elasticity of the parchment. This treatment does not increase the hygroscopicity of the parchment, and has no deleterious effect on the text or illuminations in parchment manuscripts.

In order to clean a stained vellum binding it is rubbed over quickly with a sponge moistened with dilute size, and if dried at once no harm will result.

The cleaning and repair of manuscripts is a craft that can only be mastered by experience. The simple operations of relaxing and removing creases, repairing holes, replacing missing corners, etc., should be practised on unimportant material. For repairs see pp. 92 et sqq.

Fungal attack

If parchment has become mouldy, the most convenient and effective method of fumigation is to expose it in a thymol chamber (p. 61). Larger documents may be opened out and interleaved with paper of the same dimensions that has been previously impregnated with a suitable fungicide (p. 63). This contact method is recommended where continuous protection is required over a period.

Storing parchment

The control of humidity is an essential factor in the storage of parchment. Ideally, the atmospheric relative humidity should be kept constant at about 55/60 per cent at a temperature between 60 and 75 °F. (16–25 °C.). This will prevent either embrittlement resulting from conditions that are too dry, or distortion from exposure to conditions that are too moist. Damp heat must be avoided as this causes shrinkage and encourages the growth of moulds.

It is no easy matter to maintain satisfactory conditions day and night in a private house, or in a safe or strong room, and it would have been impossible to suggest a simple remedy to help in this matter, were it not for the fact that humidity conditions can be stabilized by the presence of a bulk supply of hygroscopic material, such as cotton-wool, carpets, curtains, and textiles generally. Bare shelving in an unheated room without ventilation is no place for parchment; in the case of metal shelving there will be the added danger that moisture may condense on the metal if the ambient temperature falls. Metal safes and deed boxes are necessary in the interests of security, but are not the best accommodation unless plenty of hygroscopic material surrounds the parchment to minimize the effect of changes in relative humidity. Documents should be wrapped in paper, or preferably in textile, and textiles should be chosen with a thought to the subsidiary risk of insect attack. It has been proved that cotton and linen materials are safest.

In storing parchment documents it should be remembered that they are prone to attack by rats and mice, and precautions must be taken accordingly. Small rodents can work havoc with parchment in a very short time, and to leave a storage drawer open, even for one night, may result in damage that is irreparable. Hygiene is the best safeguard, and no foodstuffs should be left about that might attract the pests. If workmen are on the premises they should be asked to exercise care in this respect.

As to fire precautions, there should always be at hand fire-fighting equipment that would not, itself, harm the documents. Carbon tetrachloride equipment (such as is used for electrical fires), extinguishers of the methyl bromide type, and extinguishers that emit a stream of carbon dioxide gas under pressure are all perfectly safe, but the acid type of fire extinguisher is to be avoided. Asbestos blankets should be kept with the fire-fighting appliances.

PAPER

The Chinese claim the honour of being the first to discover how to make paper. They teased out silk or vegetable fibres under water, and collected the aqueous suspension on a porous support such as a stretched cloth. As the water drained away, the support was shaken, and this caused the loosened fibres to interlock and so form a thin matted sheet. When dry, such a sheet proved to be remarkably tough and serviceable.

The invention is recorded as having been made at the beginning of the second century A.D., and the earliest examples of paper that have come down to us date to within fifty years of this time. These were discovered by Sir Aurel Stein in the Great Wall of China. Some of the actual papers have been examined by one of us (H. J. P.) and were found to have been made from rags. This is an interesting fact because the fibres of the paper mulberry (*Broussonetia papyrifera*) were later preferred in the Orient as the raw material for paper-making, and it was in the West that paper made from linen and cotton rags was most in favour. Hunter,[1] who has contributed so much to our knowledge of the history of paper-making, points out that in China the soft absorbent papers made from the mulberry fibre commended themselves for brushwork and wood-block printing on one side of the paper only, whereas in Europe the requirement was for a hard paper, made from rags and treated with size, that could be used for quill-pen work on both sides of the sheet. He remarks upon the fact that it took 1,000 years for knowledge of the invention to reach Europe via the Persian Trade Route.

Quality and stability of paper

The quality and stability of paper is governed in the first instance by the raw materials from which it is made, and in Western countries many different types of cellulose fibres have been used.[2] The strongest and most durable papers are hand-made from a mixture of disinte-grated linen and cotton rags, the fibres being sized with gelatine, whereas the poorest and least durable grades of paper are those made by machinery from ground wood, pulped and sized with rosin and alum. Between these extremes lie many varieties of modern paper. One of the commonest is composed, for the most part, of sulphite

[1] Hunter, Dard, *Paper-making*, 2nd ed., New York, Alfred A. Knopf, 1947.
[2] Kantrowitz, M. S., Spencer, E. W., and Simmons, R. H., *Permanence and Durability of Paper* (containing annotated bibliography of the technical literature, A.D. 1885–A.D. 1939, U.S. Govt. Printing Office, Washington, 1940).

pulp, i.e. wood pulp chemically treated in order to remove lignin and natural resins. This paper is suitable for book printing and the printing of half-tone blocks. Modern newspapers,[1] which are not in the same class as regards permanence, contain a high proportion of crude ground-wood fibre, and only a small quantity of sulphite pulp. It is easy to determine the source of the constituents of paper by teasing out a small fragment in water and examining the fibres under low magnification. They may then be identified by comparing them with published photo-micrographs such as are to be found in a standard reference book.[2]

The following table lists some important dates in the paper industry bearing on the quality of stock:

1774	Discovery of chlorine by the Swedish chemist Karl Wilhelm Scheele	From this time, worn and discoloured rags could be bleached for use as basic material, and also finished paper could be bleached. (*Note.* Paper containing residues of chlorine compounds is impermanent.)
1793	Invention of the cotton gin	Cotton soon became the basic raw material.
1800	Experiments with straw fibres	Colour and brittleness generally resulted.
1803	Invention of Fourdrinier machine	Greatly improved turnover in paper manufacture, but weakness resulted at first from excessive shortening of fibres; later overcome.
1807	Use of alum-rosin size	Increased acidity and proneness to colour change.
1810	Filling with clay, barytes, etc.	Excess resulted in debasement.
1840	Use of ground wood pulp	Lignin present, colour and impermanence resulted.

[1] Scribner, B. W., *Preservation of Newspaper Records*, Misc. Pub. 145, Nat. Bur. of Standards, Govt. Printing Office, Washington, 1934.

[2] Armitage, F. D., *Atlas of Paper-making Fibres*, Guildhall Pub. Co., Epsom, England.

| 1850 | Introduction of soda process | These chemical treatments of wood gave a chemical wood pulp of improved quality so that a good quality cellulose stock comparable with rag cellulose became available. |
| 1857 | Introduction of sulphite process | |

1884 Introduction of
sulphate process

Acidity in paper

Although the stability of paper depends to a large extent upon the raw materials used in its manufacture, its permanence may be gravely affected by the development of acidity in the paper, since cellulose is subject to hydrolysis leading to degradation and loss of mechanical strength. Acidity may either be introduced in the process of manufacture or be acquired on ageing. Alum is used, for example, in sizing and this is an acidic substance. Also, any residues of bleaching agents left in the paper will cause acidic deterioration. Moreover, paper shares with vegetable-tanned leather a susceptibility to attack by sulphur dioxide, and in an urban atmosphere it can pick up an appreciable amount of sulphur dioxide that is converted by traces of heavy metals, in particular iron and copper, into sulphuric acid. The extent of the acidity in paper can be determined by measuring its pH (see Appendix VIII) either using the standard TAPPI[1] extraction method or the special flat glass electrode method devised by Hudson and Milner.[2] If the pH is less than 5·5, treatment to remove acidity is necessary, since otherwise the life of the paper will be endangered.

Deacidification of paper

The easiest way of deacidifying paper is to treat it with a mild alkali that will first neutralize the acid present and can then be converted into a compound that will remain in the fibres of the paper to act as a buffer to absorb any further acidity that may develop as the result of exposure to atmospheric sulphur dioxide. Uncontrolled neutralization must be avoided because, if the pH is allowed to rise

[1] TAPPI Standard T435 m-52. 1 gm. of paper is extracted in the cold for one hour with 70 ml. of distilled water, and the pH of the extract is measured.

[2] Hudson, F. L., and Milner, W. D., *Svensk Papperstichning*, 1959, **62**, p. 83 (in English).

above 9, there is risk of oxidation of the cellulose under alkaline conditions. The practical aspect of this problem was studied by Barrow,[1] who evolved a simple process of deacidification. The paper is first immersed for twenty minutes in a saturated solution of lime water (calcium hydroxide) of concentration *c.* 0·15 per cent. This neutralizes the acid, leaving a certain amount of free lime in the paper, which is then immersed for a further twenty minutes in a solution of calcium bicarbonate (concentration *c.* 0·2 per cent) so that the excess of lime is converted into calcium carbonate (chalk) which is deposited as a fine precipitate in the fibres of the paper, where it acts as a protective buffer. As an alternative Barrow[2] has suggested a one-stage process in which the paper is immersed in an 0·2 per cent solution of magnesium bicarbonate, and he has also adapted this method for the spray deacidification of books.

These aqueous methods of deacidification cannot be used for the treatment of manuscript documents in which the ink is susceptible to the action of water. In such cases a non-aqueous method of deacidification is essential, and for this purpose an elegant method has been developed in the British Museum Research Laboratory by Baynes-Cope.[3] The document is treated with a solution prepared by dissolving 19 gm. of crystalline barium hydroxide octahydrate $(Ba(OH)_2 \cdot 8H_2O)$ in one litre of methyl alcohol (this corresponds to a 1 per cent solution of barium hydroxide as the free base). The normal procedure is to immerse the document in this solution, but it may be brushed or sprayed on if the document is in a frail condition. The document is then hung up to dry, and any excess of barium hydroxide is converted by atmospheric carbon dioxide into barium carbonate, giving a final pH of about 8.

An alternative method of non-aqueous deacidification has been described by Smith[4] in which the document is treated with a 5 per

---

[1] Barrow, W. J., *J. Documentary Reproductions*, 1939, **2**, p. 47; *The American Archivist*, 1943, **6**, p. 151.

[2] Barrow, W. J., *Permanence/Durability of the Book*, 1964, **3**.

[3] Baynes-Cope, A. D., *Restaurator*, 1969, **1**, p. 2.

[4] Smith, R. D., *Library Quarterly*, 1966, **36**, No. 4, p. 175; 1970, **40**, No. 1, p. 139.

cent solution of magnesium methoxide in methyl alcohol, and then hung up to dry. In this process the magnesium methoxide is converted by the moisture in the paper into magnesium hydroxide which is the effective deacidifying agent; during drying any excess of magnesium hydroxide is converted into magnesium carbonate by atmospheric carbon dioxide, and the final pH is about 8.

Langwell[1] has proposed a method for the vapour-phase deacidification of books involving the use of cyclohexylamine carbonate. The books are interleaved with tissue paper impregnated with cyclohexylamine carbonate, and loose documents are deacidified by placing sachets containing cyclohexylamine carbonate in the box files. The active deacidifying agent is the free amine that is given off as a vapour. Some doubt has, however, been expressed about the long-term efficacy of this method of deacidification, and there is also some concern about the potential toxic hazards of the vapour.[2]

Humidity, mildew, and foxing

The control of relative humidity is of the greatest importance in places where books and papers are stored, because paper is a hygroscopic material—it absorbs moisture from the atmosphere. Excessive moisture tends to weaken the tissue,[3] and promotes the growth of micro-organisms which rot the size and cause staining. How delicate the hygrometric balance is may be gauged from a calculation that was made in connection with an extension of a quadrant book-stack at the British Museum. One thousand tons of books were calculated to absorb at least 20,000 lb. of water when the relative humidity of the atmosphere increased from 57 per cent to 63 per cent at 60 °F. (16 °C.).[4] To avoid deterioration, books and papers should be

[1] Langwell, W. H., *J. Soc. Archivists*, 1964, **2**, No. 10, p. 471; 1966, **3**, No. 3, p. 137.

[2] Du Puis, R. N., Kusterer, Jr., J. E., and Sproull, R. C., *Library of Congress Information Bulletin*, 4 June 1970, p. A-41.

[3] Carson, F. T., *Effect of Humidity on Physical Properties of Paper*, Circular C. 445, National Bureau of Standards, Govt. Printing Office, Washington, 1944.

[4] McIntyre, J., *Journal of the Institution of Heating and Ventilating Engineers*, 1937, **4**, No. 48, p. 570.

stored under conditions that are constant, say 60 per cent R.H. at 60 °F. (16 °C.).

Cellulose and gelatine size, as well as the constituents of book-binder's paste (starch, flour, or dextrin), are all excellent nutrient materials for fungi, and when the relative humidity of the atmosphere is over 70 per cent, the appearance of mould growths on paper is not long delayed. If there is an outbreak and the trouble is detected and dealt with at once by drying the affected papers little harm will ensue, but if infection is allowed to continue unchecked, the papers will be yellowed and stained with coloured spots. Some micro-organisms live on the size, and others on the cellulose fibres. Where the sizing material has been attacked, the size is destroyed, and the affected area becomes highly absorbent, like blotting-paper, and if tested by wetting, will appear dull and translucent as compared with the surroundings. When cellulytic micro-organisms are present, the surface of the paper will be eroded, and the paper may become very brittle. In both cases there is a tendency for iron salts (iron is a common impurity in paper) to be accumulated on the damaged areas, where they form rusty brown spots commonly known as foxing. But this type of staining may arise from other causes,[1] and is often due, in part at least, to the coloured products elaborated by organisms in the course of their development.

Methods of dealing with an outbreak of mould growth

When mould begins to grow,[2] the first indication is the appearance of a fine white fluff, not at first easy to discern, but soon forming furry patches of roughly circular shape, and if no action is taken, growth, once started, will be likely to proceed apace. The real source of the trouble is damp, but so long as infected material is in the room, it would be fatal to attempt to deal with the outbreak merely by raising the temperature, as this would stimulate growth and spread infection. A prior requirement is the improvement of ventilation by

[1] Armitage, F. D., *The Cause of Mildew on Books and Methods of Protection*, Bull. 8, P.A.T.R.A., Leatherhead.

[2] Plenderleith, H. J., *Archives*, 1952, **7**, p. 13.

the use of fans, etc., special attention being paid to any damp spots. Moulds must not be brushed off the books in the room; all mouldy material should first be removed, and then the room can be dried by electric heaters and fans, or by the dual-purpose machine known as a hot-air circulator, which is merely a magnified form of the familiar electric hair-drier.

Infected books and manuscripts can best be dealt with in the open air, or in a large airy room, by brushing and sunning, books being stood on edge, open, to allow free access of air, and documents flattened and suspended on stretched lines.

If the damp condition of the room can be permanently cured, and if the above instructions have been carried out, all the material may safely be returned and no further outbreak should occur, but if there is any doubt about dry conditions being maintained, then sterilization will be necessary.

(A) *Fumigation of room.* Gaseous formaldehyde may be used for sterilizing a room containing mould-infested papers,[1] provided the room can be effectively sealed for this purpose. The gas is generated by adding aqueous formaldehyde to a substance such as potassium permanganate, with which it reacts exothermically. Details of the procedure are given by Walker,[2] who recommends adding 1 lb. of aqueous formaldehyde (Formalin) to about 6 oz. of solid permanganate in a large porcelain basin or bucket. This quantity is sufficient for a room of 1,000–1,500 cub. ft. (30–50 cub. metres). As the gas is evolved briskly, the operator should make a quick exit, and seal the door on the outside. After twenty-four hours or longer, the room should be thoroughly ventilated, and any lingering odours of the fumigant dispersed by sprinkling the floor with ammonia, which converts the residual formaldehyde to hexamethylenetetramine, which is odourless. Alternatively, the sterilization may be carried out using

[1] Protein materials (parchment, vellum, leather) should, preferably, not be present as these tend to become hardened by the action of the fumigant. Despite this warning there may be cases in which the fumigation *in situ* by formaldehyde vapour could be justified as this is the most direct way of preventing moulds from spreading.

[2] Walker, J. F., *Formaldehyde*, American Chemical Society Monograph, 1944, p. 327.

7. PAGE OF DRAWINGS BY LEONARDO DA VINCI

Left: Panchromatic photograph. (To the naked eye nothing was visible)
Right: Ultra-violet fluorescence photograph showing the drawings

By gracious permission of Her Majesty the Queen

(1) Text obliterated by a darkened resin varnish
(2) Extraction with alcohol removes resin leaving yellow stain
(3) Bleaching with sodium chlorite and formalin restores legibility

(4) Dark residue of resin obtained by evaporating the alcoholic extract
(5) The book, rebound

8. PRINTED BOOK (ITALIAN, 16TH CENT.)

a paraformaldehyde heater, 5 oz. of commerical paraformaldehyde being required for a room of 1,000 cub. ft. (500 gm./120 cub. metres).

(B) *Sterilization of materials*. Two methods are available for sterilization—fumigation which is effective but confers no lasting protection, and a method involving the use of papers impregnated with fungicide of low vapour pressure which gives continuous protection over a period.

(i) *Fumigation with thymol vapour*. A suitable chamber for this purpose may be improvised from any relatively air-tight cupboard, and to be generally useful it should be large enough to accommodate in a horizontal position anything up to an imperial sheet (30 by 22 in.). The material to be sterilized is supported on a framework (stretcher covered with a net or strands of tape or twine), about 750 cm. above the bottom of the cupboard. A 40-watt electric lamp is fixed near the bottom of the cupboard, and this emits enough heat to melt the thymol crystals, which are placed some 5 cm. above it, in a clock-glass or enamel plate, supported on a wire stand. About 50 gm. of thymol is required for sterilizing the contents of a cupboard of 1 cub. metre capacity.

To use the apparatus, the current is switched on for two hours, then switched off, and the heating should be carried on for periods of about two hours every morning for fourteen days. If much material is being dealt with, the papers should be rearranged in the cupboard each morning before the light is switched on. After each treatment the door of the cupboard should be kept closed for about twenty-four hours.

In stacking the cupboard it is important to arrange for free access of the thymol vapour around the infected material—small manuscripts may be suspended, rolls set up on edge, books stood on end with their pages open fan-wise, etc. The success of the treatment depends on two factors, the concentration of thymol vapour reaching the fungus, and the drying action which attends the slight rise in temperature from the electric-light bulb.

It has been found by experiment that the method may be safely applied to prints, drawings, manuscripts, pastels, water-colour paintings, books, and also to parchment and vellum. No harm has been found to result from prolonged dosage. It should be noted that oil-paints and varnishes become softened under treatment, and for this reason the method is unsuitable for the sterilization of easel paintings and the like. The thymol chamber itself should of course be free from any internal paintwork.

Collis[1] has described the use of this method of fumigation using as the chamber a room approximately 5 metres long by 2 metres wide and $2\frac{1}{2}$ metres high in which there were six points (100-watt electric-light bulbs set in a concrete trench in the floor) for generating the thymol vapour at a concentration of about 10 gm. per cubic metre of air space.

(ii) *Fumigation with formaldehyde vapour.* Formalin (40 per cent formaldehyde) has long been known as a powerful antiseptic and germicide. It may be employed for sterilizing paper, but is not recommended for parchment, vellum, or other protein products, as these are hardened by this reagent. The papers are exposed for about twelve hours over a dish containing formalin (about 50 gm.). The sterilization must be carried out in a sealed air-tight box, and during exposure the temperature inside the box should not be allowed to fall below 18 °C. It is important also that the relative humidity should be kept above 60 per cent as moisture is essential for effective dis-infection. After sterilization the papers should be freely exposed to the air for several hours.

(iii) *Use of impregnated paper.* White blotting-paper may be impregnated by immersing it for a moment in a 10 per cent solution of thymol in alcohol, after which the excess of solvent is allowed to evaporate, leaving the thymol uniformly dispersed in the sheet. Sheets with a higher but less uniform concentration of thymol are made by scattering a handful of thymol crystals between several layers of absorbent paper and melting the crystals into the tissue by the application of a hot electric iron. Thymolized sheets, prepared by one or other process, are used for sterilizing papyrus after it has been unrolled, or for interleaving mildewed books.

[1] Collis, I. P., *J. Soc. Archivists*, 1970, 4, p. 53.

If facilities for carrying out fumigation with thymol vapour, as described in (i) above, are not available, mildewed documents may be interleaved with thymolized sheets and placed in a warm cupboard. This treatment will arrest mould growth, and sterilize the documents, and protection against mould infection will be afforded as long as some thymol still remains. The documents can then be brushed clean—preferably out of doors—and prepared for incorporation in the archives.

For the permanent protection of large parchment rolls in store, a fungicide should be chosen that is less volatile than thymol and more potent in its action. In this case the quantity of fungicide can be greatly reduced, and the paper used for impregnation may be thin and not greatly absorbent. Protective sheets are prepared by passing a roll of thin paper through a 10 per cent aqueous solution of the sodium salt of pentachlorophenol (Santobrite) or *ortho*-phenyl phenol (Topane WS and Dowicide A). Such paper provides a valuable means of protecting library material and suchlike in tropical countries where the incidence of mould growth is a serious factor in conservation. It should, however, be noted that these impregnated sheets are mildly alkaline, and may affect certain colours adversely.

If documents have become wet through accidental flooding, there is danger of mould growth occurring unless immediate action is taken. Rapid drying by heating should be avoided as this is likely to cause serious distortion of the paper. The wet documents should be mopped with an absorbent sponge or sheets of blotting-paper, and then interleaved with fungicidal sheets, and set aside to dry slowly in a warm place. In cases where there are illustrations on coated 'art' paper, the only chance of preserving them is to introduce, if possible, a thin film of polythene between the art paper and adjacent pages while they are still wet; if the sheets are allowed to dry, they will become inseparably blocked together.

Insect pests

In common with other organic materials, parchment and paper are attacked by certain insect pests, and there is no doubt that the presence of gelatine and starch increases the number of potential enemies, and that the greatest activity is associated with damp.

McKenny Hughes[1] has described the insect pests of books and papers common in Britain in a communication to the technical section of the British Records Association. He lays emphasis on cleanliness and free circulation of air as being the best deterrents, and suggests that infected manuscripts can be most simply and effectively sterilized by exposure in an air-tight cupboard containing crystals of *para*dichlorobenzene. The crystals should be present in a quantity of 1 kg. to every cubic metre of air space; the cupboard should be sealed with gummed paper, and the time of exposure should be for at least a fortnight at a temperature of not less than 20 °C.

When attack by insects is a recurrent problem, the vacuum chamber method of fumigation has much to recommend it. This has been applied on an extensive scale for the sterilization of rare books and manuscripts in the Huntington Library, San Marino, California,[2] using ethylene oxide gas mixed with carbon dioxide which has been found to be a safe and effective fumigant.

Ethylene oxide is available commerically mixed with an inert gas, as it forms an explosive mixture with air. Such commerical preparations are Carboxide or Ethoxide consisting of a mixture of 10 per cent ethylene oxide with carbon dioxide, and Cryoxide consisting of a mixture of 11 per cent ethylene oxide with 89 per cent Freon (fluorine hydrocarbons).

When isolated insect attacks occur, the accommodation—drawers, cupboards, and shelving—should be thoroughly cleaned and treated with an insecticidal solution (see p. 31) either by brushing or spraying. For the treatment of shelving it is often convenient to use an insecticidal lacquer, such as Insecta-Lac or Xylamon-BN Clear. Drawers and cupboards may also be dusted with a solid insecticide, such as DDT or BHC (Gammexane).

[1] McKenny Hughes, A. W., *Archives*, 1952, **7**, p. 19; see also Weiss, H. B., and Carruthers, R. H., *Insect Enemies of Books*, New York Public Library, 1937, which contains an annotated bibliography of the subject to 1935.

[2] Iiams, T. M., *Library Quarterly*, 1932, p. 375.

STRENGTHENING AND REPAIR OF DOCUMENTS

Documents may become weakened through neglect or storage under adverse conditions, and they may suffer material damage through careless handling. In order to restore them to a sound condition the following treatments will be necessary.

1. *Resizing of paper.* Decay of the sizing material as the result of mould growth will cause paper to become limp and to lose its characteristic quality, the so-called rattle. In this condition paper is easily damaged and readily stained, and resizing will be necessary. This can be done by applying to the paper a gelatine size, made by dissolving about 1·5 gm. of good quality gelatine in 1 litre of water to which 0·5 gm. of a fungicide such as Topane or thymol may be added. The best quality gelatine is the photographic grade, since this is entirely free from undesirable impurities of an acidic nature. It is advisable that the size solution should be freshly made, because it is a very good medium for mould growth, and it is difficult to keep it for any appreciable period of time, particularly in tropical countries, without the addition of an undesirably high concentration of fungicide. With thin documents the size solution should be brushed lightly over the paper, but thick documents can be sized by immersing them in the size solution; in both cases the documents are hung up to dry away from radiators and draughts.

If the document is in such a condition that it becomes too weak to handle easily when wet, or if it is suspected that the ink may be sensitive to water, an alternative method of non-aqueous sizing should be adopted. For this purpose a 2 per cent solution of soluble nylon in methyl or ethyl alcohol or in industrial methylated spirit is used (Appendix XVI) and it can be applied either by spraying or brushing depending upon the fragility of the paper.

2. *Removal of creases.* If the paper document is not too badly creased, the creases should be lightly damped with water, covered with a piece of silicon-impregnated release paper, and ironed out with a warm iron. In the case of very bad creasing, the document should be laid down on a glass plate, covered with a sheet of moist

blotting-paper, and set aside to dry slowly under slight pressure. The contraction of the paper against the glass as it dries should remove the creases.

3. *Repair of tears.* If the tears are extensive and if lacunae have to be made good by the insertion of patching paper, the treatment should be entrusted to an expert document repairer. Sometimes tears have been mended with self-adhesive tapes, and the result has often been disastrous because the plastic film has become hard and darkened and the adhesive has had a tendency to exude. It is essential that a good quality tape should be used; one such reasonably permanent self-adhesive tape is Magic Tape 810,[1] but even this should only be used for making a temporary repair.

A preferable method for mending tears is to use a special thermoplastic or heat-setting repair tissue which is made by impregnating a good quality fine tissue paper with an emulsion adhesive, using either an internally plasticized polyvinyl acetate (Texicote VJC 555) or a mixture of polyacrylates (70 parts of Primal AC 34 and 30 parts of Primal C/72). This tissue is prepared as follows: brush out an even coat of the emulsion adhesive on a clean piece of plate glass, lay a fine tissue on the adhesive, and leave it over night. Then strip off the tissue which will be impregnated on one side only with the adhesive and allow it to dry off between sheets of silicone-impregnated paper. To repair a tear in a document, a strip of tissue of appropriate size is laid on the area to be mended, covered with a piece of silicone-impregnated release paper, and pressed firmly with an iron or spatula heated to about 80 °C. At this temperature the adhesive is softened and the tissue is firmly attached over the tear.

4. *Lamination.* When documents are found to have lost their normal mechanical strength, and have become embrittled due to acidity in the paper, resizing is generally not a satisfactory treatment, and it will be necessary to adopt a process of lamination, in which the document is sandwiched between two sheets of transparent tissue to give mechanical support. The classical technique of lamination was that of 'silking' in which both sides of the document were

[1] Minnesota Mining and Manufacturing Co.

covered with fine silk having an open weave (known as Crepeline) using starch paste as an adhesive. This process is simple to carry out, but it suffers from the disadvantage that the silk tends to deteriorate in time. A modification that has proved more satisfactory is to use a good quality tissue paper instead of the silk. This process can be recommended for the repair of valuable documents but, being a manual process, it is time-consuming and requires some skill on the part of the operator.

In recent years a number of plastic films have been suggested for use in lamination; these permit of variations in technique, depending upon the nature of the plastic film and the manner in which it is attached to the document. They offer a rapid, routine, semi-automatic method for preserving many classes of documents, provided the modern materials used are of an approved quality. The type of film best suited to archival purposes is based on cellulose acetate containing a stable plasticizer,[1] and three basic methods of application can be used; these are: (i) heat-sealing lamination in which the film is attached by the application of heat and pressure; (ii) dry-mounting lamination in which the plastic film is supplied coated with a heat-sensitive or a pressure-sensitive adhesive; and (iii) solvent lamination in which acetone is used to soften the plastic film. The heat-sealing technique of lamination was developed in 1939 by Barrow,[2] and has proved its value, but it requires expensive equipment only to be found in large archival workshops. As an example of dry-mounting lamination there is the Morane process[3] in which a film of cellulose triacetate having a semi-matt finish can be easily applied at about 80 °C., using either an ordinary photographic dry-mounting press or an electrically heated hand iron. A simple method of lamination, which does not require any elaborate equipment, is the solvent process developed by the National Archives of India.[4] It is carried

[1] Wilson, W. K., and Forshee, B. W., *National Bureau of Standards Monograph 5*, U.S. Department of Commerce, Washington D.C., 1959.

[2] Barrow, W. J., *J. Documentary Reproduction*, 1939, **2**, p. 147.

[3] Morane Plastic Co. Ltd., Northumberland House, Gresham Road, Staines, Middlesex.

[4] Goel, O. P., *Indian Archives*, 1953, **7**; Kathpalia, Y. P., *Am. Archivist*, 1958, **21**, p. 271.

out as follows. The document is first covered on one side with a film of cellulose acetate, over which is placed a sheet of tissue paper. A swab of cotton wool moistened with acetone is rubbed over the surface; the acetone has a solvent action on the cellulose acetate, which is softened so that by slight manual pressure the tissue paper is firmly bonded to the document. This process is then repeated on the other side. However, since acetone vapour is rather toxic and forms an explosive mixture with air, it is essential that this process should always be carried out in a well-ventilated room in which no naked flames are present.

Mechanical strength is restored to weakened paper by lamination and its appearance is often improved, but the process should not be used indiscriminately, or as a substitute for the local repair of damaged documents. Further details about lamination techniques are given in the publications cited at the end of this chapter.

INK

Having considered the principal materials used as grounds for writing, attention must now be given to inks.[1]

The oldest writing-ink of any permanence is carbon ink, which, in its primitive form, was no doubt a mixture of fine soot held in suspension in oil, gum, or glue size. Carbon is fast to light, and as it is unaffected by chemical agents, it has lasted well.

The traditional writing-fluid in Ancient Egypt was a carbon ink. It was used on papyrus, wood, cartonnages, and potsherds. When papyrus is exposed to the sun, the natural biscuit colour of the reed is gradually bleached to a pale ivory, and as any writing in carbon ink is unaffected, the net result is that the ink appears to be darker and altogether more intense against the lighter ground. The binding medium of the ink (gum or glue) has probably long since decayed, but the carbon particles are locked permanently in the tissue and

[1] For a brief history of writing inks, especially of the iron-gall type, see Waters, C. E., *Inks*, Circular C. 413, National Bureau of Standards, Govt. Printing Office, Washington, U.S.A., 1936.

remain black. Chinese and Indian inks are carbon inks, and no problem is involved as regards their preservation, except when they happen to have been applied thickly to a non-absorbent ground, so that the ink adheres badly and tends to flake off. In this case the pigment may be fixed by applying a dilute solution of soluble nylon (Appendix XVI). Carbon is the basis of our modern printing inks, and of the black inks used in the etching and engraving processes. Carbon inks are still preferred for permanent writing today, and, as a class, they are referred to as manuscript inks. Black waterproof drawing inks are usually carbon inks containing a little varnish. Carbon inks in general are all unaffected by the mild cleaning and bleaching processes carried out in the laboratory.

Iron inks are in a different category. They are compounded from gallotannic acid in presence of iron, and as the tannates are obtainable from a variety of natural sources, the inks vary in quality. Also from early times iron inks have been prepared according to a multitude of recipes, and this is another reason for the wide variations in substance and permanence. In some cases the black is indistinguishable in appearance from carbon; in other cases the ink may be a rusty brown or yellow, and so faded as to make the writing almost illegible. It is not safe to assume that because a sample of writing is ancient and dark in colour, it must necessarily be in carbon ink. Iron inks have been identified which date to the second century B.C., and it is reasonable to suppose that they may have been in use before this; their discovery would approximate in time to the discovery of tanning as a means of preserving animal skins from putrefaction.

The acidity of iron-gall ink may be due to tannic acid or sulphuric acid which are present in varying amounts. Writings have been examined in which the acidity has caused the paper to become perforated and reduced to a frail membrane of lace-like appearance. This phenomenon is not confined, however, to iron-gall inks. Any acid ink may destroy the tissue in the same way, and as all sorts of mixtures have been employed as writing-inks, it is not surprising to find occasionally that even a carbon ink has been sufficiently acid to deteriorate the paper.

In bleaching a print which bears a signature, it is safest to assume that the signature is in iron ink and therefore fugitive, and to protect it before treatment by a thin wash of a 5 per cent solution of polymethyl methacrylate in acetone. This prevents the action of chemicals on the inks, and may easily be removed after treatment when the drawing is quite dry, by an application of a little of the solvent, the area being pressed afterwards with white blotting-paper.

As carbon is insoluble, the ink made by grinding it in a binding medium cannot be other than a suspension of fine particles, so that when applied to paper the medium will tend to be absorbed, leaving the particles in the interstices near the surface. With iron inks there is a greater tendency for the pigment to spread,[1] and, indeed, it is the flow of such inks that commends them for use with the pen, whereas in the case of carbon inks, the brush is the more suitable instrument for calligraphy.

In studying yellowed inscriptions that seem to be executed in iron ink, one should bear in mind that artists and writers have often been attracted by rusty colours, and at times have chosen to write or draw in materials which are recognized today as being impermanent. Such are the inks made from sepia (cuttle-fish ink), and from bistre (beech-wood soot). In cleaning and restoration work it is safest to assume that all pale rusty ink lines are fugitive. Coloured inks also are all fugitive. The most stable appear to be the reds. These vary in composition depending upon their source: some, such as madder and logwood, are extracted from plants, and others are obtained from insects, for example, kermes from Persia, grain from Poland, and cochineal from Mexico. The so-called Tyrian purple comes from several species of shell-fish. But even the reds are evanescent, and care should be taken not to expose them to any form of treatment that might result in discoloration or loss.

Before trying to protect any of these fugitive colours by applying a plastic film it is advisable to test the colours to ensure that the solvent does not cause them to run.

[1] For the effect of the migration of inks, etc., on the permanence of paper see Barrow, W. J., *Archivum*, 1953, **3**, p. 105.

Reading faded writing

When it is desired to read writing that is illegible, it is first examined by different forms of illumination with the help of light filters, in the hope that by this means details will be revealed which are not visible in the ordinary way.

A source of ultra-violet illumination in a darkened room is sometimes particularly valuable in making indistinct writing readable, and at other times the infra-red viewer may give results that are otherwise unobtainable. When an inscription is partially legible under ultra-violet light, the chances are that a photograph taken using this source will be even more rewarding; and likewise, should the infra-red viewer afford any suggestion that the writing is intensified, it will be worth while taking photographs on specially sensitized infra-red plates using a tungsten lamp source. It is quite impossible to predict in advance which method, if any, is likely to be the more effective, and the results are often entirely negative. It may be stated, in general, that the ultra-violet type of examination is more useful than the infra-red, though with dark subjects the latter is sometimes strikingly successful.

Photographic processes are of great value in studying faded or damaged drawings as they provide a means of intensifying faint lines and suppressing stains, in this way making it possible to appreciate the artist's work in facsimile. Fluorescence photographs obtained by using a filtered ultra-violet source occasionally yield surprising results as in the case of certain pages from a sketch-book of Leonardo da Vinci in the Royal Collection at Windsor Castle, one of which is illustrated in Pls. 7A and B. An ordinary photograph taken on a panchromatic plate recorded the drawing of a hand. Inspection by filtered ultra-violet radiations indicated that several drawings were still extant on the same page and it was possible, by photographing the page under ultra-violet illumination, to obtain a complete record of the drawings.

Chemical methods of intensifying writing should not be used until the possibilities of obtaining information by modern photographic processes have been exhausted.

These methods are of most significance where iron inks are concerned, but as an old faded iron ink may have spread into the paper, it is clear that chemical intensification may not always be successful, and it should only be attempted by a specialist. This problem has been studied by Santucci[1] in the Istituto di Patologia del Libro, who has described methods for which some success may be claimed. In one such procedure the document is wetted, immersed in a 2 per cent solution of ammonium polysulphide, washed in distilled water for twenty minutes, immersed in a saturated solution of basic lead acetate and then washed in 1 per cent acetic acid and finally rinsed in distilled water. The purpose of this treatment is to convert the residues of iron in the ink into black lead sulphide.

Charred documents

When a document has been carbonized by fire, it may still be possible to photograph the writing by daylight using a high-contrast blue-sensitive plate[2] or by ultra-violet or infra-red illumination.

In some cases the writing may be rendered sufficiently distinct to be read by immersing the paper in a 5 per cent solution of silver nitrate for about three hours, when the writing will appear black on a grey ground.[3] The method which seems to have met with most success, however, is that of Taylor and Walls[4] in which the document is given several applications of a chloral hydrate solution (25 per cent in alcohol), and dried at 60 °C. between each application. It is then treated with glycerine (10 per cent), dried as before, and photographed, using a contrasty non-colour sensitive plate. It is claimed that this method, even in the case of typescript or printing, has never failed to give a readable result. A comprehensive summary of the methods available has been published by the Istituto di Patologia del Libro, Rome.[5]

[1] Santucci, L., and Wolff, C., Boll. Ist. di Patologia del Libro, 1963, **22**, p. 165.
[2] Jones, G. A., Nature, 1941, **147**, p. 676.
[3] Murray, H. D., ibid., **148**, p. 199.
[4] Taylor, W. D., and Walls, H. J., ibid., **147**, p. 417.
[5] Santucci, L., Boll. Ist. di Patologia del Libro, 1953, **12**, p. 95.

FURTHER READING

BARROW, W. J., *Permanence/Durability of the Book*. Vols. 1–6, W. J. Barrow Research Laboratory, Richmond, Virginia, U.S.A., 1963–9.

DURYE, P. (Editor), *Bulletin d'Information sur la Pathologie des Documents et leur Protection*. Archives de France, Paris IIIe, France, 1961.

SOLECHNIK, N. YA. (Editor), *New Methods for the Restoration and Preservation of Documents and Books* (Trans. from Russian). 1964. Available from Office of Technical Services, U.S. Department of Commerce, Washington, D.C., U.S.A.

WERNER, A. E., 'Lamination of Documents' in *Problems of Conservation in Museums*, pp. 209–24. Allen & Unwin Ltd., London, 1969.

III

PRINTS, DRAWINGS, AND MANUSCRIPTS

AN OUTLINE OF METHODS OF CLEANING,
REPAIR, AND MOUNTING

IN the conservation of prints, drawings, and manuscripts the practical problems of cleaning, repair, and mounting are numerous and varied. While the more complex operations and delicate manipulative processes require the specialist, a number of simple methods remain that can be applied in an improvised laboratory by the amateur, and it is the purpose of this chapter to present a series of practical instructions for the collector who may be interested to carry out some of his own repairs.

Successful restoration depends on practice and experience. Old and worthless prints and drawings should be collected for experimental purposes, and repeated trials made in order to acquire dexterity in handling delicate material, and to discover the merits and limitations of the various processes described. Reagents should be tested on inconspicuous parts of the work before applying them generally, the milder processes being chosen initially and the more drastic ones only when necessary, and after carefully considering the risks involved. Thus weak solutions are tried before strong, cold solutions before hot, and mild reagents before those known to be more powerful in their action. Although technical details are given, the various processes may require modification according to the type of material undergoing treatment, and it is to be understood that the methods only apply, unless otherwise stated, to the more stable forms of art—prints, engravings, etchings, and drawings in carbon ink or in pencil when the design is not affected by immersion.

A large shallow sink provided with hot and cold running water is an essential for print cleaning but, beyond this, no elaborate apparatus is required. The sink should have a draining rack on one side, and be flanked by a fair-sized table on the other, the table having half its surface covered with 6 mm. plate glass held permanently in position by a wooden moulding of the same thickness. It is convenient to have heating facilities for paste-making in the same room. The room should be well lit with both natural and artificial lighting. Beyond storage accommodation for papers and chemicals the following completes the list of requirements:

Double saucepan and jug.
Measuring glasses.
Sponge and glass cloths.
Large photographic trays (porcelain and enamel).
A quantity of good-quality white blotting-paper.
Drawing-instruments, rules, squares, etc.
Drawing-boards and drawing inks.
Architect's soft erasers.
Flexible paper-knives.
Print-trimming knife and oilstone.
Paired sheets of plate glass of varying weight and size.
A few heavy weights.
Brushes for dusting, retouching, and applying paste.
Electric iron with thermostatic control.
Adjustable reading-lamp.
Copying-press and a capacious fume cupboard—optional.
Flat bed dry mounting press with sponge rubber on one side.[1]

EXAMINATION BEFORE TREATMENT

The paper. Examine by transmitted and reflected light, using a lens when necessary. Test the crackle on shaking.

(*a*) Is the paper very porous, soft, or spongy? It may be so soft that it would be unwise to use immersion methods of cleaning (see Japanese prints, p. 89). When paper is moistened it expands, the effect of any size or binding material is weakened, and, if carelessly manipulated in this condition, it may easily be torn.

---

[1] This is used to flatten any distortions in papers after washing or after the application of thermoplastic repair tissue (p. 66).

(b) Is the paper hard or brittle, or the surface pitted or rotten? The hardness due to size must not be mistaken for strength—test in a corner with water. Papers which have been in the tropics are frequently so brittle that they will not stand manipulation without fracture. When the surface is pitted, ink may be inclined to flake, and immersion methods should be avoided lest the ink or paint should float away. Take note of weakened areas, creases, tears, wormholes, etc.

The drawing or impression. To what category does the print, drawing, or manuscript belong? What is the nature of the ink (pp. 68 et sqq)? Is the technique simple or compound? Is any water-colour present? Does the picture bear traces of having been retouched or treated previously?

The object to be treated must be carefully examined in every detail before a course of treatment can be decided upon.

REMOVAL OF MOUNTS AND VARNISH

1. Removing cardboard backing

The card is always removed from the print: never the print from the card.

Cardboard is composed of laminated sheets, and the first operation is to insert a knife at a corner to determine the number of layers. A long flat paper-knife may then be pressed in and the laminations successively removed from the back, leaving about two of the constituent sheets attached to the print. In this condition the print is held with the back in the steam of a boiling kettle until the card becomes quite soft. It is then laid face down on dry clean blotting-paper and the card drawn slowly away by dragging gently on a corner across the part as yet undetached. In this way, if the card has been sufficiently steamed, it may be removed without straining the print. The print is now laid face down on fresh blotting-paper, and any residual adhesive carefully removed with a clean sponge. If this operation is omitted, the paper will eventually cockle. It is then allowed to dry between fresh sheets of blotting-paper under a weight such as a sheet of plate glass.

A. Before treatment, showing stains due to the action of sulphur compounds on white lead

B. After treatment with hydrogen peroxide

9. WATER-COLOUR DRAWING BY GIACOMO GUARDI (1764–1835)

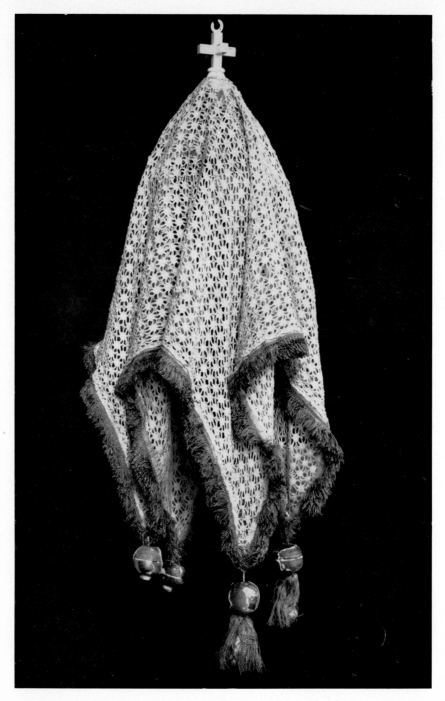

10. PYX CLOTH FROM HESSETT CHURCH, SUFFOLK. (LATE 15TH OR
EARLY 16TH CENT.)

Repaired and strengthened with terylene net

When, as sometimes happens, the backing is an inferior brown strawboard, nothing but prolonged washing will soften it. This type of board is not laminated and can only be removed by rubbing it gradually away with the fingers while wet.

2. Removal of paper backing

When completely pasted down on paper, a print cannot generally be detached by steaming. Lay it face down on glass, sponge the back of the mount with warm water. Now float the picture face upwards on lukewarm water and allow plenty of time for the adhesive to soften before attempting to detach the mount. When starch paste is hard and slow to respond to such treatment, softening may be facilitated by floating the drawing face upwards on a warm aqueous solution of an enzyme (p. 109). Remove residual adhesive and complete operations as in 1.

3. Removal of canvas backing

When a print has been pasted down on canvas fixed on a stretcher, a sharp knife is inserted at one corner and drawn along the edges to remove the canvas and print from the wooden frame.

The back of the canvas is then sponged with lukewarm water, and laid against a wet sheet of glass, the fabric being made as wet as possible and the print kept as dry as possible. After some time when the adhesive is sufficiently soft, clean blotting-paper is laid on the print, and the blotting-paper, print, and canvas inverted and placed for support on another sheet of glass. The canvas is now worked back from a corner by gently pulling it across the part as yet undetached. If the paper starts to split, and shows signs of partly coming away on the canvas, stop immediately, apply very hot water to the canvas, and wait for some time before proceeding.

Complete the operation as in 1. above.

4. Removal of varnish

A print varnished with an oil varnish may be irretrievable as this type of varnish becomes insoluble with age. The removal of spirit varnish is possible, but is rather a specialized operation requiring considerable care. The treatment given below may have to be modified to suit certain types of print.

Rub a tuft of cotton-wool in the palm of the hand (to give it a smooth surface), damp it, and lightly rub over the varnished surface. After drying, repeat the operation using turpentine instead of water. This clears the picture, and a record should be made of any colours before proceeding further.

In order to determine the most suitable solvent for removing the varnish, test a corner of the print with some methylated spirit. If this is not effective, try liquid ammonia (0·88) diluted with water (1:50). Support the print on a glass plate face up, and flood it with the chosen solvent, the action of which may be assisted by a flat camel-hair brush. Fresh solvent should be added repeatedly until it no longer becomes stained with the varnish. The print is now free from varnish although still more or less tinged faint brownish-yellow because the cellulose fibres have been stained with the darkened varnish. The print must be rinsed with water, then bleached (see below).

Plate 8 illustrates how, in the case of a printed book, it was possible to remove intensive varnish staining by the solvent action of alcohol followed by bleaching.

Old spirit varnish may be very brittle and may resist the above-mentioned solvents. However, hot water will sometimes soften it so that it flakes away. Pour boiling water into a large enamel photographic dish and immerse the print. As this method cannot easily be controlled where colours are concerned, it is risky with anything other than an engraving.

CLEANING: DRY AND WET METHODS

1. Dry methods

Although dry cleaning is not always necessary, pencil marks, etc., may become fixed in the paper if this is omitted before wet treatment is carried out.

If mildew is present, pick off the fluffy surface growths with a soft camel-hair brush, care being taken that the spores are not scattered about in the process. Many are unavoidably rubbed into the tissue of the paper. The print may be sterilized afterwards with thymol (p. 61).

For dry cleaning an architect's soft eraser may be used, or preferably Draft-Clean powder, which consists of white spherical particles of a rubbery nature that pick up dirt without dragging the surface when gently rubbed over the marks on the print. More resistant stains, such as mud deposits, may be broken up by using an electric eraser of the vibration type, or the Airbrasive unit described on p. 208 may be employed to deliver a small jet of an appropriate abrasive powder.

Dry-cleaning may be all that is required. The use of organic solvents (petrol, etc.) is not recommended except for removing specific stains. If dry-cleaning in itself is not sufficient, two courses are open— either to clean the print as a whole by immersion in water, or to apply local treatment to remove specific stains.

2. Immersion methods

The print requires support when immersion methods are employed. Some workers use a sheet of plate glass, others a flexible support of stiff paper or polythene. The print is never lifted from the water by its corners or handled while wet. It is the support that is handled, and when the support is slowly raised out of the water the print rests upon it and adheres so that it may be safely moved and if necessary turned over on to another support without being strained in any way.

A good soaking in cold water will always freshen up a print. After an hour it may be placed in a bath of hot water. Most fly-marks and mildew stains will respond to such treatment alone.

3. Cleaning with soap

In cases where further general cleaning is necessary, soap may prove to be a satisfactory cleaning agent. Carefully test the effect in a corner first. Lay the print face downwards on plate glass, damp it by contact with wet blotting-paper, then apply a little good-quality soap foam to the back with a large camel-hair mop. In larger prints a very soft badger shaving-brush is a convenient tool, and if the tips of the hairs only are used without pressure, there should be no strain on the surface of the damp paper. If the results are satisfactory on the back, the face of the print may be treated similarly. All trace of soap must be removed afterwards by thorough washing; if this is omitted, the paper may go yellow.

Alternatively the print may be soaked in a dilute solution of a non-ionic wetting-agent (e.g. Lissapol N) for half an hour and then washed.

Washing is so important, especially when soap and chemicals have been used, that it must be carried out with something of the ritual of the photographic studio.

Lead a slow current of water by a rubber tube to the bottom of the dish containing the print, and allow the water to emerge below the support. The duration of washing will depend on the nature of the foreign matter to be removed and on the type of print under treatment, but at least an hour should be allowed where bleaching solutions have been employed.

4. Drying and removal of creases

In order to dry the print, it is laid face downward on a polished glass plate, and pressed on the back with a pad of blotting-paper to remove excess moisture. It is then set up to dry slowly in a gentle draught of air. Contraction of the paper on drying against the glass will remove most creases and marks of folds (see also p. 65).

If the print has lost its mechanical strength, it would be resized at this stage (p. 65).

The processes that have been described so far will freshen up a print and in many cases this will be all that is required. It is only when staining is persistent that it is necessary to have resort to chemical methods of cleaning—bleaching, and the action of specific solvents.

BLEACHING PROCESSES

Stains that have survived ordinary washing may often be removed by the process known as bleaching. This involves either treating the stain with a substance that will break down the colouring matter by oxidation into simpler colourless compounds that may be washed away, or treating the stain with a substance that will reduce it to a colourless compound that remains *in situ*. The most effective and permanent bleaching agents are in the first category (oxidizing bleaches): chlorine dioxide, hypochlorites, sodium perborate, hydrogen peroxide, and potassium permanganate. Examples in the second category (reducing bleaches) are sodium hyposulphite and sodium formaldehyde sulphoxylate. While reducing bleaches are often effective in treating dye-stuff stains that withstand the action of oxidizing bleaches, they sometimes merely change the colour of the dye, but even if they go a stage farther and decolorize the stain completely, there is always the possibility that colour will eventually reappear owing to the subsequent oxidizing action of the atmosphere.

The simplest form of bleaching by oxidation is exposure to air and sunlight (or ultra-violet light) and this has given remarkably successful results in the case of Egyptian papyri where the writing material is a stable carbon ink.

The danger in using bleaching processes of any kind lies in the possibility of a loss of brilliancy in the inks and pigments and, if bleaching is overdone, the fabric of the paper may itself be attacked and weakened, especially when hypochlorites are used. For this reason bleaching agents must be applied under strict control and for the minimum time necessary to achieve the required results, and any excess of reagent is then decomposed with chemicals or removed immediately afterwards by thorough washing with water.

1. Use of hypochlorites

The traditional method of bleaching paper depends on the action of chlorine generated by calcium or sodium hypochlorite. The calcium compound known as bleaching powder is largely employed for bleaching the raw materials from which paper is made, and while it may also be employed for bleaching prints, sodium hypochlorite is generally preferred as it is easier to prepare. Sodium hypochlorite is known, variously, as Eau de Javelle and 'chlorinated soda'. The stock supply of sodium hypochlorite should be the commercial preparation marked '10% w/v available chlorine' and it should be stored in a coloured bottle in a cool dark cupboard, otherwise it soon loses its strength. The solution must be diluted with water before use, generally one volume being added to twenty volumes of water; in no circumstances should the strength of the bleaching bath be greater than 6:20. This liquid has a powerful bleaching action, discharging the colour from dirt, mildew stains, fly-marks, and remains of varnish. If the action is prolonged unnecessarily, the paper itself will become a staring white and there is evidence that the cellulose may be de-generated and permanently weakened. The solution, which has an alkaline reaction, tends to soften the paper, but softening may be mitigated to some extent by having at hand a bath acidified with hydrochloric acid into which the print is transferred for a few moments now and then during the bleaching. Such a bath may be prepared by adding about 4 ml. of concentrated hydrochloric acid to a litre of water. As in all processes involving the manipulation of wet paper, the use of a back-sheet or support is essential.

During the bleaching process, any writing in iron-gall inks will disappear unless protected beforehand. This is done while the paper is still dry, by a local application of a 5 per cent solution of polymethyl methacrylate in acetone. This protective film can be removed by a wash of acetone at the conclusion of operations when the print is dry.

Bleaching is only allowed to proceed until stains become faint. The print is then passed through a bath of sodium thiosulphate (photographic hypo) of 2 per cent strength to remove the residual chlorine, and washed thoroughly, when it will be found that the remaining marks gradually disappear. The hypo functions as an 'antichlor' and its employment is always desirable when hypo-chlorites have been used for bleaching.

2. Use of chloramine-T

Chloramine-T is a much milder form of bleaching agent than the hypochlorites mentioned above and its use is recommended next to that of sodium chlorite for routine bleaching. Chloramine-T possesses the unique advantage that, when applied to a print, its bleaching properties are soon lost and nothing of a corrosive nature remains on the paper. Washing may thus be reduced to a minimum but cannot be entirely dispensed with. The process is particularly suitable for water-colour drawings, coloured subjects generally, and drawings in bistre and sepia, as the reagent may be applied locally to those parts of the work that are stained without exposing the whole work to the action of the bleaching reagent.

Chloramine-T is obtainable commercially in the form of a fine white moderately soluble powder and must be kept in a well-stoppered bottle on account of its instability. Dissolve, only immediately before use, 2 gm. in every 100 ml. of water. Apply the solution to the stain with a soft camel-hair brush, cover with a pad of blotting-paper, and place under a sheet of glass. After an hour the print should be examined. Further applications may be necessary since the reagent is very mild in its action.

3. Use of chlorine dioxide

This is the safest bleaching agent to use as there is little chance of its weakening paper. Its use for bleaching prints was first described by Gettens,[1] who gave details of three methods of application suitable for the treatment of various types of material. It will suffice to describe the method recommended for bleaching prints, engravings, etchings, and drawings in carbon ink or pencil that can be safely immersed in water. This method can be used if a fume cupboard is available in which all the operations must be carried out. It is important that the fume cupboard should be well lit so that the progress of the bleaching can be observed, and it should also be provided with a drain and a supply of running water.

To prepare the bleaching solution 20 gm. of technical grade

[1] Gettens, R. J., *Museum*, 1952, **5**, No. 2, p. 116.

sodium chlorite ($NaClO_2$) are dissolved in 3 litres of water, transferred to an enamel photographic tray or a polythene dish of suitable size in the fume cupboard, and then 75 ml. of 40 per cent formaldehyde (formalin) are added. The solution will become yellow owing to formation of chlorine dioxide which is the active bleaching agent. The print lying on a glass plate or polythene sheet to act as support is immersed in the solution until the stains are removed. This will take at least fifteen minutes, but may be longer depending upon the nature of the stain. The actual concentration of the bleaching solution is not critical; it may be weakened or strengthened and 10 ml. of a wetting agent such as Lissapol N may be added if necessary.

When bleaching is completed, the print, resting on its support, is removed and washed in running water for at least fifteen minutes to remove sodium salts, but no intermediate antichlor bath is required. The print should then be left to dry on its glass or polythene support.

As a convenient alternative to the above bleaching solution there is now available a special chlorine dioxide stabilized solution (CDS) containing 9·2 per cent of active chlorine dioxide. This solution contains a mildly alkaline stabilizer, and if the solution is made slightly acid by the addition of acetic acid or dilute hydrochloric acid the active chlorine dioxide is released. For bleaching prints the solution as supplied should be diluted with its own volume of water and the bleaching carried out as already described.

It has been found that this method of bleaching with chlorine dioxide removes water-stains, fox-marks, and mildew stains, and does not give the paper a staring white appearance, as happens with hypochlorite.

4. Bleaching coloured and delicate prints

Many prints and drawings cannot be immersed in a bleaching solution without damage, notably when colours are present. In the case of a stained coloured print, the best that can be done is to lay the print face down on glass; place a pad of wet blotting-paper on the back of the stain for a few minutes and then follow this with the minimum of bleaching solution which is applied to the moistened back of the print with a camel-hair brush. It permeates the paper, having a mild bleaching action on the front. The stain should be kept under observation through the glass. When the result is satisfactory, flood the treated area with 2 per cent solution of hypo, then wash the print *in situ*, holding it against the glass all the time and at an angle to the running water. Now reverse the print, using a flexible support, and lay the support against the glass with the print face upwards, allowing a gentle stream of water to run over the picture for a short time. The print is then allowed to dry in this position.

A special method of application has been described for cleaning India proofs and very thin papers. According to this a sheet of blotting-paper is impregnated with a rather stronger solution of chlorinated soda, say 4 : 10, and allowed to become almost dry before being folded around the print and then sandwiched between two sheets of plate glass. The greatest care must be taken when removing the blotting-paper, and if there is any tendency for it to stick, it must be damped, otherwise it may bring away some of the ink and damage the print. When prints are of such a nature that they cannot be washed after this treatment, they should be exposed freely to the air for at least 2 days before being returned to the collection. It should be noted that where 'antichlor' cannot be employed, the method is not without danger to the paper, even though, judging by appearance, the result of operations seems to be entirely satisfactory.

5. Use of specific bleaching-agents and solvents

(a) *Oil, fat, and tar stains: Pyridine*. Pyridine, only the purest form of which should be employed, is an invaluable solvent for old partially oxidized oil, and for asphaltic stains, being decidely more effective than benzene.

(b) *Wax and candle-grease stains: Petrol*. Some of the grease can generally be removed with a paper-knife. The whole print is then immersed in a bath of petrol. After soaking a few minutes the stain is rubbed gently with a camel-hair brush and soon disappears.

(c) *Fly stains: Hydrogen peroxide, etc.* Stippling the spots with hydrogen peroxide (20 vols.) in an equal volume of alcohol is often effective. If this fails, try stippling with 2 per cent aqueous chloramine-T.

(*d*) *Tea and coffee stains: Potassium perborate.* Damp the area. Stipple a 2 per cent aqueous solution of potassium perborate on the stain and expose to sunlight for an hour or so. The bleaching action is slow and as the reagent is alkaline it tends to weaken the tissue. If the paper seems to be softened unduly, the action should be stopped at once by flooding the affected part with water. The final bleaching may be done by using ethereal hydrogen peroxide after the paper has been allowed to dry (see (*f*) below).

(*e*) *Ink stains.* Owing to the great differences in iron-gall inks, and even in modern inks of the blue-black type, no single process can be advocated as certain of success. A number of methods are available. Some of these may be found to bleach most of the stain, leaving a yellow tinge on the paper which, in turn, may be discharged by an entirely different process and reagent. Some of the possibilities are detailed below:

Brush with freshly prepared 2 per cent aqueous chloramine-T. If not completely effective after two or three applications, 5 per cent oxalic acid or 10 per cent citric acid may be tried, followed by thorough washing. No tannate of iron can survive any one of these methods without being bleached, and if coloured matter remains, it is likely to be carbon or the residue of some dye-stuff. Always stop the action short of complete bleaching, and take no risks as regards the possibility of rubbing up the surface of the paper.

Should a coloured stain still persist when dry, a stronger bleaching agent will be required. Damp the stain and cover with powdered sodium formaldehyde sulphoxylate. This bleaches most ink stains, iron stains, and many dye-stuffs used in coloured inks, but thorough washing is essential after such treatment.

One further method may be mentioned, strictly as a reserve process to be used in case of emergency. It must be regarded as a last resort, as it is definitely deleterious to the paper; at the same time it seldom fails. An aqueous solution (0·5 per cent) of potassium permanganate is painted over the stain where it forms a brownish-red blotch of manganese dioxide. After about five minutes cover this with a 2 per cent aqueous solution of oxalic acid. The brownish-red colour soon disappears, and the paper will usually be found to bear no trace of the original stain. Thorough washing after treatment is essential.

(f) *Blackened white lead and red lead: Hydrogen peroxide.* White lead (basic lead carbonate) is readily converted to the black sulphide by the action of sulphuretted hydrogen gas present in industrial atmospheres. Red lead, an oxide, is similarly affected and in each case stains are caused which are very disfiguring. The black sulphide may be readily oxidized by hydrogen peroxide to lead sulphate which is white and thus it is possible by simple treatment to remove the staining and restore the brilliancy of the white pigment. In the case of red lead that is superficially blackened, treatment by hydrogen peroxide results in the formation of a thin white veil of lead sulphate covering, but not concealing, the red pigment, and as it is unusual for red lead to be converted more than superficially to sulphide, the hydrogen peroxide treatment is generally all that is required to effect restoration.

The direct application of a commercial solution of hydrogen peroxide is sometimes recommended, but this is undesirable as it is liable to contain corrosive impurities. The following methods are designed in order to prevent contact of the corrosive impurities with the paper. The hydrogen peroxide solution should be poured on a stucco plate or porous tile, which is then fixed over the print about 3 cm. above it and left for a few hours. The vapour will clear the blackened pigments. Similar results are obtained by using a shallow bleaching-box with a false bottom of stucco that can be moistened with hydrogen peroxide. The print is placed in the box, face upwards, and left there until the stain has disappeared.

A method of more general application is to employ an ethereal solution of hydrogen peroxide prepared as follows. Equal parts of hydrogen peroxide (20 vols.) and ether[1] are shaken together in a

[1] Ether must be used only in a well-ventilated room free from naked lights as it is highly inflammable and asphyxiating. Residues should invariably be discarded after use.

It is decidedly dangerous to expose small quantities of ether to sunlight particularly in large closed vessels, as under these conditions unstable peroxides may be formed that have been known to cause serious explosions.

glass-stoppered bottle. The liquids are immiscible—the aqueous layer containing any impurities remains at the bottom, the ether layer rises to the top and this contains sufficient hydrogen peroxide for bleaching purposes. A glass tube (diameter *c.* 6 mm.) plugged with cotton-wool may be used for dabbing on the reagent. The tube is held in the hand, the cotton-wool dipped into the top layer *only*, and the ethereal solution is then applied to the stained areas by dabbing. Lead sulphide stains are bleached very readily by this method (Pl. 9A and B). The action of the vapour may be prolonged by having a piece of blotting-paper at hand to slip over the print immediately after applying the reagent.

It is not unusual to find painted miniatures on paper or parchment heavily stained in places where white or red lead has been used, the stains being black or deep brown and having sometimes a silvery sheen. These can be freshened up very easily with hydrogen peroxide, and for this type of work it is best to employ the ethereal solution which may be applied locally with a small brush. If there is no immediate response to the action of hydrogen peroxide, it may be that the stains have arisen from the action of hydrogen sulphide on metallic silver. Silver was often used in Persian miniature landscapes to represent water, and when once blackened by sulphide, no satisfactory method can be recommended for its restoration.

Occasionally, a black smudge of lead sulphide will be found unexpectedly on a drawing, and closer inspection will reveal it to be a residue from a previous restoration that has been carried out either in white lead or in coloured pigments that have been mixed with white lead. In such cases the hydrogen peroxide treatment works satisfactorily as, even in the case of a pigment mixture, the original hue is restored by the conversion of lead sulphide to the white sulphate.

After hydrogen peroxide treatment there is much less chance of the white lead being blackened in future, because the sulphate is less susceptible to change than the basic carbonate.

SPECIAL CASES OF CLEANING AND RESTORATION

1. Japanese prints

Few of the ordinary methods of treatment apply in the case of Japanese prints on account of the soft texture and quality of the paper. It is fortunate that this paper does not appear to be greatly attacked by foxing or mildew and that dirt is generally superficial. To clean a Japanese print lay it face down on glass and cover it with a rather larger sheet of tissue-paper (or preferably Japanese tissue which is thinner), in such a manner that one end of the tissue projects and can be held against the glass. Apply plain water all over the tissue in a series of light parallel strokes using a tuft of cotton-wool; sufficient will soak through the tissue to make the dust on the back of the print adhere and on carefully folding back the tissue this dirt will be removed. If not entirely successful, a very dilute gelatine solution (half strength, see page 65) may be substituted for the water, a fresh operation being conducted on the same lines. After cleaning the back treat the front similarly. As mauve and heliotrope pigments on Japanese prints are generally of vegetable origin and easily damaged, they should *never* be damped.

When a Japanese print is much torn, it should be completely pasted down on a sheet of Japanese paper of similar quality and strongly pressed. A good type of flexible adhesive for this purpose is made from 30 per cent rice starch and 20 per cent polyvinyl alcohol in water.

2. Japanese vellum mounts

The so-called Japanese vellum forms an ideal mount for Japanese prints. Although it is a hard paper, the surface will not bear cleaning by the ordinary dry methods as it is very easily rubbed up. A clean soft sponge or, preferably, a tuft of cotton-wool is dipped in dilute starch solution, squeezed to remove excess liquid, and passed lightly and rapidly over the surface. By this means the dirt is picked up and the mount greatly improved in appearance.

3. India proofs

The cleaning of an India proof is an extremely delicate matter on account of the ease with which the India paper becomes detached from its mount. When once detached the difference in expansion and contraction between the thin paper and its thicker mount renders it almost impossible to regain the original tension between the two when they are remounted and dried. It should be noted also that the sharpness of detail in an India proof is bound to be lost to some extent if it is necessary to wet the paper for cleaning. Stains should therefore be removed, for preference, by dry cleaning or by local treatment if possible.

Reference has already been made (p. 85) to the method of cleaning using blotting-paper impregnated with chlorinated soda. This method, as has been suggested, is open to criticism, but alternative methods milder in action would necessitate longer contact with the damp bleaching-paper and result almost inevitably in the separation of the print from its mount. If the two sheets are only partially separated, they had best be completely detached from each other by soaking and floating them apart, and then chlorine dioxide (p. 83) or a chloramine-T bath may be used to clean both the print and the mount.

In order to remount the dry print it is laid face down on plate glass; the back is pasted all over, taking care to keep the paste off the glass, and the glass is then turned over and placed against the mounting paper which has been previously damped so that the India proof adheres in its correct position. The mounted India proof is dried superficially with blotting-paper, and after about ten minutes removed from the glass. It is then allowed to dry slowly under a weight protected by sheets of blotting-paper on each side. Should the blotting-paper adhere, it may easily be removed by damping with water.

For the preparation and use of flour paste see Appendix X.

4. Pastel and chalk drawings

Pastel drawings, especially those on vellum, should be frequently inspected as they are liable to become infected with moulds. Moulds may attack certain pigments (Indian yellow; bile yellows) or they may grow on the binding medium of the powder colour—generally gum tragacanth—or on the sizing of the paper.

When mildew is found growing on a pastel it must be picked off with a fine camel-hair brush slightly moistened with pure alcohol. The picture is then sterilized with thymol. If the mould growth has caused permanent staining it may be possible to hide this by spreading the pastel pigment with a stump. Pastels should always be kept in a dry place and they should be framed in contact with a sheet of paper impregnated with thymol, Santobrite, or Topane WS.

The treatment of pastels by amateurs should be restricted to the above.

When certain types of chalk drawings (outline drawings on inferior brown paper) are mildewed they may become stained in a manner which is very disfiguring owing to the sparsity of pigment. The stains cannot be bleached as the paper would be bleached also. There is a tendency in old pastel and chalk drawings for the colour to be fixed in the paper as a result of the prolonged effect of traces of moisture upon the gum of the pastel and size of the paper; these adhesives bind the particles of pigment that are in direct contact with the cellulose tissue. Water may actually be used for cleaning drawings of this nature, as follows: float the drawing on the surface of cold water face upwards (with a paper support immersed below), and rub the spots gently after some minutes with a fine brush. If this is only partially effective after ten minutes, remove the drawing, using the support, and float it on to very hot water in the same way. This treatment is only possible with old drawings when the pastel pigment has become fixed in the tissue of the paper. The mould growths are mainly on the surface of the paper and are removable after softening on water. By this treatment the worst of the staining is dispersed.

5. Bound papers

It is sometimes necessary to remove a page from a book for treatment by one or other of the methods described above. This is done as follows—insert a wet string against the page near its hinge and close the book. After a minute the page may be torn out. When the page is ready to be returned, the torn edge is pasted and the page aligned with the fore-edge and head end of adjacent pages; this will bring the pasted edge automatically into register with the hinge from which it was torn and it is caused to adhere by placing the book in the press.

REPAIR AND RESTORATION

1. *Removing creases from paper.* When not very bad the creases should be damped and a warm iron should then suffice to remove them.

Reference has been made above to the removal of creases by drying the print against glass. In the case of very bad creases the print is damped and laid face downwards on glass. Strips of soft white paper are then pasted all round, 20 cm. on the glass and 5 cm. on the print, so that the tension may be greater as the print shrinks on drying. When the print is dry and flat, a little paste should be rubbed along the line of the crease and, if necessary, a strip of similar or thinner paper applied as a patch and allowed to dry before releasing the print from the glass. In carrying out such operations the guard papers must not be heavier or stronger than the paper to be flattened, otherwise tearing may occur.

2. *Removing creases from parchment or vellum.* With parchment or vellum the problem of creasing and warping is much more complicated and even prolonged treatment in a press is seldom effective.

A practical method of flattening parchment is first to relax it by sandwiching the membrane between two sheets of damp blotting-paper and pressing lightly for a time. The blotting-paper should be uniformly damp but not too wet. The time required for this operation will be determined by the nature and thickness of the parchment. When the membrane is limp, it is placed on a glass that has been previously polished with French chalk to remove grease, covered with a sheet of dry blotting-paper of the same size, and held against the glass by weights placed around the edges. Strips of lead about 5 cm. thick and about 20 cm. wide are ideal for the purpose, but the total weight should not be so heavy as to immobilize the parchment, since it is essential that, as the parchment dries and contracts, it should slide over the glass and take the weights with it, the centripetal pull being rather greater than the restraining action of the weights. By this means, even long-standing creases may be made to disappear. The most difficult types of membrane are those cut from near the edge of the skin, where thickness and grain are inclined to be variable, and these may need localized treatment in some form of stretching frame in which the forces can be adjusted to the requirements of the membrane. Such an apparatus has been described by Cockerell[1] and there are cases in which the frame is an invaluable adjunct in removing creases from parchment.

If such operations are practised on worthless documents it will be noticed that care is necessary to prevent ink spreading and it is a wise precaution to fix ink beforehand with an acrylic resin solution as mentioned on p. 70. When colour is present, and especially gold lettering, the membrane must on no account be relaxed. Restorations of this nature can only be conducted satisfactorily by an experienced bookbinder.

3. *Tears in paper*. If the quality of the work allows, immerse the paper in water face downwards on a glass support, and when the torn pieces have been carefully floated into their correct positions slowly raise the support and paper out of the water. When half dry, tap along the joints with the back of a spoon in order to weld the fractured surfaces together. Paste may be added as a reinforcement and also a patch if necessary.

When machine-made paper is being repaired, the grain of the patch must be aligned with that of the paper. The direction of the grain of a machine-made paper may be discovered by moistening two edges at right angles; the paper swells in the direction across the grain, and acquires a crinkled appearance along the edge.

Hand-made paper may be patched with another piece of thinner hand-made paper using rather dry paste, or with a piece of thermoplastic tissue (p. 66), and pressed very lightly.

[1] Cockerell, D., *Bookbinding and the Care of Books*, London, 1901, pp. 329 et sqq.

When an insertion is required, it should be of the same age, thickness, and surface appearance as the paper being repaired. The restorer must have at hand a reserve collection of sample papers, engravings, etc., from which to select repair material when necessary. Even when the greatest care is taken in matching the papers, some allowance may have to be made for variations of sizing, and differences of shrinkage on drying. The tendency is to make the patch too damp with paste. The edges of the insertion and the paper are chamfered as described below in the repair of parchment, and after the edges have been pasted and the insertion stuck in position the whole is flattened in the press.

4. *Tears in parchment and vellum.* When creases are absent, there is no need to soak parchment or vellum. A simple chamfered tear may be repaired by sticking the edges together and pressing under a weight till dry. Paste, however, is not a very good adhesive for parchment. The replacement of torn corners requires a much more powerful adhesive, and stronger joints are obtained when the edges are painted with the minimum quantity of dilute acetic acid (say 10 per cent). This gelatinizes the fibres so that the torn edges can be pressed intimately together.

Where there are no natural chamfers, as in a plain cut, the edges must be artificially chamfered by rubbing with an abrasive stick of chisel shape. This enlarges the cut, making it a V-shaped slit, and a patch of similar appearance but rather greater in size and thickness is cut to shape and then chamfered down to fit. It is inserted after applying adhesive to the edges, dried in the press, and then brought to the exact thickness by rubbing with a block of fine pumice. When such work is carried out carefully and the sheet rubbed over with a little pumice flour at the end of operations, the repair may be so perfect as to be almost beyond detection.

5. *Sizing and retouching.* The paper will require to be sized afresh if any retouching has to be done. Parchment size is sometimes recommended for this purpose but it has no advantages over gelatine. A good gelatine size is made by dissolving 1·5 gm. of clear gelatine in 1 litre of water. Size should always be freshly made immediately before use, and brushed thinly and lightly over the paper. Thick

papers may be sized by immersion and hung on a line to dry, away from radiators and draughts.

If any retouching is necessary, this should not exceed the absolute minimum required to conceal disfigurements due to tears and abrasions of the paper. The method should generally be by stippling save where broken lines have to be joined up. When a hard size is required, a 2 per cent solution of polyvinyl alcohol may be used.

6. *Toning.* When one page of a book has been bleached or when one of a uniform series of engravings has been similarly treated, it may appear blanched and uninteresting beside its fellows. This may be remedied in a rule-of-thumb fashion by staining the paper with a decoction of tea or coffee. Preliminary trials are made on similar paper in order to decide which stain gives the best results and to determine a suitable concentration.

MOUNTING

1. Parchment and vellum

Great care is required in mounting parchment and vellum as these are generally mounted in the damp relaxed condition and contraction on drying is considerable. If the paste is not uniformly applied around the edges, distortion will result. Assuming that there are no illuminations present, the parchment is relaxed in water and placed in sheets of dry blotting-paper between glass plates until it appears almost dry, while still retaining its suppleness. A thick mounting board is selected and four guide-marks made to show where the print is to be permanently fixed. The membrane is laid face down on glass and pasted half an inch all round the edge two or three times. It is then turned over and placed in its permanent position on the mount, and the edges pressed down very thoroughly with clean blotting-paper. It must be remembered that the edges will have to withstand a fair strain as the parchment shrinks on drying. Should the parchment have been too wet when mounted, the edges will pull away, dragging off part of the mount with them. Before drying, remove any marks with a damp sponge. After covering with two or three sheets of blotting-paper, weights are applied over the four corners and the membrane is left to dry, when it will become as tight and smooth as a drum.

Vellum is treated in similar fashion. The thinnest and finest specimens do not require preliminary soaking. It is sufficient to leave them for a short time in damp blotting-paper pressed between glass plates before mounting.

A method which affords greater control is to immerse the membrane for the required period of time in ethyl alcohol containing an appropriate small amount of water (or even in anhydrous methyl alcohol) till it becomes sufficiently relaxed for uniform stretching in a spring frame. Quantities will depend upon the nature of the parchment, its thickness and general condition.

When there is gilding or illumination, the parchment must on no account be relaxed, and in such cases manipulative processes should be left to the expert.

2. Papers

In the absence of special laminating equipment (p. 66), manuscript material is commonly mounted in guard-books.

Prints and drawings are never 'laid down' (pasted down all over) on card, but attached to the card by hinges of thin paper folded back on themselves and known as guards. When only one such hinge is used the drawing can be turned over to inspect the reverse and watermarks can be studied by transmitted light. More usually four guard papers are employed and there is then less chance of accident by careless handling.

Only the best white or ivory cards should be used for mounts. These are cut to size and increased in thickness as required by pasting cards together. The mounts should be strongly pressed after pasting.

All mounts should be finished with rounded corners to avoid the chance of damage should they be accidentally dragged over the surface of adjacent prints. This can be effected by smoothing the edges and corners with glass-paper.

Three types of mount will be described—the solid, the overthrow, and the window mount. These are illustrated in Fig. 4.

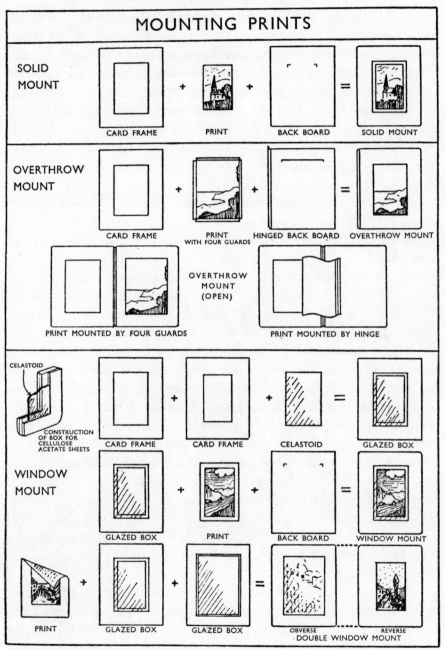

FIG. 4

(*a*) *The solid mount*. This type of mount is the one most commonly used, when there is nothing of interest on the back of the print. The print or drawing is attached by pasted paper hinges in a 'box' prepared by pasting a cardboard (3 sheet) frame to a backboard (4 sheet) of the same size as the frame. In the solid type of mount the cardboard frame does not cover any of the print. The backboard must always be thicker than the frame, the relative thickness depending on the size of the print. A comparatively large print would require a strong backboard for support, Deep 'boxes' must always be employed in mounting pastels.

(*b*) *The overthrow mount*. This type of mount is in general use where prints are hinged by one guard paper only so that the back can be inspected. It is also used when a print has a torn edge. Such a print is mounted on a backboard by pasted guards of paper and a frame is prepared of such a size as to conceal the damage. This frame is hinged to the backboard by a strip of linen so that it may be opened to the left to expose the whole of the print for examination. A hinged arrangement of this kind is known as an overthrow mount.

(*c*) *The window mount*. When drawings occur on both sides of the sheet of paper the paper may sometimes be split so that the drawings are released and they may then be mounted separately. As the operation of splitting paper is always attended by risk, it is generally preferable to adopt instead the window type of mount so that both pictures remain visible. In this case the paper is attached only by its edges between superimposed rectangular openings of appropriate size in two cards. As the drawing might easily be damaged if left unsupported it is usual to mount a sheet of cellulose acetate at one side so that it forms a transparent support. If the paper is very frail or where much ink is present that may have rotted the tissue, it may be necessary to give it additional support by adding a similar sheet at the other side.

It is a general principle in mounting a collection to endeavour to make mounts in a limited number of sizes as this is convenient both for storage and for exhibition purposes. The card surround should be of such a thickness as to protect the picture from contact with the glass when framed. If the picture is in contact with the glass, condensation effects may encourage the growth of mildew.

3. Documents with seals

When documents bearing appended seals are to be framed, they should first be inlaid in a solid card mount of such a size and thickness that the seals are backed by, and nested in, the card, so that their weight is supported. This protects them from the possibility of accident should the fabric by which the seals are attached become tendered and no longer able to sustain their weight.

Wax seals are easily broken and, if not repaired at the time, fragments tend to get lost and reconstructions become more complicated. A mixture of equal parts of rosin and beeswax is usually recommended as an adhesive for wax and, if it is a case of dealing with a simple fracture, this adhesive may be spread in the form of a hot liquid on the joints, pressing them together immediately till the parts are held securely. With heavy seals it may be necessary to insert one or two dowels before making the joint. The holes for these are made by probing with a hot needle, and the actual dowels can be made from fragments of broken needles of appropriate length and thickness. It is sometimes possible to reinforce a heavy seal by attaching a thin adhesive tape around the circumference in such a manner as to be unobtrusive, and it may be painted thereafter to match the colour of the wax.

When a seal is splintered and parts are missing, the main fragments should be brought together as above and any lacunae made up with plaster of Paris containing a little ochre and black as a rough match for the natural wax colour. Green and red colours are sometimes required. The tinted plaster should extend slightly above surface level, and after it is quite dry it is carved to match the design. It is then impregnated with a thin lacquer to stop the suction and painted to match the original. While a repair executed in this manner should not be obtrusive or out of colour harmony, there should be no effort to conceal the fact that the seal has been restored.

IV

TEXTILES

THE spinning of threads and the weaving of textiles come very early in the history of craftsmanship. Linen in southern Europe can be dated back as far as the Stone Age; in northern Europe wool was in use in the Bronze Age, and silk, which originated in China, can be traced back for more than 5,000 years. Embroidery, i.e. the decoration of the finished textiles, did not appear till much later.

Natural fibres may be of animal origin (wool, silk), or of vegetable origin (cotton, linen, hemp). Animal fibres contain keratin, a nitrogeneous compound, and, when burnt, they contract and smell of burnt feathers due to the decomposition of the keratin. Vegetable fibres are composed of cellulose; they burn easily and give off a characteristic odour of burnt paper. Thus, it is possible by a burning test to make a broad distinction between animal and vegetable fibres, but, for specific identification, individual fibres must be examined under a microscope at about 100/150 diameters magnification when, with a little practice, the main types can readily be distinguished.[1]

As textiles are of an organic nature and subject to attack by moulds and bacteria, the commonest factors that promote decay are those that favour the growth of these organisms, viz. a damp heat, lack of ventilation, and contact with decaying animal and vegetable matter. However, even under such unfavourable conditions ancient textiles may not be entirely destroyed. It is common, for example, to find fragments of textile surviving when they have been in contact with corroding copper, the corrosion products having acted as sterilizing agents. Textile remains are often found attached to the patina of Chinese bronzes, in such a condition that the fibres can be identified

---

[1] Cf. *Identification of Textile Materials*, 3rd edition, 1951, published by The Textile Institute, 10 Blackfriars St., Manchester 3.

and the weave recorded. Damp causes vegetable fibres to swell and soften, but the fact that animal fibres are not necessarily destroyed by immersion in water is proved by the survival of woollen material in peat bogs and lake dwellings.[1] Excessive heat causes desiccation and embrittlement, and exposure to bright light and noxious gases cause the type of deterioration known as tendering. The astonishingly fresh appearance of some Egyptian mummy wrappings may be due as much to the presence of salt as to the absence of light and the dryness of the surroundings.

TEXTILE ANALYSIS; PREPARATION OF RECORDS; PROGRAMME OF TREATMENT

Before beginning restoration work on textiles the first step is to carry out an examination with a pocket lens or binocular microscope, making a record of the following particulars.

The nature of the fibres of both warp and weft threads.
In spun threads, the direction of twist—S (') or Z (').
The type of weaving—tabby, twill, figured.
The count per centimetre of both warp and weft threads.
The presence of selvages.
Dye-stuffs or applied decoration—paint, gold leaf, metal threads, or embroidery.
The presence of sewing or stitch holes.

If the material is very dirty, making examination difficult, gentle blasts of air from a blow-ball or bellows may be used to remove loose dust, or in some cases a soft brush may be used. It may be impossible to record all particulars until the textiles have been washed, but it is important to get as much information as possible in the first place and make photographic records in case any evidence should be lost during treatment. The preliminary examination is important also

[1] Henshall, A. S., and Maxwell, S., *R. Soc. Proc.* (Scot.) 1951–2, **86**, p. 30. This grave was found in peat, and when excavated, scarcely anything of the body was left, but all the woollen clothing in which it had been buried was well preserved. This clothing is now exhibited in the National Museum of Antiquities of Scotland, Edinburgh.

as it forms the basis upon which decisions are taken regarding laboratory treatment.

CLEANING OF MUSEUM TEXTILES

Textiles are easily contaminated with soot and dust, and being absorbent they are readily stained by contact with substances in solution or decaying organic matter, or by the coloured substances produced by moulds in the course of their growth. Material that is dirty or stained, but is sufficiently strong to be manipulated, may be washed with water or dry-cleaned, and specific stains can be dealt with locally. It must be understood, however, that the processes recommended may require modification depending on the condition and type of textile that has to be treated, whether it be a carpet or a piece of tapestry, lace, etc. Complications may also arise from the presence of a dye or of gold thread, or because of the vagaries of the weave or make-up of the fabric.

1. Washing

The first requirement for washing textiles is a supply of soft water such as rain water, distilled water, or deionized water. Hard water is unsatisfactory as it tends to form a scum.

Old textiles are washed preferably in flat vessels. Small samples may be conveniently dealt with in photographic developing dishes, but for washing large textiles the most practical arrangement is to use a wooden tray lined with polythene and provided with a perforated false bottom. Such a tray is constructed with sides about 10 cm. high, in one of which a V-cut is made for emptying; a sheet of polythene is spread in the tray and made to take the shape of the vessel, and is then held in position around the edges by spring clothes-pegs. By this means a waterproof tank of any size can be readily improvised. A very large tank may be emptied by siphon, or preferably hinged to the table along one of its longer edges, so that the water can be run out into an adjacent sink by tipping the vessel, the action being controlled by a long screw such as that commonly used for opening and closing hinged window-lights. In emptying the tank, the polythene is pressed into the V-cut so that it forms a gutter between the table and the sink.

The perforated false bottom or, failing this, a loose sheet of polythene is useful as a support for the textiles when they are lifted out of the water.

In the case of textiles of open weave, drawn-thread work, or lace, these should be pinned down or tacked by thread to a sheet of polythene, for safety during washing.

If textiles are coloured, a spot test with water will have to be applied to each colour before washing in order to determine whether the colours are fast. Fugitive colours may sometimes be fixed either by treatment with a 5 per cent solution of common salt or acetic acid of the same strength. A stronger solution of acetic acid up to about 20 per cent may be used if necessary. A spot test should be made, and the spot absorbed in white blotting-paper to ascertain whether the salt or the acid fixes the colour. The whole textile should then be immersed in the appropriate fixing solution.

When everything is in order, the tank is filled with soft water to a depth of about 8 cm., and the textile lowered gently into it, keeping the material flat and well spread out; it is kept immersed for an hour, changing the water as required, perhaps every twenty minutes. If the mains' supply of water is soft, a gentle stream of running water may be used. This is conducted to the tank by a rubber or polythene tube and allowed to emerge beneath the support. When the running-water method of washing is adopted (in the case of a tank larger than the sink), a siphon draining system will be required.

Some of the dirt will be soluble in water, and insoluble sandy matter may be realeased by gently tamping with the fingers after the textile has been soaking for some time or by compressing several times with a sponge. When the washing is finished, the water is run off, and the support, to which the textile adheres, is raised and maintained, if necessary, at an angle to allow the material to drain. While still on the support the textile is pressed gently with absorbent towelling and it is then transferred to a backing of warm absorbent material—towelling or flannel.

When half-dry, the textile is turned over on to another polythene sheet and straightened out, the weave being adjusted so that the warp and weft threads are at right angles to each other. Fine brass pins are inserted vertically at intervals through the textile into the sheet and the pins may require adjusting from time to time as the textile dries. Drying should be carried out in a warm, well-ventilated room, and may be facilitated by using infra-red lamps or a hot-air blower.

Use of detergents. While washing in plain water can bring about a remarkable improvement in the appearance of certain textiles, the use of a detergent[1] is necessary if textiles are contaminated with grease. While a drop of ammonia may facilitate operations, soaps are not so popular for museum work as they tend to form an insoluble scum difficult to remove.

Certain synthetic surface-active agents or wetting-agents may be employed with great advantage. These are of two kinds, ionic and non-ionic, the latter type being the safer for textiles. Examples are Lissapol N, Igepal, and CA Extra. These substances can be used with confidence, provided colours are spot-tested first of all, but a warning is necessary against using any of the commercial cleansing powders and liquids that are based on them, because such patent cleaners may contain in addition soap powder, soda, or other materials that might be deleterious to fine textiles.

Another cleansing agent that can be used is a liquid soap based on potassium oleate. Although marketed primarily as a spirit soap (see below), it may equally well be used in water. It is mildly alkaline, and Beecher[2] has reported on its success as a 5 per cent solution in water for the cleaning of important tapestries.

Wetting-agents need only be used in dilute solution (as specified by the manufacturers), 1 per cent to 0·5 per cent strength being adequate for most purposes. In using detergents, they should be added in the requisite amount to the water and thoroughly stirred

[1] Hofenk de Graeff, J. H., *Studies in Conservation*, 1968, **13,** p. 122.

[2] Beecher, E. R., *The Conservation of Cultural Property*, UNESCO, 1968, Chapter 16, p. 253.

so as to form a solution of uniform strength before the textile is placed in contact with the liquid. During washing, the wash-waters are changed at least three times, and a final bath of fresh soft water completes the operation. In cases where luke-warm water may be used, the cleaning will be even more effective, but the water should never be used hot as this has a softening effect on some fibres. Thus in the case of woollen textiles certain precautions have to be taken in the washing process since they tend to shrink and harden if exposed to very hot water or to changes of temperature while wet; moreover synthetic detergents remove any natural grease still remaining in the textile. Full details will be found in the *Workshop Notes* of the Textile Museum, Washington, D.C.

Use of saponins. Saponins are widely distributed in nature among the higher plants, and their virtues as substances having mild detergent properties have long been known. They are neutral in action, froth readily with water, and their cleansing properties are due to the ease with which they form emulsions with substances of a resinous or oily nature. Plant extracts containing saponins are largely employed in the East for washing clothes. They do not seem to have any deleterious effect on delicate fabrics, and are safer to use with coloured textiles than soap. The precaution should always be taken, however, to test the colours first.

Saponin is obtainable commercially as a white powder. To use the powder a little is swished to a froth with water and this is applied with a soft brush of the shaving-brush type. To clean upholstery the furniture is supported upside down or at an angle so that when the froth has done its work and is soiled it will fall away from the textile rather than sink in. The froth is lightly worked over the surface of the textile using only the tips of the bristles of the brush, any excess of froth being removed with a soft rag, and the textile dried thereafter with absorbent towelling. By this method excellent results are obtainable without rubbing and with the minimum of exposure to moisture. For cleaning damask that is frail with age, the froth procedure may be used with appropriate variations. It will usually be found that in cases where it is safe to use water, dirt can be removed more readily with the aid of saponin, and that colours are improved in appearance and enlivened by the treatment.

2. Dry-cleaning

Dry-cleaning may be carried out by vacuum treatment in conjunction with brushing, by using organic solvents and spirit soap or by dry steam, the nature and size of the textile being the determining factors in deciding which procedure is the most suitable.

Vacuum-treatment and brushing. Old carpets and curtains that are very dusty may be improved in appearance by brushing with a soft brush (in the direction of the pile) towards a vacuum cleaner, or, alternatively, a suction nozzle with a gauze cover may be used if the fabric is strong enough to stand it. It may be added that it is sometimes possible to improve the appearance of a rug by gently rubbing fuller's earth or even baking soda into the pile, leaving it there overnight and then extracting it next day with a suction nozzle. In dealing with old rugs care must be taken to preserve the direction of the pile; if this is upset by violent local cleaning, the distorted fibres will scatter reflected light and the rug will have the appearance of being stained.

Brushes for such work should be selected with care. The bristles should be white for preference and generally long, and the degree of softness is also important. Stiff brushes do have their place among the cleaning equipment but should be used with reserve.

Solvent cleaning. The term 'dry-cleaning' is usually employed to denote cleaning by anhydrous solvents. These are less likely to affect any batter in the cloth than water, but as they may well have a greater action upon dye-stuffs it is essential that all colours on a textile be tested individually by spotting with the solvent before immersing the textile in the cleansing solution. Dry-cleaning is only given preference in cases where the presence of water is undesirable. The solvent most commonly employed is trichloroethane, a non-inflammable liquid of high volatility (B.P. 74 °C.). It should be used pure and cold, and textiles should be immersed for from ten to thirty minutes at the outside. It is further recommended that where there is a danger of dyes running, dichloroethylene (B.P. 55 °C.) should be selected as the cleaning agent in preference to trichloroethane.

It is well established that when garments are soiled with grease and perspiration they are more prone to be attacked by moth than when freshly laundered, and cleaning with solvent has the same effect as laundering in discouraging attack. It goes without saying that garments should always be cleaned before they are incorporated in the collection.

Spirit soap. The efficiency of organic solvents in removing dirt can be increased by adding a spirit soap, i.e. a form of soap that is soluble in an organic solvent. Such a preparation is the cleansing agent based on potassium oleate in which is incorporated Sextol (methyl cyclohexanol). This material (originally known under the trade name 'Howards Soap B.30' but now as 'Vulpex') is soluble in such solvents as white spirit and trichloroethane and is used at a concentration of about 1 per cent. The textile is immersed in this solution and is gently moved or pressed so as to dislodge the dirt and to dissolve grease. A final wash should be given in the solvent to remove any residues of the soap remaining in the textile. In the case of fabrics heavily stained with grease, the solution may be applied with a soft-bristle brush working from the stains towards the edges of the fabric.

Steam cleaning. For certain kinds of textiles, cleaning by steam (if properly controlled) may be much less drastic than either soaking with water or cleaning with organic solvents. Steam may sometimes be used for softening and removing stains even in the presence of fugitive colouring matter that would spread if wetted. A steam-gun apparatus that will provide wet or dry steam at option is now regarded as an essential in modern laundry practice, and it could be applied with advantage to cleaning certain kinds of museum textiles —costumes, for example, or ethnographical specimens—as it makes possible a variety of cleaning operations that would not be warranted by any other process.

3. Removal of stains; bleaching

It is not always advisable to attempt the removal of stains from old textiles. Stains of long standing may have undergone a chemical change with the formation of insoluble matter that can only be discharged by bleaching, and this process would be likely to weaken still further an old textile that had already become tendered. In certain cases, however, the removal of stains is to be recommended. In the unfortunate event of a textile being stained by accident, the staining should be dealt with quickly before it has had time to become fixed in the fibres. Iron stains commonly rot vegetable fibres, and these should be removed if the fabric is strong enough to withstand treatment. With frail old textiles, removal of stains may be a very delicate operation requiring experience and some knowledge of chemistry, but with modern fabrics, including many textiles in ethnographical collections, there is less risk of damage and, even for the amateur, a reasonable prospect of success.

In the removal of stains the first step is to ascertain the nature of the textile (e.g. wool, silk, or linen), and it is also a help to know the nature of the substance responsible for causing the stain; this may be obvious, but sometimes it will be necessary to make tests before the appropriate reagent can be selected.[1] Even so, all sorts of difficulties are liable to be encountered. The textile itself may be decorated with paint susceptible to solvents; the colours of a dyed fabric may bleed in contact with liquids; or a particular lining may cause trouble by staining the material to which it is attached. In all cases the selected reagent must be tested on an inconspicuous part of the textile to see whether it is safe to use before applying it to the stain.

The success of the operation often depends on how the reagent is applied. The general tendency is to use too much solvent and so risk spreading the stain. The smallest quantity of the reagent should be applied on a small screwed-up tuft of cotton-wool, and with a dexterous touch the stain should be lifted off rather than rubbed in. Several applications may be necessary, but if a stain is very stubborn, it is better to leave it rather than risk damaging the fabric.

[1] Moss, A. J. E., *Stain Removal*, London, Iliffe, 1950.

A. As taken from tomb

B. After unfolding and cleaning

11. FRAGMENT OF WOVEN GILT-THREAD TEXTILE FROM TOMB OF
ARCHBISHOP DE GRAY (DIED 1255) IN YORK MINSTER

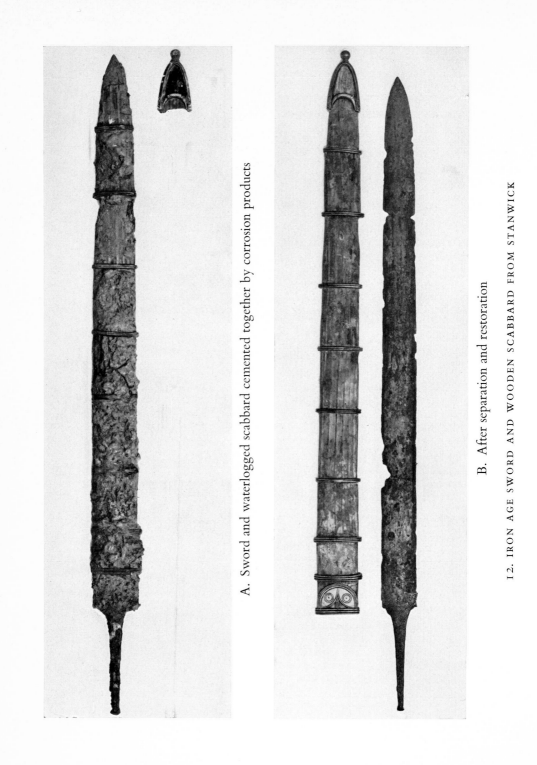

A. Sword and waterlogged scabbard cemented together by corrosion products

B. After separation and restoration

12. IRON AGE SWORD AND WOODEN SCABBARD FROM STANWICK

In certain cases a different technique is required, known as 'ringing the stain'. It is obvious that the application of any organic solvent to, for example, a grease spot, would simply result in the grease being spread over a larger area of the textile. The procedure adopted here is to stretch the textile, stained side downwards, over a glass plate covered with blotting-paper and apply the reagent to the *back* in drops from a small pipette so that it forms a ring around the stain. In this way the solvent bears in upon the stain from all sides at once, the grease is dissolved without spreading, and the resultant solution is absorbed in the blotting-paper.

An alternative method for removing grease or wax stains is to cover both sides of the stain with clean blotting-paper and apply a warm iron. This is the traditional method for removing 'candle grease'; the grease melts and most of it runs into the warm paper. Any residue is then eliminated with toluene, turpentine, or trichloro-ethane applied by ringing as described above. A blob of hardened paint or a blob of grease or mud should be carefully removed as far as possible with a scalpel or razor blade *before* the solvent is applied.

For the removal of certain kinds of stains it may be necessary to use enzyme preparations. Enzymes are naturally occurring organic substances that have a specific action in catalysing many organic reactions, including the breakdown of sugars, fats, and proteins. Mixtures of enzymes are obtainable, called 'digester powder', and this may be used for rendering certain organic stains soluble, so that they may be removed subsequently by washing. Enzymes act best in weak solutions at temperatures between 37 and 50 °C.—they are soon destroyed at temperatures in excess of 60 °C. The hydrolytic action of enzymes takes time to complete, perhaps an hour or longer, and the process is known as digestion. Enzymes are usually obtained as composite proprietary products with directions for their most effective use. For example, pepsin can be used by mixing 1 gm. of a pepsin preparation with 25 ml. of warm water and adding two drops of hydrochloric acid. This mixture is spread on a hard stain and kept moist until it becomes soft, when it can be removed by washing. In the case of very resistant stains a process involving bleaching may be necessary.

The safest all-round bleaching agent for old textiles is probably hydrogen peroxide that has been rendered alkaline with sodium silicate. The solution, comprising 250 ml. of 20-vol. hydrogen peroxide, 3 ml. of sodium silicate and, 4 litres of soft water, is sufficient for treating 1 kg. of textiles, and is compounded as follows. Dissolve the silicate in some of the water, heated as necessary, then add the remainder of the water and the hydrogen peroxide and stir till

TABLE I

Reagents	Animal fibres (silk and wool)	Vegetable fibres (cotton and linen)
Strong acids or alkalis	Never used	Never used
Dilute acids	Never nitric acid	Harmful
Dilute alkalis	Permitted	Permitted
Bleach containing chlorine	Never used	Use weak only
Hydrogen peroxide	Permitted	Use weak only
Very hot water	Never used	Permitted

uniform. It is used cold by immersing the textile for up to one working day. In the case of a very frail textile such lengthy immersion is undesirable—shorter contacts are made by washing and drying between each; retreatment with hydrogen peroxide is carried out as required.

In using solvents for the removal of stains it must be borne in mind that animal fibres are very sensitive to hot water, which causes them to shrink and lose their lustre, to excessive rubbing, and to the use of those bleaching agents which depend for their effect on the evolution of chlorine. Vegetable fibres are generally more robust, but after bleaching or using acidic reagents it is essential to wash the treated part of the textile until it is neutral. These observations are summarized in Table I.

A list of specific reagents that are commonly employed for removing stains is given in Table II which has been compiled with the object of systematizing procedure. The nature of the textile and of the stain being known, reagents are applied to the stain one after the other in the order given: thus, for example, the symbol GLA for the

TABLE II

Procedure for the Removal of Stains

List of Reagents

A	Soft water (warm)	J	Oxalic acid (1 per cent)
B	Methylated spirit	K	Acetic acid (0·5 per cent)
C	Spirit soap	L	Ammonia (0·1 per cent)
D	Trichloroethane	M	Sulphurous acid
E	White spirit	N	Pyridine
F	Hydrochloric acid (2 per cent)	O	Morpholine
G	Hydrogen peroxide (10 vols.) made alkaline with ammonia	P	Chloramine-T (fresh, 2 per cent)
H	Potassium permanganate (1 per cent)	Q	Tartaric acid (fresh, 5 per cent)
I	Sodium hydrosulphite (5 per cent) made alkaline with ammonia		

	Material stained		
Nature of stain	Wool	Silk	Cotton or linen
1. Mud	GLFA	GLA	GLA
2. Grease	D or E	D or E	D or E
3. Iron rust	JKA	JKA	JKA
4. Red ink	ABL	GJF	P or LB
5. Blue-black ink	GFKA	GKFA	P or HMA
6. Copying ink	BA	BA	BAI
7. Marking ink	CD	LG	AI
8. Fresh oil-paint	BCE or JA	BC	JA
9. Old oil-paint	NA	NA	N or OA
10. Lipstick	GLKA or QA	GLKA or KA	KA

removal of mud stains on silk is to be interpreted as follows—hydrogen peroxide (G) is applied to the mud and, if no appreciable change is seen to take place in the course of a minute or so, very dilute ammonia (L) is applied. The stain should lessen in intensity and the mud be released so that it can be sponged off with hot water

(A), taking care that it is not hot enough to destroy the lustre of the material.[1]

FUNGAL AND INSECT ATTACK

In common with other organic materials, textiles are susceptible to attacks by moulds, but if the textiles are clean and conditions are reasonably dry, trouble should not arise from this source. In the event of mould growth being discovered, it can usually be arrested by airing the textiles, and any surface growths can be removed with a soft brush. If the outbreak is extensive, the textiles may be sterilized with thymol vapour (p. 61) or by spraying with a 0·5 per cent solution of *ortho*-phenylphenol in white spirit, but sterilization may be omitted if the textiles can be washed by an immersion process. If textiles are damaged by water, as might arise from a burst water-pipe or leaking roof, mould staining might appear and the most effective first-aid measure is to expose them in a current of warm dry air. For emergencies of this kind the most suitable equipment is a hot-air blower. The use of a heater without ventilation must be avoided as it would be likely to encourage and intensify mould growths.

Insect pests also are a frequent cause of damage to textiles and they often accompany fungal attack. Animal fibres, wool and silk, provide foodstuffs for several varieties of insects, and dry conditions are no serious deterrent to their activities. Linens and cottons are normally immune from attack, and they should be segregated from the wools and silks to facilitate inspection of the more vulnerable materials. But textiles of all kinds are liable to be damaged if they should happen to be contaminated with substances that are attractive to the pests, and it is for this reason, as much as for any other, that garments are washed or cleaned before incorporation in the collection. Textiles in storage should be inspected at regular intervals according to a routine, involving unfolding, dusting, airing, and sunning, and specimens should be scrutinized to discover any traces

[1] For more extensive treatment see Holden, J. T., and Fowler, J. N., *The Technology of Washing* (British Launderers' Research Assoc.) and Moss, A. J. E., op. cit.

of insect attack—holes in the material, presence of grubs, cocoons, or loose silk threads.

There are three general ways of protecting textiles from insects. The first is to isolate the fabric—to parcel it up so that insects cannot get at it. The second is to use insecticides, and the third is to use an inhibitor that is either so distasteful to the insect or so toxic that protection is assured. This last method involves the use of a proofing reagent that can be permanently fixed on the textile fibre (see Section 3 below).

1. *Isolation of the textile.* This is only a practicable proposition in the case of individual specimens, and, even then, there is always the possibility of infection being introduced in the parcelling and of activity proceeding unrecognized. It is advisable to include a quantity of a volatile insecticide in the parcel. For wrapping textiles, good quality paper is as effective as transparent plastic, but the latter is stronger, and has the added advantage that the contents are more readily inspected.

When polythene bags are used, it is most important that the textiles are quite dry when packed as moisture cannot escape through polythene, and if the textiles are damp when packed, they are almost certain to become mildewed. The proofed bags sold for the storage of furs are also satisfactory for textiles, but in the case of susceptible material it is as well to put about a cupful of *para*-dichlorobenzene crystals in the bottom of the bag to ensure against the risk of moth eggs being present. Protection by sandwiching material passe-partout between glasses provides an alternative method of isolation, and insecticides are normally not required here as the textile is exposed continuously to view.

2. *Use of insecticides.* Apart from vacuum fumigation that can be applied on a large scale to protect costumes or ethnographical material in bulk (see 'Wood', p. 131), the most effective protection is given by the presence of a volatile insecticide such as *para*-dichloro-benzene, which, though perhaps a trifle too volatile, is otherwise satisfactory and efficient. It can be put into cotton bags and hung in wardrobes, or it may be scattered in drawers and chests between

layers of paper. This substance is very effective against the chief insect pest, the clothes-moth, and is also effective against dermestid beetle. It has, however, a rather overpowering smell which causes headaches, and as it is a liver poison it is important to avoid working for long over an open case in which this chemical is used.

For materials that cannot be protected in this way the alternative is routine spraying using, preferably, a power spray with a fish-tail nozzle, and working at a pressure to give fine atomization. The gun is held at an angle of about 45° to the textile, so that a cloud of insecticide floats on to it, rather than a direct blast which might be damaging. Many different insecticides are available for this purpose, the most satisfactory being those made up in a colourless and odourless petroleum distillate. Pyrethrum extracts have an immediate action upon moths, DDT is slower to take effect, and insecticides of a mixed type containing both ingredients are probably best (see p. 31). Very little of the spray material condenses on the textile, and there is no evidence that the regular use of the spray results in any staining or change in colour. Insecticidal dusts are liable to contaminate the material unnecessarily and are not recommended.

Another serviceable insecticide, which incidentally also has fungicidal activity, is Mystox LPLX, one of the grades of insecticides based on pentachlorophenyl laurate. This is normally supplied as a 5 per cent solution in white spirit that can be safely sprayed on the textile in a fairly liberal manner.

If spraying is carried out correctly so that liquid does not condense on the textile, there is no risk that regular routine spraying will cause any staining or will affect colours in the textile. On the other hand, insecticidal dusts are liable to contaminate the textile unnecessarily and they are not recommended.

3. *Mothproofing.* In this method of treatment certain inhibiting agents that prevent moth attack are incorporated into the textile and confer protection over a prolonged period of time. Some of the best known of these mothproofing agents are the chemicals available under the trade name 'Eulan': Eulan U 33 is used in aqueous solution and Eulan BLS in organic solvents. These mothproofers have an

affinity for wool fibres that is similar to that of dyestuffs, and Lehmann[1] has described their use for treating textiles in the West Berlin State Museums. Another substance that is also effective in mothproofing is the emulsion Mystox LSE; it can be conveniently used when textiles are washed. Beecher[2] describes the preparation of the bath by adding 250 ml. of Mystox LSE to 4 litres of water and mixing thoroughly. This gives a *c.* 5 per cent solution of the Mystox compound into which the washed textile is dipped and manipulated so as to ensure maximum penetration of the solution. When thoroughly impregnated the textile (lying on a perforated support) is raised from the bath to allow excess of the solution to drain off, and then allowed to dry in a horizontal position. If it should, however, be necessary for the textile to be tilted or hung, its position should be altered periodically during drying so as to maintain a uniform distribution of the mothproofing solution.

REPAIRING AND MOUNTING

In the past excellent and painstaking work has been carried out in the mounting and repair of old textiles by needlework, using couching or bricking techniques to attach the textiles to stronger fabric linings. An alternative was to lay the old textiles down with paste, glue, or some other adhesive, yielding results that were much less satisfactory, since this procedure was liable to be accompanied by hardening and distortion of the tissue, discolouration, and even mould growths. As a result, a prejudice grew up against the use of adhesives of any kind for mounting textiles.

The position today is quite changed; first, because of the availability of certain outstandingly useful synthetic fabrics—nylon and terylene nets in all degrees of fineness—proportionately stronger and more permanent than the natural fibres, stable chemically, and not liable to attack by moulds or insects; and secondly, because so much

---

[1] Lehmann, D., *Präparator*, 1965, **11**, No. 2, p. 187; No. 3, p. 221.

[2] Beecher, E. R., *The Conservation of Cultural Property*, UNESCO, 1968, Chapter 16, p. 260.

more is known today concerning the behaviour of synthetic adhesives. These, if carefully selected, offer types that are non-staining
and reliable in that they maintain their adhesive properties even if
applied superficially to a surface as in the dry-mounting technique,
and they may be chosen so that they are reversible, i.e. removable
at any future period of time without exposing the mounted textiles
to any appreciable strain.

Examples may now be given in both categories. The first is
represented by the reinforcement given to a fifteenth-century pyx
cloth (Pl. 10), a frail textile of drawn-thread work which was
required to support not only its own weight, but also that of four
wooden balls, one at each corner of the square. The balls were
tasselled and covered with *gesso* and gold leaf. A terylene net reinforcement was sewn on the reverse side around the central hole
where the strain was greatest, and some reinforcement was also done
at the corners; since both the textile and the terylene were of a pale
ivory colour the repair work was invisible at a distance of a few
feet. All the sewing repair work was done with terylene thread.

An example in the second category is the heat-sealing of terylene
net, gauze, or marquisette to the back of the old textile. Beecher,
who developed this process in the Conservation Department of the
Victoria and Albert Museum, has described how a suitable terylene
net, is chosen, stretched, and coated with a special thermoplastic
adhesive (vinyl acetate-vinyl caprate copolymer emulsion) using a
hot-air blower to prevent clogging the holes. This prepared reinforcement is now taken and attached to the old textile with the aid
of a warm iron (or using a vacuum table in conjunction with infra-
red lamps). The weight of the reinforcing material is chosen to suit
the type of old textile, but there seems no limit to the possibilities of
either weight or magnitude, for heavy tapestries have been successfully dealt with using this adhesive. The advantages of this process
are claimed to be the following:[1] (i) the adhesive on drying loses its
solubility in water but remains soluble in industrial alcohol, i.e.

---

[1] Beecher, E. R., in *Recent Advances in Conservation*, Butterworth, London, 1963,
p. 195.

the textile can be unmounted if necessary; (ii) no alien substance is introduced into the fibres of the old textile so that it can be draped naturally for display purposes; and (iii) there is no staining or liability to attack by micro-organisms. It remains to add that the heat-sealing can be carried out effectively at moderate heat (80 °C.) by contact for a very short time so that damage on this account is not to be anticipated. In short, this procedure is clearly destined to replace entirely the former techniques using silk net, which loses its strength in time and is subject to attack by both insects and micro-organisms.

Variations of the treatment with synthetics that have proved to be satisfactory have been recorded from various centres (Amsterdam, Zurich, etc.), notably relating to specialized problems such as the preservation of 'colours', historic flags that are today often fragmentary, being merely residues of coloured silks of extreme frailty, impossible to handle or exhibit.

It is now possible to line them almost invisibly with a fine inconspicuous net and they can then be displayed either in a frame, preferably lying flat, or, more naturally, hanging from a pole, but this must then be set horizontally so that the attendant strains are as far as possible equally distributed. It is advisable, however, to regard this arrangement as a temporary exhibition because the fabric of the flag cannot but suffer damage from any dust or spores that may be around.

An expedient adopted in Canterbury Cathedral is to show the original flag[1] of the Black Prince in a glass case by his tomb and have a perfect modern replica hanging in its natural folds from a pole that is attached to the wall above.

PROTECTION IN STORAGE AND EXHIBITION

1. *Lighting.* In studying the conservation of textiles attention should be focused on the damage that is done by unnecessary

---

[1] Restored by the Tower of London Armouries with the co-operation of the Royal School of Needlework. The original jupon has been strengthened with terylene net, dyed to match the old material.

exposure to light in causing tissues to become weakened and dye-stuffs to fade.

All natural fibres, animal and vegetable alike, are affected. The rate of deterioration varies with the quality and intensity of the light and the temperature and relative humidity of the atmosphere, but it is, above all, the invisible ultra-violet constituent that is most active in causing decay.

In the case of dyed textiles exposed to light, it is well known that certain dye-stuffs have a protective action in slowing down tendering while others actually accelerate this weakening of the tissue. The nature of the complex formed between the dye-stuff and the substrate must also be taken into account. When exposed to light, fading will occur if this complex is capable of absorbing radiant energy which brings about a molecular change. It should be noted that the spectral absorption of the complex in the dyed textile need not necessarily be the same as it is for the dye-stuff in isolation. These considerations apply with equal force to any form of lighting, natural or artificial, but owing to the relatively low intensity of artificial light sources, the rate of change of colour may be so reduced that it can only be assessed after a prolonged period of time. Long-term exposure may be just as serious in causing fading as exposure to sunlight for a correspondingly shorter time, and, in making comparisons of fading, it must be remembered that the relative humidity has been shown to have an important bearing on the fastness of dye-stuffs to light.

2. *Chemical attack.* Mention has already been made of the action of sulphur dioxide in causing the deterioration of organic materials such as leather and paper, and it is the most potent cause of the tendering of textiles. Cotton seems to be particularly prone to decay from the action of sulphur dioxide. Textile collections in cities or near industrial undertakings are likely to be best conserved when protected under glass. When the small concentration of sulphur dioxide within a case has been absorbed, little further contamination is to be anticipated until the case is opened and a fresh supply of polluted air is admitted.

Iron catalyses the changes of sulphur dioxide to sulphuric acid, and it is a common observation that where iron nails or tacks have been used to fix textiles, the material has rotted more intensively where it is next to the iron, as, for example, around the tacks used to attach a canvas painting to its stretcher. For this purpose copper tacks should be used. But ordinary dust usually contains an appreciable quantity of iron in one form or another, and this is an additional reason for adopting some form of protection for materials that are exhibited in galleries in which the air is not washed free from soluble impurities or fully conditioned.

EMBROIDERED TEXTILES

Metal threads in embroideries present a problem in that the structure of the threads will determine what is possible in the way of restoration. These threads are made by winding very fine and narrow metal strip around a core which may be of thread, hair, parchment, etc., and even gilt metal strip has been used to make gold thread by winding it over a spun thread core. Water treatment might damage several of these types; and, moreover, unless the gold is very pure, some silver and copper is usually present and it is likely to be tarnished and brittle. Silver thread may be so tarnished that its restoration is impossible.

If the gold is of good quality, the chances are that the thread will be couched, i.e. be exposed totally on the surface as a decorative element, being held in position by stitches that attach it to the foundation material. Such was the case with the gold-embroidered stole and maniples, dating from the tenth century, that form part of the St. Cuthbert relics at Durham Cathedral.[1] The work of cleaning involved removal of a hard buckram backing to which the frail old embroideries had been pasted at some time in an effort to preserve them. The buckram had shrunk, and caused the embroideries to cockle, and they were in a very brittle condition possibly due to excess of adhesive or glue from the buckram. The first step was to

[1] Battiscombe, C. F., *The Relics of St. Cuthbert*, Durham, 1956.

reinforce the embroidery by facing it with Japanese tissue. For this purpose it was necessary to choose an adhesive that would not be softened by water and that could easily be removed at the conclusion of operations without affecting the dye-stuffs. Polyvinyl acetate (dissolved in a mixed solvent consisting of toluene and acetone 95:5) satisfied these requirements, and by using this adhesive the thin tissue paper was attached as intimately as possible and the surface fixed securely. After the adhesive had dried, the embroideries were laid face down on glass, and relaxed under sheets of wet blotting-paper until the paste had softened to such a degree that the buckram could be detached. Residual lumps of softened paste that were adhering among the embroidery threads had to be picked out with forceps, and the back of the embroidery was then cleaned with saponin froth. What remained of the original lining was left *in situ*. The textiles were dried between sheets of warm blotting-paper and flattened under glass plates.

The next stage was to release the tissue paper by the application of the mixed solvent, and it was found on removal to bear an imprint of the gold embroidery in dust.[1] To clean the gold still further, fresh tissue paper was applied with polyvinyl acetate, and after one or two applications the richness of the gold threads was restored to a remarkable degree. The silk threads, however, were still very dirty. These were cleaned by several applications of saponin froth, and by this means it was possible to recover the natural sheen of the silk and to reveal colours that had been concealed by the grime of ages. The embroideries were then sterilized in the thymol chamber preparatory to mounting.

ARCHAEOLOGICAL TEXTILES

In archaeological museums, textiles are liable to be presented for laboratory treatment in all stages of fragmentation and deterioration, but perhaps the most difficult problem arises in the case of material

---

[1] The dust contained silver sulphide. This arose from tarnishing of the silver constituent of the gold alloy that had been used in making the thread.

that is freshly excavated, usually from a tomb. Such textiles may be, on the one hand, hard and brittle or, on the other, so decayed as almost to resemble a spider's web; or they may be damp so that the pattern and colours are concealed beneath a layer of mud and insect remains. But no matter what condition they are in, provided they have not completely disintegrated, they will always repay careful examination, and it is surprising what may be done in the way of preservation. As a preliminary step it may be advisable to consolidate the textile *in situ* by spraying or brushing on a 5 per cent alcoholic solution of soluble nylon to facilitate the handling of the fragile fragments and their transport to the laboratory.

The first stage of treatment is always superficial cleaning, so as to enable the textile to be examined. Loose dust may be removed by bellows, but on no account must the material be brushed. Insect remains often adhere firmly and these have to be removed with scalpel or forceps working under a binocular microscope. If a textile has been damp, it may gradually develop a white bloom as it dries owing to the crystallization of salts, and this should be held in check by spraying[1] occasionally with a fine mist of distilled water—not enough to soak the fabric and make it limp, but merely to prevent the surface from becoming white and so obscuring the structure under examination. When extraneous matter has been removed as far as possible, reverse the textile and deal with the back in the same manner.

It is nearly always possible to wash frail textiles provided they are manipulated on a support and handled as little as possible while wet. As dirt and dust have a deleterious effect, washing is always desirable, but where there are decorative attachments, e.g. metal threads or leaf, leather, etc., that might be damaged by water, washing with a spirit soap may be possible (p. 107). In all cases the textile should be photographed after preliminary cleaning, and by using an infra-red plate it may be possible to record further details of ornament that

---

[1] When fatty acids are present the textile may be difficult to wet. If there is any difficulty in wetting the textile with the water spray, a little wetting-agent (Lissapol N) should be added.

are either concealed or that are difficult to interpret by ordinary photography.

When textiles are rigid and crumpled or folded, they should be laid on a glass plate or polythene sheet and the wrinkles and folds sprayed so that they gradually become relaxed. If the material can be washed, no attempt should be made at this stage to stretch the fabric out. It is floated into shape after it has been immersed in water.

Details of the washing process have already been described. In the case of very frail textiles the porous support is preferred to the solid polythene sheet, so that water with dirt and sandy material can drain through. Alternatively, the material may be sandwiched between two sheets of terylene net fixed in a frame so that handling is reduced to a minimum. After washing, the terylene is pressed between warm dry towelling to remove excess of moisture, and when partly dry the frail material is transferred to a sheet of polythene and pinned out as described on p. 104.

Once dry all that remains is the preparation of the textile for either storage, study, or display. When the fragments are too brittle to be mounted, they can be exhibited by placing them on a sloping surface in a dust-proof exhibition case; the slope should be faced with rough silk or velvet with the pile facing upwards so that the textile fragments adhere in position. Alternatively, the fragments may be preserved in plastic envelopes, but in order to prevent damage by handling they should be tacked by stitching to a sheet of cellulose acetate before placing in the envelope.

An instructive example of preservative treatment was presented by a crumpled textile taken from the tomb of Archbishop de Grey in York Minster (see Pl. 11A). This was consolidated *in situ* with soluble nylon before being removed, as it was in a very brittle state. An initial examination of some detached fibres showed that the textile was silk and a preliminary test with a small detached fragment showed that immersion in water would cause extensive disintegration. The textile was relaxed, therefore, by being first exposed in a closed container to a high relative humidity, and then being placed in contact with moist cotton-wool interleaved with Japanese tissue.

In the relaxed condition the textile became flexible enough to be gradually unfolded. It was then bathed in acetone and dried. At this stage the soluble nylon was removed by soaking in methyl alcohol so that adherent matter previously held in position by the film of soluble nylon could be brushed off. This treatment considerably improved the appearance of the textile and revealed a striking pattern made of threads covered with silver gilt, as shown in Pl. 11B.

V

WOOD

WOOD has been exploited by man since palaeolithic times. Man has done almost everything with wood—made his home of it, made fires with it to cook his meals, used it for utensils, weapons, and implements, built ships and bridges of it, used it for making vehicles, furniture, art objects, and musical instruments, and, in modern times, transformed it into paper and even clothing. It is not surprising, therefore, that wood forms a large part of the collections in museums—particularly in ethnographical and folk museums—and its conservation is a matter of considerable importance.

Being of organic origin, wood normally decays under combined biological and chemical attack when buried in the ground, but in exceptional circumstances it has been found to survive prolonged exposure to extremes of dryness or wetness. Worked timbers exist today in the dry tombs of Egypt that date back to the early dynasties, and it is somewhat of a surprise to find that these are still sound and often so fresh in appearance that they might be taken for timbers of modern origin. Timber that has been buried in wet peat bogs for a long period of time may retain its general shape and size. The absence of air inhibits fungal attack, but profound changes may have taken place in chemical composition and microstructure, resulting in a loss of strength. Such timber can be dried, however, and its original appearance restored by laboratory treatment. In sharp contrast, wood completely decays when buried in damp sand that is well aerated. In this case decay is due in the main to fungal attack. The excavation of the seventh-century ship burial at Sutton Hoo yielded many notable treasures (now in the British Museum) but the ship itself had succumbed, leaving only rusty iron nails and a stained impression in the sand to mark where the wooden planks had rested.

13. DECORATED IVORY PLAQUE FROM NIMRÛD. (8TH CENT. B.C.)
Before treatment
See frontispiece for conditions after treatment

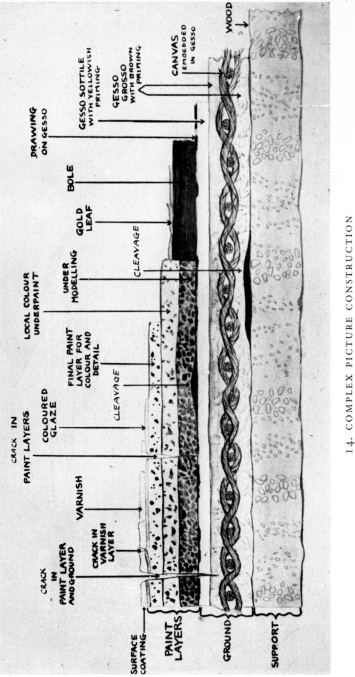

14. COMPLEX PICTURE CONSTRUCTION

Schematic representation of the stratified structure of a panel painting
(vertical section)

No such extreme changes are to be expected in wood kept indoors. Under such circumstances the commonest form of deterioration, in temperate climates at all events, is due to the dimensional changes accompanying variations in the relative humidity of the atmosphere. These result in warping and splitting, features that are related to the hygroscopic nature of the material, and to the fact that it has a grained structure.

DIRECTIONAL PROPERTIES OF WOOD

In order to study the conservation of wooden objects it is necessary to be familiar with certain characteristics of the raw material. Wood is an anisotropic substance, exhibiting different degrees of hardness, toughness, etc., in different directions. It has an organized cellular structure, and as the fibres are for the most part orientated in the same direction, grain is a distinctive feature. This varies in appearance according to the species of tree and the cut of the timber.[1] In a longitudinal median plank, two main zones are to be distinguished, namely heart-wood and sap-wood, the latter being situated towards the edges adjacent to the bark. In practice the direction of the cut is not necessarily chosen as being the most economical nor as giving the strongest timber, though both these considerations may apply; it is often selected in order to give some effect of texture or grain for ornamental purposes.

SEASONING OF WOOD

The sap-wood of a tree has a higher moisture content than the heart-wood, and when the timber is sawn into planks, the distribution of moisture in the planks varies accordingly. If left to dry out naturally, the moist parts will shrink more than the drier parts and the planks will warp. It is for this reason that they have to be submitted to a process of controlled drying known as seasoning. This consists in allowing the timber to dry out slowly under conditions

[1] In *Museum*, 1955, **8**, 3, p. 139, the relationship between cut and grain is illustrated in an admirable series of drawings.

in which distortion is prevented. But wood never loses all its moisture; the cell moisture[1] remains and, when seasoning has been completed, the moisture content of timber is found to vary with the relative humidity of the atmosphere surrounding it. The equilibrium state of air-dry timber that has been seasoned under the most favourable conditions varies in different regions. Desch[2] quotes a moisture content of 12–15 per cent as typical of timber seasoned in the United Kingdom and most regions of the United States, whereas in the more humid tropics, e.g. Malaya, 14–18 per cent is characteristic, and in hot arid regions the moisture content may be as low as 8–12 per cent.

In the early stages of seasoning sap-wood is particularly vulnerable to attack by fungi and insects, not only because of its higher moisture content, but because it contains a greater concentration of nutrients. Kiln-seasoning is general today instead of air-drying, and as it speeds up the process there is less chance of infection; it has the additional advantage that the residual moisture content of the wood can be adjusted to suit the particular purpose for which the wood is required and the climate in which it is to be used.

WARPING OF WOOD

The most important factor in preserving seasoned timber is to avoid exposing it to wide variations in atmospheric humidity. Under such conditions it alternately absorbs and gives up moisture. While this causes little dimensional change along the grain, it causes expansion and contraction across the grain with consequent warping. If one side of a plank is protected from the atmosphere, the other side will absorb or give up moisture more quickly than the protected side and warping will be intensified. Humid conditions will cause expansion across the grain on the exposed side, so that the protected side becomes concave. Conversely, where conditions are very dry the protected side will become convex. This explains the 'cupping'

[1] i.e. the moisture contained within the cells as distinct from the moisture held between the cells.

[2] Desch, H. E., *Timber, Its Structure and Properties*, Macmillan, London, 3rd edn., 1956.

that takes place in the constituent planks of a wooden panel painted only on one side, when exposed in an atmosphere that is too dry. Varying relative humidity tends to cause back and forward movements which are a significant factor in the life of panel paintings (p. 4). If a panel is restrained in a frame by glue or nails, changing relative humidity may cause the wood to crack or become distorted.

The elimination of warping is a lengthy and uncertain process,[1] although at times it has to be attempted in the interests of conservation. The operation may take several weeks or even months. The treatment consists in moistening the concave side so that water is slowly absorbed; this swells the tissue and encourages the wood to return to the flat condition, and it is then kept flat under weights until dry. But even if this operation appears at first to be successful the tendency will be for the wood to return gradually to the warped condition unless some form of cradling can be used to confine the stresses to one plane—see pp. 166 sqq.

A simple form of metal reinforcement that is often quite effective and may be applied where the wood is of reasonable thickness is to screw a series of angle irons to the back of the panel at right angles to the grain by countersunk screws passing through slots (not holes) in the metal. The edges of the slots should be slightly chamfered. This arrangement admits of lateral movements of the wood and prevents the panel from cupping. The metal and screws must be of such a nature as not to lose freedom of movement by corrosion or otherwise.

When, as in certain types of furniture, the wood is painted all over or french-polished, all the surfaces are equally protected and movement of the constituent timbers is reduced to a minimum. In the case of synthetic grainless boards that have no directional properties or plywood having an adequate number of layers, a balance of forces is achieved structurally, and warping does not occur. Large thin boards may buckle under their own weight, but this is purely a

---

[1] When wood is old and has been in a warped condition for a long time, a modification of cell structure may have occurred which precludes the possibility of a successful restoration. Wood in this condition is said to have acquired a 'permanent set'.

mechanical matter which can be dealt with by arranging for suitable supports.

ATTACK BY FUNGI

A certain degree of dampness is required before fungi can grow on materials supplying the necessary nutrients. This has already been referred to in the case of paper and leather, and it is equally true of wood. Structural timber is most prone to attack because it may become wet owing to the inadequate provision of damp-proof courses, and large wooden objects, such as canoes, totem poles, and carvings exposed out of doors, are much more likely to be attacked by fungi than objects kept indoors. The fungi attacking such timbers may be of the virulent 'dry rot' group that is so difficult to eradicate without wholesale sacrifice of the infected material. Preventive measures take the form of isolating the wood, if possible, by the introduction of a damp-proof course of slate, lead, etc., and by protecting any end-wood by impregnating it with a waterproofing agent such as linseed oil, wax, or a water-repellent silicone varnish. When timbers are exposed in the open, advantage should be taken of any possibility of deflecting water by dripstones or courses. When wood is in contact with the ground, it should be impregnated with a fungicide, and any part under ground level encased in waterproof cement.

The following fungicides are colourless and odourless and will not stain wood, brickwork, or plaster.

(A) 100–200 gm. of commercial sodium fluoride dissolved in 5 litres of water and applied cold by brush (two coats), or

(B) 100 gm. of commercial acid magnesium fluoride dissolved in 2·5 litres of water.[1]

For details of these processes and of other methods of dealing with an outbreak of dry rot, the reader is advised to consult the publications of the Forest Products Research Laboratory.[2] No satisfactory account of methods for conserving timber would be possible without

[1] A wooden tub must be used in making this solution as it attacks metal.

[2] Forest Products Research Laboratory, *Decay in Buildings, Recognition, Prevention and Cure*, Technical Note 44, 1969; *Dry Rot in Wood*, Research Bulletin No. 1, 6th n., 1960.

frequent reference to the valuable publications of this laboratory, which are based upon wide experience and research, and cover all aspects of the subject.

When moulds are growing on art objects in the museum, ethnographical specimens, etc., it will usually be found that they are feeding upon oil, grease, or the binding medium of *gesso*, rather than on the wood itself, and growth may be arrested by cleaning and applying fungicide. But the treatment should not stop here. It is equally important to take measures to prevent a recurrence of the outbreak by improving ventilation.

ATTACK BY INSECTS

Insect pests of timber are a greater menace to museum objects than moulds, because the possibility of infection is ever present. The nature of the damage will depend on the type of infestation, which varies in different parts of the world. The commonest pests in Great Britain are various types of wood-boring beetle, and the damage is done by their grubs which tunnel into the wood, converting sound tissue into powder. The grubs are popularly known as 'wood-worm'.

If the attack is not checked at an early stage, the wood may fall to pieces and may be found to be riddled with insect channels filled with powder and frass resembling fine sawdust. It is usually the presence of powder of a light colour that provides the first indication of attack; if structural timber is inaccessible, the first indication may be that a piece of timber gives way and falls to the ground, as happened in the case of a wooden rib from the roof of the North Transept of York Minster in 1934. When this occurs the attack will have already proceeded to great lengths, and it can only be dealt with by an expensive operation involving wholesale impregnation of the old sound wood with insecticides, and by making extensive replacements of the infected wood.

Furniture should be inspected regularly to ensure that it is free from 'worm', paying special attention to plywood back-boards and also to any sap-wood that may be present. It is not uncommon to find the first evidence of a wood-beetle infection in the ply-backing of a framed picture, or in the plywood that has been used to repair the back of a chest or a bureau. When discovered, infection should be dealt with at once, either by replacing the plywood or by treating it with a reliable insecticide (see p. 133).

The discovery of worm holes in wood is not necessarily an indication that insects are still active. Sometimes they die off before all the wood has been destroyed, but it is never an easy matter to be certain that activity has ceased. Clean wood dust falling from an old hole may suggest activity which, in fact, does not exist; but if an object that has been lying undisturbed with accumulations of dirty wood powder is seen to have some clean wood dust upon it, this will be a clear indication that insects are still alive in the wood. In all cases where there is any doubt, it is safer to assume the worst and the object should be lifted carefully into the open air, brushed clean, and treated with an insecticide.

Before it can be taken for granted that sterilization has been completely effective and that no viable eggs remain, the wood must be kept under regular observation during at least one complete life-cycle of the insect, but as insects develop at different rates this involves identification. For example, the powder-post beetle (*Lyctus*) breeds through from egg to adult in three months to a year, whereas in the case of the death-watch beetle (*Xestobium*)—the major pest of inaccessible structural timbers—development is much slower, taking possibly two years or more to complete. The life cycle of the common furniture beetle (*Anobium*) may also run to two years or more and that of the longhorn beetle (*Hylotropus*) is reputed to be from four to eleven years. Wood-boring insects may be identified by the size of the holes they leave on emerging to lay eggs, or by the materials attacked, or by the nature and extent of the outbreak, age of the timber, etc., but the most certain method is a microscopic study of the grub or full-grown insect and comparison with photomicrographs and drawings in the standard works of reference.[1]

[1] Forest Products Research Laboratory, Leaflet No. 3 revised 1969 (*Lyctus*); Leaflet No. 4 revised 1967 (*Xestobium*); Leaflet No. 8 revised 1968 (*Anobium*) and Leaflet No. 14 revised 1964 (*Hylotropus*).

As an aid to long-term inspection and sterilization all surface powder and the frass should be removed and the old holes filled with soft wax (see p. 133) so that any fresh ones will be at once apparent. In adding to a museum collection, the greatest care must be taken to exclude material that might introduce infection until such time as it has been sterilized. When wood is found to be attacked, treatment should be carried out as soon as possible; the longer the delay, the more difficult it will be to bring the infestation under control.

METHODS OF STERILIZATION

Insects may be killed by rise of temperature, by reduction of pressure (vacuum treatment), and by poisoning with gas (fumigation), or liquids (spraying; impregnation). It may be stated in general that fumigation methods are immediately effective but confer no lasting protection, whereas impregnation methods may be slower to take effect, but the poison remains and confers protection over a period.

Sterilization by fumigation. Sterilization may be carried out in a sealed gas chamber, and with suitable equipment it is possible to reduce the pressure to a partial vacuum before admitting the gas, which ensures that the fumigant will penetrate in a reasonable time into the objects under treatment.

Hydrogen cyanide gas is used in such a chamber at the British Museum for dealing with ethnographical material in bulk, mainly textiles, skins, feathers, and small wooden objects, for which a twenty-four hours' exposure has been found adequate. With denser materials such as heavy timber, methyl bromide would be likely to give better penetration, but methyl bromide has the disadvantage that, in dealing with ethnographical specimens which may contain feathers, leather, etc., or with upholstery containing horse hair, it tends to form compounds having a very unpleasant odour. This may be a disadvantage where objects in storage have to be frequently examined. When large objects have to be sterilized by fumigation and no special plant exists for the purpose, it may be possible to arrange for this to be carried out professionally by a firm specializing in such work.[1]

Carbon disulphide is a reliable insecticide that can be used for the fumigation of valuable objects of all kinds as it does not harm the most delicate material. It is a clear liquid at normal temperatures, having a low vapour pressure (B.P. 46 °C.) and an unpleasant odour. As it evaporates readily to form explosive mixtures with air,[2] rigid precautions must be taken to exclude naked lights and prevent smoking in any room in which this fumigant is used. Some museums are equipped with special vacuum plant for fumigating with carbon disulphide vapour. The special plant is enclosed and therefore safe and assures good penetration. It is possible to fumigate with this insecticide at normal temperature and pressure with improvised equipment. This type of fumigation is conducted as follows. Dishes of the liquid are exposed above worm-infested wood in an air-tight cupboard or box which is then sealed up, the doors being pasted round with adhesive paper or polythene tape. A polythene bag may be used instead of a cupboard provided it can be adequately sealed with tape. Liquid carbon disulphide should be used in the proportion of 100 ml. to each cubic metre of air space in the chamber. The liquid volatilizes in the course of a few hours, and the heavy vapour pours down over the wood and tends to accumulate near the base of the cupboard. The time of exposure required for fumigation is from two to three weeks, and a fresh amount of liquid carbon disulphide should be added at the end of the first week to take the place of that which has evaporated. After fumigation the unpleasant smell disappears on exposing the wood to air for a short time.

It will be obvious that fumigation by carbon disulphide is particularly effective for sterilizing boards that can be treated in a horizontal position in a shallow box, and as this fumigant is without action on

[1] Rentokil Laboratories Ltd., 7 Morocco Street, London, S.E. 1.

[2] Carbon disulphide is a dangerous chemical and fumigations involving its use are best left in the hands of trained personnel.

paint or varnish the method is very useful for the treatment of worm-eaten panel paintings.

Liquid carbon disulphide should be stored in a cool place and protected from daylight as this causes the liquid to develop acidity.

For the sterilization of wooden objects that are not decorated with fugitive colours, a non-inflammable solution of one part of carbon disulphide in four parts of carbon tetrachloride may be recommended. While this is not quite so toxic to insects as pure carbon disulphide, equally satisfactory results are obtainable either by using a greater concentration or extending the period of exposure.

Sterilization by impregnation. Impregnation with liquid insecticides may be carried out by using a pipette or a syringe to inject the liquid into the holes. Alternatively, the insecticide may be brushed in. Large undecorated timbers may require to be drilled in inconspicuous parts to enable the insecticide to penetrate.

Suitable liquid insecticides are those containing DDT, BHC (gammexane), pentachlorophenol and its derivatives, chloronaphthalenes, or the metallic naphthenates. Many reliable mixtures are available commercially.[1] If applied thoroughly to all insect holes, the impregnation method may be as effective as fumigation, but before using an insecticide it should be tested to make sure that it is non-staining and that it does not soften paint or damage any decorations on the wood with which it might come in contact.

For filling the holes after treatment, the best material is usually a soft wax to which an insecticide has been added. A suitable preparation for filling the holes can be made by stirring DDT powder into molten beeswax, bleached or appropriately coloured to match the timber. When solidified, the wax paste may easily be spread into the worm holes with a blunt knife. If the wood requires strengthening (see below) this ought to be attended to prior to waxing.

Sterilization by spraying. While spraying is not very effective for killing pests that have already bored their way into wood, there is

[1] See *Wood Preservations Register*, published by *Timber and Plywood*, 194–200 Bishopsgate, London, E.C. 2.

evidence that spraying with a 2 per cent aqueous emulsion of DDT can prevent the spread of an outbreak of *Lyctus*.[1]

Proofing of wood against insect pests. Proofing is essential in the case of timber that may be exposed to attack by termites ('white ants')— the most injurious wood-feeding insects known. Creosote conforming to a standard specification[2] is used for this purpose but to be entirely effective the wood should be impregnated under pressure, and the creosote retained by the timber in certain minimum amounts. Metallic naphthenates are also used for pressure impregnation. For the protection of museum objects of wood such as furniture that cannot be impregnated under pressure, the only alternative is to saturate the wood as completely as possible by dipping or brushing, using a non-staining insecticide that will penetrate deeply into the timber. Protection is limited in proportion to the depth of penetration of the preservative. Such an insecticidal mixture may be prepared by dissolving pentachlorophenol in a petroleum distillate. This leaves the wood clean after treatment, but it is emphasized (F.P.R.L. Leaflet No. 38) that a certain minimum period of immersion is necessary if this treatment is to be entirely effective. For thin wood where glue is absent a hot 4 per cent aqueous solution of zinc chloride or sodium fluoride may be used, the object being dipped into the solution; but with aqueous solutions penetration is less effective and the degree of protection usually less satisfactory than that obtainable by the use of petroleum solutions or chloronaphthenates.

STRENGTHENING TIMBER

Wood that has been weakened by the attack of fungi or insect pests may be strengthened by impregnation with a consolidating agent or it may be reinforced mechanically. The nature of the specimen and the condition of the timber will determine which of the two

[1] Forest Products Research Laboratory, Leaflet No. 43, 1964.

[2] British Standard Specification Number 144. See also Forest Products Research Laboratory Leaflet No. 38 which gives an account of the habits and habitat of termites. References are given in this leaflet to the problem as it presents itself in Australia, India, Malaya, West Indies, and U.S.A., as well as in Great Britain.

methods is likely to be the more satisfactory, but in many cases it
will be found that both mechanical strengthening and consolidation
are required in order to restore solidity. When this is the case
impregnation may sometimes precede reinforcement, but sometimes
it will be more appropriately applied after the wood has been
mechanically strengthened.

Consolidation by mechanical reinforcement

Of the mechanical methods for strengthening timber, the following are the most important.[1]

1. Dowelling either with metal or wooden pegs, and refacing if
necessary with wood.

2. Inlaying across cracks with solid X-shaped wedges to prevent
the cracks from opening; or covering the joints by 'buttons' of wood,
i.e. small palettes c. 7 cm. by 5 cm. glued across the cracks.

3. Reinforcing with wooden splints, glued and/or screwed to the
old wood. Special bracket irons, angle irons, etc., may be useful in
repairing furniture.

4. Stopping irregular cavities with a gap-filling cement (see
repairs, p. 140).

Consolidation by impregnation

Methods of consolidation by impregnation may be applied to all
porous materials and are particularly suitable for dealing with intricate shapes, carvings that have suffered erosion by exposure, or wood
that is riddled with worm holes. Impregnation is carried out by
immersion, injection, or the solutions may be applied with a brush.

Where the surface is covered with loose *gesso* and gold leaf it can
only be satisfactorily consolidated by impregnation with a substance
that penetrates easily, and synthetic consolidating agents dissolved in
organic solvents are recommended in this case. Painted *gesso* is in the
same category, but the paint must be tested to ensure that it will not
be softened or dissolved by the solvent. If there is any sign of its

[1] This matter, in so far as it concerns painted panels, is given detailed attention in
Museum, 1955, **8**, 3, p. 139.

being attacked it may be possible to change the solvent for one less active, or waxing may be the preferable technique.

Impregnation by wax. When mechanical repairs are necessary they are always carried out before the wood is waxed. For many purposes the wax-bath is a most effective form of treatment, but for large objects special equipment is required. The bath may be a capacious, rectangular iron tank, heated electrically and thermostatically controlled so that the temperature of the wax is not allowed to rise above predetermined limits. There should also be an independent safety device to switch off the electric supply in case of failure on the part of the thermostat. Block and tackle will be required for raising and lowering heavy objects, and with this equipment it is possible to deal conveniently with life-sized wooden sculptures.

The composition of the wax mixture may be varied but the main ingredient is usually unbleached beeswax to which has been added a resin in quantities not exceeding 50 per cent.

The object to be impregnated, which must of course be quite dry, is lowered into the molten wax and kept beneath the surface by weights or otherwise. As the temperature gradually rises the air is expelled in a stream of bubbles and wax enters the pores of the wood. Any traces of moisture are driven off by maintaining the temperature at about 105 °C. till bubbling ceases, and it may then be allowed to rise to about 120 °C. The time of immersion depends on the porosity and bulk of the timber. When the impregnation is considered to be complete the heating is shut off, the object raised from the tank, and the hot wax allowed to drain away. Finally, surplus wax is removed from the surface with turpentine.

Waxing by immersion has been developed on a large scale in the Walters Art Gallery, Baltimore, by Rosen,[1] and it is also applied with much success in the Institut Royal du Patrimoine Artistique, Brussels, as a routine method of treating church furniture, architectural material, wooden carvings, and the like.

For the impregnation of small objects the wax immersion process can be carried out using improvised equipment, but a note of warn-

[1] Rosen, D., *Journal of the Walters Art Gallery*, 1950–1, p. 45.

ing is necessary about a potential source of danger when the tank is heated from below. If moisture has been introduced it will accumulate at the bottom of the tank as the wax solidifies; on reheating, steam pressure may be generated beneath the semi-solid wax and may cause an explosion. This danger can be mitigated by placing a metal rod upright in the wax as it cools; the rod is withdrawn and most of the water decanted away before the wax is reheated. It must also be remembered that the molten wax mixture is inflammable, and that serious burns can be caused by splashing. When wax is being melted over an open flame, an asbestos board should be at hand to place over the vessel in the event of the wax catching fire.

Wax-resin mixtures are inert and very stable, and being waterproof they afford protection against damp. They are thus of value in preventing movements in wood due to changes in the relative humidity of the atmosphere. Waxing has certain disadvantages, however, unless the objects are kept in cool surroundings. Even if the surface of a waxed object has been cleaned after immersion in the bath so that only the thinnest film of wax remains, there is a tendency for wax to creep out gradually from the inside, and in a matter of time the surface will become sticky and tend to collect dirt. In addition, if a waxed object is exposed to the sun or exhibited in a glass case that is lit internally, the specimen may develop an objectionable gloss with rise of temperature. A further disadvantage of wax mixtures is the fact that they have a high refractive index and lower the tone of colours. The optical qualities of light colours are best conserved by using materials having a lower refractive index than wax, and in certain cases colourless synthetic resins may be preferred.

Impregnation by synthetic resins. In recent years a number of synthetic resins that can be used as consolidants have become available. In this type of work a factor of paramount importance is that the consolidant should be capable of thoroughly penetrating the weakened wood. When solutions of synthetic resins, such as polyvinyl acetate or polymethacrylates, are used for this purpose, they suffer from the disadvantage that they can only be used as relatively dilute solutions in an organic solvent so that repeated applications are necessary in order to get an adequate amount of the resin into the wood. Also, owing to the fact that the solvent has to evaporate from the wood, it is difficult to achieve the degree of penetration necessary to ensure that the consolidant is deposited throughout the wood and not merely concentrated in the surface layers. There are, however, two particular types of synthetic resins that offer a new approach to this problem. These are the epoxy and polyester resins that do not require the use of a solvent. These can be readily applied by brushing or injection as mobile liquids—consisting of the resin plus an appropriate hardener and accelerator—that readily penetrate the structure of the weakened wood and solidify *in situ* at room temperature. Another important advantage of these non-solvent resin systems is that they are very versatile, so that the properties of the resin system can be altered to suit the particular requirements of the work in hand; thus the setting time can be varied within wide limits by choosing a suitable hardener and varying the amount of the accelerator, the physical properties of the solid resin formed after setting can be varied by the addition of a plasticizer, and finally the viscosity of the resin-hardener system in its pre-set form can be adjusted as desired by suitable choice of a particular resin.

As a specific example of the use of an epoxy resin for the consolidation of a fragile wooden object, we may consider the case of a ceremonial double-faced four-horned mask for use in the *Ikem* play, which was carved in about 1900 by an Ibo artist at Oziutem (Southeast Nigeria). When this was received in the British Museum Research Laboratory, it had been so thoroughly attacked by insects that the bulk of the mask was reduced to a mere shell and the nose and one ear were almost detached. Consolidation leading to restoration of mechanical strength was readily achieved by injecting into the mask a resin formulation consisting of the following: Araldite CY 219, 50 parts; hardener HY 219, 25 parts; accelerator DY 219, 1 part; dibutyl phthalate, 10 parts. Subsequently this particular formulation has been successfully used for the consolidation of many wooden objects in a fragile condition. As well as being used as liquid systems for impregnation, these epoxy and polyester resins can be mixed with powdered inert materials and made available as pastes which, when mixed with a liquid hardener, set at room temperature to a hard solid; in this form they can be used for making good parts of a wooden object which may be missing, as they can be readily shaped with ordinary wood-working tools. Thus in the case of the Nigerian mask referred to above, holes and gaps where the wood had been completely eaten away were made good with the epoxy resin Araldite AV 121. A convenient polyester paste that can also be used for the same purpose is the material available commercially under the trade name Bondafiller.

REPAIRS AND MAINTENANCE

The first requirement for wood repairs is a good adhesive that is easy to apply and which will make a strong joint. Calcium caseinate is a powerful adhesive for wood; it was used in the Middle Ages for furniture-making and for joining planks together to make into broad panels as supports for painting. A good-quality hide glue is more convenient in practice, and can yield joints that are strong enough for most purposes. The tendency nowadays, however, is to choose one of the modern synthetic resin adhesives. These set by chemical action when mixed with a hardener to give very strong joints. Four main types are recognized, namely:

> Urea Formaldehyde (U.F.) adhesives.
> Phenol Formaldehyde (P.F.) adhesives.
> Resorcinol Formaldehyde (R.F.) adhesives.
> Epoxy resin adhesives.

The first three tend to shrink on setting but the epoxy resins are characterized by the fact that they set without undergoing any appreciable contraction in volume.

The application varies according to the manner in which the hardener is mixed with the resin before use.

(1) The hardener is mixed with the resin in the stated proportions before the adhesive is applied to the joint.

(2) The hardener is applied to one side of the joint, the resin applied to the other side, and the two held together till the adhesive sets, or

(3) the adhesive is supplied as a dry powder consisting of resin plus hardener to which it is only necessary to add water before use.

Detailed instructions are supplied by the manufacturers in each case.[1] In making a choice of adhesive it may be of significance that the R.F. hardener is neutral, whereas the others are acidic or alkaline.

If, in addition to repairing a joint with an adhesive, it is necessary to fill irregular cavities in such a manner that the filler will itself confer strength, a modern gap-filling adhesive must be used, one of the most satisfactory being Aerolite 300, a U.F. resin. If it is merely a question of filling up a hole, Bondafiller may be used, or a viscous celluloid[2] syrup in which has been incorporated a porous filler such as sawdust or pumice powder. Glue and sawdust may sometimes be all that is required, and awkward holes may be filled in with shaped balsa wood inserted with an adhesive. In pegged repairs of this nature, extra wood must always be allowed and the excess cut or filed away after the adhesive has finally set.

Veneers and inlays tend to suffer from desiccation of the glue which causes them to lift; in this condition they are easily damaged with a duster and they should be temporarily secured with adhesive tape. This is a case where early attention is amply repaid. The process of laying back damaged veneer is a matter for the specialist—amateur repairs are seldom very permanent or satisfactory—and for the job to be done properly, it requires the use of a flexible glue[3] and the appropriate irons, the veneer being flattened and maintained under pressure until the adhesive has hardened.

Marquetry can be kept from drying up by rubbing occasionally with a little non-drying oil. Olive oil answers well for the purpose.

[1] See also Houwink, R. and Salomen, G. *Adhesion and Adhesives*, 1965.

[2] Celluloid fillers must be applied in thin layers allowing time for the material to set between each application, otherwise shrinkage may be considerable.

[3] Animal glue can be rendered flexible by the addition of starch derivatives, e.g. sorbitol.

A. Encrusted with a corroding copper alloy which has afforded it cathodic protection

B. After treatment

15. SILVER-SPOUTED BOWL FROM UR OF THE CHALDEES (*c.* 2500 B.C.)

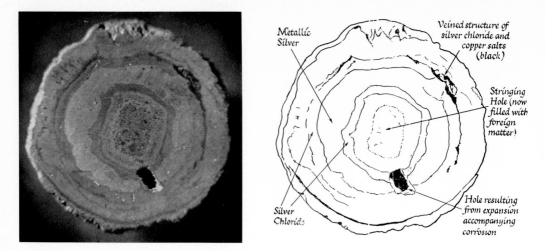

16. CROSS-SECTION OF A CORRODED BEAD OF BASE SILVER FROM UR OF THE CHALDEES, SHOWING STRATIFICATION

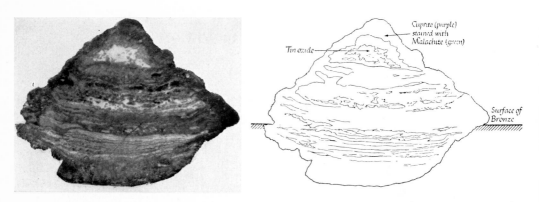

17. CROSS-SECTION OF PYRAMIDAL OUT-GROWTH KNOWN AS 'WARTY PATINA' FOUND ON A CORRODING CHINESE BRONZE

The light areas are tin oxide and the dark areas mainly cuprite. The multi-layered structure indicates that the incrustation is of great age

Almond oil is used for cleaning the wooden parts of violins and other musical instruments that are decorated with inlays. Wooden furniture having a good surface, whether French-polished or wax-polished, should be kept in condition by rubbing at intervals with a soft cloth. The original polish is always worth preserving whether applied to veneer or solid timber and it improves with time. Furniture polish coats the surface with a thin film of wax. This is a good thing, but wax should not be allowed to accumulate in cracks or crevasses as it will detract from the appearance and collect dirt. For cleaning polished furniture, of whatever kind, a suitable emulsion can be made by shaking together, vigorously, half a pint each of linseed oil, turpentine, and vinegar, to which is added a small teaspoonful of methylated spirit. This mixture is comparatively inexpensive; it removes dirt and polishes in the same operation, and is harmless if applied in moderation.

WATERLOGGED WOOD

When wood has remained buried for long periods in wet soil or peat, it undergoes serious deterioration arising from bacterial degradation of the cellulosic components of the cell walls; much of the finer cellulose tissue disappears, but the thicker lignin structures remain and these preserve the shape of the wood and often the general surface appearance. It is not uncommon to come across wooden objects from lake dwellings or from wells that appear to have survived for generations with little disfigurement, dark in colour but preserving their shape and ornament in minute detail. The loss of the finer cellulose tissue does not cause much alteration in the gross volume of the wood, but the porosity is much increased and the wood is able to absorb water like a sponge. When filled with water it is very heavy, and in this waterlogged condition it may be unable to bear its own weight so that if carelessly handled it may fracture across the grain. Objects in this condition must be lifted on a rigid support or splint and wrapped at once in polythene sheeting—so that they can reach the laboratory in the condition in which they were found. So long as the objects are kept wet they will keep their shape, but if allowed to dry without being specially treated, the weakened cellular tissue that is held apart only by water will collapse and the specimens will then be damaged beyond recovery.

The conservation of waterlogged wood is one of the archaeologist's major problems.[1] It involves, firstly, the removal of the large excess of water by a method which will prevent any shrinkage or distortion, and, secondly, the incorporation into the wood of a material which will act as a consolidant and confer mechanical strength to the wood. Many methods for the treatment of waterlogged wood have been tried in the past with varying degrees of success. Those which have aroused most interest and which seem to offer the best chance of success are the following.

Treatment of small- to medium-sized objects

1. *Alum method*. The principle underlying this method is based on the fact that alum (potassium aluminium sulphate, $K_2SO_4 . Al_2(SO_4)_3 . 24H_2O$) is a salt which has a much greater solubility in hot water than in cold water; it will in fact dissolve in its own water of crystallization at 96 °C. This means that if the excess of water in the wood is replaced by a solution of alum at an elevated temperature, then on cooling the alum will crystallize out inside the wood and will stabilize the weakened cell-walls. In practice, the waterlogged object is immersed in a saturated solution of alum maintained at a temperature of 92–96 °C. in a copper or iron vessel. It is left totally immersed in this hot solution for a sufficient period of time to ensure adequate impregnation. An average time is at least ten hours, but a longer period will be necessary if the wooden object is bulky or if the wood has a close grain. The object is then removed from the alum bath, washed quickly with warm water and set aside to cool. Any residual white deposit of alum which crystallizes out on the surface is brushed off when the object is dried. This method was the earliest used for the treatment of waterlogged wood, and it has a fair record of success, but it is rather drastic and sometimes fails.

[1] Christensen, B. B., *Conservation of Waterlogged Wood*, National Museum, Copenhagen, 1970.

There is evidence that the best results are obtainable with hard-woods rather than softwoods and that success depends on the use of a sufficiently concentrated hot solution of alum, and on securing adequate penetration. An example of the satisfactory application of the process to thin slats of yew is described in detail by Moss[1] in the preservation of an Anglo-Saxon wooden bucket.

2. *Alcohol–ether method*.[2] This method is essentially similar to the routine used for the drying out of biological specimens. The water-logged wooden object is first immersed in successive baths of ethyl alcohol (industrial methylated spirits can also be used) until all the water has been replaced by alcohol, the progress being followed by measuring the specific gravity of each bath. When all the water has been replaced by alcohol, the object is then immersed in successive baths of diethyl ether, so as to replace the alcohol by the ether. When this has been accomplished, the object is dried very quickly by plac-ing it in a vessel which can be rapidly evacuated so that rapid vola-tilization of the ether occurs. Ether was chosen because it has a very low surface tension (0·17 dyne/cm., compared with 0·72 dyne/cm. for water). This means that when the ether evaporates, the surface tension forces are too low to cause any appreciable collapse of the weakened cell walls. If necessary, dammar resin can be dissolved in the final bath of ether so that the dammar will be deposited in the pores of the wood to act as a consolidant. This method has proved to be very successful, but it is only economically practicable for the treat-ment of relatively small objects. Also alcohol and ether—particularly the latter—are highly inflammable materials, so that extreme pre-cautions have to be taken to guard against fire risks. Furthermore, the low boiling point of ether (35 °C.) would be an additional prob-lem militating against the use of this method in tropical countries.

3. *Arigal-C method*. This method depends upon the use of a special melamine-formaldehyde resin to impregnate the waterlogged wood. The object to be treated is first washed in water to remove the acidic

[1] Moss, A. A., *Museums J.*, 1952, **52**, p. 175.
[2] Christensen, B. B., *Om Konservering af Mosefundne Traegenstande*, National Museum, Copenhagen, 1952.

substances which are present in the wood as the result of the degradation which has taken place. After this preliminary washing the object
is immersed in a 25 per cent aqueous solution of the melamine-
formaldehyde resin (Arigal-C). The object is left immersed in this
solution until the excess of water has been replaced by the resin
solution and thorough impregnation of the wood has been achieved
—a process which, in the case of bulky objects, may take many weeks.
Then the object is removed from the bath, to which a special hardener
(catalyst) is added. The wooden object is replaced in the bath, which
is placed in a vacuum container and the pressure reduced to 80 mm. of
mercury. After about 35–40 hours the liquid resin is converted to a
solid which consolidates the cell walls and thereby confers mechanical strength on the wooden object. Further experimental details and
the results achieved by this method will be found in the publication of
H. Müller-Beck and A. Haas,[1] who introduced this method for the
treatment of specimens of prehistoric wooden objects excavated from
waterlogged neolithic strata.

4. *Polyethylene glycol wax method.* The polyethylene glycols are
synthetic materials having the generalized formula: $HOCH_2$.
$(CH_2OCH_2)n . CH_2OH$. The early members of the polymeric
series are liquids, the intermediate members are semi-liquids of the
consistency of vaseline, and the higher members with value of n
greater than 35 are wax-like materials. Although these materials
have the physical properties of waxes, they are distinguished from
other waxes by the fact that they are freely soluble in water. The
particular material having suitable properties for the treatment of
waterlogged wood is the polyethylene glycol wax of grade 4000,
which is a hard, white, non-hygroscopic solid with a melting point
of 53–55 °C. Using this material it was possible to develop a reliable
method, which was also simple to carry out since the removal of the
excess of water in the waterlogged wood and the consolidation of
the wood could be achieved in one operation.[2] The waterlogged
object is cleaned to remove all dirt on the surface and placed in a

[1] *Studies in Conservation*, 1960, **5**, p. 150.
[2] Organ, R. M., *Studies in Conservation*, 1959, **4**, p. 96.

container with a close-fitting lid which is filled with a 12 per cent solution of wax at room temperature. The container is placed in a ventilated oven and the temperature is gradually increased until after a period of weeks it has reached 60 °C. During this time the wax slowly diffuses into the wood, displacing the water in the wood, and the supernatant solution slowly evaporates through the slight space between the lid and the container, so that at the end of the operation the wooden object is just covered with molten wax. The object is then removed and allowed to cool. When cold, the wax on the surface of the object is removed by brushing with hot toluene. In carrying out this method it is important that the dimensions of the container should be such that the actual quantity of wax present will be more than enough to cover the object at the end of the process. Polyethylene glycol waxes are commercially available under a number of different trade names; the following are among the best known: Carbowax, P.E.G., Polywachs, and Modopeg.

Treatment of large wooden objects

The above methods for the treatment of wooden objects in a waterlogged condition involve the use of fairly elaborate equipment. This may present a difficult problem when large wooden objects such as boats and canoes have to be treated. The very size of such objects may well preclude the use of any of the above impregnation methods because of the cost of constructing a suitable-sized container and of acquiring the large quantity of materials required. However, large objects of this type will usually be found in such a state that they still possess a reasonable degree of mechanical strength. For this reason it is possible to consider an alternative method of treatment which does not involve the use of elaborate equipment or large quantities of chemicals. Immediately after excavation the object is wrapped in damp sacking, placed in a cool cellar, and allowed to dry out slowly—the sacking being damped periodically as required. This slow-drying process is allowed to proceed for at least a year and, if properly carried out, there will be no undue warping or shrinkage of the wood. When the wood has dried out, the object can be stabilized by brushing on a material which will penetrate the wood to an extent sufficient to ensure consolidation. For this purpose an epoxy resin has proved suitable; the actual formulation to be used is the same as that given above (p. 138) for the consolidation of the Nigerian ceremonial mask. This is a mobile fluid which is readily absorbed by the wood and solidifies *in situ* at ordinary room temperature. Successive coats should be applied until there is no further absorption of the resin preparation.

RESTORATION OF THE STANWICK SCABBARD

An unusual type of restoration was successfully accomplished in the case of the iron sword discovered in its wooden scabbard by Sir Mortimer Wheeler in the excavations at Stanwick, Yorkshire, in 1952. This was a unique object dating to the first century A.D. (Pl. 12). As it was waterlogged, it was dispatched by the first train to London packed in a mass of wet newspapers, and it was this prompt action that made its preservation possible. Reference is made later (p. 292) to the corrosion of the iron sword by sulphate-reducing bacteria and to the preservation of the weapon. The following details relate to the preservation of the wooden scabbard.

The scabbard was made from two slats of ash of a maximum thickness of 3·5 mm. and tapering towards the edges. These were held together by a series of bronze rings of symmetrical eye-shape set at intervals, and decreasing in size from the mouth-piece to the chape. As the sword could not be withdrawn from the scabbard, in which it was firmly held by its iron sulphide corrosion products, the alum method could not be used for preserving the wood. This acidic substance in reacting with the sulphide might have caused disintegration beyond control. It was decided, therefore, to remove the scabbard from the sword by dissection under water. The varying width of the bronze fittings afforded the possibility of their removal from the chape end; this proved to be a delicate but not a difficult task, and the bronze mouth-piece was finally released from its own end.

After the removal of the bronze fittings the wood was detached with the aid of scalpels from one side of the sword-blade and floated on to a glass plate cut to the length of the scabbard. The blade was then reversed and the remaining wood removed and floated on to a second glass plate.

The specimens were then treated by immersion in a series of alcohols of increasing strength in order to eliminate the water. The treatment was carried out in boxes made specially from tin-plate. The alcohol in the wood was eventually replaced by amyl acetate, the final immersion being carried out in a solution of celluloid dissolved in equal volumes of amyl acetate and acetone to a strength of about 5 per cent. Throughout these operations, the wood remained on the glass-plate supports and was not handled until it had been strengthened. This work took about fourteen days, and on the evaporation of the solvent, the thin porous wood was found to be toughened quite satisfactorily.

For the reassembly of the scabbard it was necessary to prepare a core of such dimensions that, with the old wood in position, the bronze rings would slip on from the pointed end, and the reconstructed scabbard would conform to original dimensions. But here a difficulty arose due to minor irregularities in the shape of the metal fittings. This necessitated the use of a resilient core which was made as follows: a piece of wood was cut slightly thinner and narrower than the sword, and to this was fixed along its length a piece of thin steel cut from a flexible steel rule, the attachment being made with a bandage soaked in shellac. This core was then impregnated with a solution of nitrocellulose and the old wood of the scabbard was attached to it on both sides with Durofix, the contact being made as intimately as possible. The rings could now be slipped on from the pointed end, there being some slight elasticity in the core in consequence of the action of the spring in its interior. When the adhesive hardened the core became rigid and some minor repairs with a mixture of celluloid and sawdust completed the restoration.

It was, of course, never intended to return the sword to its scabbard; the two were subsequently mounted side by side on a wooden baseboard to form an exhibit, interesting in itself and convenient for purposes of study.

VI

BONE AND IVORY

FROM earliest times bone and ivory have exerted a peculiar fascination for the craftsman. Bone was the more easily come by and, as it was available in a variety of shapes and degrees of hardness, selected pieces could be fashioned into all sorts of useful objects—fish-hooks, arrow-heads, tools, and implements. Ivory, though of standard shape, was the more suitable material for fine work and lent itself to decorative treatment. It could be carved, etched, stained, painted, gilded, inlaid with metals and with precious and semi-precious stones; it could be used, moreover, for inlaying in wood, and for veneering. When a material was required for the finest carving, the choice fell on ivory rather than on bone. Thus, ivory was in demand for the plaques and reliefs that were used for diptychs and bookbindings. It was also ideal for carving figurines and statuettes, and specimens are extant that date back to the earliest dynasties of Egypt. A great wealth of ivory-carving has survived from early Christian times in the West, and many fine works in ivory have also come down to us from remote civilizations in China and the Near East. Although bone was more generally used for utilitarian purposes, it was often brought into service for ornamental purposes as well, owing to the relative scarcity of ivory.

When worked and decorated, the two materials may be so much alike that they cannot be distinguished by mere inspection, and identification is then a task for the specialist. It is not possible by chemical means alone to distinguish bone from ivory. In both materials the main inorganic constituents are the same, namely calcium phosphate associated with carbonate and fluoride, and the organic tissue of both is ossein; while the latter varies in quantity, it is usually present to at least some 30 per cent of the total weight.

Microscopic examination will, however, permit of a differentiation, since bone and ivory both have a cellular structure, and the micro-structure of each is definitive.[1] In cross-section, bone shows a rather coarse grain with characteristic lacunae, whereas ivory, being composed of the hard dense tissue known as dentine, is more compact and is characterized by the presence of a network composed of tiny lenticular areas resulting from the intersection of systems of striations that may be seen radiating from the centre of the tusk. In favourable circumstances this can be observed without sectioning by studying the surface with a pocket lens.

The main factors bearing on the conservation of bone and ivory may be deduced from a consideration of their physical structure and chemical composition. Bone and ivory are anisotropic having directional properties and for this reason they are easily warped upon exposure to heat and damp; furthermore, they are decomposed by the prolonged action of water due to hydrolysis of the ossein, and the inorganic framework is readily disintegrated by acids. Being porous and of light colour, bone and ivory are easily stained. They tend to become brittle with age and they lose their natural colouring when exposed to sunlight. When burnt, they become grey or blue-black (bone-black and ivory-black are two well-known pigments), and when buried in the ground for prolonged periods of time they are greatly weakened and may be disintegrated either by salt incrusta-tions or by water; in the latter case they are converted ultimately to a sponge-like waterlogged material similar to waterlogged wood. Under other circumstances they may become fossilized. With the onset of fossilization the organic content gradually disappears and the re-maining calcareous matter becomes associated with silica in the form of quartz and with mineral salts derived from the ground. When bone and ivory are in good condition it is possible to preserve them by taking very simple precautions, but when they are in a fragmentary state, waterlogged, or fossilized they can only be cleaned, strength-ened, and stabilized; a satisfactory restoration may be impossible.

[1] Perriman, T. K., 'Pictures of Ivory and other Animal Teeth, Bone and Antler', *Occasional Papers on Technology*, No. 5, 1952, Pitt Rivers Museum, Oxford.

Two general features should be considered before discussing detailed methods of preservation and restoration. These relate to size and colour. Bone and ivory are usually only available in pieces of limited size, so that large objects made from these materials will of necessity be composite in structure. In the case of ivory, for example, when a large object does not conform to the shape of the tusk, the artist may add portions by dowelling or jointing (tongue and groove, half-lap, etc.) and, when any warping of the component pieces occurs, the greatest strain will tend to be imposed on the joints. This is particularly noticeable in the case of books that have covers made of ivory; a clasp or even a pair of clasps may have been fixed to keep the covers shut and the pages flat, but should swelling of the pages occur (and this is by no means unusual if they are of parchment), the strain on the ivory covers may be considerable and the bindings may open along the joints. This type of accident is caused by the cumulative effect of damp which causes the pages to swell, but similar accidents may be the direct result of exposing the ivory to sunlight or to heat. Joints may open, veneers may warp, and if warping is serious, it may be impossible to restore the original shape.

Old ivory often has a yellow colour and this is accepted as a form of natural patination which may help to enhance the appearance. On the other hand, coloration may have been artificially applied, as is often done by the Japanese carver of netsuke, who displays the greatest originality in arriving at a surface effect that will show his handiwork to the best advantage. The greyish colour of burnt ivory has already been mentioned, and in some of the Nimrûd ivories there seems reason to suppose that the burning was intentional and was carried out with the object of achieving a particular colour effect. Staining may be due to a residue of some former embellishment executed in a fugitive dye-stuff that has decomposed; in this case the residual colour may show some signs of regularity or of pattern work which may be of interest and value to the specialist as evidence of a decoration that once existed but no longer survives. There also arises the problem of adventitious staining which may be due to a variety of causes. When there is no sign of regularity in the staining its origin may be obscure; it may possibly be due to some photochemical effect or to contact of the bone or ivory with another material. Rust stains and copper stains can be helpful in the reconstruction of a broken object by showing which pieces originally fitted together, or in calling attention to the previous existence of hinges or metal attachments. In the case of the Franks whalebone casket in the British Museum, staining of this kind was particularly valuable to those engaged in its reconstruction. Finally, there may be disfiguring stains arising through use or accident. Stains may be removed by appropriate chemical treatment, but since there are so many possible causes of coloration in bone and ivory objects, the greatest caution is necessary before undertaking any treatment that might result in the loss of important characteristics; only in exceptional cases can the removal of stains be justified, because although chemical treatment may discharge the stain, it may result in damage to the texture and patina of the ivory, and thus magnify the disfigurement.

METHODS OF CONSERVATION

Removal of surface dirt

Having referred to the damage that can be caused to bone and ivory by exposure to water, it may seem illogical to assert that washing with soap and water can be carried out without danger. This can, however, be done if the objects are in good condition, and if they are dried with soft towelling immediately after treatment, so that the wetting is confined to the surface. The use of water containing a detergent (soap, or one of the new surface-active agents) is indeed essential for the removal of soot and grease, but the object must not be allowed to remain in contact with the aqueous solution longer than is absolutely necessary, and for this reason the washing is carried out with a brush rather than with cotton-wool or a sponge. The hardness of the brush and the length of the bristles is also important; too soft a brush would only prolong the time necessary for cleaning. The brush must therefore be selected with some care to suit the job in hand, taking into account the strength of the object and the amount of grime to be removed.

If the condition of the object precludes the use of water, dry-cleaning using a spirit soap solution (p. 107) may be attempted. This arises, for example, in the case of partially decayed ivory or bone, especially when the polished surface skin has deteriorated and there is evidence of cracking.

Removal of soluble salts

Ivory or bone objects recovered from a salty environment will contain absorbed soluble salts that will tend to crystallize out, causing possible disintegration of the objects. These salts must be removed by washing the objects in successive baths of distilled water, but great care must be exercised, because repeated washing may be injurious if the objects are in a poor state of preservation. Hence consolidation of the object by brushing on a 5 per cent alcoholic solution of soluble nylon is an advisable precaution prior to washing.

The success that can be achieved by careful washing may be illustrated by reference to the particularly difficult problem that arose in connection with the cleaning of salt-incrusted and semi-fossilized ivories from Egypt. These may be very absorbent and, if placed in water even for a few minutes, they tend to split and to warp, making the task of removing the salts extremely difficult. However, the cleaning of such ivories ceased to present any real difficulty when it was discovered that it was not necessary to remove all the salt but only the surface deposits, and that success depended on the speed of operations. In a typical instance a cracked ivory, disfigured by a salty incrustation, was placed in a shallow earthenware dish, and covered with distilled water. This water was discarded and replaced with fresh distilled water at intervals of five *seconds*, four or five washings being considered to be sufficient. The ivory was then immediately washed in 80 per cent alcohol for thirty seconds, followed by two washings in 95 per cent alcohol or industrial methylated spirit for a similar period. Finally, the object was immersed in ether for one minute, and dried in air. By this procedure the entire clean-

ing was completed within three minutes, the ivory having been
exposed to water for a very short time, and it survived without
any apparent change of shape or extension in the cracking. Such
treatment may seem to be too quick and easy to have any permanent effect, but, in fact, it has been applied on many occasions in
dealing with salty ivories from Egypt and Palestine. The results have
been entirely successful, and the times have been cut down well
below those stated where specimens were particularly frail or fragmentary.

Removal of insoluble salts

The treatment of bone and ivory objects that are covered with incrustations of insoluble salts such as calcium carbonate (chalk) or
calcium sulphate (selenite) poses a special problem. The complication that arises in the removal of calcium carbonate is that in this
case the use of acid is essential to decompose the carbonate, but
during decomposition the effervescence due to the evolution of
carbon dioxide gas would inevitably result in disintegration of the
ivory. This difficulty is overcome by applying the acid locally only,
i.e. no more than a square centimetre is dealt with at a time. Ivories
incrusted with carbonate are cleaned under a binocular microscope
at about 10 diameters magnification, applying a 1 per cent solution
of hydrochloric acid with a small water-colour brush repeatedly. As
effervescence ceases, the excess of liquid is mopped up either with a
second brush or with shreds of blotting-paper applied with forceps.
The acid must be used in quantities just sufficient to soften the incrustation, which is then removed with a needle. Finally, in order to
eliminate the last traces of acid, the ivory is washed in several changes
of distilled water for a few seconds at a time, and then dried by
the alcohol and ether method already recommended for delicate
material.

Occasionally one comes across an ivory that is incrusted with
calcium sulphate (selenite). This incrustation can be distinguished
from the more usual calcium carbonate by the fact that it is not
decomposed by acids; it is, in fact, so insoluble that it cannot be

removed by chemical means. Any attempt to do so would involve a long soaking process which would cause the ivory to disintegrate. The only procedure that can be recommended for removing calcium sulphate from ivory is to reduce the incrustation mechanically by the use of dental equipment—inverted cones and burrs. Needless to say, such treatment can only be undertaken if the ivory object is sufficiently robust to withstand the mechanical stresses involved.

In describing the different methods of cleaning bone and ivory, emphasis has been laid on the importance of cutting down the time during which they are exposed to the action of chemicals and even of water, but in an exceptional case it may be necessary to break these rules in order to save a fine specimen. Such action is only justifiable when the risks to be taken are fully understood, so that treatment can be suitably modified to reduce these to a minimum, and when there is a reasonable hope of success. An interesting example is provided by the restoration of a well-known Egyptian ivory figurine in the British Museum, once thought to represent Menes of the First Dynasty.[1] This ivory had been broken in antiquity; the parts were incrusted and held together with calcium carbonate which, in crystallizing, had opened up the structure to form a series of strata interspersed with carbonate, so that the object was both swollen and deformed. In order to restore the object to its original shape it was necessary to clear away all the carbonate from the cracks; therefore the cleaning could not be confined to the surface as is normally the case. Actual soaking in dilute hydrochloric acid followed by washing was necessary. It was foreseen that effervescence during the acid treatment would probably cause the specimen to disintegrate, and this eventuality was prevented by previously impregnating the ivory under vacuum with a solution of celluloid (2 per cent) and allowing it to dry. The celluloid solution had the effect of slowing down the penetration of the acid, thus holding the effervescence in check. When the calcium carbonate had dissolved, the constituent pieces fell apart. These were washed in distilled water, dried through alcohols to benzene, and then impregnated with a solution of dammar resin dissolved

[1] Figure illustrated in Plenderleith, H. J., *The Preservation of Antiquities*, 1934.

in benzene, using the vacuum technique already described. Re-assembly of the fragments, using a viscous solution of dammar resin in benzene as the adhesive, presented no problem and the original shape was recovered. After restoration the figurine was found to be more complete in regard to its ornamentation than had been pre-viously suspected. Only one major gap remained and this was filled in with a mixture of beeswax and carnauba wax and tinted with thin oil-paint to match the biscuit colour of the ivory. It should be noted that when cracks in ivory arise from warping it is not desirable, in general, to fill them in, because under different environmental con-ditions they may tend to close up, and if this natural tendency for the cracks to close is prevented by the presence of a filler, it may cause the ivory to rupture. However, in the present instance a small por-tion of ivory was missing, leaving a fissure that caused a structural weakness. This weakness was overcome by the filling which, at the same time, had an aesthetic value in minimizing the disfigurement.

Consolidation

When an ivory or bone object is in a dry, powdery condition, it can be readily consolidated by impregnation with a 5 per cent solu-tion of a suitable transparent synthetic resin, notably polyvinyl acetate or polymethacrylates, in toluene. If only surface impregna-tion is necessary, the solution can be applied by brushing; it will probably be found that two or more coats may be necessary, but care should be taken to ensure that each coat is allowed to dry out before the next one is applied. If these solutions are judiciously applied, the object should not have an unpleasant sheen. However, if it is essential for aesthetic reasons to preserve a matt appearance, it is advisable to use a 5 per cent solution of soluble nylon (Appendix XVI) in alcohol as the consolidant.

If the object is in a very fragile condition, it will be necessary to secure thorough impregnation in order to impart adequate mecha-nical strength. This can be achieved by carrying out the impregna-tion under vacuum in an apparatus such as that illustrated in Fig. 5. The object is put in a container filled with the impregnating solution,

and the container is placed inside a vacuum vessel that is attached
to an ordinary laboratory water pump. When the pressure inside
the vacuum vessel is lowered, air in the interstices of the object will
escape and the impregnating medium will readily penetrate the object.
When no further air bubbles escape from the object, the vacuum
is slowly released by opening the tap on the vacuum vessel. The

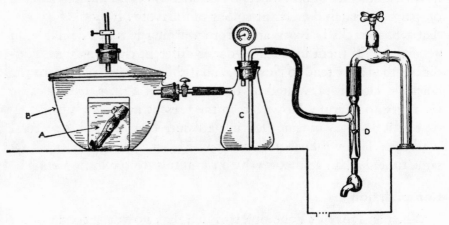

FIG. 5. Apparatus for Vacuum Impregnation

A. Impregnating medium containing the object.   B. Vacuum vessel.
C. Trap with pressure gauge.   D. Water pump attached to mains supply.

object is then taken out of the solution and allowed to drain on a wire
frame.

For the consolidation of ivory or bone found during excavation in
a wet soft condition, Purvis and Martin[1] and McBurney[2] speak
favourably of the use of an emulsion of polyvinyl acetate to strengthen
the object both before removal from the ground and immediately
after; Bedacryl L (a polymethacrylate emulsion) also works well.
These emulsions can be readily transported as a concentrate for field
work and diluted with water to the required consistency before use;
they are stable so long as they are protected from frost.

[1] Purvis, P. E., and Martin, R. S. J., *Museums J.*, 1950, **49**, p. 293.
[2] McBurney, C. H. M., *Arch. News Letter*, 1954, **5**, p. 47.

A. As received in the Laboratory

B. After cleaning

18. SILVER GILT PATEN FROM TOMB OF ARCHBISHOP DE GRAY
(DIED 1255) IN YORK MINSTER

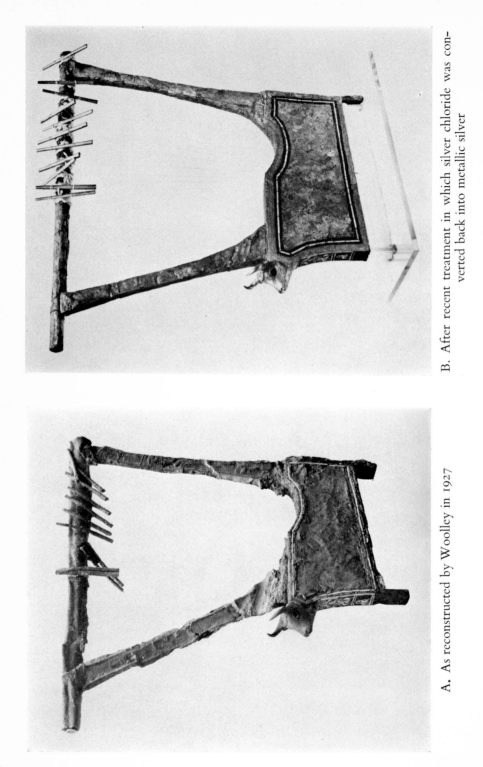

A. As reconstructed by Woolley in 1927

B. After recent treatment in which silver chloride was converted back into metallic silver

19. SILVER LYRE FROM ROYAL GRAVES, UR OF THE CHALDEES (c. 2500 B.C.)

A. Application of temporary facing to front of the soundbox

B. Application of synthetic resin and silver wires to back of the soundbox prior to electrolytic reduction

20. STAGES IN THE TREATMENT OF THE SOUNDBOX OF THE LYRE

A. As excavated—the silver, inlaid with gold and niello, completely covered with corrosion products

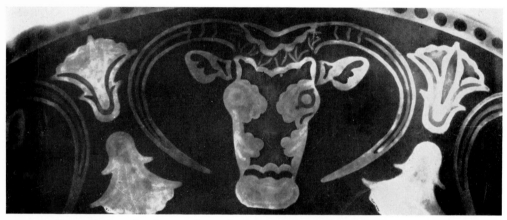

B. Radiograph of part of cup disclosing inlay under corrosion products

C. After treatment and restoration

21. THE BULL CUP FROM ENKOMI (*c.* 1400 B.C.)

REPAIR OF IVORIES

For the repair of broken ivory objects a suitable adhesive that can be safely recommended is one based on nitrocellulose and available commercially under the trade names 'Durofix' and 'H.M.G.' This possesses the following advantages: ease of application, reliable adhesive properties, and subsequent ease of removal with a solvent. This last property is particularly important because it means that adjustments can easily be made during the repair work if this should prove necessary. This type of adhesive is certainly preferable to aqueous adhesives, such as glue or isinglass, since these tend to soften under humid conditions, particularly in a tropical climate, and this may lead to a disastrous loss of strength in the adhesive joint. By using Durofix a complicated repair like that of the ivory comb of St. Cuthbert, which has split into numerous fragments, could be undertaken with confidence and with the knowledge that under museum conditions the repair would be, to all intents and purposes, permanent.

In repairing ivory or bone objects an important point that must be borne in mind, particularly if the objects consist of thin pieces, is that the individual fragments should all be kept under controlled conditions of relative humidity whilst the repairs are being carried out. If this is not done, it may be found that the separate fragments have shrunk in different amounts and can no longer be fitted together properly. The separate fragments should therefore be kept in closed containers inside which the same relative humidity is maintained by using a suitable chemical.

Particular care must be taken in handling ivories when there are features of interest that must be preserved; for instance the carved ivory plaques of the Christian era that have prayers written on the back in ink, and others that are coated with wax as a ground for writing with a stylus. There are cases where damage has been caused in the moulder's shop when making plaster replicas of ivories. Moulding is not necessarily dangerous provided the moulding materials can be used cold. The temptation to use a warm jelly mould or warm rubber latex, which is so convenient for dealing with under-cuts, must be resisted, as such treatment may cause cracking or stain-ing. The best material to use is a cold-setting silicone rubber; there are a number of grades of this material and the easiest to use is the fluid grade (Silastomer K 9161) to which a catalyst is added to promote the setting reaction. This mixture can be poured slowly over the ivory object and allowed to set for twenty-four hours, after which the flexible mould can readily be removed. Perfect replicas may be obtained by the use of silicone rubber and, when expertly handled, this material imposes no strain on the ivory.

RESTORATION OF AN INLAID PHOENICIAN IVORY

During an excavation at Nimrûd in 1952, Professor Mallowan recovered a number of magnificent ivories from the bottom of a well, dating from the period of Assur-nasir-pal II (883–859 B.C.) and, by drying them slowly and uniformly, he was able to preserve their shape and prevent serious cracking. It may be of interest to describe the subsequent treatment that was applied to one of them—a master-piece of exquisite carving, embellished with gold and incrusted with lapis lazuli and carnelian (Frontispiece).

When this reached the British Museum Research Laboratory it was covered with fine clay (Pl. 13), and an X-ray examination showed the presence of deep cracks which were widest at the back, or external side, of the tusk, but, fortunately, scarcely apparent on the decorated side. The clay was carefully scraped from the back and, as this revealed a surface without decoration, it was rigidly secured (as a first-aid precaution to prevent any further opening of the cracks) by backing it with layers of broad adhesive tape, the equivalent of surgical strapping. The front was then dealt with, working under a binocular at a magnification of 10 diameters. First the upper layers of clay were removed with needles to expose the sculpture. Many fragments of gold leaf were recovered from the clay; these were washed with 1 per cent nitric acid and then with water, and set aside for subsequent replacement. The ivory was further cleaned with pellets of blotting-paper held between pointed forceps and moistened with detergents in order to peptize and release the clay with the minimum of strain, and later the surface was washed and polished by the same technique, doing small areas at a time. The final stage in the restoration was the replacement of the loose fragments of gold leaf in their correct positions on the cleaned ivory, using Durofix as the adhesive.

The background of this superb object—thought to be part of a throne—is decorated with an all-over floral pattern consisting of alternating flowers and seed capsules, the stems and sepals being covered with fine gold. The forms are deeply carved and the thin walls that outline the flowers are also gilt so that they appear like metal cloisons framing the lapis lazuli inlays of the petals. The seeds (or buds?) are represented by polished carnelians of dome shape, serrated at the base to engage with the gilt ivory calyces. This rich background forms a canopy for the main carving below, a scene in high relief depicting a lioness in the act of killing a Nubian. The ivory body of the animal is unadorned, and powerfully modelled. It stands out in sharp contrast to the relaxed human victim with his gleaming golden loin-cloth, and spikelets of crisp curly hair, an effect obtained by fixing gilt-topped pegs into the head which was stained black beforehand. In spite of the loss of much of the gold overlay and the blue and red incrustation, this ivory carving still gives the effect of a faceted polychrome jewel.

The following technical points relating to the construction of the ivory were noted during the cleaning and are of special interest. The lapis lazuli inlays are of varying thickness, but the recesses in the ivory are of uniform depth. Consequently, it was found necessary to bed the inlays in a cement so that their polished surfaces would be level with the cloisons. This is the only case known to the authors where a blue cement has been used for inlaying lapis lazuli. It is composed of lime putty coloured to match the lapis lazuli by the addition of copper frit and where inlays are missing the ivory is often stained by a residue of this frit cement. Another interesting observation was made on examining the *back* of fragments of gold leaf from the ivory.

Traces of a brownish film were clearly visible on the gold under the microscope. This material which was of organic origin and swelled in water, becoming very sticky, appeared to be the original adhesive employed in laying the gold leaf. It is difficult to believe that a reversible colloid could have survived in such circumstances but apparently this was the case, and it was due no doubt to the protection from air and moisture afforded by the coherent film of gold.

HORN, ANTLER, ETC.

Many of the methods that have been described for the treatment of bone and ivory apply with slight modification to kindred organic materials that are frail or porous, such as tortoise-shell, horn, and antler. These may be washed in the same way as ivory.

In the case of horn, which is usually thin and hollow, the surface may be strengthened and prevented from flaking by impregnation with polyvinyl acetate and it may be possible to confer added strength by attaching a plastic tape or bandage to the inside surface of the horn. Only part of the interior can be covered if a horn is intact, but this will be the thinnest part and the part, therefore, that has the greatest need of reinforcement.

Antler usually has a spongy central tissue covered with a continuous outer rind. Under conditions of prolonged burial the spongy tissue generally decays and only the outer rind survives. Thus the antlers of the Sika deer that once crowned a Chinese wooden deity were found to have lost all their spongy tissue; they were hollow and partially collapsed. The surface skin had survived, however, and it was possible to support this with a wire core bound with cotton-wool and reinforced where necessary with a filling of nitrocellulose and cork dust. The antler picks or levers found in flint workings in the chalk are usually dry, and in this case may be treated by pouring dilute polyvinyl acetate lacquer through the porous tissue. It should be noted that this may leave an unpleasant shine on the outside of the antler unless the surface is swabbed with toluene and the antler allowed to dry in toluene vapour. This can easily be done by suspending it in a tall vessel containing a couple of ounces of the solvent.

Although jet and amber are not chemically related to bone and ivory, their treatment may be referred to here as they are washed according to the methods outlined above for ivory. While fossil amber is insoluble in organic solvents it is not easily distinguished in appearance from other resins that are soluble and for this reason it is advisable to avoid the use of alcohol and ether altogether in cleaning objects of resinous origin.

Finally, a special warning is necessary in dealing with jewellery that may be inlaid with materials such as shell, mother of pearl, and coral (which consist essentially of chalk). These substances are decomposed by acid; where there is any doubt about identification, cleaning-agents of an acidic nature must at all costs be avoided.

VII

EASEL PAINTINGS

EASEL paintings are defined as paintings on panel or canvas in tempera or oils, and they present unique problems in conservation because of their variety and complexity of structure. The pictorial image is, however, the important thing—colour and optical quality have to be studied in relation to conservation—and it is for this reason that the care of valuable paintings is regarded as being the most exacting and responsible of all museum curatorial activities. Restoration is a matter for the expert as it involves an appreciation of aesthetic quality as well as a specialized training lying outside the field of ordinary museum work; but the curator must himself be familiar with all aspects of his subject, and the present chapter is designed to provide such technical information as may help him to appreciate the fundamental factors involved in the care of paintings whether in the gallery or in the restoration studio. It deals with the structure of paintings, with the ills to which they are subject, and with methods available for their conservation.

STRUCTURE OF PAINTINGS

An easel painting cannot be regarded merely as a coloured surface. Although painting techniques may have changed through the centuries, the basic fact remains that, from the physical point of view, a painting is a stratified structure built up in a series of layers each of which may exhibit complexities of its own as shown diagrammatically in Pl. 14. There is first of all the support, a prepared panel or canvas; on this is spread the ground, which consists essentially of a white inert substance in a glue medium. On Italian panels the inert substance was usually calcined gypsum (Ital. *gesso*), but northern painters favoured the use of chalk. For the application of gold leaf, a special ground was used in which the inert constituent was a species of clay known as bole. The paint layer overlies the ground and it consists of an aggregate of pigment particles in a binding medium. In tempera painting[1] the medium was egg yolk or the whole egg, but later, drying oils were more commonly used. Finally, there is usually a layer of varnish and this surface coating serves a twofold purpose: it protects the paint layer against atmospheric contamination and also confers upon it an enhanced brillance. When a picture is in a sound condition, its various layers are fused and interlocked, the closest study revealing no sign of cleavage.

The character of the painting is mainly influenced by the nature of the binding medium and, as the medium carries the whites and blacks and other pigments, its stability is crucial to the life of the picture. By the test of time, egg-tempera and oils have proved themselves satisfactory media for easel paintings, but they suffer in varying degrees from a tendency to shrink and to become brittle with age. When a picture reaches a certain age, its surface usually becomes patterned with a series of micro-cracks which have picked up foreign matter and reveal themselves as dark hair-like lines most readily discernible in the lighter passages; these lines intersect and form a complicated network known as *craquelure*. Many factors contribute to the general appearance of *craquelure*, but in the main it is due to the natural shrinkage of the medium on ageing and the inability of the brittle aged film to withstand the slight rhythmical movements of the support.[2] The forces thus imposed on the paint layer may cause a *craquelure* which extends through both the painted layer and the ground; different types may be recognized as characteristic of painting on wood panel or on canvas.

While superficially the *craquelure* on a painting may often appear

---

[1] Cennino Cennini has described the whole process of tempera painting in his famous *Treatise* published in 1437 (date of earliest surviving text). Cennino D'Andrea Cennini, *Il Libro dell' Arte (The Craftsman's Handbook)*, translated by D. V. Thompson, jr., New Haven, U.S.A., Yale University Press, 1933.

[2] Movements in response to changes of the relative humidity of the atmosphere (see later).

to resemble the intentional crackle of a glaze on oriental pottery or porcelain, it differs in this respect that it is an acquired characteristic and develops slowly; it is not regarded as a disfigurement, and rarely is it of such a nature as to introduce instability.

Two subsidiary types of *craquelure* may be mentioned. One is due to faulty technique, such as the application of a layer of quick-drying paint over a slow-drying paint; this type of so-called 'youth' *craquelure* is usually restricted to certain passages of the painting. The other condition is due to a faulty choice of material and is known as 'alligatoring', a term used to described the system of wide depressions in the paint layer resulting from the use of bitumen or asphaltum, a material that is soluble to some extent in the binding medium and has notoriously bad drying properties.

In contrast with *craquelure* which is a more or less normal condition in old pictures, cracking and cleavage are serious forms of deterioration which affect canvases as well as panel paintings. A crack has the appearance of a crevasse in the paint layer, running inwards at right angles to the surface, and it usually penetrates through all the layers of the picture. It is caused by flaws in the ground or support. Cleavage, the more insidious form of deterioration, is due to loss of adhesion between the superimposed strata of the picture; it manifests itself in the formation of blisters which, if they be allowed to fracture, will lead eventually to the loss of paint.

While cracking and cleavage may be found in pictures of any age, they are to be seen most frequently in old pictures where the binding media have lost much of their original elasticity as a result of chemical changes, and are no longer able to adapt themselves to movements of the support occasioned by exposure to environmental changes. Both these conditions are revealed particularly when there are sudden extreme changes in the relative humidity of the atmosphere. The conservation of the paint layer depends in the first instance on the condition of the supports, whether panel or canvas, and their reactions to the environment.

PAINTINGS ON PANEL

Church furniture of painted wood was in common use in Italy from very early times, and an obvious development was the use of flat painted panels for wall decoration and for altar pieces. When large panels were required they had to be made by joining planks together, and for this purpose a cement was used made from lime and cheese which is, essentially, calcium caseinate. If the planks were thick enough, they were pegged as well with iron or wooden dowels. Very heavy panels were often additionally reinforced with cross-bars, either inserted wedge-fashion into a converging channel cut across the grain, or fixed in some other way to the back. Such reinforcement was not possible in the case of thin panels especially when, as in the side leaves of a triptych, they were painted on both sides. Panels completely protected on both sides by paintings have proved to be very durable, whereas thin panels painted only on one side have been less able to withstand the influences that cause warping.

The mechanical behaviour of painted panels is closely related to the environment to which they are exposed:

1. When conditions of storage or exhibition are kept constant as regards temperature and relative humidity, a panel tends to attain a state of equilibrium and no warping, cracking, or movement of any kind need be anticipated.

2. When a picture is transported to a locality where the environmental conditions are different from those to which it has been accustomed, a certain amount of movement will take place. In a composite panel that is unprotected at the back, each constituent plank will tend to cup, and at this stage cracks may make their appearance on the painted surface opposite the joints.

3. In a picture gallery where the air is not conditioned, day-to-day variations in temperature and relative humidity are to be expected, but normally these do not impose any great strain on the support. However, in addition, there are the long-term variations of a seasonal nature to be considered. When artificial heating is brought into action in the autumn and discontinued in the spring, the

environmental changes may be considerable. These changes impose strain on the support and for this reason care must be taken especially in the spring and autumn to look for any signs of cracking and blistering or weaknesses in the paint overlying the joints in composite panels.

Temperature and relative humidity are the most important factors in the life of a panel painting. Exposure to extremes of temperature will cause desiccation and shorten the life of the picture, but extremes of relative humidity are the more potent and insidious cause of trouble, wood being a bad conductor of heat but responding quickly to damp and dryness. In the conservation of panel paintings, however, it is, above all, *variation* of relative humidity that has to be guarded against as this causes intermittent movements of the support that give rise to cracking and cleavage of the ground and paint layers.

Easel paintings have also been carried out on several other types of support—metals, slate, marble, etc. Of these the metals are the most important despite the fact that ground and paint layers do not adhere well to the non-porous surface. Metals are, moreover, good conductors of heat, and for this reason paintings on metal are more prone to damage by variations of temperature than by variations of the relative humidity of the environment.

Panel paintings: mechanical damage and treatment

1. *Cracking*. The most sensitive kind of easel painting is undoubtedly the large wooden panel, especially when it is made up from thin planks and painted only on one side. Such a panel is prone to mechanical damage. It may be fractured even by lifting or moving it carelessly. A less obvious cause of trouble may be the position of the picture on the wall, where it is perhaps exposed to a mild draught of air from a door or window, and the changing relative humidity will ultimately cause it to crack. This tendency to cracking explains why so many panel paintings have been treated in the past with a cradling or parquetry reinforcement at the back. The cradling has been applied with the twofold object of giving mechanical strength to the panel and of confining its movements to one plane so as to prevent twisting or warping. Cradling consists of a series of wooden slats

('stretchers') fixed rigidly at intervals in the same direction as the constituent planks, i.e. along the grain of the panel; these stretchers have slots to accommodate another series of wooden slats ('runners') arranged at intervals at right angles to the grain and in contact with the panel. While the stretchers are fixed, the runners should have freedom of movement to allow for slight expansion or contraction of the panel, but so often the runners themselves become warped and immobilized, with the result that the cradling becomes the prime mover, and the panel has to adjust itself as best it may. For this reason, if a cradling has to be applied to strengthen a picture, it should be kept as simple as possible.

Other ways of reinforcing a panel are by inserting X-shaped wedges, or inlays across the joints of planks in order to prevent their opening, or to trust to a series of 'buttons' glued across the joint to hold the crack. Buttons are palettes of wood about 10 cm. by 5 cm. by 1 cm., the size varying with the conditions. A common type of reinforcement is that achieved by gluing textile to the back of the panel, and this is often found where a panel has been enlarged by the artist in the course of painting the picture. Rubens often varied the proportions of his smaller panels, and reinforced the backs in this way. When a thin panel has been enlarged it is seldom that the different members are in harmony, and warping often occurs. Some of these enlarged panels are so warped that it is difficult to contain them in their frames. Not infrequently textiles were fixed on to the face of panels before applying the painting ground, and this is a sound technique because it not only strengthens the panel, but at the same time provides a good key for the painting ground.

When a panel painting is observed to develop a convexity on the painted side, or a series of convexities or undulations corresponding to its constituent members, this should be regarded as an emergency requiring immediate attention. The trouble may arise from one of two causes:

Firstly, it may be due to the fact that the picture has recently been hung in a dry room or been exposed to heat, e.g. by sunning or by being placed near a radiator.

Secondly, if a picture has attained a state of equilibrium under conditions that are rather damp, say in a large private house, and has been lent to an exhibition, exposure in the drier conditions of the gallery may cause dehydration at the back, which is unprotected by paint, with consequent cupping of the panel (see 'Wood', p. 126).

In both cases the picture should be taken at once to a cool basement room where conditions are known to be damper and laid flat, face downwards. The picture may usually be left in its frame, but any nails or metal cleats around the edges that might restrain the natural tendency of the panel to revert to its original shape should be removed. A restorer with experience of panel work should then be consulted. He may consider that it will be sufficient to leave the panel to recover over a period of time, or that some special form of treatment is required. Recovery, which in the natural course of events may take many months, can be assisted by the judicious application of pads of damp blotting-paper to the unpainted side.

After the panel has recovered its shape and been given any necessary reinforcement, cracks may remain on the painted side, and these will require to be filled with stopping. Various materials may be used for stopping, one of the commonest being a putty made from plaster of Paris and glue to which has been added a little stand oil. After the crack in the painting ground has been filled in, the surface of the stopping is painted in the colour and texture of the original, taking care that the new paint is level with the adjacent surface (see 'Inpainting', p. 180).

When a panel painting is being sent from its normal environment to an exhibition, it is a wise precaution to protect it on the back with a material that is impervious to moisture, e.g. polythene sheet, fixed with polythene tape. Protection of the back in this way tends to counteract the effects of changes in relative humidity and warping is prevented. This precaution is only necessary when the panel is removed from the environment to which it has become accustomed. On its return home the sheet should be detached as there is no advantage in covering the back when the panel is known to be stable in its home surroundings.

2. *Cleavage and flaking paint.* Cleavage may take place between any of the adjacent strata of the painting. When it occurs in isolated areas it will commonly result either in the appearance of a blister or in paint becoming loose on the surface.

When cleavage is widespread, the condition is more serious. Extensive cleavage is an indication that the panel is no longer able to fulfil its function as a support, and consideration has then to be given to the possibility of its replacement, either by a fresh panel, or by some structural material that may serve the purpose more suitably. This type of operation, known as 'transfer', is one of the greatest delicacy, and is only undertaken as an extreme measure by an expert.

When loose paint is found on the surface of a picture, action must be taken at once to prevent it falling off. If movement of the picture is likely to result in loss of paint, emergency measures should be taken while the picture is still on the wall by sticking mulberry tissue over the damaged areas using dilute gelatine as the adhesive. If the glass cannot be detached from the front, the picture will have to be taken down carefully and removed from its frame. It is then laid face upwards in preparation for treatment. The cause of flaking may be the breakdown of an old repaint or tension in the panel resulting from an advancing crack in the wood, but there is no doubt that, fundamentally, such instability is caused by exposure to uncontrolled changes in relative humidity (see p. 4).

The flaking paint is reattached to the picture by injecting an adhesive under the raised paint—usually either a dilute solution of gelatine or a mixture composed of beeswax and resin—and applying gentle pressure and heat so as to flatten the paint. This work must be carried out with dexterity as the glue quickly becomes tacky and the wax-resin adhesive shows a tendency to set prematurely. Operations can be greatly facilitated by using the appropriate tools. Fine brushes and spatulas are required, and an electrically heated steel spatula having a gently curved blade is an invaluable instrument in preventing the adhesive from setting too soon. The degree of heat should be controlled within narrow limits so that the instrument can be employed to soften and flatten the paint without changing the shape of the fractured edges.

It is important to draw attention to the danger of fingering a blister before treatment, as the paint is brittle and under compression, and it may easily fly to pieces at a touch.

PAINTINGS ON CANVAS

The advantages of a textile support for easel painting came to be recognized in the fifteenth century with the discovery of the possibilities of oil painting, and from this time onwards canvas was destined to become the principal form of painting support. It had the merit of lightness and flexibility. A painting on canvas could be carried as a banner and, within limits, it could be rolled, so that the large easel painting was no longer static in the sense of being an elaborate piece of furniture that must remain where it had been erected.

Canvas is the fabric in general use today for easel painting. It is woven from spun threads of cotton, linen, or hemp, in tabby or twill weaves, and the fibres are protected from direct contact with the oil by a sizing of glue. The canvas is then primed in such a manner as to preserve the texture by covering it with a thin ground of linseed oil and white lead. This painting ground provides a uniform surface to work upon and one that will reflect light, so that the artist can exploit to the full the translucent quality of his paints. The canvas is stretched in a wooden frame provided with wedges in the corners so that it can be tightened or slackened at will.

A stretched raw cloth canvas tightens when damp and expands when dry, but the effect of glue sizing and of priming and painting reduces such movements to a minimum, and may even cause them to operate in the reverse direction, some expansion taking place in damp conditions and some tightening in dry conditions. Very large thin canvases are those most liable to sag in their stretchers and, if allowed to do so, they may easily take on a permanent warp, especially noticeable towards the corners, where undulations appear that soon collect dust. It is not a good thing, however, to tamper much with the stretcher keys after they have once been adjusted to a reasonable mean. It may be that the site occupied by the picture is exposing it to too high a temperature or relative humidity. The picture should be rehung elsewhere for a year and kept under observation. Should there be no improvement it may be necessary to have the canvas removed from its stretcher and replaced in contact with a stretched raw cloth canvas. The additional canvas at the back will give support to the picture and slow down its response to atmospheric changes in relative humidity.

It is clear that in the case of canvas, the environment plays a part in conservation second only to its influence on panel. While the oil ground and the superimposed paint layers on a canvas are more adaptable to movements of the support than the *gesso* ground and paint layers on wood, the elasticity of the oil is gradually diminished with the passage of time; the paint layer becomes brittle and is easily cracked by movements of the support, due to changes in relative humidity.

An accidental knock at the back of an old canvas may cause local stretching, and result in the formation of a series of concentric cracks in the ground and paint layer, a disfigurement not necessarily very serious, unless accompanied by cleavage and blistering of the paint.

It is characteristic of canvas that it tenders with age, and gradually becomes weakened so that it is easily punctured or torn. Tendering may be due to a variety of causes but a major factor is certainly the cumulative action of sulphur dioxide absorbed from the atmosphere and its conversion to sulphuric acid by the catalytic action of iron.[1] A canvas may become so rotten with age that it can no longer bear the strain where it is held to the stretcher by tacks. In this case it may be sufficient if the edges only are strengthened, and this is done by a process known as strip-lining. Eventually there will come a time when the whole fabric gets so frail that it can no longer be regarded as a satisfactory support, and then consideration has to be given to

[1] In tacking a canvas to a stretcher copper tacks should always be used.

the possibility of backing it with fresh canvas, a process known as lining or, more generally, relining.

Canvas paintings: mechanical damage and treatment

1. *Patching holes*. Holes in canvas are repaired by backing the canvas with a patch, and filling either with stopping or with an insertion depending on the size of the hole. If the canvas is puckered it will have to be relaxed with moisture and flattened, and it may be necessary to remove hard paint from loose threads with a paint remover in preparation for the repair. In the case of a small hole the picture is laid face down on glass with the damaged area in contact with an oiled paper. A patch is prepared from a piece of raw cloth canvas larger than the hole, and it should be 'chamfered' by pulling several threads from the weave all round, thus thinning the edges so that the shape of the patch will not appear on the front of the painting. A suitable adhesive is a mixture of warm beeswax and resin, the patch being fixed with a warm iron; or a flexible emulsion resin adhesive may be used. The picture is then turned over, the oiled paper removed, and the hole stopped with putty made from whiting and linseed oil in preparation for inpainting.

If the hole is large, it is filled in by inserting a piece of primed canvas of the same weight and weave as the original canvas. The weave of the inserted piece is aligned with the threads of the canvas, the contour traced, and the piece cut to the exact size and shape of the hole; it is then fitted in position, and secured temporarily on the front by Sellotape. A patch is applied to the back as already described, and stopping is used on the front if required before inpainting.

2. *Mending tears*. When tears in the canvas have to be mended, the torn edges are first brought together working from the back so that the weave can be distinctly seen, the broken threads being lined up, and the tear secured with Sellotape. The picture is turned over and the tear secured on the front. Then working from the back again, the Sellotape is removed and a patch applied as described above. In applying a long and awkward patch with a glue-paste adhesive, care must be taken not to stretch the material too tightly as on drying

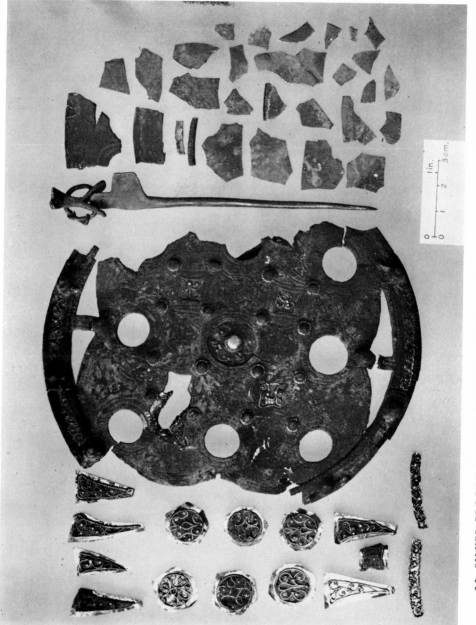

22. SILVER BROOCH FROM CANTERBURY SHOWING ITS CONDITION BEFORE RESTORATION

23. SILVER BROOCH FROM CANTERBURY AFTER RESTORATION

it may shrink and pucker the canvas. In using aqueous adhesives puckering of the joint due to differential shrinkage is a frequent cause of embarrassment. Polyvinyl acetate emulsion or epoxy resins are less liable to cause trouble in this respect; they have the merit that they are used cold, and no great pressure is necessary in order to make good the joint. Wax-resin adhesives may also be used, and in this case the patch is applied, as mentioned above, with a warm iron.

3. *Strip-lining*. When the canvas support is in good condition generally, and only the edges are weakened where they have been attached to the stretcher, these can be strengthened by applying strips of canvas to the back of the painting. Raw cloth canvas is used of the same weight and texture as the picture. The strips are cut to fit, allowing slightly more material at the outside edges for fitting over the stretcher; the inside edges must not extend beyond the width of the frame, and these edges are 'chamfered' as in preparing a patch. A strong adhesive is necessary for strip-lining, and the glue-paste mixture may be used, but the best cement for this purpose is an epoxy cold-setting resin, as this does not shrink on setting, and there should be no tendency for the canvas to cockle. Should its removal ever be necessary, however, this could not be accomplished by heat or solvent action, but only by rubbing down from the back with glass-paper. Whatever adhesive is used, the repaired canvas must be put in a press or kept under weights until the joints are secure.

4. *Relining*. Relining is for canvas paintings what transfer is for panels: it is a method that can be used for saving a picture that is threatened by the failure of its support. Most old paintings of any importance have already been relined.

In relining, the painted surface is first reinforced with tissue paper applied with an aqueous adhesive; then, any previous relining canvas is removed. If a painting is being relined for the first time, the old canvas is smoothed down before a new canvas is applied. Relining is a major studio operation, but it is only by virtue of the fact that it can be expertly accomplished that so many Old Master paintings survive in such excellent condition today. This work is never attempted unless it is deemed to be essential for the survival of the picture and then it is only undertaken by a qualified expert. Apart from the general risks involved in relining, the chief danger is that characteristics of the artist's technique may be impaired; for example the *impasto* may be flattened and a tonality introduced that is foreign to the work, but in recent years the technique of relining has been improved and brought more under control. When heat is required, it is applied either by electric irons thermostatically regulated or by the use of a hot table,[1] and much ingenuity has been devoted to evolving methods of protecting the *impasto* during relining, involving the use of vacuum relining tables.[2]

The glue-paste adhesives that were originally in universal use have largely been replaced by various wax-resin mixtures containing inert materials such as China clay, powdered chalk, etc. Wax relining has several advantages: the wax consolidates the paint layer by impregnation through the cracks from back to front, it avoids the complications that may result from using aqueous cements, and it can be easily removed at any time without strain when further relining is required. It is possible to carry out relining without heating by using a cold-setting emulsion adhesive and this has the advantage over glue that it remains permanently flexible. It is only applicable, however, in cases where the paint layer is in such good condition that it does not require to be consolidated by impregnation with wax.

In the preceding paragraphs treatment has been prescribed for dealing with certain types of deterioration arising primarily from failure of the panel or canvas support. It falls now to consider how far the paint and varnish layer may suffer damage in themselves or from what may be regarded as surface agencies.

THE PAINT LAYER

The paint layer is composed of insoluble particles of pigments mixed together in the greatest complexity, each particle being surrounded by an impervious film of medium. In egg-tempera and oils

[1] Ruhemann, H., *Studies in Conservation*, 1953, **1**, p. 73.

[2] See *Studies in Conservation*, 1959, **4**, p. 73 (de Wild, A. M.); 1960, **5**, p. 1 (Slabczynski, S.) and 1960, **5**, pp. 17–20.

the medium isolates the pigments from moisture and noxious gases. This is not so in the case of water-colours or gouache, in both of which gum arabic is the essential binding medium. White lead, which in water-colour is so readily blackened by the action of sulphuretted hydrogen in the atmosphere (p. 87), is immune when ground in oil or egg-tempera.

Pigments that are chemically incompatible in water-colour may often be mixed in oils with much less chance of their interacting with each other, and when resin is added to the oil it is even possible to use colours made from mixtures of pigments containing sulphur and copper without fear of subsequent chemical interaction which would lead to loss of brilliance. This has always been well known, and El Greco, for example, mixed such potentially incompatible pigments freely by employing isolating resin varnishes. It would seem therefore that in easel paintings there is no problem as regards the preservation of the pigment constituent of the paint layer. Whenever chemical changes have occurred, they are usually irreversible. Two of the commonest examples to be found on Old Master paintings are associated with ultramarine and copper resinate green.

Ultramarine is occasionally found to have lost its brilliance and to have become mottled white in appearance. This is due to the action of acid, probably arising as a legacy from some ill-advised process of cleaning in the past. In water-colours this so-called 'ultramarine sickness' has even been traced to acidity in the paper support.

In many early paintings it has been observed that areas that were originally a brilliant green have now assumed a dirty brown colour. This is due to a chemical change which copper resinate greens undergo, particularly in alkaline conditions. Since alkaline reagents (e.g. soap, wood, ash, ammonia) were used in the early days for cleaning paintings, these may be responsible for the browning that is so often observed. Alkalis can also destroy the colour of Prussian blue, a pigment widely used in the palette with yellows in composing mixed greens, and in this case also there is a tendency for the greens to go brown and there is no possibility of restoring the original hue.

It is questionable whether the amount of sulphurous gases present even in industrial atmospheres would be enough to affect pigments bound in oil or tempera, but it is a different matter when soot, which is greasy and contaminated with sulphuric acid, is allowed to accumulate on a painting: it becomes ingrained in the *impasto* and *craquelure* and the weave of the canvas, and causes deterioration of all the materials with which it is in contact. Dust in any form is harmful and for this reason paintings that are of any value should never be hung against the chimney-breast of an open fire, or above a radiator; apart from the undesirable temperature and humidity conditions in these situations, the dirt problem is intensified by convection currents. The main reason for keeping pictures under glass is to protect the paint layer from noxious gases and from dust more effectively than can be done by the varnish itself. When a picture gallery is air-conditioned glazing is unnecessary.

As an oil painting matures there is a tendency for it to go down in tone; the medium becomes more translucent and darker in colour. The increased translucency is due to an increase in the refractive index of the oil on ageing, and this cannot be prevented. The main form of deterioration in the paint layer, however, is that caused by the darkening of the oil medium. Linseed oil is a complex mixture of fatty acid glycerides, certain of which (e.g. linolenic) tend to become dark in colour on ageing. When an oil painting is kept in a dull light the rate of darkening is intensified, and although the main cause of such darkening is usually due to the deterioration of the varnish (see below) the change in the medium itself is a factor of importance. The pernicious practice of rubbing over the surface of a painting indiscriminately with linseed oil under the mistaken idea that this will help to preserve it merely aggravates the tendency to darkening and cannot be too strongly condemned. Darkened oil paint may be restored in large measure by exposing the picture to sunlight which bleaches the discoloured ingredients of the oil. The medium of tempera painting is in a different category. It has no tendency to darken or lose its optical qualities and, as it has a comparatively low refractive index, delicate nuances of colour can be appreciated in this medium to a degree impossible in oil painting.

THE VARNISH LAYER

The final coat of varnish is applied to a picture to enhance its appearance, to give depth and luminosity to the colour, and unity to the composition. At the same time it gives the picture some mechanical protection and shields it from direct contact with the atmosphere. But varnish is impermanent, and as it decays and is removed and replaced many times during the life of an Old Master painting, it is necessary that it should be of such a nature that it can be easily removed, even in the decayed condition, without exposing the paint layer to the action of solvents that might soften it, and without involving any mechanical strain that might weaken it. It is hardly necessary to say that a varnish must also be transparent and remain so, and it must be tough; and to be of maximum optical value it should have a high refractive index approximating to that of the dried oil films (c. 1.53). Further qualities are required, but the few enumerated above are sufficient to restrict the field to what are called the spirit varnishes, i.e. those made from resins that are directly soluble in volatile solvents such as turpentine or white spirit, and that on evaporation of the solvent leave behind a film of resin having the desired qualities. Of the natural resins, mastic and dammar come nearest the mark, and in spite of certain deficiencies are in most general use today. Certain synthetic varnishes have recently been introduced and these are discussed in detail later (p. 183).

Varnish deteriorates by blooming[1] and by becoming brittle and opaque.

(a) *Bloom*. This word has been used to describe the dull bluish-white appearance that develops in a transparent film and leads to a cloudiness. The precise cause of blooming is not known, and while many factors may be involved, damp is certainly a major factor in the blooming of varnish. Dammar and mastic are sensitive to moisture which affects the varnish film after it is dry, causing it to become clouded with a bluish-white mist. The blooming of varnish may also be caused by the use of inferior materials or incorrect solvents in its formulation.

[1] Brommelle, N., *Museums J.*, 1956, **55**, p. 263.

If dealt with in the early stages, bloom can be removed from the surface of the picture by rubbing with a soft silk pad, either dry or with a little wax polish, but if left unattended, the bloom tends to work its way into the film and it can then no longer be removed by surface treatment.

In the case of pictures that are prone to bloom, a palliative may be found in the use of a microcrystalline wax polish (see Appendix XV). For the precautions necessary to prevent bloom forming during re-varnishing, see pp. 181–3.

(b) *Embrittlement and loss of transparency.* So far as our present knowledge goes, all spirit varnishes based on natural resins become brittle, disintegrate with age, and develop a yellow colour. The yellowing is most pronounced in varnished pictures that are exposed to a bright light. While daylight prevents oil paint from yellowing it has the opposite effect on dammar and mastic varnishes. Daylight is essential for the life of a painting in the oil medium, but exposure for long periods to direct sunlight is not recommended as this causes premature ageing of the varnish and hastens the day when its replacement will be necessary.

In old pictures that may still retain a coating of oil varnish, e.g. an oil-run copal, the decay of the varnish is accompanied by crazing which may communicate itself to the underlying paint and cause serious damage to the picture.

Whatever the nature of the varnish the breakdown of the film exposes a much larger surface area for the condensation of moisture and accumulation of dirt, and when the varnish has become badly discoloured and porous and is no longer protective its removal is imperative.

STANDARD STUDIO TECHNIQUES

1. Removal of varnish

Films of soft resin varnishes (mastic and dammar) are removed from a painting by applying solvent on swabs of cotton-wool to small areas at a time, the dissolved varnish being absorbed by the wool and the swabs changed frequently during the course of the work. The choice of solvent is crucial as it must dissolve the varnish without affecting the underlying paint. Many solvents for resin are available—alcohol and acetone are the two most generally used—but they must be diluted with a restrainer (turpentine or rectified petroleum) in such proportions as to ensure that the liquid has no action on the paint layer, but dissolves the varnish without undue friction. In order to adjust the proportions of solvent and restrainer, cleaning tests are first made on the edge of the picture. It may be found that a mixture of alcohol and turpentine in the proportion of 4 vols. to 20 vols. removes the varnish without affecting the paint; a 2/20 mixture may be equally satisfactory, whereas a 1/20 mixture may be found to be effective only on continued rubbing and this is undesirable as it would be likely to damage *impasto*. In such a case the 2/20 mixture might seem to be the best to employ. This would then be tested on varnish overlying small areas of bright colour, e.g. vermilion (which is usually most sensitive), using for the purpose of the test a wisp of cotton-wool twisted round a match-stick. The swab is closely examined in order to discover whether, as a result of cleaning, any pink colour has been communicated to the cotton-wool. If so, the cleaning solution is too strong and it must be further diluted with turpentine. When the mixture has passed these tests satisfactorily, parts of the painting are selected and rectangular areas cleaned of varnish in order to form an estimate of the condition of the underlying paint and the change of tonality that may be anticipated as a result of cleaning. This preliminary routine is a necessary prelude to the cleaning of any important picture.

In stripping a picture the restrainer must always be readily accessible. In practice, the operator can hold the cleaning swab in one hand and the restraining swab in the other, so that should there be any indication of the softening of the paint, as by the appearance of a trace of colour other than brown on the cleaning swab, he can flood the area with restrainer and arrest the action. The areas are finally wiped over with the restrainer to remove the last of the solvent and any softened residues of varnish that may remain on the picture. In the case of high *impasto* or resolute brush-work, such as is found in paintings by Rembrandt, hollows may be filled with old dark varnish while the raised portions are light and possibly abraded. The cleaning of such paintings requires time and patience as the work may have to be carried out very largely by using small wisps of cotton-wool on match-sticks as described above, rather than larger swabs held in the fingers.

The experienced restorer will be able to estimate beforehand what the paint layer can stand in the way of cleaning. He will recognize the existence of any soft resins used by the artist in the course of painting the picture, and ensure that such a painting is not damaged by his cleaning solutions. He will consult with the curator regarding the removal of any repainting that dates from a former restoration. In cleaning a picture it is often found that previous repairs have been concealed by unnecessarily large areas of repainting, and the removal of such restorations, followed by inpainting of the stopping only, will usually be desirable.

2. Inpainting

The term 'inpainting' is used in picture restoration to emphasize the fact that the original paint is sacrosanct and must not be covered with modern additions of colour. The only exception is where the picture is abraded and part of the design rubbed away; here it may be necessary in the interests of aesthetics to retouch the paint layer with colour—a delicate operation for which paints are employed that can readily be removed if necessary. Where inpainting is required, either in oil or tempera paintings, the medium that is chosen is egg-tempera. This is applied irrespective of the original technique because it is not subject either to darkening or to increase in transparency; the oil medium, as has been mentioned, is subject to both. Tempera has the one disadvantage that it becomes insoluble, but this is no serious inconvenience when it is applied to areas of stopping only. In case it should ever be necessary to remove the modern paint, it may be applied over an isolating varnish of dammar in turpentine and this is the technique generally adopted, each coating of tempera being given a thin coating of dammar varnish before the next is applied. As the dammar can always be softened by the use of resin solvents, this makes it possible to remove the retouchings at any time.

In order that the quality of the inpainting should be in harmony with the rest of the picture, it is necessary that the transition from stopping to finished painting should follow the same course as that adopted by the artist. Thus, the stopping should be coloured to match the ground of the painting; if drawing or under-modelling is present, this should be reproduced on the stopping, and the under-painting and glazing should be built up as nearly as possible in the manner adopted by the artist himself. The inpainting should be carried out using stable powder pigments ground in the medium and it is important that the finished restoration should be of slightly lighter hue than the adjacent passages of paint, a dark retouching being much more obtrusive than a light one. The aim should be not to deceive; it should be to conceal forms of damage that would distract the attention and by their presence make it impossible to appreciate the picture as the artist intended. A trained eye can usually detect restorations but, should the matter be in doubt, suspicions can often be confirmed by inspection of the painting in a darkened room under ultra-violet radiation, or by infra-red photography, or X-radiography.

After the painting is dry the picture is ready for revarnishing.

3. Revarnishing

As already mentioned, mastic and dammar varnish are the picture varnishes in most common use. It is difficult to decide which is the better as the resins themselves are complex mixtures[1] and subject to much variation in quality. Mastic seems to give the more brilliant finish, but it requires a turpentine solvent which may be one reason why it becomes so yellow on ageing. Its use was abandoned by the National Gallery in 1949 in favour of dammar varnish,[2] which, in contrast to mastic, may be dissolved in white spirit and is believed to be less prone to yellowing.

[1] Mills, J. S., and Werner, A. E. A., *Journal of the Oil and Colour Chemists Assoc.*, 1954, **37**, p. 131.

[2] Lucas, A., and Brommelle, N., *Museums J.*, 1953, **53**, p. 149.

Dammar picture varnish is made from selected dammar resin by dissolving it in white spirit without the aid of heat. The resin is suspended in a gauze bag in the solvent contained in a covered jar, and the liquid shaken or stirred at intervals over a period of some weeks. A suitable concentration would be about 115 gm. of dammar in 500 ml. of white spirit. A little stand oil is added, finally, to act as a plasticizer to toughen the film and to help brushing-out qualities, but never in excess of 5 per cent.

A picture should never be varnished until the paint is quite dry. The surface must be free from dirt, grease, and wax, and to ensure this it is rubbed over lightly with white spirit and allowed to dry before beginning operations. The varnish may then be applied by brush or spray. The work should be carried out in a warm dry room free from dust and draughts; care should be taken that the varnish is not chilled but is several degrees above the temperature of the room.

If a brush is used, it should be a special varnish brush made with bristles of the finest quality and kept exclusively for the purpose. The varnish is applied to the picture thinly in a series of overlapping squares, say 20 cm. by 20 cm. (depending on the size of the picture), using first horizontal strokes and then immediately afterwards vertical strokes. In this way any excess of varnish is removed and a film is left of uniform thickness free from brush marks. A second coat may be applied if considered necessary after the first has dried, but the aim should be to apply the thinnest varnish film consistent with realizing the desired optical effect.

When the spray is used—and spraying has much to commend it especially when there is high *impasto*—the fan-shaped type of nozzle is best. The pressure and the distance of the jet from the picture have a bearing on success and will be determined to a large extent by the viscosity of the varnish. In using the spray the jet must not be too near the painting, because it will then deliver varnish that is too liquid to control; on the other hand, if it is too far away, it will tend to give a matt effect by covering the surface with minute spots or scales of resin that are too dry to coalesce, thus affording no protection.

In theory, the thinnest uniform coating should be obtainable by spraying, but in practice a uniform coating is difficult to achieve without building up a film that is at least comparable in thickness with that obtained by brushing.

When a picture has been varnished it is allowed to remain on the easel till the varnish is dry; it should then be kept under glass for a few weeks until the varnish becomes really hard, when there will be less tendency for the surface to bloom.

Synthetic resin varnishes. Various types of synthetic resin are now available and research is constantly proceeding with the aim of producing a synthetic varnish suitable for paintings that will have all of the required characteristics (p. 177) and none of the demerits of natural resins.[1]

One of the first synthetic resins to be tested was polyvinyl acetate which has been used for many years on quite an extensive scale in the U.S.A. The choice of solvent is important as there are many solvents for this substance that are too active for application to oil paintings. Alcohol only should be used for preparing a varnish for brushing purposes and the standard solution is made by dissolving 20 grammes of polyvinyl acetate in 100 ml. of ethyl alcohol[2] without the application of heat. This may take a long time but solution is facilitated by stirring and shaking. The standard solution may be diluted, if necessary, to half or quarter strength, by adding ethyl alcohol. This formula is given by Bradley[3] together with a reliable spray formula for a polyvinyl acetate varnish composed as follows:

Standard solution of polyvinyl acetate in ethyl alcohol (20 per cent w/v)	250 ml.
Ethyl alcohol	250 ml.
Cellosolve acetate (or cellosolve)	100 ml.
Diacetone alcohol	35 ml.

[1] Thomson, G., *Studies in Conservation*, 1957, **3**, p. 64.

[2] Of strength 96 per cent. It should be noted that polyvinyl acetate does not dissolve in absolute alcohol.

[3] Bradley, M. C., jr., *The Treatment of Pictures*, Cambridge, U.S.A., Art Technology, 1950.

Attention has also been devoted to the esters of polymethacrylic acid, which have the advantage that they are soluble in hydrocarbon solvents, but the discovery that they tend to cross-link and become insoluble precludes their use.

These two types of resins are linear polymers of relatively high molecular weight. Hence, for a given solids content, the viscosity of their solutions is high and this gives rise to practical difficulties in their application. These can be overcome by using a varnish based on polycyclohexanone[1] which is a polymer of low molecular weight similar in physical properties to the natural resins. This is made up in white spirit and yields a relatively non-yellowing film which, unplasticized, is rather glossy and rather brittle. The glossy nature of the film is no disadvantage as the optical quality can easily be adjusted after the varnish has dried, by the application of wax polish (see below). The brittleness, however, is a problem that has to be overcome by the addition of a plasticizer, and several formulations are on the market.

4. Wax varnishing

Wax varnishes are merely polishes, because even if applied thinly to the painting by brush, the wax residue that remains on the picture after the solvent has evaporated is polished by using a soft long-bristled brush. The resulting gloss may be enhanced, if desired, by further polishing with a soft cloth. The surface of a wax varnish even when polished is duller than that given by resin or synthetic varnishes, and wax may be applied over these to reduce their high gloss. Resin and synthetic varnishes are never applied over wax.

A common formula for wax varnish contains 100 gm. of white beeswax dissolved in 500 ml. of distilled turpentine with the aid of a water-bath maintained at about 60 °C. An improved form is the wax mixture made from microcrystalline wax and polythene wax (see Appendix XV). This leaves a surface that is relatively non-sticky and the wax may be used either as a polish or, in the case of smooth painting, for eliminating ingrained dirt.

[1] This material was available commercially as Resin AW2, now known as Ketone Resin N; an English equivalent is Resin MS2.

In order to wax-polish a picture, the surface is first rubbed very gently with a piece of soft silk to remove any dust. Some of the polish is then placed in the palm of the hand, where it quickly softens. A piece of cotton-wool wrapped in thin silk is charged with the softened wax, and used to polish the picture with the minimum of pressure. In the case of a picture ingrained with dirt, the polish is applied direct, using the cotton-wool without the covering rag. The waxed cotton-wool collects the dirt, and finally the surface may be polished (using a new covered pad) by the method described initially. Large canvases may require some support from the back (by a pad of papers or the like) during cleaning and polishing.

EXCEPTIONAL FORMS OF DETERIORATION

1. *Insect attack on panels*. Painted panels are sometimes found to be attacked by wood beetle (*Anobium*), the larvae of which tunnel into the wood to emerge eventually from the surface as fully developed insects. Activity may be recognized by the appearance of holes or frass and, if action is not taken in time, the support may become so weakened that cleavage of the paint results.

When insect pests are found to be active, the painting should be at once isolated to prevent adjacent pictures becoming infected. It must then be sterilized, using an insecticide that will not damage either paint or varnish, the most satisfactory form of treatment being fumigation with carbon disulphide (see p. 132). To confirm that sterilization has been successful, the panel should be inspected at intervals of six months after fumigation. If the old insect holes are filled with wax at the time of fumigation, the appearance of any new ones will be readily detected.

2. *Fungal attack on canvas*. A canvas that has been relined with a glue adhesive is prone, under conditions of damp heat, to be attacked by moulds. The appearance of fluffy white growths, visible especially on dark passages of paint, is an indication of fungal activity, and if observed through a reading-glass will likely be found growing on the glue where it is exposed in the *craquelure*. To arrest and prevent

further growth, the surface of the painting should be rubbed over lightly with soft pads of cotton-wool and the picture exposed to sun and air. This may be all that is required. The glass, however, should be sterilized, before it is replaced, by cleaning with cotton-wool that has been moistened with formalin. In very bad cases it may be necessary to use formalin on the actual painting, but this should be left to the discretion of the restorer who will know from his experience or can discover by testing whether the picture is in a condition to be treated with aqueous solutions. The back of the canvas must also be considered and may be given permanent protection against mould growth by the use of a non-volatile fungicide such as Santobrite or Topanews (p. 30).

FURTHER READING

CONSTABLE, W. G., *The Painter's Workshop*. Oxford University Press, 1954.

FELLER, R. L., STOLOW, N. and JONES, E. H., *On Picture Varnishes and their Solvents*. Revised edn. Press of Case Western Reserve University, Cleveland, 1971.

MAYER, R., *The Artist's Handbook of Materials and Techniques*. Faber & Faber, London, 2nd edn., 1962.

RUHEMANN, H., *The Cleaning of Paintings*. Faber & Faber, London, 1968.

STOUT, G. L., *The Care of Pictures*. Columbia University Press, 1948.

PART II

METALS

VIII

GENERAL INTRODUCTION

THE conservation of museum objects of metal is a study in itself. Metals form a heterogeneous though well-defined group of materials, almost all subject to corrosion—that is, to the loss of metallic properties with the formation of mineral incrustations. This is due to a series of chemical or electrochemical reactions, and disintegration may be slow or accelerated depending on the nature of the metal and the conditions to which it is exposed. Metallic corrosion is accompanied by a change in appearance calling attention to the fact that a chemical change has taken place.

Before beginning a course of treatment it is necessary to know something about the nature of the corrosion. This is often induced by the action of some active agent, such as chloride present in the ground, that has entered into chemical combination with the metal, and the main aim of any method of treatment will be to remove the corrosion products by suitable chemical means applied in the laboratory under scientific control. The effect of such treatment may be striking, as when an object that is disfigured by a gross incrustation of minerals can be so dealt with that its original metallic condition is restored; but such an extreme change in appearance need not be the inevitable result of chemical treatment. There are many cases where it will be necessary to treat a corroded object without affecting the patinated surface, which must be retained because it is aesthetically pleasing, and there are other cases when the mineralization cannot be removed because the extent of the corrosion is so great that its removal would seriously endanger the object. Thus the nature and condition of the antiquity must be taken into account in determining what freedom of action exists and to what degree its stability can be assured with the minimum of change.

In dealing with corroded metals there are, in fact, three possible methods of treatment: the use of chemical reagents, the use of electro-chemical and electrolytic reduction, and mechanical methods; and while it will be convenient to study these methods individually, it should be understood that they are not necessarily mutually exclusive, but may be applied as occasion demands in combination. Thus, the use of chemical reagents and reduction methods are each dependent for ultimate success upon the application of certain forms of mechanical treatment (brushing, washing, etc.) and there are many cases where the best results can be obtained only by a combination of all three processes. Metals have individual characteristics; they are susceptible to different chemical reagents, they corrode in different ways, and in doing so they form different kinds of incrustations that must be recognized and studied before it is possible to decide upon the best method of treatment. Chemical methods involving the use of specific reagents can only be described in dealing with the metals themselves. By contrast, the methods of reduction and the mechanical methods are of general application to all corroded metal, and these processes are therefore described in this chapter as a preamble to the study of individual metals of antiquity.

In considering what treatment to apply, a preliminary physical examination is of the greatest importance. This is carried out with the aid of a lens and, if necessary, by exploring with a needle or in the case of ferrous metal by using a magnet. It is necessary to form some estimate of the thickness and regularity of the encrusted layer, strength of the residual metal, presence of ornament, taking special note of fine detail and of any cracks. To reveal the presence of hidden ornament in cases where the metal is heavily corroded, it may be necessary to use X-rays. Methods of treatment are based upon this preliminary assessment, and tables are given at the end of each chapter (save in the case of gold), to assist in deciding what may be the best procedure, but whether the suggested methods are, in fact, the best to apply in the circumstances can only be decided by the knowledge, experience, and skill of the operator.

If metals are considered as raw materials, it is noteworthy that few are found in nature in the free or uncombined state. They occur in combination with non-metallic elements in the form of minerals, and these provide the ores from which the metals are extracted by smelting. Minerals, rather than metals, are thus the stable forms under natural conditions, and it is to these minerals that metals tend to revert, especially when they are buried in the ground for prolonged periods of time. It has been observed that, other things being equal, the more easily a metal is won from its ores, the greater is its stability. Thus, metallic tin which is obtained with the minimum expenditure of energy from the oxide (cassiterite) shows less tendency than copper to become reoxidized. Because of its relative stability, tin has been used as a coating for protecting copper vessels from at least the beginning of the Christian era, and even in this attenuated form it is often found to have survived in excellent condition.

When metals are buried in the ground, the rate of corrosion is intensified according to the degree of acidity of the soil, its porosity, and the presence of naturally occurring soluble salts. These substances in the presence of moisture conduct electricity and are known as electrolytes. Metallic corrosion is an electrochemical phenomenon. The absolute strength of electric currents flowing over corroding metal can be measured, and by comparing such measurements with the rate of corrosion, change of weight, etc., it has been shown that the whole complicated cycle depends on electrochemical principles.

Metals that have been buried and have already suffered some degree of corrosion have a comparatively porous surface and are thus liable to retain traces of salts. Often these salts are sealed up in what appears to be a stable incrustation, but should they be exposed to moisture and oxygen they are likely to give rise to fresh activity, with consequent pitting of the surface and possibly serious disfigurement. In some cases there is a progressive growth of the surface minerals which takes place at the expense of the metallic core; in others, the mineralization is compact and stable and, after preliminary development, it tends to inhibit further change. Where development has been slow and uniform the intricacies of shape and ornament are preserved and the appearance of the object may even be enhanced by the colour and texture of the patina. A patina that has developed slowly may sometimes be evidence of antiquity and a fine patina will determine the market value of an object. It is necessary, therefore, in considering the treatment of metal objects to consider also the preservation of their patinas when these may be taken as evidence of age or have in themselves an aesthetic value. The patinas of Chinese bronzes, for example, which have matured through the years in ground substantially free from soluble salts, have an irresistible appeal for the collector; but the danger is that mineral patinas which are apparently quite stable may become unstable if exposed to damp , and when corrosion becomes active it is necessary to use special methods to arrest it without serious loss of surface appearance.

Burial in the earth, however, is by no means essential for the corrosion of metals. Even when objects are kept indoors, moisture and oxygen are enough in themselves to cause dulling of the surface due to the formation of a layer of oxide. The results of attack by sulphurous gases that are present in industrial atmospheres are even more readily apparent, yielding the darker films of sulphide known as tarnish; but disfigurations of oxide and sulphide are purely superficial and readily amenable to treatment.

The individual metals of antiquity are few in number—gold, silver, copper, lead, tin, and iron, but they have been mixed together as alloys, intentionally or otherwise, from remote periods. Thus, electrum (an alloy of gold and silver) is much more common than pure gold, and ancient silver almost invariably contains copper. Copper and tin were alloyed intentionally to make the more useful metal called bronze, and lead was often added to the mixed metal. But there is evidence that tin was not always distinguished from lead by the early metallurgists; analyses sometimes reveal the presence of both or even a preponderance of lead when this could only yield an alloy that was less serviceable for the purpose intended. Some of the earliest examples of bronze from Ur of the Chaldees contain such a small quantity of tin that it is doubtful whether the composition was intentional and it may therefore be misleading to use the term 'bronze' in this connection. Lead and tin have themselves been alloyed together from remote periods. Copper and zinc were alloyed intentionally in Roman times for coinage, but here again, there are isolated examples of brass occurring in earlier civilizations (China), and to what extent this was intentional can only be determined by further study. The manufacture of steel is a comparatively modern process, but the carburization of iron was discovered many years previously at the armourers' forge, where iron and slag were hammered in the presence of carbon and wrought, possibly by chance, into steel, an alloy superior to all others for the manufacture of sword-blades.[1] Such a chance occurrence might possibly provide a basis for the celebrated sword-blades of fable and legend!

Metallic corrosion has been described as an electrochemical phenomenon. This action can be demonstrated where two dissimilar metals are in contact in the presence of a conductive solution of a salt—the essentials of a simple electric cell; under these conditions the baser metal is corroded preferentially as long as the two are in electrical contact, the more noble metal surviving by what is called 'cathodic protection'. By conducting such experiments with different pairs of metals it is found that the metals can be arranged in order of their nobleness from gold downwards, through silver, copper, lead, tin, and iron, the baser metal always being sacrificed in the presence of an electrolyte where it is in contact with another metal higher up in the series.[2] An interesting example of survival by cathodic protection is that of the frail but perfect silver bowl discovered at Ur of the Chaldees among a mass of copper bowls (Pls. 15A and B). The fact that only the silver bowl survived was significant, and the condition of the copper bowls was such as to confirm that they had been preferentially corroded in accordance with this theory. For the same reason, bright inlays of copper or its alloys are sometimes found

[1] See Bird, V., and Hodges, H., *Studies in Conservation*, 1968, **13**, p. 215, on the metallurgical examination of two iron swords from Luristan.

[2] It should be noted that when metals are alloyed, as in stainless steel, the position of the alloy in the electrochemical series cannot be determined even approximately.

embedded in heavily rusted iron swords and knives, iron in relation to copper being the baser metal.

It is not only the conjunction of two different metals that promotes electrochemical decay. Where two or more metals are alloyed together as tin and copper are in bronze, the susceptibility to corrosion is greater than in the case of an unalloyed metal and, when once it has set in, the decay of bronze proceeds more quickly than is the case with copper alone. In the same way base silver is corroded more intensely than pure silver. Indeed, it is no uncommon occurrence to find that an object having the appearance of being a corroded bronze proves on examination to be made of base silver, the copper constituent having corroded preferentially and covered the white metal with a heavy green deposit, thus concealing the true nature of the alloy. In such cases treatment can be applied to remove the green incrustation, revealing the underlying silver enriched in appearance in proportion to the quantity of copper that has been leached from the alloy in the process of corrosion.

From these considerations it follows that different metals are at different electric potentials relative to a surrounding electrolyte, and it is then but a step to the idea that if different potentials could be established on one and the same metal (e.g. by local inclusions in the surface, varying porosity and concentration of the electrolyte, etc.), an electric current would flow leading to an electrolytic form of decomposition. This has proved to be the case, and in some measure may serve to explain the more catastrophic forms of corrosion such as the rusting of iron and also the behaviour of metals that have been subjected to the periodic action of saline water.

REDUCTION METHODS

1. Electrochemical reduction

In this method of reduction nascent hydrogen acts as the reducing agent in what is essentially a chemical reaction, but the generation of the nascent hydrogen involves the use of zinc and caustic soda in contact with the metallic object undergoing treatment so that an electrochemical process is also involved. The reaction is carried out in a Pyrex beaker or enamelled container with the aid of heat. Heat promotes chemical action, and thus enables results to be obtained reasonably quickly.

Materials. The zinc is used in granulated form or in the form of a coarse powder, so as to present a large surface of contact with the object under treatment. It may also be used in the form of zinc wool and wrapped around the object. Zinc dust is not as a rule so effective, as it tends to clog together.

Granulated zinc may be purchased as such, ready for use. If required as powder, the granulated zinc is pulverized in an iron mortar to the requisite grain size, and it may then be passed through a sieve of about 30 mesh to the inch, which yields a granular powder sufficiently fine for the most delicate operations. The advantages of using zinc wool is that it can be wrapped round the object, thus ensuring good electrical contact; on the other hand, the object is concealed by the wool during treatment, and the progress of the reaction is more difficult to follow.

Commercial flake caustic soda is dissolved in water and the strength of the solution should be not less than 10 per cent. When in contact with excess of zinc this solution will be 'spent' after about an hour's heating, i.e. evolution of hydrogen which is the potent factor in effecting reduction will then have ceased. It is usual, therefore, to employ stronger solutions, say up to 20 per cent, for objects that are heavily corroded. It is better to change such solutions occasionally rather than to work with solutions in excess of 20 per cent concentration.

Method of procedure. Heavy objects such as axe-heads, spear-heads, and the like are buried under a heap of granulated zinc in an enamelled basin, covered with the caustic soda solution, and the liquid boiled for an hour or so over a gas-ring or Bunsen burner in a fume cupboard as the vapours evolved are irritating. During this time, distilled water is added, as required, to maintain the volume of the solution at the original level. Delicate objects such as fibulae are buried in zinc powder, covered with a 10 per cent solution of caustic soda, and heated over a steam bath for an hour, taking the same precautions to maintain the volume of the solution.

The result of such treatment is to soften the incrustation. In the case of bronzes, the green colour will disappear, and it will be found possible by brushing under a stream of water to remove much of the brown, muddy deposit, revealing a metallic surface upon which are retained any details or ornament. If the metallic surface is not entirely clean, it will be necessary to repeat the reduction with fresh zinc and caustic soda. It is not permissible to leave any remains of mineralization unreduced as they seal in traces of chloride, and the only satisfactory method of eradication is by further reduction followed by brushing and washing. If traces of chloride are allowed to remain, a further outbreak of corrosion is inevitable, sooner or later. In some cases the mineralization may be found to be covered by a film of metallic copper which will make them more difficult to remove. It is most important, however, that they be removed. This plating out of copper is not so liable to occur when the reduction is carried out in boiling solutions, as the plating action is discouraged by the mechanical agitation.

In cases where residual incrustations cannot be removed even with a steel or glass brush they will have to be picked or scraped off. This often requires the exercise of much patience, using a magnifier and mounted needle, and going over the whole surface a small area at a time, picking off residual lumps of incrustation to expose the pockets of greenish-white pasty material (cuprous chloride) that underlie them. A subsidiary reduction is then required to ensure that salts exposed by this treatment are rendered soluble so that they can be washed out. This operation must be conducted with thoroughness and is described in detail on pp. 200–3.

In the course of reducing objects with zinc and caustic soda, the soda is spent and must be discarded, but a quantity of zinc remains, and, as it is rendered largely inactive owing to the formation of a film of oxychloride and carbonate, it tends to accumulate in the laboratory. It may be recovered for further use by washing it with water acidified with hydrochloric acid, then with distilled water, and drying.

Variations in procedure. The electrochemical reduction process as outlined above admits of several useful variations:

(i) If the object is encrusted with lime or chalk in addition to the normal mineralization, it will be necessary to treat it first in a solution of Calgon (p. 255) to remove the lime or chalk before proceeding with the reduction.

(ii) Where local treatment only is required, as in exposing an inscription on the base of an Egyptian bronze statuette, reduction may be done by repeatedly applying a paste of zinc powder and sulphuric acid of 90 per cent strength. Alternatively, the paste may be made *in situ* on the surface of the object by applying a few drops of the acid and mixing in a small quantity of the zinc powder with a glass rod or a tuft of glass bristles held in a piece of glass tubing.

(iii) Silver objects which are not heavily coated with horn silver respond well to reduction with zinc and hot formic acid, and even more readily when aluminium granules are used instead of zinc.

The main advantages of electrochemical reduction are that it requires no apparatus beyond what is readily available or can be easily improvised, and with the modifications described above it provides the means of reducing metal objects locally when desired. It is, however, subject to the limitations that apply generally to all methods of reduction.

2. Electrolytic reduction

This method of reduction, which is normally preferable to that of electrochemical reduction, involves the use of an electric current. The corroded metal object is made the negative electrode (cathode) in a suitable electrolyte such as sodium carbonate solution, the positive electrode (anode) usually being of stainless steel; under these circumstances the reducing action is then dependent on the application of an electric current. When current passes, hydrogen is evolved at the cathode with the result that the incrustation is gradually reduced and saline matter eliminated. As the reduction progresses, chlorides are transferred from the cathode to the anode. This method can be very effective in cleaning badly encrusted metals of all kinds, but unless conditions are made to conform to accepted standards (as described below), complications in the form of secondary reactions may ensue.

Equipment. The electric supply must be direct current, either from a secondary cell or accumulator, or it may be A.C. transformed from the mains to about 12 volts and rectified (see Diagram, Appendix XVII). It is the current in the circuit that is the most important factor, however; this depends upon the resistance of the electrolyte and the size of the electrodes, but will vary during the process as the resistance of the incrustation on the object alters under treatment.

In practice, sodium carbonate of about 5 per cent strength is usually chosen as the electrolyte, and two anodes are hung equidistantly, one on each side of the cathode, and only a few inches from it. Under such standardized conditions the rate of reduction will then depend mainly on the current density which can be regulated by a variable resistance to approximately 10 amps per square decimetre of cathode area, so as to give a steady vigorous evolution of gas. This figure is not critical for iron or steel objects. For copper and silver objects, however, the current density should not be allowed to fall below 2 amps per square decimetre, otherwise there is a tendency for a film of metal, usually copper having a salmon-pink colour, to be deposited on the surface of the object in the region of the chloride-containing incrustation, and this is difficult to remove. At first the resistance of the incrustation may be considerable, but in the course of treatment, after perhaps an hour or more, a rise in amperage will indicate that the resistance of the incrustation has fallen, and this should be compensated by increasing the external resistance in the circuit.

Method of procedure. A convenient arrangement is as follows: A glass tank or one constructed of polythene or of wood lined with polyester resin and glass fibre is filled to a suitable depth with 5 per cent sodium carbonate and brass bars are laid across the top from which the electrodes are suspended by copper wires, thus allowing of easy adjustment. The object is attached to the negative pole of the electric supply, whilst the anodes are wired together and joined to the positive pole through an ammeter and an adjustable resistance.

The anodes should be removed occasionally and washed to remove scale and incrustations which tend to form on them; it is also desirable that separate sets of anodes should be used for the reduction of different metals so as to avoid any risk of plating out. The use of stainless steel anodes avoids the complications previously encountered with anodes made from sheet iron, which tend to be heavily attacked during electrolysis. Graphite and carbon anodes suffer from the disadvantage that they break down in alkaline solution, depositing a black film on the object, and attempts to brush this off only burnish it into the surface. Sometimes it is advisable to tie nylon bags round the object being treated if additional support should be required, or if there is any chance of metal inlays, etc., falling off into the solution. Another refinement is to cover the surface of the electrolyte with floating glass capsules or short lengths of polythene tube, called croffles, in order to minimize the escape of caustic spray which, though not excessive, tends to irritate the throat.

In reducing a corroded object the duration of treatment will depend upon the nature of the incrustation, but its removal can be facilitated by taking out the object from time to time and brushing and scraping the surface under running water. The object should be removed while the current is still running. In no circumstances should it be left in the tank after the current is switched off, otherwise it may become plated with any metallic impurity present in the electrolyte.

Caley[1] has referred to a complication that is liable to interfere with the cleaning of bronzes that contain much lead. The lead is distributed in the alloy in the form of globules, and as these are gradually dissolved by caustic soda, the bronzes become pitted. Also the electrolyte tends to build up a concentration of lead plumbite. Lead may then be replated on the objects as a grey coating. Usually this is easily brushed off, but an electrolyte contaminated with lead salts might well plate this metal on to other objects treated subsequently, with undesirable results. He recommends that, when necessary, the lead salts be removed from the electrolyte by plating lead on to a large sheet of copper attached as a temporary cathode to the cathode

[1] Caley, E. R., *Technical Studies*, 1937, **6**, p. 194.

bar which normally carries the objects under treatment. The lead coating is easily stripped from the copper sheet later, by passing it through a bath of 10 per cent nitric acid, and after washing in water it is ready to be used again should occasion require.

This serves to draw attention to the importance of keeping the electrolyte clean. Lead can easily be detected in the electrolyte by withdrawing a small sample in a test-tube and adding dilute sulphuric acid, until it is slightly acid. If a white precipitate of lead sulphate is formed, this is an indication that the electrolyte is contaminated with lead, which must be removed by the method described above; alternatively a fresh lot of electrolyte should be made up.

INTENSIVE WASHING TECHNIQUE

When an incrustation has been broken down by reduction there will remain on the surface of the metal a sludge of insoluble oxides and metallic powder; this will also contain chlorides as well as a residue of the electrolyte employed in the process. The sludge is removed by brushing the object under running water, and while this will remove most of the superficial soluble impurities at the same time, it is not by any means sufficient to deal with those impurities within the metal. It will be readily understood that when an incrustation has grown upon metal, the metal underlying the incrustation will be microporous, and will behave as if it was a mass of capillary tubes, which will retain a residue of chlorides that are not easy to remove. They can be eliminated by prolonged soaking in changes of distilled water, and the process may be speeded up by using hot water, but unless the capillaries can be flushed with the distilled water, there will always be the chance of chloride being retained in the pores of the metal in sufficient amounts to cause a fresh outbreak of corrosion at a later date under humid conditions.

Such considerations have been examined theoretically by Organ,[1] and as a result of practical tests carried out under controlled conditions, using a conductivity meter, he has been able to recommend

[1] Organ, R. M., *Museums J.*, 1955, **55**, p. 112.

a form of intensive washing and also a particularly sensitive method of carrying out the silver nitrate test, i.e. the test that is used in practice to determine when objects are free from chloride. In this method it is recommended that the washing should be carried out with distilled water, by alternate heating and cooling, at least in the early stages, to ensure permeation. The heating causes any air or liquid in the capillaries to expand and partly leave the metal, and on cooling fresh water is sucked in. In dealing with a batch of bronzes, it is convenient to use a steam oven, in which are placed Pyrex beakers of distilled water containing the objects. The oven is kept at about 98 °C. during the working day, the temperature being allowed to fall overnight. This alternate heating and cooling ensures that the capillaries in the metal are flushed with water, and the progress of the washing is followed by measuring the electrical conductivity of successive baths of wash-water until it reaches a minimum value.

In the final stages of washing, when testing for chlorides is of the greatest significance, it is essential to be able to detect the presence of the merest traces of chloride remaining in the wash-water. Organ has emphasized the importance of applying the test under optimum conditions. The volume of wash-water should not be much in excess of that required to cover the object, which should be left in contact with the wash-water for some time. Then the test is carried out under the following standard conditions which give the most sensitive results. About 10 ml. of the water to be tested are poured into a tall narrow cylinder standing on a black surface, and several drops of dilute nitric acid are added. The cylinder is then stoppered with a glass stopper and inverted several times in order to mix the solutions. At this stage the liquid should be clear when examined in a good side lighting. Five drops of 2 per cent silver nitrate are then added, mixed as before, and time allowed for any opalescence to appear. Under these conditions one part of chloride per million of solution may easily be detected in a column 10 cm. high.

A convenient precise method for determining the actual concentration of chloride in the wash-water can be carried out using a specific-ion electrode for chloride that has recently become available commercially.[1] It is merely necessary to immerse this electrode in the wash-water, when the concentration of chloride can be read off on a scale. The instrument must, however, be first calibrated against chloride solutions of accurately known concentration.

The washing procedure described above is of wide application to metals and many siliceous materials, notably to baked cuneiform tablets, but this method is not suitable where lead objects are concerned. Hot distilled water reacts in a few hours with lead to form lead hydroxide which would cover the metal with a milky white film. A special procedure is required for washing lead objects (see p. 269).

DRYING OF METALS

Two methods are commonly employed for hastening the drying of metals—heating and desiccation. Heating in an oven at 105 °C. is the simpler process, and is satisfactory for iron objects of all kinds. It is satisfactory also in the case of silver and copper alloys that are smooth and non-porous. Porous metal, however, takes longer to dry, and base silver and copper alloys that are at all porous may acquire a disfiguring film of oxide in the oven. Although oxide films may be removed by glass-brushing, this introduces another operation, and one that can be avoided if drying is done in a desiccator. Drying can be accelerated by passing an object through a bath of acetone and then placing it in a desiccator from which the air can be evacuated. A capacious vacuum desiccator is a very useful piece of apparatus to have in a conservation laboratory. It is filled with silica gel (see Appendix XI) and evacuated as required by means of a vacuum pump attached to the main water supply (see Fig. 5, p. 156). The vacuum desiccator is used not only to dry objects, but also to store them under dry conditions until such time as they can be lacquered or protected with wax.

[1] Orion Research Inc., 11 Blackstone Street, Cambridge, Massachusetts, U.S.A. Available in U.K. from Electronic Instruments Ltd., Richmond, Surrey.

MECHANICAL METHODS

When a metal object is showing signs of active corrosion, there can be no question that the only way of checking the activity and effecting a permanent cure is to employ chemicals, but this involves using certain 'mechanical' operations as well, in order to facilitate the action of the chemicals and their removal at the conclusion of the treatment. Mechanical methods may be employed directly for cleaning oxidized or tarnished metals, where it is merely a question of removing surface staining; they may also be employed in dealing with rust fragments that are completely oxidized, and no longer subject to chemical change.

Even with the most primitive workshop facilities it is possible to make a simple kit of tools that will be adequate for most purposes.

Making needles and chisels

The commonest tools are needles and small chisels, and the most satisfactory are those that one makes oneself. Needles may be mounted in wooden or metal handles, or in a small pin-vice or mandrel. They should be short and stiff and of varying thicknesses. An etcher's needle, as sold for dry-point work, is a useful instrument for general purposes.

A series of chisels and scrapers can be made from old files that have been annealed in the fire, or from pieces of silver-steel rod of round, square, or rectangular section. The cutting edges are made first of all by grinding, and then the tools are given heat-treatment to adjust the hardness prior to sharpening. The heat-treatment is conducted in two stages as follows:

Hardening. Heat about 2 cm. length of the chisel at the sharp end to bright redness, avoiding over-heating, then immediately quench the metal by dipping the point in water and moving it about rapidly. This will make it dead-hard and brittle, and it will be dark in colour. Polish the metal on a fine emery paper until it is silvery white in order that the temper colours may be observed in the subsequent operation.

Tempering. To toughen the hardened metal, heat the polished chisel 1 cm. or even farther from the cutting-edge—very gently and under strict control—and watch the temper colours moving towards the cutting-edge in the sequence—yellow, straw, purple. Aim to arrest operations by throwing the tool into cold water when a middle-straw colour extends from the cutting-edge some distance up the chisel. If the colour of the cutting-edge has gone to the purple stage, the chisel has been overheated, and the hardening and tempering operations must be done again.[1]

Finally, clean and sharpen on a carborundum slip or oilstone.

Mechanical methods may be defined as picking, chipping and scraping, grinding, cutting, brushing, shot-blasting (grit-spraying), polishing, and burnishing.[2] These will now be considered *seriatim*:

Picking

Picking is a technique apparently so commonplace as to seem unworthy of further description, but there is much more to it than would at first appear. It is not often realized that a force of 1 lb. exerted by means of the point of a needle 1/5000 inch in diameter is equivalent to a pressure of several tons to the square inch. A needle is thus a very potent tool and the correct method of handling it is shown in the diagram (Fig. 6). If pressed near the edge of a brittle surface, the edge will chip off, and the nearer to the edge it is pressed, the less the pressure required to remove tiny flakes from the rust escarpment. Considerable masses of rust can be eliminated, grain by grain, by using a needle in this manner; this is a labour of patience and the operator must be content to advance very slowly, using the minimum of pressure. Any attempt to hasten proceedings by pressing the needle too far from the edge, places unnecessary strain on the

[1] A pale yellow colour represents razor hardness and the metal is brittle; a blue or purple colour implies flexibility as required for springs and hack-saws. Intermediate straw or brown colours are an indication that the steel will be tough enough for use as a chisel and will keep its cutting-edge.

[2] See Maryon, H., *Metalwork and Enamelling*, Chapman & Hall, London, 3rd ed. (revised), 1954.

A. Before treatment—corroded coins fused together as the result of a fire

B. After separation in citric acid and cleaning by reduction

24. HOARD OF ENGLISH SILVER PENNIES (EDWARD I AND EDWARD II)

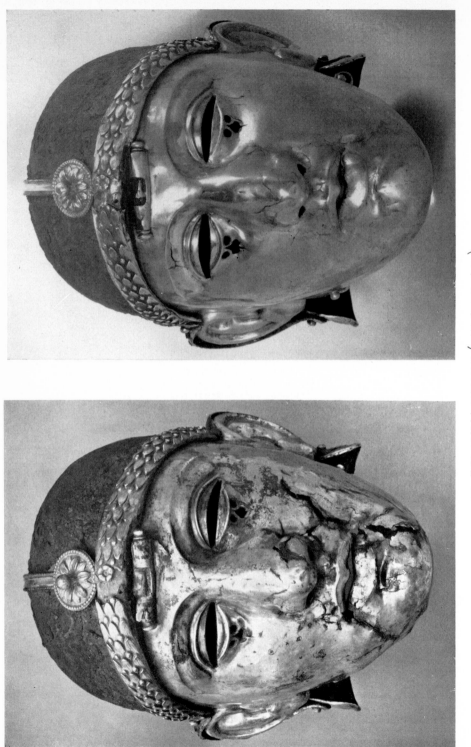

25. THE EMESA HELMET (1ST CENT. A.D.)

Left: As received in the Laboratory. *Right*: After treatment and reconstruction

object and may end in disaster. The needle may be used on occasion as a tiny lever or even as a scraper.

Chipping and scraping

When metallic excrescences have to be removed this can be done by using a small chisel and jeweller's hammer, or a chisel mounted for use as an engraving tool. When the object is very thin and brittle,

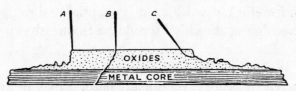

FIG. 6. Mechanical Removal of Rust

(A) Needle held at the correct angle and in the right place (at edge of oxide layer).
(B) Needle held at the correct angle but in a position liable to fracture the metal core.
(C) Angle and position of needle both incorrect.

chisels are not employed as they are liable to fracture the specimen: it is safer in such a case to use the needle or fine engraving tool, but dental burrs may at times be useful to help to reduce thick lumps of oxide.

When incrustations have been softened by reduction, it is useful to be able to remove them in the wet condition, and in cases where it would be unsafe to use metal tools, lest they should cut into the surface, a sharpened stick may be employed, cut to a chisel edge. Cane tools are also useful as scrapers, and these may be used to rub the surface of an object undergoing treatment with zinc and caustic soda, in order to observe the progress of the reduction.

A convenient mechanical instrument for chipping off corrosion products is the so-called electrically driven Vibro-tool,[1] which has a vibrating head carrying a needle or chisel that can be used to exert a continuous pressure easily controlled by the operator. If an area of corrosion should unexpectedly collapse, the Vibro-tool remains in position as no manual pressure is being exerted, and there is less risk of the needle or chisel skidding across the surface as may occur in

[1] Obtainable from Burgess Products Co. Ltd., Sapcote, Leicestershire, England.

the case of manual tools before the operator has time to release the pressure he is exerting. Of course a certain amount of care is necessary to ensure that the instrument is used properly, but with a little practice it can prove a most satisfactory means for mechanical cleaning. It should be noted that the cutting heads supplied commercially are not suitable for conservation purposes; instead a small pin-vice should be cut down and fitted into the tool to hold a needle or small chisel. Also, for efficient working it is essential that the point of the needle or the edge of the chisel should be frequently sharpened.

Grinding

When excrescences are exceptionally hard, it may be preferable to grind them away. For this purpose a small wheel or inverted cone may be used on a dental drilling-machine; alternatively, the grinding may be done with slips of carborundum which can be obtained in various shapes and degrees of roughness. Grinding, however, must not be lightly undertaken, as it can destroy markings in the rust—textile marks, wood grain marks, etc., which may be of significance. On the rusted blade of a sword, for example, they may indicate that a scabbard had been present and decayed *in situ*; or markings on the tang of the weapon may be all that remains to show how the hilt was constructed. It is also necessary to add a warning that grinding may give iron oxide a dull metalic polish so like that of metallic iron itself that it becomes difficult to distinguish between the two.

Cutting

Cutting by using a hack-saw is only employed as a means of separating two objects that are corroded together into a solid mass, and which could not otherwise be separated. Such a mass may be cut as a preliminary to chipping and picking. Slit-saws are sometimes useful, or fret-saws, or even a copper wire hardened by stretching, fixed in a frame and fed with carborundum powder in oil. The quillon of a sword that had slipped along the tang in antiquity and was rusted firmly into position in the wrong place was released by working a small hole through the rust between quillon and tang, inserting the copper wire and 'sawing' a slit through the rust along the tang. The wire was found to be much more effective for the purpose than the finest fret-saw since it was more flexible.

Brushing

Brushing is a frequent accompaniment of all other mechanical processes, its object being to eliminate foreign matter and reveal the progress of the work. Where a good solid iron core remains and objects can be dealt with chemically, occasional brushing in a stream of water is essential to eliminate the by-products of the reaction, which tend to adhere to the specimen in the form of a sludge. Different kinds of brushes can be selected to suit the type of work in hand. Hard nylon tooth-brushes are invaluable for use on bronzes after reduction. If a steel brush is used, it must be dried thereafter or it will rust. A motor-driven brush can lead to a great saving of time when objects are strong enough to stand this treatment. When wire brushes of appropriate coarseness are used, either hand or motor-driven, they will help to scrape away loose rust, but care must be taken that the bristles do not penetrate too deeply into softer parts of the incrustation. Rotating wire brushes, if soft enough,[1] smear the products of reduction over the metal and make the surface appearance more uniform. In some cases it is safer to use graded steel wools rather than brushes. The finest grades are very gentle in action, especially when used with a little oil. Glass brushes are used for fine work such as jewellery or for polishing silver inlays in iron—they are indispensable in the laboratory. For removing hard rust from soft metal inlays, there is no more effective tool than a carborundum pencil, or a slip of this abrasive that has been rubbed down to a point. It enables the rust to be pushed off without rubbing the surface of the inlay.

Shot-blasting (Grit-spraying)

One of the most effective methods of dry-cleaning is to use a jet of particles of fine grit blown from a modified form of spray gun,

[1] A warning is necessary against the indiscriminate use of brass brushes as they tend to impart a yellow brass colour to other metals.

as in the shot-blast cabinet. Several types of cabinet are available commercially. Fine work may be cleaned in the dental cabinet, using a spray of bauxite grit, and at the other extreme, heavy metal castings are dealt with by using various grades of powdered cast iron, but bauxite is suitable for most museum purposes. It is possible by varying the grade of bauxite, the pressure, the distance of the nozzle from the object, the angle of attack, etc., to carry out a variety of cleaning operations quickly and efficiently. This type of cleaning is never used where soft metals are present as it would give them a matt surface. It is useless, therefore, for gold, silver, and lead alloys, but it can be very useful for the removal of mud and soft corrosion products from bronze and iron. Indeed it can safety be employed for the removal of siliceous deposits and dirt from certain kinds of smooth bronze patina without harming the surface. Shot-blasting has also proved to be the best means of removing surface incrustations of various kinds from baked clay tablets (p. 328).

A more refined form of shot-blasting or grit spraying is the air-brasive process in which abrasive particles selected from a range of sizes (10 to 50 microns) and of various degrees of hardness (e.g. aluminium oxide, dolomite, glass beads) are carried through a small nozzle in a stream of air delivered through a hose at pressures that can be adjusted between 40 and 80 lb. per sq. in. (3–6 kg./cm.^{2}). The Airbrasive unit[1] is a very versatile tool because of the many variations that are possible in size of particles, driving pressures, and choice of abrasive powder to suit the particular work in hand. It can be recommended for the mechanical cleaning of many other types of archaeological and ethnographical objects[2] in addition to metals.

Polishing and burnishing

Polishing is done with the finer grades of abrasives such as emery-flour, rouge, diamantine. These are used either as powders or made up with tallow in paste form. Special cloths impregnated with such

[1] Obtainable from S. S. White Industrial Division, 10 East 40th Street, New York 16, N.Y.; Elliott Brothers (London) Ltd., Century Works, Lewisham, London, S.E. 13.
[2] Gibson, B. M., *Studies in Conservation*, 1969, **14**, p. 155.

materials can also be obtained. Abrasives are available in emulsified form as metal polishes, or compounded with paraffin and cotton-wool as polishing wools. The degree of abrasion depends not only on the size of the particles, but on the nature of the abrasive—carborundum powder, for example, being harder and having a greater cutting action than pumice powder of the same degree of fineness. Levigated alumina is a finishing abrasive by means of which a high polish can be obtained on metal that has been previously rubbed up with a series of coarser grits. The final effect of brilliance can be obtained on steel only by burnishing to eliminate all porosity from the surface. This is done either by using a cloth wheel on a buffing-machine or, in the case of fine work, a hard polishing-stone, e.g. haematite, the so-called bloodstone. A chain burnisher is very seldom used, and then only for coarse work in exceptional cases. Burnishing and polishing by abrasives, although of great importance in cleaning jewellery, or in removing rust spots from otherwise bright armour and accoutrements, are, however, techniques of limited application. In cases where the rust is not of a spotty nature, but present as a continuous layer of fine dust on a coat of mail, for example, it should be removed as far as possible with a stiff brush, if the metal is strong enough to stand this. No attempt should be made to attain a bright finish by burnishing with an abrasive, as the links will almost certainly have been weakened by rusting. In such cases sufficient protection is given, after cleaning, by the application of a thin film of wax, which, when brushed, leaves a dull shine of satisfactory appearance that acts as a foil for any embellishments. This type of treatment and finish, by brushing, waxing, and polishing, has been applied with considerable effect in cleaning sword guards and t'suba where the steel is covered with fine ornament and often inlaid with gold and silver.

The most perfect examples of the armourers' craft in existence are, without question, Japanese swords, and if these become spotted with rust, the use of tools or of etching or abrasive materials in an effort to remove the rust does more harm than good. All that can be done is to try to minimize the disfigurement caused by the dark spots of rust on the mirror-like surface of the steel by alternate applications of kerosene and lanolin, and by rubbing with silk or a Selvyt cloth. The surface may be protected thereafter with a thin film of a neutral microcrystalline wax (see Appendix XV). Care is necessary to avoid possible accident, as the swords are often exceedingly sharp.

REPAIRING METAL ANTIQUITIES WITH SOLDER

Metals that are uncorroded may be joined together by soldering, i.e. by alloying them with another metal of lower melting-point that can be made to flow through the joint and, on solidification, act as a bond of union between them. Full details of the process are given in textbooks on metal-working,[1] and it will suffice here to state some general principles that apply to soldering as a method of repairing antiquities.

There are two principal kinds of solder, hard solders which may contain many different metals and melt above 600 °C., and soft solders that are composed of a mixture of lead and tin. In those cases where the nature of the metal permits, it is preferable to use a hard solder as this gives a secure joint. Suitable hard solders which have been successfully used are Easy-Flo silver solder and Sil-fos. For soldering small objects the 'Little Torch'[2] is particularly useful as it gives a needle-point flame that can be precisely adjusted to give an intense heat over a very small area. In other cases it will be necessary to use soft solders, in particular the material known as tinman's solder, Grade K (B.S.S. 219), which contains three parts of tin and two parts of lead. Its melting point is so much lower than that of either tin or lead that it can be used for repairing either of these metals as well as other metals of antiquity, which are in such a condition that a hard solder cannot be safely used.

The surfaces to be joined must be clean, i.e. free from oxidation and tarnish and any other impurity that will prevent the molten solder from coming into intimate contact with the metals with which

[1] e.g. Maryon, H., op. cit.

[2] From Tescon Corporation, 2633 S.E. 4th Street, Minneapolis, Minnesota 55414, U.S.A.

it is to unite. But even the heat required in the process of melting soft solder would cause the metal to become oxidized unless it is protected; it is necessary therefore in the process of soldering to use an oxide-solvent, called a flux. Fluxes are of two kinds: the first contain chlorides such as zinc chloride and ammonium chloride, while the second include those based on resins and fats. The former are very effective but difficult to remove completely afterwards, and for this reason are likely to give rise to subsequent corrosion; the latter are less efficient but do not cause corrosion.

In repairing antiquities, the non-corrosive fluxes are to be preferred, but we are then faced with the difficulty that while the old-fashioned resin fluxes are adequate for work on new metal (as in joining electrical cables, where absence of corrosion is an important factor), they are intractable where there is intercrystalline oxidation as in the case of ancient metal. A compromise is thus necessary, and it is to be found in the proprietary materials sold as 'non-corrosive' or 'activated resin' fluxes. These still require the joints to be clean, but are easier to work than the simple resin fluxes.

COMMERCIAL FLUXES AND SOLDERING FLUIDS

As it is important to have a working knowledge of the properties of fluxes used in the repair of metals, the following notes relating to some of the commonest that are commercially available may be of interest. Comments are based upon workshop experience rather than laboratory testing.

Corrosive fluxes

(1) Baker's Soldering Fluid. This is recommended for general-purpose work, such as repairs to tin, brass, copper, or iron articles, and for joining and backing-up electrotypes. The joint requires thorough washing.

(2) Fryolux. This solder paste is very useful for tinning two surfaces that have to be closely fitted, such as a piece of brass tubing telescoped into another piece. Useful for 'sweating' screw heads into their sockets.

(3) Multicore, ARAX. This flux is very good for general-purpose work and can be used with stainless steel.

(4) Solderine. This does not have the same self-cleaning properties as 1, but is satisfactory on surfaces that can be very thoroughly cleaned before application. It is less corrosive than 1, 2, and 3.

Non-corrosive fluxes

(5) Multicore Solder Paste, Cored Ersin Solder, and Liquid Ersin Flux. All three have been found satisfactory on cleaned surfaces, the Cored Ersin Solder being ideal for electrical contacts.

(6) Alcho-Re. This solder paste has been found to be satisfactory when applied to surfaces made spotlessly clean beforehand.

When ancient metal is found to be very difficult to solder, the best flux to use is probably a mixture composed of 70 parts of zinc chloride and 30 parts of ammonium chloride. This has the advantage of melting at 180 °C., but it is very highly corrosive. When it is used in making a joint, the object should be washed immediately afterwards in water acidified with a few drops of hydrochloric acid in order to decompose any insoluble zinc oxychloride that may remain on the joint, and it should finally be thoroughly washed in water made faintly alkaline with a little washing soda.

Soldering is required most frequently in repairing brittle metals, e.g. speculum or ancient silver, or in mending fine work such as that on brooches, handles, etc., where leverage would tend to rupture joints made by adhesives. Soldering is often used as a temporary fixing in 'tacking' cracked metal together as is done in the reconstruction of crushed metal objects. When the original shape has been re-established, a permanent soldered joint can be made to take the place of the temporary fixings which are easily removed. (Cf. treatment of the Emesa silver helmet, p. 234.)

In exceptional cases it may be necessary to apply a modern metal patch to an antiquity. This should bear an unobtrusive but distinctive mark to indicate that it is modern; a small depression, for example, such as can be made by using a spring-loaded centre punch.

Soft solder can be given a coating of copper by degreasing the solder with trichloroethane and then rubbing it with a moistened crystal of copper sulphate. The copper surface thus obtained is less obtrusive than the white metal. Soft solder that has been applied to silver can be concealed by degreasing and then silver-plating. This is done by 'ragging', i.e. plating with a glass rod anode around which is wrapped silver wire in contact with a small piece of soft rag moistened with a cyanide electrolyte.[1] The solder is rubbed with the rag whilst a small current is passing (at about 3 volts) and it gradually becomes covered with a thin coating of silver.

Summary

The general methods of treatment that are applied in dealing with corroded objects have been described, namely, reduction methods (electrochemical and electrolytic), mechanical methods, washing, drying, and repair. The action of chemical reagents in arresting corrosion and cleaning and restoring metal objects is of equal importance as a general method of treatment, but, as reagents are selective in action, they are dealt with in the specialized chapters that follow.

[1] For the composition of solutions and methods of operation see *The Canning Handbook on Electro-plating*, W. Canning & Co. Ltd., Birmingham, 18, 20th edn. 1966.

IX

GOLD AND ELECTRUM

GOLD is found in nature in the metallic condition as a rich yellow, soft metal, commonly associated with quartz and certain sands. It does not corrode, it is not dissolved under natural conditions, but it is often found alloyed with the baser metals, silver and copper. The presence of silver in gold gives pale-coloured alloys in which the degree of paleness is in proportion to the amount of silver present, and such alloys have been known since the time of Pliny as 'electrum'. Both gold and electrum have been used for coinage and jewellery from the earliest times.[1]

When gold is found alloyed with copper, there is usually some silver present as well, and although such alloys may be very pale yellow or even greenish yellow when freshly cast or cleaned, they lose their pallor after years of burial in the ground and acquire a warm yellow hue. This is known as surface enrichment and is due to the action of salts in removing the baser metals from the surface of the alloy, leaving a film of pure gold.

It is usually desirable to preserve the rich colour, even though it may only be a surface enrichment, and in cleaning, care should be taken not to rub the surface because its quality is easily lost. Incrustations of lime can be removed from the gold by applying very dilute nitric acid (1 per cent) locally with a match-stick, a small brush, or a capillary glass tube. Siliceous or muddy incrustations on gold may be removed by soaking in a 2 per cent solution of a surface-active agent such as Lissapol N. Organic remains are softened by immersion for a few minutes in caustic soda (2 per cent) and removed with a match-

[1] Sutherland, C. H. V., *Gold. Its Beauty, Power and Allure*, Thames & Hudson Ltd., London, 1959.

stick. If incrustations resist these attentions, they may sometimes be disintegrated by using a fine jet of steam.

Gold is sometimes found having a clear purplish red or rose-pink colour. In the eighteenth to twentieth dynasties of Egypt, a striking rose-pink colour was imparted to gold used for personal ornaments, horse-trappings, and sequins. On opening a box of royal robes in Tutankhamun's tomb, for example, it was observed that the garments had been decorated with sequins in a variety of shapes and, although the textiles had perished, it was clear that in one instance at least a garment had borne a stitched panel of massed sequins regularly positioned, rose-pink alternating with yellow gold, to give a diaper effect, thus proving that the pink colour was not an effect of age. A pink sequin from the Tutankhamun robe was analysed and found to contain in addition to silver and some copper, 0.85 per cent of iron which was the colouring constituent. The pink colour was confined to the surface of the sequin back and front.

Attempts to reproduce this coloured alloy were successfully carried out by R. W. Wood,[1] who fused gold with iron and obtained an alloy having the same colour and micro-structure as the sequins. If this was the technique applied in the early dynasties of Egypt, it would be necessary to suppose that the iron was introduced in the form of a mineral from which it could be released when in the crucible, as the melting-point of iron is 1,535 °C. An independent examination of the sequin problem made at the British Museum Research Laboratory has shown that when gold containing silver and copper is fused with iron pyrites and soda, some of the silver and copper combines with the sulphur in the pyrites and rises to the surface of the molten gold as a dross, leaving the gold alloyed with iron. When this gold is hammered into sheets and given heat treatment, it develops a superficial colour characteristic of the Egyptian sequins. Iron pyrites (M.P. 1,171 °C.) has about the same melting-point as pure gold (M.P. 1,063 °C.) and often has the yellow metallic appearance of gold, for which it might easily be mistaken; indeed it has been called 'fool's gold'. If by chance some of this material were inadvertently mixed

[1] Wood, R. W., *J. Egypt. Arch.*, 1934, **20**, pp. 62–5.

with gold scrap for the crucible, it would be possible for the rose-pink colour to be developed accidentally. If such were the case, it would explain why this particular technique appeared sporadically in these dynasties and was later forgotten.

Gold coins sometimes have what appears to be a variety of this same rich red patina, but here it is an acquired characteristic, the colour having developed by contamination and possibly heating during the life of the coins. At its best this adventitious red can be very handsome, and is regarded by collectors of coins as a valuable patina worth preserving, but it is easily rubbed off and when once lost it is virtually impossible to restore the rich colour by artificial means.

Although gold is so durable, it is a very soft metal and can be beaten out to form the thin leaves used for manuscript illumination and for applying to *gesso*. It can, moreover, be dissolved in mercury fairly easily to give gold amalgam. This substance has the consistency of butter and when rubbed over clean silver or copper, it adheres. The mercury may be readily volatilized by heating and the silver or copper thus becomes covered with a continuous layer of gold. The process is known as 'mercury gilding' or 'fire gilding'.

It was interesting to find both techniques used together on the dragon heads that ornamented the periphery of the shield from the Sutton Hoo ship burial, now in the British Museum. The original heads were executed in bronze that had been gilt by the mercury gilding process, but certain repairs had been made in antiquity and some of the heads had been replaced by models in *gesso* covered with gold leaf.

Gold is likely to be found as decoration on armour and accoutrements, on buckles, on bronze statuettes, especially in the eyes of the figures, and on silver dishes, in which case it may be limited to the embellishment of reserves of ornament. Silver so decorated is said to be 'parcel gilt'. This type of decoration was exploited in Persia during the Seljuk period for the embellishment of horse-trappings, rose-water sprinklers, incense-burners, vases, dishes, and caskets. When gold is present in reserve ornament on silver, special care is required in cleaning because the gold is thin and the surface soft, and the gold reserves could be easily damaged by the cleaning materials used to remove tarnish from the surrounding silver.

CLEANING GILT METAL

Metals that are gilt should not be reduced because of the danger of losing the gilding, but if the gold overlies solid copper or bronze, it is sometimes safe to apply the Rochelle salt process (see p. 250) for cleaning the base metal. If the base metal is encrusted with corrosion products, however, and it is known that a film of gold exists beneath or among them, the only possible line to take is that of mechanical cleaning, using needles under a binocular microscope at a magnification of some ten diameters. Very dilute nitric acid (1 per cent) can be used to clean the surface of the gold when it is exposed to view, but acid should not be used to soften the base incrustation, otherwise the ornament may become detached. To reveal the gold can be a long and arduous task, but the results are rewarding if the shape and decorative appearance can be recovered. In the case of silver-gilt objects covered with copper corrosion products derived from the base silver alloy the incrustation can be removed by local treatment with a 5 per cent solution of formic acid applied with a swab of cotton-wool.

When gilding is present on bronze statuary that is exposed to soot deposits and accumulations of dust, it requires occasional cleaning, and as dirt of this nature is usually acidic, it responds readily to washing with dilute ammonia. The statuary should be well washed with water thereafter. This simple type of cleaning was applied to the royal effigies in Westminster Abbey, and the results were very satisfactory.

CRUSHED GOLD OBJECTS

Objects of gold are often found in a distorted condition when they are dug from the ground, and there may be a strong temptation to try to fold the metal back into shape. This must be resisted as it is not the easy task that it appears to be. Pure gold is readily malleable, but when it is alloyed, as it usually is to some extent, the metal becomes brittle on ageing, and mechanical manipulation should only be undertaken after scientific examination has shown that the metal is of such a composition that reshaping can be considered a reasonably safe procedure in the hands of an expert.

Many examples of the restoration of crushed golden objects, by careful annealing and tooling back to shape, are provided by the material excavated at Ur of the Chaldees by Sir Leonard Woolley. One of the finest specimens is the wig-helmet of Mes-Kalam-Shar, made from a single plate of 15 carat gold, and weighing slightly over one kg. A more intricate reconstruction was that of the gold bull's head forming the frontal ornament of a lyre. This was brought to the Laboratory as a complex, held together by wax and bandages, so that the relative position of the various pieces could be studied at leisure. The gold mask, ears, and horns were first recovered, and as the gold, though badly crushed, was much thinner than that of the helmet, it was correspondingly easier to manipulate. The original shape of the animal's head was re-established, and having done this it was possible to reset the eyes and reassemble the various pieces of carved lapis lazuli forming the beard.

The special tools used for such work are metal and wooden stakes, levers of various kinds, mallets of box-wood, hide and horn, and shaped sand-bags of leather.[1]

[1] Maryon, H., op. cit.

X

SILVER

SILVER is a soft white lustrous metal which fuses at about 960 °C. It is found locally in the metallic condition (as native silver), but is more generally distributed in mineral form, two of the commonest minerals being argentite (silver sulphide), and cerargyrite (silver chloride), commonly known as 'horn silver'. The sulphide is black in colour, and the chloride a dirty purple or slate grey. The pure metal is malleable and ductile, and is capable of taking a high polish, and for this reason has always attracted the craftsman. It has enjoyed a deserved popularity in most countries of the world for objects of personal adornment and decorative metal-work. Gold and silver have been used for coinage throughout the ages, and for this reason the ratio of values has always been a significant figure, the relationship fluctuating with the scarcity of one or other metal. Partington[1] quotes a number of examples illustrating how the relative values changed at different periods and in different localities, observing that in the earliest periods of civilization gold was the commoner metal, because it could be obtained from rivers, whereas silver had to be obtained from the hills where it occurred, not as a surface deposit, but buried, often deeply, in the ground.

Both gold and silver were in general use at Ur of the Chaldees in the Early Sumerian Period, at a time when silver was a rarity in Egypt. Indeed, silver was never available there in any quantity until the Graeco–Roman period, and it is not surprising, therefore, that the robbers who entered Tutankhamun's tomb were found to have concentrated first upon the silver.

[1] Partington, J. R., *Origins and Development of Applied Chemistry*, Longmans, London, 1935.

PATINA AND CORROSION

In silver objects there is generally a clear-cut distinction between the corrosion products derived from relatively pure silver and those from base silver alloys containing an appreciable amount of copper. In the former case the products are silver sulphide and silver chloride, whereas in the latter case the copper corrodes preferentially, giving rise to cuprite and malachite. A distinction must also be drawn between corrosion products that are bulky and unsightly and those that are laid down as a thin uniform layer which may enhance the aesthetic appearance of the object. Thus one occasionally comes across objects of ancient silver having a shiny black patina of silver sulphide, and this is worth retaining for its decorative quality. A thin uniform film of silver chloride can also form the basis of an agreeable patina, as in the case of silver objects excavated from soils containing little chloride. T'ang silver from the *loess* has sometimes a beautiful patina of a chalky texture and pale lilac colour, stained pink and green with cuprous oxide and malachite respectively. As this patina is stable and enhances the appearance of the object, it is desirable to preserve it. If the patina is concealing fine ornament, a compromise is necessary, however, and it may then be permissible to expose the ornament by rubbing with a mild abrasive. The impregnated cloths that are sold for polishing metals are suitable for this purpose (Duraglit, etc.) provided the appropriate grade of cloth is used, i.e. one for cleaning silver: those sold for cleaning copper and brass are too drastic in action and would abrade the metal unnecessarily.

When silver objects have been buried for long period of time in salty soil, they are largely transformed on the exposed surfaces into stable silver chloride (horn silver) usually having a grey earthy appearance of no aesthetic value, but occasionally having a compact surface that may enhance the appearance of the object. Also deformation may be considerable, owing to the expansion accompanying the change from metal to mineral, but, as it is stable, treatment is only required to improve the appearance of the object, to expose details of ornament, or to recover the original shape of the object.

26. SILVER HANGING BOWL FROM ST. NINIAN'S ISLE, SHETLAND, SHOWING
CONDITION WHEN EXCAVATED

27. EQUIPMENT USED FOR THE
CONSOLIDATION WITH EPOXY
RESIN SHOWING BOWL MOUNTED
ON TURNTABLE

A. Interior

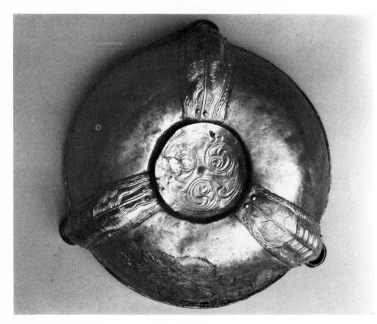

B. Exterior

28. SILVER HANGING BOWL FROM ST. NINIAN'S ISLE, SHETLAND, AFTER
REMOVAL OF CORROSION AND CONSOLIDATION

Horn silver is tough and the object will remain robust as long as the incrustation of silver chloride is left in position, so that it must be borne in mind that the object may be much weakened if the silver chloride is removed. Another factor of importance is that silver which has suffered long-continued corrosion may have a discontinuous stratified structure, so that when the corrosion products are removed the remaining silver will be in a very fragile condition. This is clearly seen in the sectioned silver bead from Ur (Pl. 16). Both these factors had to be taken into account in carrying out the special treatment of the St. Ninian's silver hanging bowl (see p. 237). In some cases corrosion may have gone so far that little silver metal remains; it will then be necessary to adopt a special treatment of consolidative reduction (see p. 224).

ELECTROCHEMICAL REDUCTION OF SILVER OBJECTS

Electrochemical methods may be applied to remove corrosion from silver. Besides the aluminium and soda method referred to for removing tarnish (p. 240), a number of other methods are available that give satisfactory results in dealing with corroded silver. For example, it may be that in using 30 per cent formic acid as a solvent the cleaning has not been entirely effective; in the event, zinc or aluminium powder may be added and the mixture heated for a time. An alternative to the formic acid and zinc is to use zinc and caustic soda, which has a more pronounced softening effect on the corrosion. The horn silver becomes slimy after a time, and the object considerably weakened; brushing during reduction must be gentle and frequent, especially towards the latter stages. The reduced silver chloride incrustation takes the form of a white spongy deposit which is easily removed, and the residue can be consolidated by burnishing with a glass rod to restore the metal-like quality. The object is then boiled in several changes of distilled water, or allowed to remain under running hot water for several hours, but in any event the washing is completed in several changes of distilled water until all chlorides are removed. The intensive method of washing (p. 200) can also be applied to silver.

After treatment, the silver is dried in an oven at 105 °C. and it should be kept there for some hours, as the surface of reduced silver tends to be porous. It may sometimes be preferable to dry in a vacuum desiccator (see p. 202), as oven-drying tends to produce a film of tarnish.

ELECTROLYTIC REDUCTION OF SILVER OBJECTS

1. *Normal reduction methods.* When silver objects are covered with a fairly thick layer of silver chloride or silver sulphide and there is a good solid core of metal underneath, reduction may be carried out in the usual manner using 5 per cent caustic soda solution as the electrolyte and iron electrodes. The superficial layer of the corrosion products is reduced to powdery silver that is brushed off, so as to reveal the underlying uncorroded silver. A variation, particularly to be recommended in the case of this metal, is to use formic acid of 15 per cent strength as the electrolyte, instead of caustic soda. This method was very useful in dealing with the following rather unusual specimen. The silver casing attached to a Greek vase of blue glass was badly corroded, and as the vase was of such a shape that the silver could not be removed for treatment it was necessary to select a method that would clean the silver without harming the glass. Choice fell upon electrolytic reduction in 15 per cent formic acid, using anodes of stainless steel, and the result was considered to be entirely satisfactory. A caustic soda electrolyte could not have been used here as it would have been likely to attack the glass.

Stainless steel anodes are not an essential in using formic acid— indeed prolonged electrolysis in formic acid leads to the steel being attacked and there may then be a deposition of iron on the silver. With iron anodes in formic acid this deposition would take place even more quickly. There are no such complications when using anodes of graphite or carbon with formic acid. Good results are obtained, for example, using carbon anodes with a 12 volt supply adjusted to give a current density of 1 amp. per sq. dm.

During the electrolytic reduction of a base silver object any copper minerals in the incrustation are reduced to metallic copper, and there is a tendency for a film of copper to be left on the object. This film can be removed (after washing to remove the electrolyte) by immersing the object in a 20 per cent solution of silver nitrate in distilled water. By this means the film of copper is replaced by silver powder which is easily brushed off. If, however, much copper is present, the object should be first treated with formic acid (p. 228) before reduction.

Another variation that may be employed where it is desired to remove small areas of silver chloride or where it is inadvisable to immerse the object in the electrolytic tank is to carry out local reduction by the 'rag' method.

For this purpose a small swab of cotton-wool moistened with a 30 per cent solution of formic acid is placed on the area of corrosion, and a fine metal rod (such as a stainless steel sewing needle), used as the anode, is pressed into the swab and another needle used as the cathode is held against an area where uncorroded silver is present; the normal source unit for direct current with an e.m.f. of 12 volts is used. The swab is changed when it becomes saturated with the products of reduction, and each time this is done the area being reduced is washed with a swab moistened with distilled water, dried with a piece of tissue paper, and inspected to see how the reduction is progressing. Treatment is continued until reduction has been completed. Care must be taken to ensure that the two needles do not touch free metal, otherwise there will be a short circuit; also the amount of electrolyte must be sufficient just to wet the area under the swab without allowing any excess to run across the object. If any silver sulphide is present in the corrosion, this will produce hydrogen sulphide which will tarnish the cleaned silver. This tarnish can, however, be easily removed in the normal manner. This treatment was particularly successful in the treatment of silver-gilt patens and chalices removed from the tombs of Archbishop de Grey and Archbishop Ludham in York Minster (Pl. 18).

2. *Consolidative reduction.* When an object of high silver content is so heavily corroded that little silver metal remains, as may happen

in some cases, it may be sufficient to carry out mechanical cleaning to expose surface features, but such treatment will not restore the original appearance of the silver. If it is desired to do so, then a special method of consolidative reduction must be used, whereby the silver is reduced throughout its thickness to massive metallic silver.

The essential feature of this process of reduction is the concept of 'dissolve and deposit' which is achieved by the use of partially

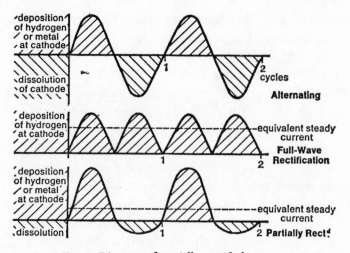

FIG. 7. Diagram of partially rectified current

rectified current; this type of current will successively reduce, then dissolve, and then deposit, all these reactions following each other rapidly at the frequency of the electric supply, as indicated diagrammatically in Fig. 7. At the same time the reduction must be carried out at a very low current density to prevent the evolution of copious hydrogen gas that would tend to disturb the reduced silver. Details of the circuit required are given in Appendix XVIII.

An instructive example of the value of this new method of reduction was the treatment devised by Organ[1] for the silver lyre found by Woolley in 1927 in the Great Death Pit of the Royal

[1] Organ, R. M., in *Application of Science in Examination of Works of Art*, Boston, Massachusetts, Museum of Fine Art, 1965, pp. 126–44.

Graves at Ur believed to date from 2500 B.C. After excavation the pieces of the lyre, many of them in a crushed condition, were reinforced with layers of bandage and reassembled on a new wooden framework (the original framework had completely decomposed during burial in the ground), using paraffin wax as consolidant and adhesive, and put on display in the British Museum (Pl. 19A). Although the form of the lyre was recovered in this way, it no longer had the appearance of having once been made of silver. This was indeed not surprising, because during the long period of burial in salty ground the original silver had been completely converted into silver chloride and now had a dark-brown colour. The question therefore arose as to whether it would be possible to improve its appearance by restoring the silver colour. This was a difficult problem owing to the extensive mineralization of the silver, and when a fragment of the lyre was examined under the microscope in cross-section, it was found that the lyre, which at the time of burial had presented a sequence of wood, silver, soil, and matting, had been converted into a sequence of corrosion layers consisting of silver chloride, calcareous matter, and an outer incrustation of soil, calcareous matter, and silver chloride. It was evident that a satisfactory method of treatment must satisfy three important criteria: firstly, conversion of the dirty-brown silver chloride into massive bright metallic silver; secondly, the restoration of sufficient ductility to the regenerated silver to permit the distorted pieces being bent back into shape; and thirdly, the preservation of any surface markings that were of archaeological significance. Numerous experiments were carried out on other fragments of completely mineralized silver excavated at Ur, details of which are given in Organ's publication, and eventually a satisfactory procedure was worked out. This involved the following sequence of operations:

(a) Paraffin wax used by Woolley was removed with hot toluene by refluxing in an extractor.

(b) The wax-free pieces were soaked in 30 per cent formic acid to remove adherent calcareous material.

(c) Fine silver wires were attached to the back of the pieces using polymethacrylate resin (Tensol 7) to conduct the electric current and to reinforce the fragile pieces.

(d) The reinforced fragments were immersed in a 3 per cent solution of sodium hydroxide and connected to the negative terminal of a control unit for electrolytic reduction, using a carbon rod fitted inside a sleeve of porous polythene as anode. Electrolysis was carried out at a current density of 10 mA/dm² using partially rectified current for periods of up to three or four weeks until the whole surface of the piece had become silvery in colour when it was immediately removed. Details of the circuit for partially rectified current are given in Appendix XVIII.

(e) After removal from the electrolytic tank the pieces were rinsed in cold distilled water only until the electrical conductivity of the last bath of wash-water was found to be about 15 micro-mhos.

The pieces were then dried at room temperature and the surface of the regenerated silver polished lightly with a fine glass-bristle brush.

When treating the two faces of the sound-box slight modifications were necessary owing to their large size. The wax was removed in stages by dabbing the front surface with swabs of cotton-wool moistened with toluene, and then a temporary facing of mulberry paper was attached using an aqueous solution of polyvinyl alcohol. The reinforced sound-box was then removed from the wooden backing used by Woolley, thus exposing the waxed backing of bandages. These were removed with toluene and the same series of processes detailed above were carried out. (See Pl. 20).

In order to permit the pieces to be reshaped, a process for impregnating any voids in the regenerated silver with more Tensol 7 was adopted, and the impregnated pieces were heated gently to a temperature of about 130 °C., at which the Tensol 7 would soften, so that the pieces could be bent into shape while still hot. After reshaping, any excess of Tensol 7 remaining on the surface of the silver was removed by swabbing with chloroform. Finally a special framework was made in Perspex, and the various pieces of the lyre were re-attached to it using a special wax-resin mixture of high M.P. composed of 25 parts beeswax and 75 parts Cosmolloid 80H. As well as illustrating the value of consolidative reduction, this example also shows how a complex problem of restoration can be carried out in a logical manner. Pl. 19B shows the lyre reassembled after treatment.

COPPER INCRUSTATIONS ON SILVER

Reference has already been made (p. 193) to the cathodic protection of silver in the presence of corroding copper. A common result of such action is the formation of a heavy deposit of copper corrosion products on the silver that is itself uncorroded, and this may be difficult to remove. The usual procedure is to get rid of as much as possible of the incrustation by mechanical methods (picking, grinding, etc.) first of all, and then to endeavour to eliminate the rest by the action of selective solvents. Some examples will now be given to illustrate the treatment of silver objects by the application of solvents, selected because of the specific properties they possess.

(i) *Ammonia*. In the presence of air ammonia slowly dissolves copper and it may be claimed that no reagent is more effective for cleaning silver that has become encrusted with a massive deposit of copper by long contact with the baser metal. Ammonia, however, must be used with restraint where silver chloride is present, because it dissolves this substance and, if applied to corroded silver, would leave the metal in a much weakened condition. It softens organic remains such as residues of wood, skin, textiles, etc., and is thus a general cleaning-agent where such types of incrustation are concerned. It is used in concentrated form (density 0·88) in a fume cupboard.

(ii) *Potassium cyanide*. This is highly poisonous and seldom required, but it is a very potent stain remover. It is *not* applied in the form of a solution and it should on no account be used where acid is present or be allowed to come in contact with the skin. For removing stains from silver, a small pellet of the potassium cyanide is held with forceps and rubbed on the wet silver, and in dissolving a little of the silver it will at the same time remove most stains.

(iii) *Formic acid.* This has the particular merit that it may be used to dissolve copper compounds without affecting silver or silver chloride.

A striking illustration of the use of formic acid was in the treatment given to a silver cup dating from the fifteenth century B.C. from Enkomi-Alasia in Cyprus which was covered with a green encrustation.[1] This incrustation had originated partly from the copper constituent of the silver alloy and partly no doubt from contact with base metal in the ground, and it gave the impression that the cup was made of bronze (Pl. 22A), concealing the fact that it was actually of silver elaborately decorated with niello and gold. The nature of the object having been discovered by X-ray examination, (Pl. 21B) formic acid was selected as the cleaning agent, and after a successful experiment on one of the fragments, the cup was immersed for twenty minutes in a boiling solution composed of one volume of commercial formic acid and two volumes of water. By such treatment the green incrustation was removed, leaving patches of cuprite and reduced copper which yielded eventually to local applications of ammonia (0·88). The ornament around the cup was revealed in surprising freshness, the niello for the most part being in excellent condition and the gold inlays rich in colour without showing any evidence of blanching (Pl. 21C). The silver proved on analysis to be alloyed with 3·4 per cent of gold and 9 per cent of copper.

(iv) *Silver nitrate.* For removing a thin film of metallic copper from silver, the use of a solution of silver nitrate is preferable (see p. 223).

(v) *Ammonium thiosulphate and thiourea.* A useful process for the removal of thick horn silver (silver chloride) is to glass-brush[2] the surface with a 15 per cent aqueous solution of ammonium thiosulphate containing 1 per cent of Lissapol N. The thiosulphate may be replaced by 5 per cent thiourea although this requires to be rubbed more vigorously and is best reserved for cast silver such as buckles and ornaments that are rigid enough to withstand the mechanical stresses involved. The thiourea method is, however, very mild in its

---

[1] Schaeffer, C. F. A., *Enkomi-Alasia* (Excavations 1946–50), 1952, Klincksieck, Paris.

[2] If the brush is provided with a metal holder, it should be washed frequently otherwise the holder will soon become corroded.

chemical action and can be perfectly controlled. It can be used where niello decoration is retained in horn silver, and for this reason alone it forms a very useful addition to the methods available for conservation.

(vi) *Citric acid.* This is a convenient cleaning-agent for corroded copper, and hence for base silver covered with green corrosion compounds. It has the merits of being non-poisonous and odourless, but it must be used with a certain reserve as it is a non-selective stripping agent, and even in 5 per cent aqueous solution may tend to overclean. It is used as a pickle for separating objects such as base silver or copper coins that have become corroded together (see below).

It should be noted that in certain circumstances it may be necessary to use more than one reagent. Thus, for example, in the case of the silver lamp (Pls. 15A and B) the bulk of the copper incrustation was cut away, but a resistant layer of metallic copper remained firmly adhering to part of the frail silver. The removal of this necessitated prolonged treatment in ammonia followed by local treatment with potassium cyanide. After all traces of the incrustation had been removed the lamp was dark in colour; it was given a bath in warm formic acid (about 30 per cent strength) for a short time (twenty minutes) to brighten the metal and, after washing and drying, the silver was toughened in the furnace as described later.

COMPOSITE OBJECTS

Silver has been used so widely in decoration that all sorts of problems are presented in the conservation of objects of a composite nature containing the metal in conjunction with other materials.

In dealing with silver inlays it is safest to adopt the mechanical methods which have already been described (p. 203). If chemical treatment is essential, it may be necessary to isolate the inlay with a wall of plasticine or clay, but there is always the danger of chemicals seeping beneath the inlay and presenting a problem in washing. When washing after treatment is impossible, as with a fretted silver ornament set in lacquer, cleaning can only be satisfactorily accomplished by the use of abrasive cloths. The problem of revealing silver inlays in rusted iron generally resolves itself into adopting methods for removing the rust which tends to overrun and obscure the silver. Niello, a black decoration, has been used for ornamenting silver from very early times. Pliny[1] refers to the technique having been employed in Egypt, though few examples have survived. There are, however, black decorations still extant on the dagger-blades from Mycenae dating to 1500 B.C. and the niello technique is well established in Roman, Byzantine, and Anglo-Saxon art. Examples of black inlays from many sources have been subjected to laboratory examination by Moss[2] who developed micro-tests for their identification and showed that prior to the eleventh century niello corresponded with the mineral acanthite (silver sulphide), whereas subsequently a fusible mixture of silver and copper sulphides was used that corresponded to the mineral stromeyerite. Lead sulphide (galena) was sometimes present in addition.

Niello ornament might be difficult to discern on heavily tarnished silver, or might even be eclipsed by the spread of incrustation; it is necessary, therefore, to add a warning that the application of any electrochemical process would reduce the black surface of the niello to metal, and thus destroy the decoration. Should doubt exist, electrochemical methods are best avoided; but if the reduction has been brief, the black colour of the niello can be exposed again by the judicious use of metal polish, the reduction effect being purely superficial owing to the high electrical resistance of the niello relative to that of the silver.

Another factor to be taken into account when there is niello decoration is that the niello may be lying between layers of corrosion. In such cases the use of chemical reagents or any electrochemical or electrolytic process of reduction is out of the question. Recourse must be had to careful mechanical cleaning under a binocular microscope to pick off the upper corrosion layer so as to reveal the niello decoration. If such treatment is carried out correctly, the result

---

[1] *Natural History*, Book xxxiii, 131.
[2] Moss, A. A., *Studies in Conservation*, 1953, **1**, pp. 49–62.

can be very rewarding, as is evident from the great improvement in appearance of an elaborately decorated brooch found at Canterbury. Pl. 22 shows the brooch before treatment and Pl. 23 after treatment.

CLEANING SILVER COINS

Old silver coins that have been found in the ground provide examples of decay which will vary according to the quality of the alloy and the nature of the soil.

Identification of the coins is a primary requirement, and treatment is carried out with a view to making the ornament distinct and the inscription, if any, readable. It is sometimes the case, however, that an inscription is more legible in the corroded state, and for this reason it should be studied before treatment. After such preliminary study, a hoard of coins is assorted into groups according to the different forms of treatment required. In some cases corrosion may have proceeded in such a manner that the surface of the coin is black and wax-like, and very little metal remains. This is characteristic of a sulphide incrustation, and such coins had best be treated only by washing and drying. When the surface is cracked or the coin is very porous it may be reinforced by impregnation with a microcrystalline wax.

More usually, a preponderance of metal remains, and the incrustation is due to silver chloride; but silver coins are generally debased and the incrustation will be found to be mixed with the products of the corrosion of the copper present in the silver alloy. The coins may then be adhering firmly together in masses. A conglomerate of this nature may be broken down by formic acid treatment or by soaking in 5 per cent citric acid, although sometimes the individual coins are more easily released by reducing the mass with zinc and caustic soda. The alkaline Rochelle salt process (p. 250) has advantages where the silver is greatly debased with copper, but in this case the coins must be carefully brushed from time to time since the cuprite which cements them together is dissolved by the Rochelle salt exceedingly slowly and then only in the presence of air.

In the British Museum Research Laboratory, where coins frequently arrive for treatment in hoards, they are dealt with in a machine constructed on the principle of the ball mill. This apparatus takes the form of a deep rectangular tank made of polyvinyl chloride mounted at an angle of about 45° from the vertical ('tumbler tank') and arranged to revolve slowly about its longer axis. It is driven by an electric motor. For cleaning base silver coins the tank is filled with an appropriate reagent such as 30 per cent formic acid, and a few loose coins are added to act as hammers when the tank revolves and so help to separate other coins from the conglomerate mass. As the tank revolves the contents fall four times from the flat walls during every revolution and these movements assist the chemical action so that the coins are soon separated. Individual coins are washed with water thereafter and dried in hot sawdust in the tumbler tank; they emerge clean and with a slight polish which seems to heighten the contrast of light and shade and thus enable lettering and ornament to be more easily studied.

Before the installation of the tumbler tank, electrolytic reduction was employed, and while this procedure was found to give equally satisfactory results, it involved more labour. It was applied, for example, in cleaning a hoard of 15,000 silver coins from Dorchester. During reduction the coins required continuous attention and had to be frequently removed and brushed in order to prevent the reduced incrustations from being deposited as a resistant metallic film on the coins. The small mass of corroded silver coins shown in Pls. 24A and B had become agglomerated as a result of fire. The mass was loosened to a considerable extent by soaking for some hours in a 5 per cent solution of citric acid, final cleaning being done by placing the coins in stirrups of copper wire suspended from the cathode bar of the electrolytic tank.

RESHAPING OF CRUSHED SILVER OBJECTS

Ancient silver objects are often recovered from excavations in a fragmentary or in a crushed condition, and since the silver will usually be in a brittle condition, it will be necessary to toughen it and make it ductile before the repair and reshaping of the object can be carried out. Normally the silver can be toughened by annealing at a dull red heat. The operation requires dexterity and experience, because silver melts at about 960 °C. and there may be impurities present that lower the melting-point of the metal considerably. The metal begins to glow at about 600 °C. If there are any mineral compounds of silver and copper present, such a temperature cannot be attained without fusion. Silver chloride, for example, melts at 455 °C. and cuprous chloride (nantokite) at 422 °C. Where doubt exists, or where the silver is very thin, the minimum of heat should be used. Toughening actually begins to take place at about 250 °C., and if the silver is placed in an oven, the temperature of which rises in about two hours to 400 °C., this should suffice for most purposes.

In the case of sound metal, free from salts, the silver may be heated in an electric furnace, the temperature of which is adjusted to 600–650 °C. The best results are obtained in the electric furnace: if a gas furnace is used, it is difficult to prevent the silver from blackening unless all fumes can be excluded during heating. When silver is debased with copper, heating will cause the formation of a black surface film of copper oxide. Staining due to oxidation is, however, easily removed in a bath of sulphuric acid (5 per cent).

In the case of silver that has been crushed out of shape, heat treatment is always applied before any attempt is made to bend the metal. When once toughened the metal may be worked back gradually to shape with the fingers, or with wooden tools covered with chamois, a process requiring much patience because the softened metal hardens again on cold working, and repeated heat treatment may be required as the work proceeds. When dents have to be removed from modern silver, there is more latitude, and it is usually possible to rub out small deformities, without preheating, by the use of shaped tools manufactured for the purpose. The most useful are bloodstone burnishers mounted in brass sockets on stout wooden handles. There is no question of using these on old silver, however, until it has been previously toughened.

The largest of the silver salvers from the Sutton Hoo ship burial was excavated in a crushed and very brittle condition. It was toughened by heating it repeatedly with a large blowpipe flame and restored to shape with the fingers, and later with the help of a hide mallet. When a free flame is used in this way heating should be carried out in a darkened room, as it is impossible otherwise to detect when the metal begins to glow, and part of the object might easily be inadvertently over-heated.

Occasions may arise, however, when heat treatment at 600 °C. will not suffice to toughen the silver. This occurred, for example, in the case of a silver libation vessel excavated at Nuri in the Sudan in a fragmentary condition. In this case experimental heat treatment of small pieces at increasing temperature was carried out, and it was found that the silver was only toughened by heating to a temperature of 900 °C., i.e. about 50 degrees below the melting point of the alloy. Despite this fact it was possible by annealing the vessel at this temperature in a neutral atmosphere, followed by quenching in water, to toughen the silver so that the fragments could be reshaped and soldered together.

RESTORATION OF THE EMESA HELMET

An unusual and very interesting problem involving the conservation of silver in juxtaposition to iron was provided by the Emesa helmet, a treasure from Syria (Pl. 25), and as it presented certain novel features its restoration will be described in detail. When received, this fine helmet, with its silver visor in the form of a human face, was at first taken to be a ceremonial piece, but, as pointed out by Seyrig,[1] the protection afforded by the iron skull-cap was continued by a lining of iron of substantial thickness 1–6 mm. underlying the visor and conforming exactly to its shape. The probability is therefore that the helmet was intended as head armour to protect the wearer under war conditions; the iron cranium was dented as if by a heavy blow. The silver was found on examination to be very brittle

[1] Seyrig, H., 'Le Casque d'Émèse', *Annales Arch. de Syrie*, 1952, **2**, Nos. 1 and 2.

and cracked in many places; the major cracks had been filled with a dark stopping material in an effort to reinforce the silver, as shown in the photograph. The iron backing of the visor had rusted and the swollen metal pressing behind the brittle silver had been responsible for distorting the features and forcing the cracks open, in some cases to as much as 4 mm. A state of strain had set in which, if not released, could only lead to further deterioration as the silver itself was only 0·5 mm. in thickness. A necessary preliminary to treatment was the removal of the visor from the helmet; this proved to be easy because the hinge, although no longer movable, was already detached from the head-piece and the two parts were merely held together by wire. After temporary consolidation by applying transparent Sellotape across the cracks in the mask, the visor was bedded in a thick pad of cotton-wool, and the layer of rusty iron was cut away from the back in the region of the mouth and lower jaw. It was in this region that the silver was weakest and most distorted through contact with the corroding iron. It was clear that no satisfactory restoration would be possible unless the silver could be toughened. A pilot experiment was carried out on a tiny detached fragment and as this gave re-assuring results the visor was heated in the electric furnace for three hours, the temperature rising slowly during this time to a maximum of 310 °C. Heating was stopped at this point. The silver was now darkened, partly by the burning of the mixture of rust and wax that had been used in a previous restoration to fill the cracks and partly by the blackening of residual rust that remained attached to it. The rust was removed by brushing with a 9 per cent solution of oxalic acid (see p. 288) before the final heat-treatment as additional heating would have made the iron compounds too insoluble to remove later. Further heating for eighteen hours at 600 °C. and thirteen at 650 °C. was necessary before the silver was considered to be sufficiently toughened to stand up to the manipulation that would be necessary in closing the cracks. In order to strengthen the visor in the areas where the iron backing had been cut away, the underside of the silver was cleaned and given temporary reinforcement by applying patches of silver gauze across the cracks with soft solder. The gauze took the shape of the silver very readily and could be fixed without involving any pressure. The front of the visor was then carefully cleaned with Duraglit cloths to remove all of the dark oxidation products and it was then in a condition for the restoration work to begin.

The first operation was to restore the shape of the lower jaw by dealing with the cracks, one series at a time. The temporary patches of silver gauze were removed, and the silver was manipulated to get the edges of the cracks to meet exactly, then fresh patches of gauze were applied, and fixed permanently in position across the cracks on the underside, using soft solder with a non-corrosive flux. This was a long and exacting process but well worth all the care expended upon it because, as the work advanced and the cracks disappeared one by one, the visor became noticeably stronger and more rigid, and the likeness nearer to that shown in the earliest photographs.

It should be emphasized that it was the toughening of the silver that made this type of restoration possible; if for any reason it had not been possible to toughen the silver by heat treatment, it could not have been manipulated. In its brittle condition the only possible action would have been to try to reinforce the inside, and fill the cracks from the front. It is fortunate that the more permanent type of restoration could be carried out on the Emesa visor, and that it was not necessary to use filling material, as this tends in time to become a conspicuous disfigurement. Care was taken to leave no solder on the front of the mask; it appeared inevitably as thin lines in the repaired cracks, and these were concealed by the local application of a surface coating of silver, applied by 'ragging' with a pointed silver anode tipped with cotton-wool moistened with potassium cyanide (p. 227).

It now only remained to replace the rusty iron that had been removed from the back of the visor. This material, after cleaning, was still in the form of sizeable fragments that could be returned to position in contact with the silver, where they were consolidated with Durofix.

The major fractures that remain in the silver after restoration no longer weaken the structure, nor do they cause serious disfigurement.

29. CHINESE MIRROR OF HAN DYNASTY

The hair-like cracks result from stresses in the brittle
speculum metal set up by oxidation

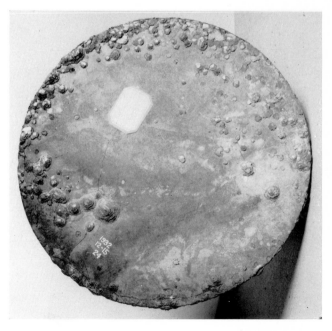

30. CHINESE MIRROR OF HAN DYNASTY FROM THE
HUAI VALLEY

The oyster-shell pitting is characteristic of advanced
spotty corrosion on a brittle speculum metal

31. EGYPTIAN BRONZE FIGURE OF ISIS AND HORUS (PTOLEMAIC PERIOD)

Left: As excavated (plinth is modern). *Centre*: After treatment with Rochelle salt and caustic soda. *Right*: After final treatment

It would have been possible to deal with all the cracks, but this would have meant removing practically all of the iron from the back of the visor, and, as much of the iron was in sound condition, this large operation was not considered justified. The interest and value of the object depend as much on the variety and perfection of the craftsmanship displayed in its construction as on its actual appearance. With the removal of the loose and swollen rust, where the strain was greatest, and the consolidation of the iron and silver in the lower part of the face, the helmet is now considered to be in a stable condition.

The small holes beneath the eyes in the visor had been designed so that the wearer could look down to the ground in front of him, but evidently they were not enough, and it is amusing to find that they had been enlarged, in each case, by a narrow notch cut in the central lobe, no doubt in an emergency as this adjustment is not the work of a craftsman.

THE RESTORATION OF THE ST. NINIAN HANGING BOWL

An interesting example of the cleaning and consolidation of a fragile silver object involving the use of modern synthetic resins was provided by a silver hanging bowl found—along with a number of other silver objects—on the site of a ninth-century church on St. Ninian's Island in the Shetlands (Pl. 26). This object was in a very frail condition, the silver being paper-thin and sandwiched between thick layers of copper minerals derived from the preferential corrosion of the copper in the base silver alloy. Three ribs of heavy silver gilt were symmetrically arranged around the rim, and a preliminary examination suggested that treatment should be limited to improving the appearance of the silver gilt ribs; these were cleaned by the local application of hot 30 per cent formic acid. For this the bowl was supported over a small dish standing on a large mirror and the acid was applied from beneath with swabs of cotton-wool in order to prevent it from flooding over the surface of the bowl and attacking the thick coating of mineral.

Later it was realized that this bowl was of great archaeological importance, because it was the only surviving example of a *silver* hanging bowl to have been found in the British Isles, and that therefore an effort should be made to restore its original appearance. The inside of the bowl was less mineralized than the outside, and it was cleaned mechanically using a spray of bauxite. Before the outside could be cleaned it was necessary to strengthen the bowl, since its strength was due almost entirely to the outer coat of mineral. For this temporary reinforcement it was decided to use a viscous solution of polystyrene that on drying would leave a stiff supporting film, but would ultimately shrink away from the bowl and could be removed. For the application of this reinforcement the bowl was mounted on a small turntable (Pl. 27) so that it could be rotated facing upwards or downwards or at any intermediate angle. When the reinforcement had become hard, it was possible to clean the outside of the bowl in the same way as the inside had been cleaned, and then the temporary reinforcement was released. The question that now had to be decided was the type of synthetic resin that would be most suitable for making a permanent reinforcement. It must have the following properties: (i) be colourless and transparent, (ii) be strong but not brittle, (iii) adhere well to the silver, but not react with it chemically, (iv) be easy to apply, and, finally, (v) be dimensionally stable so that undue shrinkage with the development of contractile forces would not occur, as this would cause deformation of the fragile bowl. The only material satisfying these criteria was an epoxy resin, and after experimental trials a formulation was adopted consisting of 10 gm. Araldite Casting Resin F, 1 gm. of Hardener 951 and 1 gm. of dibutyl phthalate. The method of applying this was essentially the same as that used previously. Further details are given in a publication by Organ,[1] and the success achieved can be assessed from Pl. 28A and B showing the interior and exterior of the bowl after treatment.

The conservation of this object presented a problem of peculiar difficulty because its mechanical strength was largely dependent upon

[1] Organ, R. M., *Studies in Conservation*, 1959, **4**, p. 41.

the unsightly encrustation of minerals that nevertheless had to be removed because it gave a false impression of the original appearance of the object. Any incautious attempt at surface cleaning by chemical reagents could have been disastrous—successful treatment depended upon a full assessment of the condition of the object, and the choice of the correct type of synthetic resin for reinforcement of the bowl— an instructive example of modern scientific conservation.

TARNISH

On exposure to city atmospheres, silver is readily tarnished by the formation of a thin surface film of silver sulphide, and for this reason polished silver requires regular cleaning. The sulphur which tarnishes the silver may be carried in the air in the form of sulphuretted hydrogen from flue gases either industrial or domestic, its action being particularly noticeable in foggy weather. There are other, perhaps not so obvious, sources of sulphur contamination. It may be impossible to keep silver bright in places where there are vulcanized rubber floor-coverings or where a case has a rubber seal of the draught-excluder type. Cheap paints may contain volatile sulphur impurities that will tarnish silver, and even certain types of dry paint film may be potential sources of trouble. Casein is a common constituent of water paints and this is subject to bacterial action that releases sulphur compounds that will tarnish silver. Emulsion paints should not be used to decorate cases that are designed for the exhibition of polished silver unless they can be guaranteed as free from casein. Paints based on lithopone are also suspect. The safest paints to employ are either cellulose paints or good-quality oil-paints based on titanium white. These should contain enough lead-driers to act as a sulphur barrier and prevent any sulphur compounds that may be present in the oil film contaminating the air in the case. A more insidious source of trouble is contact of the silver with textiles that have been 'finished' by treatment with chemicals containing sulphur. Such textiles may contain as much as 200 parts per million of reducible sulphur, whereas all that is required to cause visible discoloration is 2 parts per million, and they should not be used in exhibition cases in which silver objects are displayed.

Tarnish is easily removed with plate powder or rouge cloths, but for antique silver which requires regular cleaning such abrasives are not recommended as they would tend in time to cause damage by wearing down stamp marks and fine ornament. The same applies to Sheffield plate or silver-plated ware, where drastic cleaning or the use of chemicals might result in exposing the underlying base metal. In these cases it is safer to confine routine cleaning to rubbing with a soft cloth and a little French chalk, moistened to a paste, if desired, with methylated spirit containing a few drops of ammonia.

For silver that has been neglected and is heavily tarnished, the following simple electrochemical method of treatment may be used. Place the silver in contact with aluminium, cover it with a dilute solution of caustic soda or sodium carbonate (washing soda)— a solution of 5 per cent strength is ample—and allow it to remain until the stain has disappeared. It can then be washed in running water and polished with a soft cloth or cotton-wool. Alternatively the method of local electrolytic reduction (p. 223) may be used, if the areas of tarnish are not too extensive.

If the tarnish is only superficial, a chemical solvent for tarnish called Silver Dip is available, and this gives excellent results provided the silver is not left in the solution longer than necessary and is washed thoroughly. For cleaning silver inlays the solution is applied with cotton-wool swabs. It should always be used fresh, otherwise silver dissolved in Silver Dip will deposit on base metals.

Tarnishing may be prevented by the exclusion of sulphur in any form. This is easier to achieve with silver in storage than when silver is on exhibition, as protection may be afforded by wrapping in several layers of soft tissue paper, and if the silver has been polished and washed beforehand it will be likely to remain bright for a long time. Alternatively, the silver may be kept in polythene bags having an air-tight seal. A recent advance has been the introduction of an anti-tarnish paper—a soft velvety paper that has been impregnated with chemical substances (copper compounds, chlorophyll, etc.) so that it will absorb hydrogen sulphide from the air, thus leaving correspondingly less sulphur to attack the silver. Anti-tarnish papers should not be in actual contact with the silver or there may be staining by transfer of the sulphur, but as external wrapping papers they cannot be other than advantageous.

Silver should be exhibited in a dust-free case, provided with a breathing channel to allow for the expansion and contraction of the air that occurs with change of temperature. This channel which is usually filled with cotton-wool should contain in addition a loose plug of anti-tarnish paper. The efficiency of such papers when placed actually inside a case has been found to vary, however, because they tend to become easily desiccated. Actually they are more effective when freely exposed to the varying temperature and humidity of the atmosphere; nevertheless, when a bulk supply of anti-tarnish paper can be included in a closed case, it reduces the rate of tarnishing even under dry conditions. This has been established in a series of tests in which the protected silver was found to remain bright for up to a period of several months after unprotected silver had visibly blackened.

Where silver is displayed in a closed glass case on shelving draped with Shantung silk that has been passed through a 10 per cent solution of lead acetate,[1] dried and ironed, it may remain bright for many years, as demonstrated by Bengt Bengtson in the Nordic Museum, Stockholm.

With certain designs of exhibition cases it is possible to arrange a tubular filter-vent, through which sulphur-free air can be introduced by blowing from outside to replace the contaminated air in the case. The joints of the case are then sealed with polythene tape. A suitable blower can be improvised from a vacuum cleaner, the bag being replaced by a filter tube charged with material that will absorb sulphuretted hydrogen, e.g. pumice granules that have been previously treated with copper or lead acetate and glycerol.

When silver objects have been cleaned to remove tarnish, the

[1] This method was first suggested by Professor J. Tandberg; the lead acetate solution should contain 2 per cent of glycerol and about 1 per cent of ammonia.

TABLE III. SILVER ALLOYS

For method of use
see p. 190

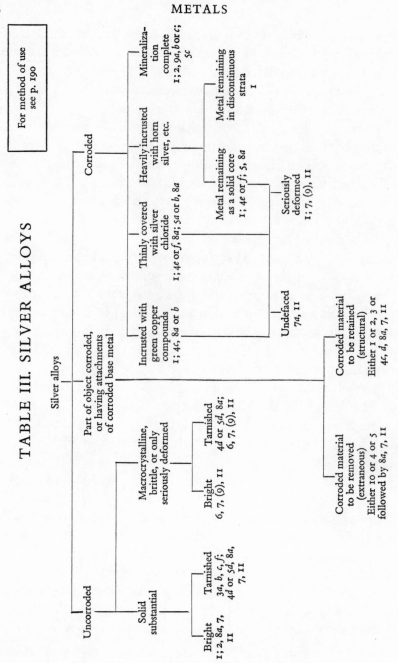

Silver alloys

Uncorroded

Solid
substantial

Bright
1; 2, 8a, 7,
11

Tarnished
3a, b, c, f;
4d or 5d, 8a,
7, 11

**Part of object corroded,
or having attachments
of corroded base metal**

Macrocrystalline,
brittle, or only
seriously deformed

Bright
6, 7, (9), 11

Tarnished
4d or 5d, 8a;
6, 7, (9), 11

Corroded material
to be removed
(extraneous)
Either 10 or 4 or 5
followed by 8a, 7, 11

Corroded material
to be retained
(structural)
Either 1 or 2, 3 or
4a, d, 8a, 7, 11

Corroded

Incrusted with
green copper
compounds
1; 4c, 8a or b

Thinly covered
with silver
chloride
1; 4e or f, 8a; 5a or b, 8a

Heavily incrusted
with horn
silver, etc.

Mineraliza-
tion
complete
1; 2, 9a, b or c;
5c

Undefaced
7a, 11

Metal remaining
as a solid core
1; 4e or f, 5, 8a

Metal remaining
in discontinuous
strata
1

Seriously
deformed
1; 7, (9), 11

1. No treatment.

2. (a) Warm soapy water; (b) Lissapol N froth.

3. Mild abrasives: (a) French chalk; (b) Rouge; (c) 'Plate powder'; (d) Pumice or emery powder; (e) 'Metal polish'; (f) Duraglit; (g) Special cloths.

4. Solvents:
   (a) Concentrated aqueous ammonia.
   (b) Potassium cyanide.
   (c) Hot formic acid (30 per cent).
   (d) Silver Dip.
   (e) Ammonium thiosulphate plus Lissapol N.
   (f) Thiourea plus Lissapol N.
   (g) Citric acid (5 per cent).
   (h) Silver nitrate (20 per cent) for removing a copper coating from silver.

5. Reduction:
   (a) Electrochemical.
   (b) Electrolytic (normal).
   (c) Electrolytic (consolidative).
   (d) Local ('ragging').

6. Annealing and reshaping.

7. Protective finishes: (a) Lacquer: Frigilene, Incralac.
   (b) Microcrystalline wax polish.

8. Washing. Media for diffusion of soluble chlorides: (a) Distilled water.
   (b) Sodium sesquicarbonate (5 per cent).

9. Consolidants: (a) Cosmolloid 80 H.
   (b) Bedacryl 122X.
   (c) Polyvinyl acetate.
   (d) Soft solder.
   (e) Metallic reinforcement.

10. Mechanical: (a) picking, (b) chipping, (c) grinding, (d) brushing, (e) grit spraying, (f) polishing, (g) burnishing.

11. Storage and exhibition. Dust-free case with sulphur-free atmosphere.

most practical way to prevent further tarnishing is to apply a thin coating of an impervious lacquer. A number of such lacquers are now available, and lacquers that are of the right quality and consistency are almost invisible if they are correctly applied. Among the commercial lacquers that have been found to have excellent protective properties are Frigilene and Incralac.

Before lacquering, the silver must be cleaned and degreased, and while cleaning can be done by any of the methods recommended, a word of warning is necessary as regards the washing process to remove grease. Many proprietary detergent preparations are available today that are excellent for household cleaning, but some are entirely unsuitable for silver, as they contain phosphates which react with the silver to form a resistant brown stain. It is better to degrease the polished silver by washing it in hot soapy water, or the pure detergent Lissapol N may be used; the silver is then rinsed in running water and dried. After degreasing, care should be taken not to spoil the surface by touching it with the fingers. When quite dry the silver is ready to be lacquered.

Lacquer may be applied by spraying, dipping, or brushing. The brushing technique is probably the simplest. A soft clean brush is used and the lacquer should be sufficiently thin to spread without leaving brush marks. It must not be allowed to collect as a thick film in any hollows where it would catch the light and reveal its presence by a shine foreign to that of the silver. It is useful to have a solvent at hand which can be used, if need be, to remove any surplus. Lacquer can be prevented from collecting in hollows by stippling with a brush or by using a gentle puff of air from a blow-ball.

XI

COPPER AND ITS ALLOYS

COPPER derives its name from Cyprus which was the Roman source of the metal, *aes cyprium* being the 'bronze from Cyprus'.[1] It is, however, an element, and it occurs in nature in the metallic condition as well as in the form of many minerals, chief of which are cuprite (cuprous oxide), chalcocite (cuprous sulphide), chalcopyrite (copper-iron sulphide), and the basic carbonates, malachite and azurite or chessylite.

Metallic copper resembles silver in being sensitive to sulphur which causes it to become covered with a film of tarnish consisting of copper sulphide. It differs from silver, however, in being sensitive also to oxygen; pure copper oxidizes very readily when exposed to moist air, whereas, under similar conditions in air that is free from sulphur compounds, silver remains unchanged. Thus it happens that while silver objects in the museum tend to tarnish, copper objects are more usually covered with a thin film of oxide which confers on them a dull appearance. The oxide film does not increase appreciably in thickness with time and for this reason it may be regarded as protecting the underlying metal; oxidation may be so slight that the metallic appearance of the metal is maintained and there is no disfigurement; but if the metal is alloyed with tin, lead, or zinc and the constituents imperfectly mixed, the oxidized surface may be patchy and give rise to a rather unpleasant appearance. The restoration of the metallic condition is not, however, a major problem as the thinly oxidized metal may be cleaned with metal polish or by immersing the object for some hours in dilute sulphuric acid (5–10 per cent), washing afterwards, in each case, drying, and rubbing up

[1] Rickard, T. A., 'The Nomenclature of Copper and its Alloys', *J. Royal Anthropological Inst.*, 1932, **62**, p. 281.

with a soft cloth. But the brilliancy is soon lost and to preserve
a burnished surface, even under museum conditions, it is usually
necessary to cover it with an impervious film of lacquer.

When buried in damp soil, copper and its alloys soon lose their
metallic appearance. The oxide layer increases in thickness, and
cuprous oxide becomes compacted into the purplish-red mineral
known as cuprite; this, in turn, may become encrusted with basic
carbonates that are green or sometimes blue in colour corresponding
to the minerals malachite and azurite. Such incrustations are stable
when free from chloride and they protect the underlying metal
from further corrosion.

It does not follow, however, that all green incrustations are stable.
Appearance has little to do with stability, even though it be true that
a thin coherent deposit is more likely to be stable than a heavy porous
incrustation that would tend to behave like a sponge and absorb
moisture and soluble salts from the soil. When more than one metal
is present, as in the tin bronzes,[1] it is only to be expected that incrustations will be more complicated both in composition and structure
and therefore more liable to contain and retain salts. Contamination
is the rule rather than the exception because soluble salts are widely
distributed in nature, in the soil as well as in the sea, and for this
reason they are usually present in excavated material.

It was noted in the case of silver (p. 220) that when this is buried
in salty ground it tends to become covered with an insoluble shell of
stable silver chloride. In the case of copper and its alloys, however,
the presence of chlorides in the ground presents an acute problem
from the point of view of conservation because an unstable cuprous
chloride is formed as a corrosion product that can react with moisture
and give rise to progressive corrosion under humid conditions in
museums, with the result that the surface becomes powdery and
spotty. So common are these features in corroded bronzes that the
appearance of characteristic pale green powdery spots is referred to as

[1] Gettens, R. J., *J. Chem. Education*, 1951, **28**, p. 67. In this paper the reactions that
take place during corrosion of a tin bronze are described and the morphology of the
incrustation illustrated in a series of photomicrographs.

'bronze disease' whether occurring upon copper or on any of its alloys.

It is not surprising that 'damp' has been mistakenly credited with being the cause of corrosion since serious outbreaks of active corrosion have been observed to take place in damp weather. But as the features of bronze disease cannot be reproduced even under damp conditions when chlorides are absent, it is clear that moisture is only a subsidiary factor. In fact these spots grow because the cuprous chloride (nantokite) is hydrolysed, forming hydrochloric acid that reacts with uncorroded copper metal under the combined action of moisture and oxygen to form the pale green powdery basic cupric chloride (paratacamite). Since the initial hydrolysis is a reversible reaction, the corrosion will continue to progress until this hydrolysis is arrested. The main objective, therefore, in conservation must be to eliminate or to immobilize the cuprous chloride. Here we are faced with two difficulties. Cuprous chloride cannot be removed by mere washing with water. Not only is it insoluble but it is also inaccessible as it occurs in greatest concentration, not in the upper, but in the deeper layers, of incrustation. In practice, chemical methods can be used to neutralize the cuprous chloride, but its inaccessibility introduces a serious problem. A corroded bronze has a banded structure (Pl. 17), the metal core being surrounded by layers of massive cuprous oxide interspersed with powdery tin oxide, and these layers underlie an external shell of basic carbonates. Chlorides may be present in the green surface shell, but in a heavily corroded bronze concentrations of cuprous chloride are found in the absorbent layers of tin oxide, and even in the micro-cracks and fissures that can be shown by metallographic technique to exist in the interface between metal and cuprous oxide.

In view of these facts there are two approaches to the problem of treating the chlorides present in a mineralized bronze. One is to decompose the incrustation so that the deep lying cuprous chloride can be laid bare and removed. There are many laboratory methods by which this may be accomplished and they are generally referred to as stripping methods. On the other hand, there are times when it would be quite unthinkable to sacrifice the patina of a bronze, and, if corrosion has set in, then special techniques must be used to reach the cuprous chloride and render it innocuous, i.e. to stabilize the bronze without unduly altering its appearance.

In the study of ancient metals it will be noted that bronzes have survived for thousands of years even though their porous incrustations have been impregnated with salts. The explanation must be that an equilibrium had been established between the corroded bronze and its environment in the ground, and it is to this that we must attribute survival. Excavation destroys the equilibrium, however, and exposure to new and very different environmental conditions provokes changes that are often profound. It may sometimes happen that a bronze can undergo a second acclimatization to the museum environment, without visual change, but it is more usual for further corrosion to take place in the process, and if neglected, equilibrium will in many cases only be re-established at the expense of complete disintegration. All bronze objects should, therefore, be sent for laboratory treatment as soon as possible after excavation.

When electrochemical or electrolytic methods can be adopted, the objects will be restored to a stable condition and to something resembling their original uncorroded appearance. But it will only be possible to apply such reduction methods when a substantial metallic core remains and when its mechanical strength is beyond doubt. In the absence of a metallic core the aim will be to arrest decay by the use of selective chemical reagents. In the case of a finely patinated bronze also, the prospect of arresting decay without destroying the patina will depend upon the nature and distribution of the corrosion, and also upon what success can be achieved in localizing the action of the chemical reagents during treatment. When conditions are dry, chloride activity will be at a minimum and if bronze disease should break out and can be dealt with in its early stages, there will be less chance of its getting out of hand. In this type of problem the following points are important: (1) to treat the spots in the early stages, (2) to dry the bronze well thereafter, and keep it dry, and (3) to be alive to the necessity of giving further treatment in good time should further spots make their appearance.

The intimate connection between damp and corrosion is illustrated by the interesting case of a Greek bronze head of a Barbarian

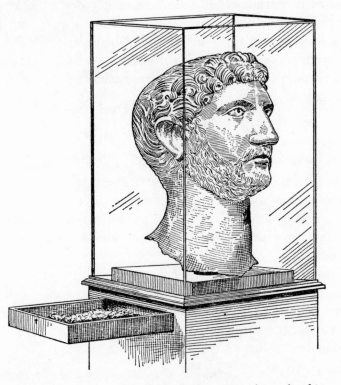

FIG. 8. *Preservation in dry air*. The drawer in wooden pedestal is filled with silica gel so that, when closed, the drying agent is in direct contact with the air in the glass case through perforations behind the plinth

dating to 400 B.C., which had a very fine patina that had never given any trouble. Suddenly it showed signs of corrosion and the cause was traced to damp from a leaky roof that had entered the wall against which the bronze had been exhibited. The spots were excavated individually with dental tools and, when the bronze had been carefully washed and dried, the cavities were filled with lacquer.

No further outbreak was detected until the following winter when a series of new spots had to be treated, but these were neither so intense nor so obtrusive as before. There has been no further trouble, nor indeed is any expected, as the specimen has now been mounted in a case of the island type kept permanently dry by silica gel (see Appendix XI). Such an arrangement is shown diagrammatically in Fig. 8. In instances of this kind it is often better to accept the risk of further outbreak and be prepared to attend to the specimens again, rather than adopt drastic measures that would be certain to change the character of the piece.

METHODS OF TREATMENT

1. When incrustation can be sacrificed

When the incrustation on a bronze object is unsightly, actively corroding, or may be covering inscriptions or concealing decorative details, it will be advisable to 'strip' the bronze, i.e. remove all the incrustation, provided, of course, that there is a solid core of metal still remaining.

This can be done by using chemical reagents such as alkaline Rochelle salt or alkaline glycerol to remove the basic cupric carbonate, dilute sulphuric acid to remove cuprous oxide (cuprite), followed by electrolytic reduction to eliminate cuprous chloride.

The chemical solutions are prepared as follows:

Solution 1. Alkaline Rochelle Salt. Dissolve 50 gm. of commercial flake caustic soda in one litre of cold water and dissolve 150 gm. of Rochelle salt (sodium potassium tartrate) in this solution.

Solution 2. Alkaline glycerol. Dissolve 150 gm. of commercial flake caustic soda in one litre of cold water and add 50 gm. of glycerol to this solution.

Solution 3. Dilute sulphuric acid. Slowly add 100 gm. of concentrated sulphuric acid to one litre of cold water in a Pyrex beaker, stirring continuously.[1]

---

[1] The acid must always be added to the water, and not vice versa; water should never be added to strong sulphuric acid as this might cause serious accident due to spurting accompanying the sudden evolution of heat.

In order to carry out the treatment the encrusted object is allowed to soak in solution 1 or 2 in a covered container of glass or porcelain, either in the cold or, if it is desired to hasten operations, in a steam-bath until the incrustation is softened, when most of it can be removed by brushing. The colourless Rochelle salt solution becomes deep blue in reacting with the incrustation.

After the first part of the treatment, a brownish-red residue of cuprous oxide (cuprite) will be found firmly adhering to the metal, and it does not respond well to brushing. It is usually associated with pasty cuprous chloride. Sometimes there is also a layer of metallic copper which has been deposited within the incrustation during the process of corrosion. This copper (referred to as redeposited copper) tends to seal up the minerals beneath it, and protect them from attack by the reagents. If redeposited copper is observed, this complicates the treatment because it is insoluble in Rochelle salt and in dilute sulphuric acid, and it must be removed mechanically. This is not always an easy matter and it takes time, but unless all of the copper deposit is picked off at this stage, there can be no guarantee that the process will give permanent results.

The object is then placed in solution 3 in a container of glass or porcelain. It is set aside in a warm place with occasional brushing, and examination with a pocket lens, until as much as possible of the cuprite has been eliminated together with a sludge of copper powder.

A peculiar condition that sometimes arises and may be seen under the lens is one in which cuprite forms a crystalline mosaic with copper crystals on the apparently intact surface of the cleaned metal. As this film may have chlorides trapped beneath it, it must be broken down in the final operation, to ensure the removal of chlorides by electrolytic reduction, which is carried out as described on pp. 197 et. sqq. After reduction the object is subjected to the intensive washing process (p. 200), dried, and lacquered.

An alternative method for the chemical stripping of bronzes is to use a 10 per cent solution of commercial Detarol (trisodium salt of N-hydroxy-ethylene-diaminotriacetic acid). The object is immersed in this solution, which removes both the malachite and cuprite incrustation, if necessary, the solution should be changed when it becomes too highly coloured. When the reaction is completed, the object is taken out and rinsed under running water; it is then ready for electrolytic reduction, followed by intensive washing, drying, and lacquering.

2. When patina or incrustation should be preserved

More difficult problems are presented by well-patinated bronzes showing bronze disease, by bronzes so extensively mineralized that no solid core of metal remains, and by bronzes in which the decorative features may be completely mineralized. If such objects are in need of treatment, the aim must be to stabilize them by arresting the corrosion while retaining their general character. Three general methods can be used for this purpose. These are as follows:

(i) *Use of sodium sesquicarbonate.* In this method the object is first given a preliminary mechanical cleaning to remove adherent dirt and superficial corrosion products, and then allowed to soak in successive baths of 5 per cent sodium sesquicarbonate solution until a stage is reached when the solution is shown to be free from chlorides.[1] In the initial stages when the chloride is being removed fairly rapidly, the solution should be changed every week, but in the later stages the time between changes can be extended. One problem that may occur during treatment is the formation of a secondary deposit of malachite on the surface of the object; if this occurs, the object should be taken out and the deposit brushed off. The total period of treatment will depend upon the nature of the object and the amount of cuprous chloride present; in many cases it may extend over many months. It is bound to be a slow process because the sodium sesquicarbonate has to diffuse through the incrustation before it comes in contact with the deep seated cuprous chloride, and can neutralize the hydrochloric acid formed by hydrolysis to produce soluble sodium chloride that is washed out.

In order to study the course of this reaction more precisely an

[1] The test is carried out as described on p. 201, but sufficient nitric acid must first be added to neutralize the solution, i.e. until effervescence ceases.

A. Condition after removal of corrosion products

B. After consolidation with polymethacrylate resin (Technovit 4000 A)

32. BRONZE BOWL FROM BIRDLIP

A. In corroded condition

B. After consolidative reduction

33. LEAD COINS AND BULLAE

investigation of the stabilization of fifteen bronze objects was recently carried out in the British Museum Research Laboratory.[1] The elution of the chloride was followed by determining the actual chloride concentration in the solutions by polarographic analysis. It was found that the chloride concentration showed an initial sharp rise, reaching a maximum after soaking for two to three weeks; this was followed by a fairly sharp decrease during the next two or three months which became gradually less until a final constant concentration below 50 parts per million was reached.

After sesquicarbonate treatment is completed, the object is washed in changes of cold distilled water until the final bath is shown to be neutral when tested with a suitable indicator (Appendix VIII); the object is then dried and waxed in the usual manner.

(ii) *Use of silver oxide*. The aim of this method devised by Organ[2] is to expose the cuprous chloride and to form over this a stable seal of silver chloride. To achieve this all the spots of bronze disease are first excavated with a sewing needle ground to a chisel-edge under a low power microscope, care being taken to ensure that the loose green powder that is removed does not lodge in areas of sound corrosion. Then a paste of pure analytical reagent grade silver oxide moistened with industrial methylated spirit is rubbed into the exposed layer of cuprous chloride and into the edges of the excavation with a match-stick cut to a point. The treated object is then deliberately exposed to an atmosphere having a relative humidity of about 78 per cent by placing it in a closed space in which is placed a dish containing a slurry of crystalline photographic 'hypo' (sodium thiosulphate). Under these conditions the cuprous chloride will react with the silver oxide forming cuprous oxide and silver chloride, both of which are stable salts and will seal off the cuprous chloride against attack by moisture. If the treatment has not been adequately carried out, light green spots of corrosion will appear, and it will be necessary to repeat the treatment, applying a further quantity of silver oxide until the object shows no signs of active corrosion when

[1] Oddy, W. A. and Hughes, M. J., *Studies in Conservation*, 1970, **15**, p. 183.
[2] Organ, R. M., *Museums J.*, 1961, **61**, p. 2.

exposed to the high relative humidity. This dry method of treating bronze disease should be used in cases where the object cannot be safely exposed to aqueous solutions, e.g. a bronze with enamel inlay.

(iii) *Use of benzotriazole*. This method which has been recently described by Madsen[1] for stabilizing bronzes showing active corrosion is carried out as follows. The object is first mechanically cleaned to remove adherent soil, etc., paying particular attention to areas of corrosion, and any previously applied lacquer or wax is removed by soaking the object overnight in a mixture of equal parts of acetone and toluene. Then the object is immersed for 24 hours in a 3 per cent solution of benzotriazole in industrial methylated spirit under vacuum. The vacuum is then released, the object removed, dried, and wiped with a swab of cotton-wool moistened with industrial methylated spirit to remove any excess of benzotriazole on the surface of the object. The object is then exposed under normal ambient conditions and examined to see if any spots of corrosion reoccur. If this happens, the above treatment is repeated until no further corrosion is evident. The object is then in a stable condition. Tests on this method carried out in the British Museum Research Laboratory showed that it gave satisfactory results on objects that are not too heavily corroded, but that if very active corrosion was present, even many repeated treatments failed to stabilize the object. This method has the advantage, however, that it is quicker to carry out than the sodium sesquicarbonate method. It would seem, therefore, that a preliminary washing in sodium sesquicarbonate solution to remove the major part of the chlorides followed by the benzotriazole treatment may prove the most satisfactory method for treating badly corroded bronze objects.

The reason for using benzotriazole depends upon the fact that benzotriazole is known to react with clean metallic copper to form a very thin film of a chelate compound that protects the copper against atmospheric attack, and Madsen implies that the same mechanism is the basis of his method of treatment. However, this chelate com-

[1] Madsen, H. B., *Studies in Conservation*, 1967, **12**, p. 163.

pound is unstable under acid conditions that exist at the centres of bronze corrosion, where, moreover, cupric ions, and not metallic copper, are present. Benzotriazole forms an insoluble complex compound with cupric ions, and it is, therefore, more likely that the precipitation of this insoluble complex over the cuprous chloride forms a barrier that prevents the ingress of moisture that activates cuprous chloride promoting bronze disease. The mechanism is thus analogous to that of the silver oxide method.

3. Removal of calcareous deposits. Use of sodium hexametaphosphate (Calgon)

Bronzes are sometimes covered with calcareous deposits, and while these may be removed with dilute nitric acid this is undesirable where there is fine work, or where metal is very thin, as the acid treatment is rather drastic. In all cases it is preferable to remove the deposits by soaking the bronze in a 5 per cent solution of sodium hexametaphosphate (Calgon),[1] which in time releases the deposits of calcium and magnesium salts by complexing them to form soluble salts. Stronger solutions up to 15 per cent may be used. This hastens the reaction, and warming the solution hastens matters still further, but not without risk to the patina. On the other hand, where the patina is not of importance, Calgon solution can be used to remove the green incrustation completely, merely by continuing the treatment for long enough. Calgon has the merit that it may safely be employed for cleaning the surface of copper alloys that are in such an advanced state of decay that no metallic core remains. For this reason it is a useful material to have in the restoration laboratory.

CHINESE BRONZES

Chinese bronzes comprise alloys of the gun-metal and bell-metal class, containing tin in the proportion of 10–20 per cent. Such alloys were used for the massive funerary bronzes. The mirrors are of speculum metal, a white bronze which may contain tin in quantities up to about 30 per cent. Lead is commonly present as a minor

[1] Farnsworth, M., *Technical Studies in the Field of Fine Arts*, 1940, **9**, p. 21.

constituent in all Chinese bronzes; its presence seems to have little effect on stability, though when present in quantity it tends to lower the tone of the patina.

In alkaline soils which contain little chloride, the corrosion of copper and its alloys takes place more slowly and more uniformly than when much chloride is present, and the products of the reaction, as we have seen, are more likely to be stable. They may, in fact, constitute a beautiful patina well worth preserving, either for aesthetic reasons or as evidence of antiquity. Such are the patinas found on Chinese bronzes. They may be thin and enamel-like, moderately encrusted, or massive, and they may vary in colour from white or the palest turquoise to the positive greens and blues characteristic of malachite and azurite; a warmer tone is contributed by the presence of cuprite in the lower layers and when exposed at the surface may add a colour varying in hue from pale ochre to deep reddish-purple. In advanced stages of corrosion the remaining metal may be cracked and frail, but the progress of mineralization has not always been so destructive, and specimens have survived for 3,000 years that are beautifully patinated and can still be described as robust.

Chinese bronzes seldom require chemical treatment to ensure their preservation. They may sometimes be improved in appearance by mechanical treatment to remove mud or gross incrustations and reveal concealed features of ornament or inscription. Indeed, the bronzes that reach western markets have sometimes a mineral surface suggesting that a form of mechanical treatment has already been applied to remove incrustations and expose to view the more subtle hues of the under layers and, in particular, the pale turquoise layer of tin oxide. This oxide, which, in the absence of chloride, is usually laid down as a thin coherent film, is normally white, but as it is very readily stained with copper compounds, it forms the basis of smooth shiny coloured patinas that are stable and much admired and sought after by collectors.

The speculum alloys are characterized by brittleness and this accounts for some of the features of corrosion peculiar to the mirrors.

When the brittle core is unable to adjust itself to the increasing strain resulting from expansion accompanying the change from the metallic to the mineral condition, cracks begin to make their appearance. Sometimes they are superficial and hair-like (Pl. 29), in which case they tend to become centres of corrosion, from which copper compounds spread out over the adjacent metal without necessarily attacking it. The rate of decay is slow, however, compared with that found in bronzes containing less tin. Sometimes corrosion takes place in isolated spots, and when this happens in the case of speculum the surface of the metal becomes cracked around the spots in a series of small concentric rings, so that each spot looks like a tiny oyster-shell, and further cracking may even lift the spots clear of the surface where they remain as hard excrescences (Pl. 30). Such pitting is characteristic of speculum metal that has at one time been highly polished; it may be taken as indicating considerable antiquity in the specimen, and there is no evidence of any change in the appearance of the spots under museum conditions.

DECORATION IN GOLD, SILVER, AND TIN

The conservation of copper alloys is often complicated by the presence of decorations in other metals, chief among which are gold, silver, and tin, and it is important to preserve as much as possible of these other metals. Decorations may easily be concealed in a heavy incrustation on a corroded bronze and it is very important, therefore, to be on the look-out for evidence of ornament, as this might be of great archaeological significance. The discovery of such decoration will obviously have an important bearing on the method of treatment that is employed.

Copper alloys may be gilded with gold leaf or gold amalgam. Whichever process has been adopted there is always a problem when the metal underlying the gold has corroded, because the gold becomes covered with copper compounds so that its presence may not at first be recognized. Gold is insoluble in the chemical reagents normally employed for cleaning bronzes, but if these reagents should attack the corroded bronze lying underneath the gold, there is nothing to prevent the gold being lost. If, from a preliminary examination, the presence of gold is suspected, it is preferable to deal with the gold first and the bronze, locally if necessary, afterwards. A useful reagent for cleaning the gold is formic acid (30 per cent), as this softens carbonate incrustations and enables the extent of the gilding to be assessed. Drops of the solution are applied with a match-stick to the encrusted gold, preferably under a binocular microscope, and absorbed with the dissolved incrustation in blotting-paper; to assist the action of the acid, any insoluble minerals are first carefully removed with the help of a needle. Working in this manner it is possible, in time, to expose all of the gilding. As a final operation, the gold may be fixed with lacquer after washing and drying.

Examples are found among Chinese bronzes of the T'ang and later periods where the film of gold is coherent and alloyed to solid bronze by the mercury gilding process. In these cases, alkaline Rochelle salt may be used as the cleaning-agent. Where there is gold embellishment and the underlying base metal has expanded by oxidation, however, the gold may be porous, and an object in such a condition cannot safely be treated with Rochelle salt or, indeed, by any chemical process as any chemical action on the base metal would be likely to loosen the gold which would float off. Mechanical picking has to be resorted to and is carried out under the microscope, particular attention being given to base metal deformations with a view to recovering as far as possible the original shape and the artistic appearance of the object.

Silver and tin decorations on bronze survive without corroding, but in each case preservation may be difficult. Reference has already been made (p. 193) to the cathodic protection afforded to silver by contact with copper in the presence of an electrolyte, and to the fact that a base-silver alloy having a green incrustation may be mistaken for bronze and be dealt with as such (p. 194). When white metal is observed in treating an object having a green incrustation, the action should be arrested by washing the object with water. The partially cleaned specimen should then be closely inspected with a magnifying glass to determine whether there is any pattern-work before deciding what modification of treatment, if any, is necessary in the circumstances. If the white metal proves to be silver,[1] the probability is that a warm 30 per cent solution of formic acid, applied locally to the white metal, will be the most suitable treatment, but mechanical methods should be exploited as well. When a bronze is embellished with silver it is generally desirable to preserve the patina of the bronze and in such cases it may be better to switch over to sodium sesquicarbonate. If the bronze has been reduced, it should be boiled in distilled water for some hours at the conclusion of the treatment to darken it, if necessary, so that the dark metal will act as a contrast to the silver.

Should the white metal prove to be tin it is likely to be in the form of a thin coating and in this case reduction methods would be inadvisable. Tin is found on bronze cooking-vessels, on ornaments such as fibulae and in association with red 'sealing-wax' enamels and inlays on the escutcheons of Saxon hanging bowls, while, in China, it was used for elaborate inlays on Han bronzes—chariot fittings, belt fasteners, and sword guards. On all of these objects a heavy incrustation of copper minerals is best removed from a film of metallic tin by the application of mechanical methods of treatment—by the use of needles working under a binocular microscope. On the other hand alkaline Rochelle salt may be made to give satisfactory results but there is then no guarantee that all of the tin will be preserved when it is attached to metal that has already corroded.

Extreme caution is necessary when beginning work on freshly excavated material. This is well illustrated by some of the objects from the ship burial at Sutton Hoo in East Anglia, a notable example being the large dragon from the shield which was concealed under a green muddy incrustation. The mud was removed with the aid of a small stencil brush moistened with a little detergent, and the object was found to be gilt-bronze having local areas washed with tin, and

[1] A simple test for silver is to place a drop of 15 per cent sulphuric acid on the metal and to add a tiny crystal of chromium trioxide to the drop and wash off after one minute. A red stain (silver chromate) left on the metal indicates that silver is present. The stain may be easily removed with dilute ammonia followed by washing with water.

it was inlaid with garnets; in the course of operations it was revealed that the tail of the dragon was an ancient restoration composed of chalk and glue overlaid with gold leaf. Here any treatment involving immersion in an aqueous solution would have been disastrous as the chalk and glue ground would certainly have been softened or damaged.

When dealing with fine metal-work that is decorated with gold, silver, or tin, dry or semi-dry methods of cleaning should always be applied in the first instance. There remains the possibility, however, that wet methods may ultimately have to be used to ensure permanent conservation. Also, whatever standard form of treatment is applied, it may be necessary to introduce modifications at any stage of the work to suit the particular requirements of the specimen.

The restoration of an Egyptian bronze statuette of Isis and Horus (Pl. 31) may be cited as an example of how technique has sometimes to be modified to meet particular requirements. This bronze was heavily encrusted, the white patches showing in the first photograph being an indication of bronze disease. Preliminary examination revealed that the eyes were inlaid with thin sheet gold, but the gold was considered to be sufficiently firmly attached to remain unaffected by the reduction of the incrustation.

Treatment was begun by immersing the bronze in a solution of alkaline Rochelle salt. The solution was changed frequently with intermittent brushing, until the green coating had all disappeared and had given place to reddish-brown cuprite. This took three days and details of the features were now becoming apparent, as shown in the central illustration (Pl. 31). Mechanical cleaning was then carried out very thoroughly prior to soaking in sulphuric acid (15 per cent); the acid treatment went smoothly and seemed to remove all the cuprite. Thus, a remarkable improvement in appearance was achieved in a comparatively short time, but it was clear, having regard to the coarse incrustation that had been removed, that the metal must be in a highly porous condition and the entire elimination of chloride would be difficult.

The bronze was therefore placed in a nylon bag (as a precaution lest the gold should fall from the eyes) and reduced continuously for seventy-seven hours in the electrolytic tank using a solution of caustic soda as the electrolyte, with periodic brushing. This treatment disclosed the existence of an inscription around the base. The inscription was cleaned out as far as possible with a needle, and the bronze was then ready for washing. Washing was carried out by the method described on p. 200 and had to be continued for six months before the final traces of chloride were eliminated. The specimen was dried, and the gold on the eyes which had survived perfectly was burnished. Although the bronze was now stable and clean, the appearance was unsatisfactory, as the metal had a mottled pale straw colour, and this made it unattractive as a museum exhibit. This discoloration was dealt with by the device of applying warm plasticine as a coating all over the bronze and leaving it there overnight. (Only some brands of plasticine are effective, and these contain traces of sulphur compounds which impart just the right degree of tarnish.) The metal had now a rich brown-black colour. It was washed with methylated spirit to remove grease, and lacquered with Ercalene. Finally a little chalk was rubbed into the inscription so that the characters would be more apparent against the darkened surface of the metal. The restoration being completed, the object was remounted on its plinth.

CRUSHED COPPER OBJECTS

When thin copper alloys are buried in the ground, they are liable to be crushed by the weight of earth that covers them. Before any attempt is made to restore the shape, the metal must be softened by heating and plunging into cold water. Over-heating will cause extensive oxidation of the surface and it is better to soften little and often during the bending process rather than attempt to achieve too much in one single operation. Where there are several dents, the order in which they are removed is sometimes of importance and the operator works, as a rule, from the main body of metal towards the extremities, endeavouring to recover the shape with the minimum of movements of the old metal. As for tools—pin vices, wooden cramps, clothes-pegs are all useful, but where the metal is thin enough, the most sensitive control is that given by the hands, the softened metal being pressed against shaped wooden stakes held firmly in a vice. Cracks may be reinforced at the back with soft solder (p. 210).

REPAIR OF DAMAGED BRONZE OBJECTS

Bronze objects are often recovered from the ground in such a condition that certain areas may have completely corroded away. In such cases it will be necessary to replace these missing areas. This can be done using metal sheets or resins, either alone or reinforced with glass fibre. If metal sheets are used, these are first shaped to fit the contours of the object and then fixed in position. If the object is in a sound condition, this can be done by soldering, but if any corrosion is present an epoxy resin adhesive should be used.

Irregular gaps are more easily repaired with a suitable cold-setting synthetic resin. A good example to illustrate this method of repair is provided by a Romano-British bowl from Birdlip, which at some stage had been completely stripped of mineral; but so much of the original metal was missing that the bowl, although chemically stable, was physically weak, and scarcely able to support its own weight (Pl. 32A). The resin used to strengthen the bowl was Technovit 4004a, a special cold-setting polymethyl methacrylate. This consists of a powder and a liquid which set in about twenty minutes at room temperature when well stirred together; it has the advantage that while setting it passes through a pasty stage when it can be worked into shape. The method employed was to warm and shape a sheet of dental wax against the outside of a sound area of the bowl, then to slide it round to the missing area and fix it to the metal by applying a hot spatula. Technovit was then brushed on to the inner surface of the wax and the edges of the metal, three layers in all being applied. When the Technovit had hardened the wax was removed and any excessive thickness of resin tooled off. By using this method it was possible to restore all the missing areas and part of the rim, as can be seen in Pl. 32B. Other resins that can also be used in this method of repair are the polymethacrylates Plexigum and Tensol 7, and the polyester resins Bondafiller or Crystic. If it is necessary to give additional strength, the polyester resins can be reinforced by the incorporation of fibre glass matting which is available in various thicknesses.

TABLE IV. COPPER ALLOYS

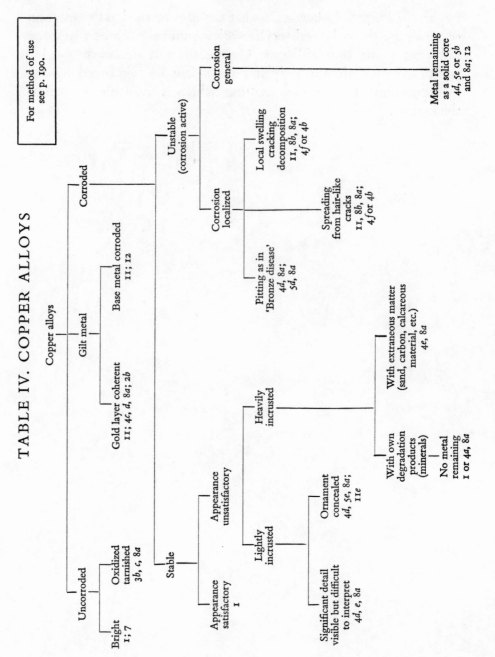

For method of use see p. 190.

1. No treatment.

2. (a) Warm soapy water; (b) Lissapol N froth.

3. Mild abrasives: (a) pumice or emery powder, (b) 'metal polish'; (c) Duraglit; (d) special impregnated cloths.

4. Chemical reagents:
    (a) Sodium sesquicarbonate (5 per cent).
    (b) Benzotriazole.
    (c) Formic acid (30 per cent) applied dropwise.
    (d) Alkaline Rochelle salt followed by sulphuric acid (10 per cent).
    (e) Sodium hexametaphosphate (Calgon).
    (f) Silver oxide.

5. Reduction
    (a) Aluminium and caustic soda.
    (b) Zinc and caustic soda.
    (c) Zinc and dilute sulphuric acid.
    (d) Zinc and sulphuric acid (90 per cent)—for local use only.
    (e) Electrolytic in sodium carbonate.

6. Annealing and reshaping.

7. Protective finishes: (a) Lacquer: Ercalene, Incralac, Bedacryl 122X.
    (b) Paraffin wax or microcrystalline wax bath.
    (c) Microcrystalline wax polish.

8. Washing. Media for diffusion of soluble chlorides: (a) Distilled water.
    (b) Sodium sesquicarbonate (5 per cent).

9. Methods of darkening: (a) Boiling for a long time in distilled water.
    (b) Brushing under a running tap with a little very dilute ammonium sulphide.
    (c) Encasing in plasticine.

10. Consolidants: (a) Nitrocellulose. Durofix.
    (b) Bedacryl 122X.
    (c) Polyvinyl acetate.
    (d) Soft solder.
    (e) Paraloid B72.
    (f) Molten wax.

11. Mechanical: (a) picking, (b) chipping, (c) grinding, (d) brushing, (e) grit-spraying, (f) polishing, and (g) burnishing.

12. Storage and exhibition. Dust-free dry case.

XII

LEAD, TIN, AND PEWTER

LEAD and tin are soft white metals, and though very similar in appearance, they are easily distinguished by their relative density—lead being almost twice as heavy as tin—and by the fact that clean lead makes a black mark when rubbed on white paper and tin does not. Lead is subject to corrosion in cases where tin is resistant and many organic acids which attack lead have no action on tin. Tin can be used with perfect safety for coating copper cooking-vessels and, in the form of foil, as a hygienic wrapping for foodstuffs.

Tin becomes oxidized, however, as a result of prolonged burial in the ground. In these circumstances the greyish film of stannous oxide which initially forms on the metal gradually gives place to white stannic oxide. The characteristic corrosion product of lead is the basic carbonate which is also white, but the two are readily distinguished by applying a drop of dilute nitric acid which causes the lead incrustation to effervesce, whereas the stannic oxide is unaffected.

Alloys of lead and tin are known as pewter, the hardest variety of which contains about 80 per cent of tin and 20 per cent of lead. Roman pewter contains about 80 per cent of tin, but the proportions of tin and lead in pewter have been found to vary considerably throughout the centuries, owing to scrap metal having been so often melted down and refashioned. Modern pewters are in a different category. Lead is usually absent, its place being taken by antimony and possibly some copper, with the result that these alloys are much harder and less subject to oxidation than the traditional alloys.

LEAD

Museum objects of lead are normally covered with a thin film of oxide. When this has grown slowly in pure air, it has a dull grey appearance, and acts as a protective patina: when the film of oxide has grown in impure air (air that is contaminated with traces of organic acids, paint fumes, etc.) it is discontinuous and non-protective; a certain milkiness may then make its appearance on the surface, and in time active corrosion breaks out with the formation of basic lead carbonate. The carbonate is loosely adherent and the corrosion is accompanied by a considerable increase in volume. It is for these reasons that lead objects often suffer serious disfigurement unless the corrosion is checked in the early stages.

When lead objects are excavated from the ground they are commonly found to have a white incrustation. This is composed of lead compounds formed by chemical action between the metal and saline matter, and also by the action of oxygen and carbon dioxide dissolved in the ground water. Even when such an incrustation appears to be stable, it is often so unsightly as to be unacceptable on specimens for study and exhibition.

The aim of laboratory treatment is therefore either to arrest corrosion, or to improve the appearance of the lead. Carbonates and other salts must be removed, and then the cleaned metal is preserved either by exposing it in an uncontaminated atmosphere so that it will build up its own protective film of oxide (see above), or, more usually, by sealing the surface with a film of wax. A serious complication arises from the fact that the expansion of the surface on corrosion causes micro-cracks to form in the underlying metal, and these have to be cleared of impurities if the results are to have any permanence.

METHODS OF TREATMENT

1. Electrolytic reduction

(a) *Normal reduction.* In the case of fairly massive lead objects the standard process of electrolytic reduction can be carried out to remove superficial corrosion. The object is made the cathode in either a 5 per cent solution of sodium hydroxide or a 10 per cent solution of sulphuric acid as electrolyte using an anode of iron or preferably stainless steel, and a current density of 2–5 amp/dm² is maintained. Owing to the susceptibility of lead to solvent action by the electrolyte certain precautions must be taken, namely:

(i) The current must be switched on before the object is immersed in the electrolytic tank, and under no circumstances must the current be switched off while the object is immersed in the tank.

(ii) There must be an immediate evolution of hydrogen gas when the object is immersed in the tank. This indicates that a proper electrical contact has been made with the lead through the corrosion layers. If this does not happen, the object must be taken out and an area of corrosion products cleared away so as to provide the necessary contact.

(iii) Heavy lead objects should be supported in the electrolytic tank to prevent any risk of their becoming detached from the electrodes, or the supporting wire cutting into the soft metal.

If these precautions are observed, electrolytic reduction will give very satisfactory results.

(b) *Consolidative reduction.* In the case of thin lead objects such as coins, medals, and bullae or inscribed scrolls that have been stored in bad conditions and have suffered attack by volatile organic acids, it will be found that they have often corroded so badly in the course of time that they have become extremely fragile and all surface detail is a mass of corrosion products. Under such conditions removal of the corrosion products would involve loss of the inscription, thus rendering the objects worthless; it is necessary, therefore, to use a special method of consolidative reduction by which the basic lead carbonate can be converted into a compact mass of lead. For this purpose the object is tightly compressed between two polyurethane foam pads to support it and cathodically reduced in a 10 per cent solution of sulphuric acid or a five per cent solution of sodium hydroxide at a current density in the range of 100–200 milliamp/dm². It has been found that sulphuric acid is preferable and gives better results, but if this acid electrolyte is used, the anode must be of lead in place of the iron or stainless steel used in the case of sodium

A. Before treatment

B. After treatment

34. PEWTER MEDAL OF THE CAPTURE OF THE BASTILLE

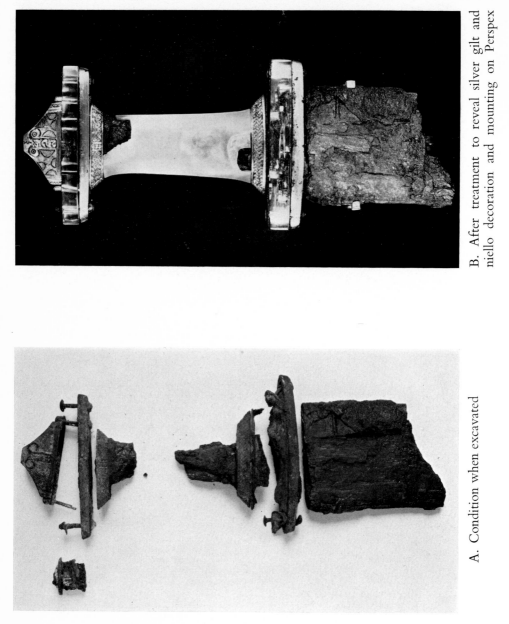

B. After treatment to reveal silver gilt and niello decoration and mounting on Perspex

A. Condition when excavated

35. HILT OF IRON SWORD FROM AN ANGLO-SAXON BURIAL, COOMBE

hydroxide and a lead wire is wrapped round the object to serve as the cathode; however, in the case of smooth lead objects, e.g. inscribed scrolls, it is preferable to use a strip of lead covering the whole surface of the object so as to prevent the lead wire from possibly making a mark on the surface of the object. Also when using sulphuric acid as the electrolyte, the period of reduction will be longer than that required under alkaline conditions; it may take up to three weeks or longer, depending upon the size of the object. If sodium hydroxide solution is used as the electrolyte, the end of the reduction will be indicated by the evolution of small bubbles of hydrogen from the surface of the object, but this will not be observed when sulphuric acid is used as the electrolyte, and the object must be taken out and inspected periodically to determine when the reduction has been completed. Details of the circuit required for this technique of consolidative reduction are given in Appendix XVIII. The kind of result that can be achieved by this method of consolidation is illustrated in Pl. 33A and Pl. 33B, which show the condition of some lead tokens before and after treatment.

(c) *Washing procedure.* Washing to remove residues of alkali or acid cannot be carried to completion in water alone, and a special procedure of controlled washing using indicators to follow the course of the washing is necessary. This is carried out in two stages as follows: first, place the object in a bath of very dilute sulphuric acid prepared by adding four drops of 15 per cent sulphuric acid to 1 litre of water. The pH of this solution will lie between 3 and 3·5; the reduced lead object is placed in this solution and after about a minute the pH is measured with Universal Indicator paper when it will be found that the pH has increased to about 7. This process is repeated in successive acid baths until finally no alteration in the pH of the acid solution is observed when the object is left in the solution. Usually about five or six baths will be necessary and the whole operation takes about ten minutes. This washing removes all the alkali, but leaves the object slightly acid, and this residual acidity must be removed in the second stage. For this purpose the object is immersed in successive baths of cold distilled water, having a pH of about 6, for periods of about one minute. At first the pH will rise as the acid is washed out, but after about five or six baths it will be found that the pH will remain constant at a value of about 6. Objects that have been reduced using sulphuric acid as electrolyte only need washing through the second stage.

(*d*) *Finishing*. When washing has been completed, the lead object is removed from the final washing bath with polythene tongs or tweezers (it should not be handled if possible at this stage to avoid absorption of grease, etc., from the hands), mopped dry with a soft clean cloth and quickly dried either with a hot-air blower or by passing through a bath of industrial methylated spirit. The object is now glass brushed, if necessary, to improve its appearance, and then transferred to a bath of molten paraffin wax or preferably molten microcrystalline wax, such as Cosmolloid 80H. When no more bubbles of air appear around the object, it is removed from the molten wax and placed on absorbent tissue paper or blotting paper so that the excess of wax can drain away. Any local pockets of wax remaining in hollows can be remelted with a hot-air blower and removed with small wads of blotting-paper.

2. Use of ion-exchange resins

A notable contribution to the preservation of lead objects was made in the British Museum Research Laboratory when it was discovered that lead carbonate and chloride could be removed from the metal by the use of ion-exchange resins.[1] The principle of this method, which has long been known as a means for softening hard water, i.e. removing dissolved calcium salts, depends upon the fact that special synthetic resins which possess ion-exchange properties will take up lead ions.

The process is very simple. All that is necessary is to place the corroded lead objects in contact with granules of an appropriate ion-exchange resin, such as Amberlite IR120, cover with distilled water and keep hot, changing the resin if necessary until the white incrustation disappears. Metallic lead is unaffected, but the incrusta-

[1] Organ, R. M., *Museums J.*, 1953, **53**, p. 49.

tion of basic lead carbonate which gradually dissolves is removed from the system; the lead ions are taken up by the resin in exchange for hydrogen, and carbon dioxide is evolved from the hot liquid. The ion-exchange method has the advantage that no chemicals have been introduced into the system, and therefore subsequent washing of the lead is unnecessary. Although the initial outlay in resin is rather expensive, the method is economical because the resin may be regenerated after use by treating it with nitric acid to dissolve out the absorbed lead, and washing it with distilled water till the washings are neutral to litmus paper: the resin is then in a condition to be used again. The apparatus is shown diagrammatically in Fig. 9. The method has the further advantage that, when specimens are badly swollen and the cracks filled with a resistant white deposit of basic carbonate, it is not essential to remove this, as in using ion-exchange resins the carbonate has not been contaminated with chemicals. Nevertheless it will usually be desirable, for the sake of appearance, to remove all of the carbonate if possible.

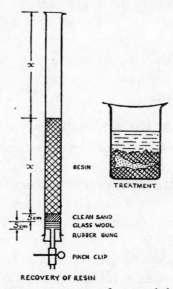

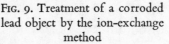

FIG. 9. Treatment of a corroded lead object by the ion-exchange method

However, if certain areas of carbonate prove very resistant, the treatment should not be prolonged unnecessarily in an attempt to remove such resistant corrosion, because the ion-exchange resin does have a slow solvent action on the already cleaned metallic lead, and this is undesirable because it gives the lead an etched appearance. Indeed, since the ion-exchange method can only be conducted in the presence of water, and as distilled water has a certain solvent action on lead, the rate of cleaning should be speeded up whenever possible. To facilitate this, any hard incrustations of carbonate occurring in cracks should be opened up by picking with a needle.

The use of ion-exchange resins is advocated for the treatment of small objects—coins, medals, weights, badges, sling stones, etc.— where there is no deeply incised decoration. But it must be realized that the granules of the resin cannot form intimate contact if the width of incised lines, grooves, etc., is less than the average diameter of the resin granules. In using this method it is essential that any surface coating of shellac or other varnish should be removed before treatment is commenced. Another point to be noted is that, in the case of inscribed objects, the method can only be used if the corrosion is superficial; otherwise consolidative reduction must be used.

3. Use of chelating agents

The treatment of corroded lead seals attached by means of a silk cord to parchment documents, such as, for example, papal bulls, presents a special conservation problem, because from an archival point of view it is not desirable that the seals should be removed from the document for treatment by any of the methods already discussed. This problem has been recently investigated by Kühn,[1] who has devised a method whereby the lead seal can be treated *in situ* without using acids, alkalis, or hot water. The reagent in question for removing all basic lead carbonate is a 10 per cent solution of the disodium salt of ethylene-diamino-tetraacetic acid (available commercially under the trade names Titriplex III and Disodium Deterate, or obtainable directly from many chemical suppliers). The process is simple to carry out. Small areas of the silk cord are first impregnated with a wax solution, the purpose of which is to prevent the solution being absorbed through the cord by capillary action; then the lead seal, resting on two glass rods, is immersed in the above solution, and left there until all the superficial basic lead carbonate has dissolved. This may take up to twenty-four hours depending upon the degree of corrosion, but in the case of heavily corroded seals it may be necessary to renew the solution a number of times. The solution is only very slightly acid and has no appreciable solvent

[1] Kühn, H., *Museumskunde*, 1960, **29**, p. 156.

action on lead itself. When the lead seal is free from corrosion products, it is removed and washed in successive baths of ordinary tap water. It is then dried and waxed in the manner already described (p. 270).

4. Acid treatments

As the white incrustation that develops when lead corrodes is essentially carbonate, it is readily dissolved by acids.

Dilute nitric acid was formerly recommended for removing incrustations of lead carbonate from antiquities, the cleaning effect being immediate. It seemed that excess of acid could be neutralized with alkali, such as caustic soda, and the soluble residue removed with water, leaving a clean metallic surface which, on drying and waxing, would remain permanent under museum conditions. This, however, has not proved to be the case. It appears that, after a lapse of several years, lead so treated acquires a milky appearance, and the method is no longer considered satisfactory.

Experiments using acetic acid have given even less permanent results judged on a time basis. This is not surprising as lead corrodes very readily in presence of acetic acid vapour and carbon dioxide. This, indeed, forms the basis of a commercial process for the manufacture of white lead.

Caley[1] has described a method of treating corroded lead objects in which they are soaked in a cold 10 per cent solution of hydrochloric acid followed by soaking in a 10 per cent solution of ammonium acetate. The advantage of using ammonium acetate is claimed to be two-fold; it dissolves lead dioxide which is insoluble in hydrochloric acid, and it acts as a buffer to protect the lead from the action of any trace of hydrochloric acid that may remain from the first bath. Although this method can give satisfactory results, and Caley has reported on fifty-six lead objects treated in 1937 that were in perfect condition seventeen years later, it has no particular advantage over the method of electrolytic reduction.

[1] Caley, E. R., *Studies in Conservation*, 1955, **2**, p. 49.

STORAGE OF LEAD OBJECTS

The susceptibility of lead to attack by organic acids is one of its principal characteristics. The effect of carbonic acid in presence of acetic acid vapours and of humic acids has already been noted. Tannic acid is equally corrosive, and an exudation of tannic acid from oak cupboards and drawers is credited with causing the intensive corrosion to which lead objects are subject when stored therein. Coins and medals, beggars' badges, crosses, inscribed scrolls, etc., have been found converted completely to amorphous masses of white powder as a result of their being kept during past generations in oak cupboards. Nor are other woods necessarily innocuous. To be harmless, the timber must be well seasoned, and if any doubt exists, it should be sealed with a resistant lacquer. This applies particularly to nests of shallow drawers where there is a large surface of wood and limited ventilation. Well-seasoned mahogany is probably the safest wood to use for cupboards and cases designed for the storage of lead objects.

Organic acid vapours liable to cause corrosion are also derived from certain adhesives used in the making of cardboard boxes and the cardboard cataloguing discs sometimes attached to, or stored with, the objects, and also adhesives used for the passe-partout mounting of thin lead scrolls between sheets of glass. Any adhesive may be harmful to lead if in the course of time it breaks down, forming volatile acidic decomposition products, and it should be remembered that only a very small concentration of acid is needed to start off corrosion, which then proceeds very extensively. Also the waxing process (p. 270) does not guarantee protection over a long period of time. Some lead seals, treated and waxed in the British Museum Research Laboratory, were placed in their original cardboard boxes when returned to the Manuscripts Department, and after four years many of them showed signs of further corrosion.

Any material likely to be used in the storage of lead must be tested to see if any acidic organic vapours are given off. This can be done by placing a piece of bright lead in intimate contact with the material, and leaving it for about six months in a warm place. If there are no signs of corrosion after this time, it is safe to assume that the material is harmless. It has been found that the best method for storing small lead objects, such as coins, medals, etc., is to put them into polythene envelopes or polystyrene boxes. However, these must not be stored in drawers of oak or unseasoned wood.

TIN

Tin has been described as being very stable under normal atmospheric conditions, but when buried in the ground and exposed to moisture and oxygen over a long period it loses its lustre, becoming granular and grey in appearance. This change is due, in the main, to oxidation. The oxide layer may have a greenish hue when traces of copper are present. A more advanced stage in the corrosion is the conversion of the grey stannous oxide to a higher form, stannic oxide, which is nearly white in colour, but it is probable that this only occurs as a secondary reaction in the presence of soluble salts.

Tin is often found as a thin silvery layer on bronze, especially in jewellery and suchlike. This has been applied to the bronze in much the same way as a plumber applies soft solder. The bronze has been cleaned and fluxed to prevent it oxidizing, heated to a temperature slightly above the melting-point of tin (232 °C.), and the molten white metal then wiped over it with a rag charged with tallow. Thin washes of tin are easily destroyed both by acids and alkalis, and when found on ancient metal objects these should be cleaned by mechanical methods if possible.

Solid objects of tin, e.g. plates, jugs, coins, and medals, are cleaned either electrochemically or by electrolytic reduction in the usual caustic soda electrolyte. Corroded tin coins have been found to respond well to electrochemical reduction in the cold, using either zinc, aluminium, or magnesium powder and caustic soda.

The problem of corroded tin is often confused with an allotropic change that takes place in the metal at low temperatures, known as 'tin pest'. This is, however, a different phenomenon from that of ordinary metallic corrosion. It is speedier in action, and more catastrophic in its results, for the metal actually changes its crystalline state and falls into a coarse grey powder. The destruction of everything of archaeological interest is thus complete, and restoration is impossible. It is fortunate that true 'tin pest' occurs very rarely, and only in exceptional circumstances has it been identified with any certainty as occurring in the case of museum objects. When an object of tin shows signs of decay these are almost invariably the result of metallic corrosion, and are therefore amenable to treatment, as was the case with the sarcophagi in the Kapuzinergruft in Vienna.[1]

Special care is required in dealing with heavily oxidized tin that bears incised ornament because in such cases the detail may be entirely in the oxide layer, which must therefore be preserved, and, of course, reduction would destroy this. A case in point is the Hartogs plate in the Rijksmuseum, Amsterdam. This famous plate was recovered after more than eighty years of exposure on the coast of Australia, and it has been supposed to be a victim of 'tin pest' because of its frail condition. It was shown, however, by micrographic examination that the weakness had resulted simply from prolonged metallic corrosion. Oxidation of the surface had been accompanied by a considerable increase in volume, and this had resulted in strains that tended to make the oxide layers split away from the core of metal, threatening the loss of the inscription. In such cases, reduction is out of the question, and the only possible treatment is to consolidate with microcrystalline wax (p. 270). Fortunately, in the case of the Hartogs plate, there was no indication that corrosion was still taking place, and chemical treatment was therefore not required.

In the case of tin coins that have been struck and bear a raised inscription, however, conditions are different. During corrosion the inscription is preserved at the expense of the worked metal constituting the flat part of the coin. This is an interesting case of the debasement of a metal in those parts that have been subjected to the greatest mechanical strain. Thus in struck coins the inscription may be clarified by careful reduction as was done in the case of corroded

[1] Lipl, F., *Studies in Conservation*, 1962, **7**, p. 89.

tin coins from Malaya[1] where good results were obtained by using magnesium powder and caustic soda.

Embedding lead and tin in plastic materials

When a lead or tin coin is of unique interest but is so weak or fragmentary that the remaining pattern is likely to succumb to any process of cleaning, the only way of saving it is to embed it in a transparent plastic. This can be done with a polyester resin (e.g. Crystic) which sets at room temperature without the use of pressure. Purves and Martin[2] have described the method of embedding biological material in such a resin, and Miss Plesters[3] has given full details of its use for embedding paint fragments that are to be prepared as cross-sections. When it is desired to preserve coin fragments, the most convenient shape of the polymerized resin block is one that may be kept in a coin cabinet, i.e. a disc, which should be highly polished to offer minimum interference with vision. As there is a certain shrinkage when the resin sets, it is very difficult to prepare such a polished disc by simply allowing the resin to set in a mould with polished plain faces. Hence it is usually necessary to work and polish at least one of the flat faces.

If an electrically heated press is available, a thermoplastic resin may be used, and the embedding operation is greatly facilitated, since blocks may be prepared of uniform size that only require final polishing. A methacrylate resin called Transoptic[4] has been found to give reproducible results under these conditions. The powdered plastic should first be spread on white paper and examined carefully, any dust or foreign matter being removed. The object is then washed in chloroform, air dried, and thoroughly dried over silica gel. (Avoid touching with the fingers after washing with chloroform.) A circular mould, 2·5 cm. in diameter, is then partly filled with the powder and the object placed gently on top. An equal amount of powder is

[1] Plenderleith, H. J., and Organ, R. M., *Studies in Conservation*, 1953, **1**, p. 63.
[2] Purves, P. E., and Martin, R. S. J., *Museums J.*, 1949, **49**, p. 293.
[3] Plesters, Joyce, Ibid., 1954, **54**, p. 97.
[4] Organ, R. M., in *Recent Advances in Conservation*, Butterworth, London, 1963, p. 128.

added and the plunger of the mould inserted. The mould is then placed in the press and heated gradually to 150 °C. without applied pressure. Heating is discontinued, the pressure raised to 2,000 lb. per sq. inch (140 kg./cm.²), and the mould cooled to 40 °C. while maintaining the pressure. Cooling may be hastened by a water-cooled jacket. The clear resin block containing the coin is then removed and may be finished off by polishing with I.C.I. Perspex Polish, grades 1, 2, and 3 being used successively on Selvyt cloths.

If at a later date it is desired to remove the embedded object, the block is soaked in chloroform. Transoptic swells and dissolves; the polyester resin is crazed, and in each case the object may easily be removed without any risks of damage. The thinnest lead foil has been mounted in Transoptic and demounted without distortion.

PEWTER

Pewter vessels depend to a large extent upon their patina to give them an appearance of dignity and maturity; chemically cleaned pewter has the appearance of lead and so in the conservation of pewter objects it is essential to avoid overcleaning. Where the metal is merely stained or covered with a film of oxide and it is a question of improving the appearance, a rub with a mild abrasive such as rottenstone applied with an oily rag will be all that is required.

When pewter carries a fine design hidden by a thin deposit of lead carbonate, as in the case of the Bastille medal (Pls. 34A and B), it can be treated either by electrolytic reduction or by the ion-exchange process. These remove the corrosion product while preserving the finest details of the design.

Old pewter is occasionally found to have wart-like growths of incrustation on the surface, possibly arising as a result of localized contamination with salts. If these spots have a hard skin and are not showing signs of active corrosion, it may be safer to leave them alone than to attempt to get rid of them (e.g. by grinding) because the material underneath may be mainly tin oxide which is often very crumbly. If exposed to the air, moreover, the under-layers of such spots may begin to corrode actively. If corrosion is already active and treatment essential, electrolytic reduction may be carried out. This will remove all corrosion products but the appearance of the object will suffer because the surface will be left full of small depressions or pock-marks. In such a case the only course that can be recommended is to fill the depressions and make good the surface with wax.

Reduction is the safest procedure, however, when searching for the original pewter marks under a layer of heavy incrustation. Such marks are easily damaged by scraping as the underlying metal may be softer than the incrustation. Tankards and flagons are often marked beneath the lip, and care should be taken with capacity marks on the side of vessels, and makers' and owners' marks under the base. When the site of the mark is known or suspected, local reduction with zinc and caustic soda may be all that is required.

An example of the unexpected discovery of a pewter mark occurred in the case of a plate brought up from the sunken galleon in Tobermory Bay. This had a thin greyish-white incrustation and was apparently devoid of documentary interest. A short reduction in the electrolytic tank, however, revealed a stamp on the under surface of the plate, and it was sufficiently legible to be recognized by the Duke of Argyll as indicating that the plate was of Portuguese origin.

TABLE V. LEAD AND TIN ALLOYS

For method of use see p. 190.

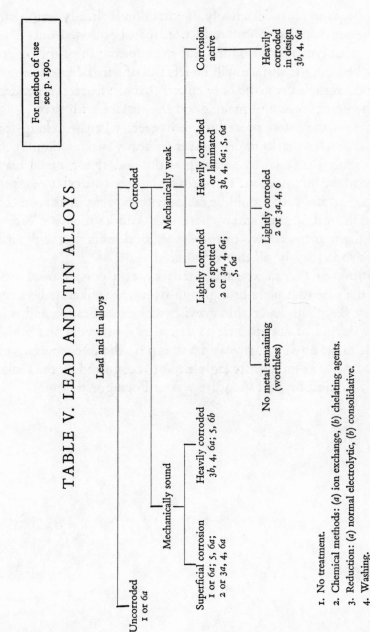

Lead and tin alloys

- Uncorroded
  1 or 6a
- Corroded
  - Mechanically sound
    - Superficial corrosion
      1 or 6a; 5, 6a;
      2 or 3a, 4, 6a
    - Heavily corroded
      3b, 4, 6a; 5, 6b
  - Mechanically weak
    - Lightly corroded or spotted
      2 or 3a, 4, 6a;
      5, 6a
    - Heavily corroded or laminated
      3b, 4, 6a; 5, 6a
      - Lightly corroded
        2 or 3a, 4, 6
      - No metal remaining (worthless)
    - Corrosion active
      - Heavily corroded in design
        3b, 4, 6a

1. No treatment.
2. Chemical methods: (a) ion exchange, (b) chelating agents.
3. Reduction: (a) normal electrolytic, (b) consolidative.
4. Washing.
5. Mechanical cleaning: (a) picking, (b) chipping, (c) grinding, (d) glass-brushing, (e) grit-spraying, (f) burnishing.
6. Protective finishes: (a) wax, (b) impregnation with synthetic resin.

XIII

IRON AND STEEL

IRON occurs in the metallic condition in meteorites where it is associated with small quantities of nickel, cobalt, copper, etc., and the
oldest iron objects that have been subjected to chemical analysis have
been shown by the presence of these trace elements to be of meteoric
origin. Terrestrial iron is of rare occurrence as the metal is so readily
oxidized and converted to minerals, and these are abundantly distributed throughout the earth's crust.

Objects of iron and steel provide some of the most intractable
problems for the conservator, because of the variety and complexity
of their corrosion products. Iron corrodes easily, the corrosion products are unsightly, and the swelling and deformation of the objects
may be severe.

Rusting. Iron is readily attacked by oxygen in presence of moisture
to form rust—a name derived from the characteristic orange and
red compounds that appear as the first products of corrosion. These
consist at first of a mixture of ferrous and ferric hydroxides, but on
further oxidation the rust becomes substantially a hydrated ferric
oxide, in which some carbonate is usually present as well.

This might seem to be fairly straightforward, but when salts are
present that can act as electrolytes, the chemical reactions that cause
corrosion are reinforced by electrochemical reactions, and mineralization is greatly accelerated. It was noted in introducing the subject
of corrosion (p. 194) that when a metal was partially protected from
aeration by patches of oxide, etc., certain areas became anodic and
others cathodic so that, in fact, the corroding metal behaved in the
presence of an electrolyte as if it were a number of tiny galvanic
cells. This is a feature of iron corroding in the presence of sodium
chloride, the anodic areas dissolving to form ferric chloride whilst

the cathodic areas become alkaline owing to the formation of sodium hydroxide. A film of hydrogen gas begins to accumulate on the cathodic areas, and as this has a comparatively high resistance to the passage of electric currents, its presence tends to slow down the reaction. In presence of oxygen, however, the hydrogen is continuously removed, the two gases reacting to form water or hydrogen peroxide. Thus the electrolytic action is enabled to proceed and it continues until the area is covered with a deposit of rust formed by the interaction of the ferric chloride and sodium hydroxide. New areas then take on the roles of anode and cathode and since sodium chloride is regenerated at the same time as the rust is being deposited the cycle of reactions can continue. This is an important factor in the conservation of iron as it means that we are faced with the same conditions that confront us in the treatment of 'bronze disease', namely, that stability cannot be assured until all the chloride has been removed from the corroding object.

It has been mentioned that the accumulation of a film of cathodic hydrogen slows down the electrochemical action, but that the action of oxygen in breaking down this film makes it possible for the corrosion to proceed. It does not follow, however, that, in the absence of oxygen, iron will necessarily remain uncorroded. The film may be broken down in another way, namely by bacterial action, and this introduces a novel factor that is important in studying the corrosion of ferrous metals. Iron and steel are often found to be very badly corroded when buried, under anaerobic conditions, in heavy clay containing sulphates. In this case corrosion has been traced to the presence of sulphate-reducing bacteria which act in a two-fold manner: firstly, converting the sulphates to sulphides which attack the iron, and secondly, breaking down the hydrogen film and thus making it possible for corrosion to continue. When corrosion takes place under such circumstances the surface of the iron is found to be covered with a black crust of iron sulphide, and the clay surrounding the object is also stained black. Should there be any doubt about the nature of the deposit, iron sulphide is easily detected by its reaction with acids to liberate sulphuretted hydrogen recognizable by its characteristic odour of rotten eggs. The first of the sulphate-reducing bacteria to be made the subject of laboratory experiment was *Vibrio desulphuricans*, but many new varieties have since been isolated and it is probable that there are several species.[1] This type of corrosion is very prevalent and in a common cause of the destruction of iron pipes buried in clay.

Reference should also be made to the action of sheath-forming bacteria (e.g. *Gallionella ferriginea*) in promoting corrosion by differential aeration.[2] These bacteria form a blistered structure of tubercles that is a common feature of heavily corroded iron, and sulphate-reducing bacteria may also be active in the anaerobic areas beneath this cellular structure.

PRELIMINARY EXAMINATION

When an iron object comes to the laboratory for treatment, a careful examination is necessary to determine the condition of the specimen before a course of action can be decided upon. If a massive incrustation of dry rust is free from chloride, it may be stable under museum conditions, or if rusting has proceeded to the limit and no metal core remains, even if the oxide is swollen and fissured, the specimen will also have reached a stage of stability and no treatment will be required. On the other hand, if corrosion is still taking place, the chlorides present will have to be removed in order to prevent further deterioration of the object. Therefore the first question to decide is whether there are any signs of chemical activity.

An examination is first made of the surface. Corroding iron does not display the range of colour that is apparent in bronzes that are 'diseased', but even so areas of active corrosion may often be detected by the fact that they have a slightly different colour and texture from those of the surrounding metal or incrustation. But changes of colour and texture do not necessarily indicate in themselves that corrosion

[1] For an interesting résumé of this work see Butlin, K. R., 'Bacteria that Destroy Concrete and Steel', *Discovery*, 1948, pp. 151-5. The general principles of metallic corrosion are broadly surveyed by Vernon, W. H. J., in *Research*, 1952, 5, pp. 54-61.

[2] Burgess, S. G., *School Science Review*, 1952, 34, p. 175.

is active. Dampness on the surface of the object is, however, a sure sign, because when chloride is present in contact with iron it gives rise to ferric chloride which is hygroscopic, and beads of brown liquid may be found on the surface of otherwise dry rust; even a comparatively thin film of rust will show signs of dampness due to chemical activity if chloride is present.

For assessing the internal condition of an iron or steel object, X-radiography is particularly useful. Iron oxides are relatively much more transparent to X-rays than the solid metal, and X-radiographs reveal the distribution and extent of oxidation more certainly and directly than any other method; they enable one to estimate the depth of pitting, and hence to decide on the best method of treatment, and also will reveal the presence of any inlay.

But only in rare cases can radiographic methods of examination be considered an essential and their application in any case is limited by the thickness of the metal. Whether facilities are available for X-radiography or not, a careful examination is always carried out, first with a magnet in order to form some estimate of the extent of the metal core, and then by a needle or metal probe, used with the aid of a lens, in order to reveal the extent and condition of the rust layers and discover, if possible, the existence of any decoration hidden beneath the incrustation. Other tests are made instinctively, e.g. the balance of a rusty blade as an indication of the regularity or otherwise of the corrosion, and an estimate of weight for bulk (relative density) which, with the magnet test, should help in determining the extent of oxidation.

TREATMENT OF IRON OBJECTS

From the preliminary examination it will be decided in which category to place the objects, and guidance as to subsequent procedure may then be obtained by consulting Tables VI and VII on pp. 292 and 294.

Where a substantial core of metal remains in the heart of the rust, reduction methods can be employed without the cleaned object being

Condition as
excavated

Radiograph disclosing
outline of inlays
under rust

Preliminary exploration

Obverse. Mars

Equipment employed for removing the
rust. Radiograph (*extreme right*) used as
guide

Reverse. Military standards

36. FRAGMENT OF A ROMAN SWORD FROM SOUTH SHIELDS (*c.* 200 A.D.)

37. 7TH-CENTURY FRANKISH IRON BUCKLE INLAID WITH SILVER

Left: Before treatment. *Right*: After treatment

mechanically weakened, but if, as in the case of a thin and heavily rusted blade, the metallic core is discontinuous, reduction methods are best avoided.

When small objects no longer have a metallic core they are very brittle, and as any treatment would be likely to weaken them still further, objects in this category are best left alone. Sometimes interesting ornament may be hidden in a mass of rust, and can never be revealed by cleaning because of the frailty of the specimen. In such cases photographic evidence may be made available by radiographic methods, using X-rays or radio-isotopes.[1] At other times a little careful work with a needle under a binocular microscope may succeed in revealing something of special interest. When this can be done without undue risk it is worth while in specimens that are designed for exhibition in public galleries.

Laboratory attention may not be required in order to ensure the stability of a specimen, yet it may be desirable in order to improve the general appearance. Apart from the matter of ordinary repairs, treatment may be required for any of the following reasons—to reveal the original contours or shape; to expose ornament existing in the rust, or decorative inlays that are hidden by the incrustation; to study the method of construction, or, in general, to reveal evidence which, in the absence of such treatment, would be likely to remain concealed. Such evidence may sometimes be obtained by radiography, but more generally by the application of mechanical and chemical methods used either alone or together. Mechanical methods are of special significance in dealing with corroded iron and steel.

Reduction. The standard practice with iron objects is to apply reduction methods whenever possible, i.e. when a good continuous core of metal remains, and there are no complications in the way of inlays or non-metallic attachments. The normal procedure is to apply electrolytic reduction using caustic soda solution as the

[1] Moss, A. A., 'The Application of X-rays, Gamma Rays, Ultra-Violet and Infra-red rays to the Study of Antiquities', *Handbook for Museum Curators*, Part B, Section 4, Museums Association, London, 1954.

electrolyte and iron or stainless steel as the anode. Electrochemical reduction with zinc and caustic soda solution can also be used.

Difficulty is sometimes found in making a good electrical contact with corroded iron objects, and it may be necessary, by scraping away the rust, to expose some uncorroded metal for this purpose. Electrical contacts may have to be made in several places in preparing large objects for electrolytic reduction.

As a matter of interest, electrolytically reduced iron often steams when first rinsed after removal from the tank. This is due to the rapid oxidation of pyrophoric iron, and a case is on record where a large piece of black reduced rust, when picked off, actually glowed and burned through the french polish on the bench! This, however, is very exceptional.

When reduction is completed, the object is removed from the tank, rinsed in cold water to remove the sludge consisting of re-duction products, etc., and then boiled in successive changes of distilled water until the wash-water is free of chlorides as indicated by the silver nitrate test. The washing should be carried out as rapidly as possible to prevent rusting. The object is dried in a warm oven for at least twenty-four hours, or under an infra-red heater, brushed, and then given a protective finish (see below).

Caustic soda treatment. Where chemical corrosion is observed to be taking place on an object that is too frail for electrolytic reduction, it may be treated by boiling the object in successive baths of dilute caustic soda solution (not more than 1 per cent), followed by boiling in changes of distilled water. The results may be satisfactory when the treated object is kept in a dry place, but with this method there is a chance that chlorides may remain in the under layers, and the result of caustic soda treatment is therefore not necessarily permanent.

Sodium sesquicarbonate treatment. As an alternative to caustic soda a 5 per cent solution of sodium sesquicarbonate may be used at room temperature, the volume of solution being just sufficient to cover the object. During the first week the solution should be changed daily, as most of the chloride is washed out rapidly, but in the later stages

weekly changes will be sufficient. The progress of the reaction is
followed by testing the solution for chlorides (p. 201). When the
presence of chloride has reached a minimum, the object is left in a
final bath for four weeks, and then tested for chloride. If this test is
negative, this indicates that the treatment is completed; otherwise
further treatment must be continued. At the end of the treatment
the object is dried and waxed as already described. Waxing is
preferable to a lacquer for giving mechanical support to a frail
object.

The duration of the treatment depends on the nature of the object
and the amount of chlorides initially present. In experiments carried
out in the British Museum Research Laboratory[1] in which the actual
concentration of chlorides was determined, it was found that in one
case where the initial concentration of chloride in the first bath was
635 parts per million, treatment for twenty weeks was necessary
before the chloride concentration was reduced to a minimum value
of 8 parts per million, whereas when the initial concentration was
54 parts per million only eight weeks were necessary to reduce the
concentration to 5 parts per million.

Use of rust softeners, solvents, and inhibitors. Thin rust spots on burnished steel may often be softened by keeping the steel under paraffin
oil for a few hours, and then rubbing locally with worn emery paper
of fine grade or even a match-stick, but care must be taken to remove
all the paraffin oil or fresh rust is likely to be formed. The paraffin
oil is removed with a dry cloth, and replaced with a lubricating oil,
and this is eventually removed by dry rubbing, any thin residual
film of lubricating oil being harmless. The substance known as
'Plus-Gas Fluid A' is even more effective than oil in softening rust.
Unless rust spots are removed, they tend in time to bite deeply into
the metal. At these points anodic attack is taking place, and this
localized chemical action is a stimulus to greater activity. It is important, therefore, in maintaining collections of armour and the like,
to be aware of the danger of rust-pitting, and to take action in good
time to remove the rust. Where salts are absent, and atmospheric

[1] Oddy, W. A., and Hughes, H. J., *Studies in Conservation*, 1970, **15**, p. 183.

relative humidities are at 50 per cent or under, rusting is not a serious problem, but moisture readily condenses on cold metal surfaces, and condensation is always a menace if there should be a sudden drop in temperature. Also in a city atmosphere, condensed moisture might well contain sulphur dioxide which would promote rusting. A smear of lanolin (wool fat) has proved to be a good protective agent for burnished steel, but as it leaves the surface of the metal sticky, it is only of practical value when the steel is protected by being enclosed in an exhibition case. A thin layer of non-sticky wax is to be preferred for museum objects (see Appendix XV).

Certain commercial rust removers come within the category of rust solvents,[1] and these are of special value for derusting objects that are either too heavy or too large and unwieldy for treatment by electrolytic methods. Some have the added advantage of being rust inhibitors, i.e. they leave a protective film on the surface of the metal after treatment. Rust solvents may be applied by brushing, and when the solvent action has gone far enough, either the surface is wiped clean without washing, or in other cases any remaining chemicals are washed away. In using these commerical preparations the makers' instructions must be followed implicitly.

In these rust inhibitors the active constituent is often a derivative of phosphoric acid which forms an inert film of ferric phosphate on the surface of the metal. In this connexion it is interesting to observe that objects of iron or steel are occasionally found in the ground in a substantially uncorroded state after years of burial. This may sometimes be explained when they are from a burial site, and have been exposed to the action of phosphates from adjacent bones. The protection given by tannates, which may have their origin in decomposing leather or oak bark, is even more marked.

Rust may be removed by the use of a solvent such as a 9 per cent solution of oxalic acid, but it is often more convenient to use a complexing reagent, which has the property of combining with the iron dissolved from the rust; the iron is then said to be sequestered. Some of the most effective complexing reagents are derivatives of

[1] e.g. ACP Deoxidine, Jenolite, Ferroclene.

ethylenediamine tetra-acetic acid (EDTA), and these include a range of compounds that will complex iron under either acid or under alkaline conditions. Detarex HM is claimed to be the most powerful complexing agent for dealing with iron salts, but Detarex C is of greatest interest as it can be used in the presence of caustic soda which slightly dissolves rust to form ferrites. This is extremely effective on freshly deposited rust, but less so on aged and especially on heated iron oxide. In these difficult cases it is a help to add sodium hyposulphite ($Na_2S_2O_4$).[1] A solution which has been used with good effect contained 30 ml. Detarex C, 30 gm. caustic soda, and 6 gm. sodium hyposulphite per litre of water. The method of application is to keep the rusty object immersed in a hot solution until such time as the rust is dissolved to the required extent, the object being throughly washed, dried, and waxed thereafter.

Protective finishes. Whatever chemical method is adopted in cleaning iron and steel objects, the subsequent washing to remove residual chlorides is likely to cause the metal to become somewhat rusty and discoloured. After drying this can be removed by brushing. There then arises the question of what type of protective finish is likely to be most effective. In the past sealing agents such as oils, fats, and vaseline were used, but these are not satisfactory because they leave a sticky surface, and may be difficult to remove from objects that have suffered extensive corrosion and have a pitted or flaky surface. It is preferable to use either a microcrystalline wax (Cosmolloid 80H) or a lacquer. Waxing is done by immersing the object in the molten wax until no more air bubbles are evolved from the object; if immersion is not feasible the wax is applied locally using an industrial type of hot-air blower, or an electrically heated spatula. Any excess of wax can be removed by placing the object on absorbent paper and heating it with a hot-air blower. If the object is fairly robust, an organic lacquer, such as Ercalene, can be applied by brushing. The final colour can be adjusted, if necessary, by adding a small amount of a suitable pigment to the wax.

[1] Formerly known as hydrosulphite. This is not to be confused with photographic 'hypo', which is sodium thiosulphate ($Na_2S_2O_3$).

Certain chemical substances have the property of preventing the corrosion of iron and steel in enclosed spaces without being in contact with the metal surface at all. These are known as Vapour Phase Inhibitors (V.P.I.),[1] but it is not safe to use them indiscriminately, as, however effective they may be with ferrous metal, some have been found to attack copper alloys and others soft solder. It is likely therefore that the use of wax or lacquer will continue to be the most popular type of finish for archaeological specimens.

PATTERNS IN SWORD BLADES, DAMASCENE WORK, ETC.

A feature of the Japanese sword-blade is the pattern latent in the steel, arising from the method of forging by folding and twisting the red-hot billet of metal according to a pre-arranged formula. A series of intricate cloud, wave, and other patterns may thus be repeated along the length of the blade, and good examples are greatly esteemed by the connoisseur and must be preserved. Should the metal be allowed to become dull, the pattern may become indistinct and finally disappear. Reference has been made (p. 209) to the conservation of such weapons. The following note refers to a method of restoring a lost pattern, using the reagent called 'nital' prepared by dissolving 1·5 ml. of concentrated nitric acid (Analytical Reagent, Sp. Gr. 1. 42) in 100 ml. of alcohol (industrial methylated spirit). First remove any grease with a soft rag moistened with toluene or trichloroethane. Then moisten a swab of surgical cotton-wool with freshly prepared nital solution[2] and apply it uniformly to the blade, rubbing backwards and forwards from hilt to point. This is done beside a running tap under which the blade is plunged to arrest the etching of the acid. Sometimes this solution develops the pattern within a few seconds; at other times several short applications may be necessary before the desired result is obtained. The blade should be closely inspected after each washing; as an excessive use of the

---

[1] Biek, L., *Museums J.*, 1953, **53**, p. 110. For summary of tests see Bennister, H. L., *Research*, 1952, **9**, p. 424.

[2] Rubber gloves should be worn.

reagent might blur the pattern, it is very important to avoid carrying the action too far. The blade must finally be washed under the running tap for about half a minute and carefully dried with a soft cloth.

Japanese swords should be kept *slightly* waxed. If the waxing is overdone, there is a possibility that dust will accumulate, and as great care must be taken to ensure that the scabbards are kept free from any dust that might cause scratching, it is better not to wax at all than to apply wax too liberally. The formula using microcrystalline wax given in Appendix XV is suitable. The smallest quantity is brushed uniformly over the burnished metal with a moderately stiff brush. Then as much as possible of this is removed by brushing with a softer brush having longer bristles.

The textured patterns in damascened blades often have the appearance of 'watered silk', an effect obtained by long heating and light forging, producing what is known as spheroidization of iron carbide in a pearlite structure. Damascened blades should be treated with the same care as is afforded to Japanese swords.

The coarser pattern effects sometimes found in swords of the eighteenth century, and typically in the Malayan kris, are obtained by variations in relief of the different elements of the pattern. This is attained by an etching process and in general such blades provide no complication as regards preservation.

PRESERVATION OF RUST

When iron is completely converted to massive oxide and no free metal remains, the specimen is stable and no laboratory treatment is required for its preservation. When the rust is in a granular rather than a massive condition, however, there is always the possibility of disintegration due to the crystallizations of salts, and in this case the specimen will have to be washed free from salts before its stability can be assured; the surface may have to be consolidated by impregnation before washing as is done in the case of brittle pottery and stone (see p. 330).

TABLE VI

NOTES ON THE TREATMENT OF IRON AND STEEL OBJECTS

TWELVE REPRESENTATIVE SPECIMENS

Object	Features	Treatment	Result
1. Coat of mail.	Loosely adherent red rust; some links very thin.	Derusting solutions considered dangerous in this case; dry brushing, and brushing lightly with wax.	The cleaned chain had a black appearance and dull shine.
2. Welwyn fire dogs.	Large, heavy, and broken in two.	Cleaning in part by electrolytic reduction, in part by derusting solutions, and in part by picking. Repaired by metal splint screwed to the old metal.	The broken parts reassembled, and details of structure revealed.
3. Romano-British steelyard.[1]	Iron beam and lead weight badly corroded.	Reduction with zinc and caustic soda.	Restored. Method of use and capabilities of the instrument rediscovered.
4. Stanwick sword.[2]	Corroded and encrusted with iron sulphide, due to action of sulphate-reducing bacteria.	Electrolytic reduction. Mounted on a base-board having a recess of the shape of the sword.	Shape recovered; object frail but complete.
5. Sutton Hoo sword.	1. The blade fragmentary and largely mineralized. 2. The tang. 3. Gold hilt ornaments.	X-radiography. Mechanical treatment. Reassembled with hilt in a Perspex mount in such a manner that each piece is detachable.	Design of the pattern-welded blade recorded. Main structure of the hilt revealed and position of ornaments established.
6. Sutton Hoo shield boss.[3]	Encrusted with carbonate and rust concealing ornament in gold, bronze, tin, and garnets.	Dilute nitric acid (1 per cent), locally, and detergents—washing and drying through alcohol and ether baths, and finally lacquering.	The original state recovered as far as possible, and much interesting ornament revealed.

	Condition	Treatment	Result
7. Sword hilt from Anglo-Saxon burial at Coombe.[4]	Fragmentary; rust concealing decoration in silver gilt and niello.	Careful picking with needle under binocular microscope; local electrolytic reduction with formic acid; dried and lacquered; mounted in perspex.	Decoration in silver gilt and design in niello revealed. (Pls. 35A and B.)
8. South Shields sword.	Fragmentary masses of rust, apparently insignificant.	X-radiography to reveal inlay. Mechanical treatment to remove overlying rust.	Inlaid figures of Mars and of Roman standard revealed. The brass[5] inlays exposed to view on either side of the blade. (Pl. 36 illustrates the progress of the work.)
9. Japanese sword guards.	Inlays and design practically concealed by superficial rust.	Careful picking and use of motor brushes with mild abrasives; rust softeners where necessary. Final waxing.	Design and inlays revealed.
10. Merovingian buckles.	Silver inlays covered with rust.	X-radiography to reveal pattern. Rust picked off under binocular microscope.	Silver pattern completely revealed on a ground of black iron. (Pl. 37.)
11. Merovingian purse mount.	Frail rust; no metal remaining.	X-radiograph indicated object too frail for any form of treatment.	Contour established, and intricate ornamental inlays of noble metal recorded by radiography.
12. Sutton Hoo axe.	Fragmentary; massive rust; no metal remaining.	Cross-sections of fragments indicated original shape of haft and head; also the existence of a ring at end of handle. Original shape recovered by picking and grinding.	Reconstruction based on evidence that was only discovered by patient microscopical studies.

1 Moss A. A., Antiqs. J., 1940, 20, p. 385.
2 Wheeler, Sir Mortimer, The Stanwick Fortifications Research Report, 17, 1954. Antiqs. J., London.
3 Maryon, H., Antiquity, 1946, 20, p. 21.
4 Davidson, H. R. L., and Webster, L., Mediaeval Archaeology, 1967, 11, p. 1
5 While this material could not be sampled for analysis, a brass of similar appearance on a Roman scabbard in the British Museum, of the first century A.D. and bearing the image of Tiberius, was spectrographically examined and proved to be an alloy of copper and zinc containing a lesser quantity of tin; traces of silver, lead, and iron were present. It is possible that the two Roman alloys correspond with the metal known as orichalcum (Plato, Critias, 114 E) obtained from a naturally occurring mineral.

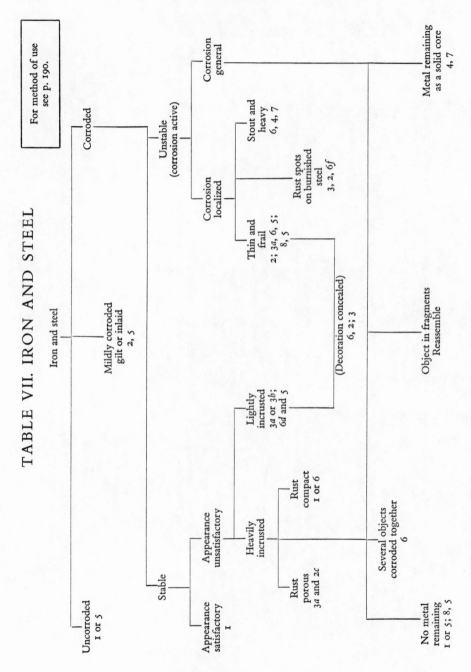

TABLE VII. IRON AND STEEL

For method of use
see p. 190.

Iron and steel

Uncorroded
1 or 5

Corroded

Mildly corroded
gilt or inlaid
2, 5

Stable

Unstable
(corrosion active)

Appearance
satisfactory
1

Appearance
unsatisfactory

Heavily
incrusted

Lightly
incrusted
3a or 3b;
6d and 5

Corrosion
localized

Corrosion
general

Rust
porous
3a and 2c

Rust
compact
1 or 6

Thin and
frail
2; 3a, 6, 5;
8, 5

Rust spots
on burnished
steel
3, 2, 6f

Stout and
heavy
6, 4, 7

(Decoration concealed)
6; 2; 3

Several objects
corroded together
6

No metal
remaining
1 or 5; 8, 5

Object in fragments
Reassemble

Metal remaining
as a solid core
4, 7

1. No treatment.
2. Mild abrasives:
   (a) Fine emery powder; (b) carborundum powder; (c) steel wool.
3. Rust softeners:
   (a) Paraffin oil; penetrating oil; 'Plus-Gas Fluid A'.
   (b) Petroleum jelly; lubricating oil; clock oil.
   (c) Lanolin mixtures.
   (d) Deoxidine, Jenolite.
   Rust solvents:
   (e) Oxalic acid.
   (f) Citric acid half neutralized with ammonia.
   (g) Deoxidine, Jenolite.
4. Reduction: (a) zinc and caustic soda. (b) electrolytic reduction.
5. Protective finishes: (a) lacquer, (b) microcrystalline wax.
6. Mechanical: (a) picking, (b) chipping, (c) grinding, (d) scratch-brushing, (e) grit-spraying, and (f) burnishing.
7. Washing in hot distilled water to remove soluble chlorides.
8. Washing in hot caustic soda or cold sodium sesquicarbonate.

When the removal of rust might cause the collapse of the specimen, it should be preserved. It should also be retained if its removal would be likely to result in serious disfigurement. A common example is the spotty surface sometimes found on a reduced iron object; the spots are due to compacted masses of ferric oxide occupying pits in the metal, and if these were dug out, the smooth surface would be made unsightly, and they are, therefore, left *in situ*. When salts have been removed as far as possible, and the object has been given a protective coating of wax or lacquer, the risk of corrosion breaking out again under museum conditions is extremely slight.

Iron rust may have an evidential value. It is never safe to proceed to reduce a rusty object without making a careful examination to ensure that there are no features peculiar to the rust that will be sacrificed in the process. Thus, a rusted shield grip may retain fragments of a leather belt, or the oxidized surface of a sword may provide the only evidence of the structure of the scabbard or the hilt. Textile imprints in rust may be important, and even the off-prints from reeds or grasses with which the corroding object was in contact. Compacted rust is to be regarded, therefore, as possibly retaining evidence that might otherwise be unobtainable, and laboratory treatment, on occasion, may have to be directed to the preservation of this evidence, rather than to the restoration of the object as a museum specimen.

PRACTICAL EXAMPLES

In the absence of a personal examination, it is never possible to give more than an indication of what treatment would be likely to be the most desirable in any particular instance, but some further guidance may be obtained by studying case sheets. Brief practical notes are given in Table VI relating to a dozen iron objects selected as being representative of different stages of mineralization, in the hope that they may illustrate the application of methods already described, and at the same time be useful for reference.

PART III

SILICEOUS AND RELATED
MATERIALS

XIV

STONE

SINCE early in the present century the preservation of stone has engaged the attention of scientists the world over. The phenomena of decay are commonly to be seen on public buildings and outdoor monuments: weathering, which weakens the stone though it may sometimes enhance its appearance; staining, which may result in permanent disfigurement; and the crystallization of salts, which in some cases may cause powdering of the surface, cracking, and even complete disintegration. Deterioration may be traced to bad technique such as carelessness, or lack of knowledge or experience in the handling of stone by architects or builders, but it is more often due to natural causes. In this case, the most that can be done is to try to find a way of mitigating the damage, by washing, or periodic steam cleaning, or, it may be, by some form of impregnation.

While some reference will be made to the treatment of outdoor stone monuments, it is principally the preservation of stone objects indoors that will be dealt with here. This is the simpler task, and although it introduces problems, it may fairly be claimed that most of them are capable of solution.

MINERALS

The earth's crust is composed of minerals associated together to form rocks, and, while the rocks have been used as such for building and sculpture, certain of the minerals have attracted the artist-craftsman from earliest times because of their special qualities for fine work, e.g. hardness, texture, and colour. In the Far East and in the Americas, minerals such as jade, rock crystal, and malachite were used for fine carvings; in the Middle East, lapis lazuli, turquoise, and carnelian were employed extensively for inlaying furniture and for the decoration of metal objects; and alabaster provided the Egyptian craftsman with an attractive material from which to fashion the lamps and unguent pots that were an essential furnishing both of the temple and of the tomb.

Minerals, as a class, may be regarded as inert, and objects fashioned from them are unlikely to need attention other than periodic cleaning, which can be done in some cases by washing with warm soapy water, or by brushing with spirit.

There is, however, one exception, and this is the mineral called marcasite which is sometimes used for inlays. Marcasite is a sulphide of iron, being a variety of iron pyrites, and it has a similar brassy appearance. It is very liable to decomposition which takes place as a result of oxidation in the presence of moisture, the sulphide being converted to ferrous sulphate which forms a white feathery incrustation on the surface, sulphuric acid being produced at the same time. Treatment may take the form of washing, or, in bad cases, soaking in dilute ammonia prior to washing; and since the acid is, of course, the major factor in causing decomposition, washing is continued until acid can no longer be detected on testing the wash water with litmus.

When fossils contain decomposing marcasite and calcium carbonate they are often beyond recovery, because the acid resulting from the decomposition of the marcasite reacts with the calcium carbonate causing disintegration. Such fossils are said to be 'pyritized', and the best method of treating them is to expose the fossil to the fumes of strong ammonia in a closed vessel. This neutralizes any free acid, but the treatment may take many months and even then can never be guaranteed to be completely successful as it may not be possible for the ammonia fumes to reach all of the acid. After washing in water, drying is conducted quickly through baths of alcohol and ether, and the fossil is then impregnated with a lacquer to exclude air and moisture. For this purpose a silicone lacquer is very suitable, as it is a water repellent; good results have also been obtained by using polyvinyl acetate in a mixed solvent of nine volumes of toluene to one volume of acetone.

A. Before treatment—the shape almost obliterated by salt crystals

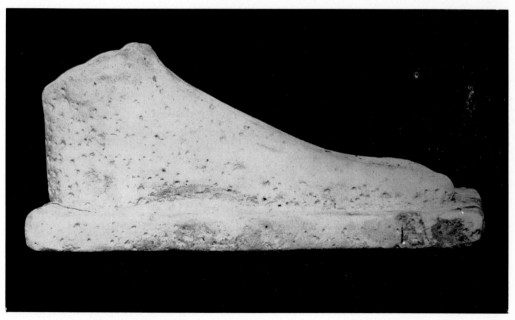

B. After treatment—revealed as the model of a left foot

38. EGYPTIAN SCULPTOR'S TRIAL PIECE OF A FOOT IN LIMESTONE
(PTOLEMAIC PERIOD)

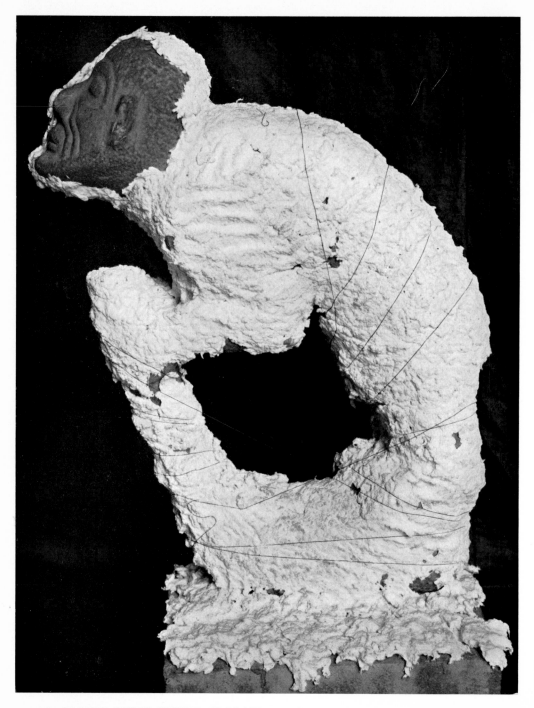

39. CARVED STONE FIGURE, PROBABLY HUAXTEC CULTURE, FROM MEXICO
Coated with paper pulp to remove soluble salts

IGNEOUS ROCKS—GRANITE AND BASALT

Of the igneous rocks, granite and basalt are most widely distributed. These are generally hard, non-porous, and very stable under a wide variety of conditions. Granite contains over 66 per cent of silica, and is an acidic rock, whereas basalt is a basic rock containing less than 52 per cent of silica. Between these two extremes there are many well-defined rocks of an intermediate silica content. Many have been used for monuments in antiquity and have survived weathering extremely well.

A problem is presented, however, when such stones are brought away from their natural surroundings and exposed in the open to weathering of a nature that is foreign to them. Cleopatra's Needle, a granite obelisk from Heliopolis, now on the Embankment in London, was observed to have suffered a marked deterioration in its condition on being taken from the dry atmosphere of Egypt to the humid atmosphere of England. A like deterioration was observed in a similar granite monolith that was taken from Egypt to New York, and it was found necessary in each case to treat the stone so as to prevent access of moisture.

A study of the London monolith made in 1952[1] showed it to be a typical granite composed of crystals of quartz, feldspars, hornblende, and some white mica. While the stone was originally of a pink colour, it had become badly stained with a black film. This proved to be mostly carbonaceous in nature, but it contained an inorganic residue which consisted mainly of iron oxide and silica. Light coloured patches marked places where flakes of the stone had become detached by the action of frost which was regarded as the prime cause of the deterioration. Conservation involved cleaning, drying, and waterproofing the stone. Cleaning proved to be difficult; the roughened surface of the granite necessitated the use of scrubbing brushes and even wire brushes, and it was found that the application of an organic solvent was essential to soften the black film before it could be removed. The solvent was composed of nine volumes of carbon

---

[1] Burgess, S. G., and Schaffer, R. J., *Chemistry and Industry*, 1952, p. 1026.

tetrachloride and one volume of benzene emulsified by the addition of a surface-active agent, e.g. 1 per cent of Lissapol N. When the cleaning was completed and the natural colour restored, the stone was hosed down and allowed to dry; it was then given two applications of a 10 per cent solution of paraffin wax (M.P. 50 °C.) in white spirit. After the solvent had evaporated, the stone was warmed gently, using a blow-lamp, with the object of getting the wax into the cracks and porous sections, and thus excluding moisture. This worked well, and the stone, inasmuch as it has been waterproofed, is now protected from the action of frost which was the main object of treatment. The staining by soot, however, cannot be prevented, especially with a surface as rough as this Egyptian granite, and within three years the stone had become as black as ever.

Basalts are more homogeneous than granites, and they seem to be less liable to deterioration. Certain monuments of lava from British Honduras were observed to be very crumbly on the surface after having been exposed in the portico of the British Museum for a few years and had to be brought indoors. These stones are porous and therefore prone to damage by frost, but how far the industrial atmosphere may have contributed to their deterioration is hard to assess.

Such incidents serve to illustrate the general principle that when an object is exposed out of doors it is liable to suffer deterioration from causes that are beyond control, and although the object may never have been intended for a museum, it may be necessary to keep it indoors so that it will be protected from dirt and the rigours of a climate that will hasten its destruction.

SEDIMENTARY ROCKS—SANDSTONE AND LIMESTONE

The problem of preserving sedimentary rocks is essentially one of overcoming surface frailty. The particles of grit of which they are composed are cemented together in a matrix which, if disrupted, leaves the particles free to fall away in powder. On the other hand, some stones develop a natural skin or patina which may afford a certain degree of protection. However, if calcareous sandstone or limestone is exposed to an urban atmosphere containing sulphur dioxide which is eventually converted into sulphuric acid, the formation of calcium sulphate soon weakens the surface to such an extent that the surface tends to flake off. Experiments made in an effort to strengthen such a surface by applying so-called stone preservatives have proved to be unsuccessful. Indeed, studies in stone preservation have brought out the fact that the application of impervious surface films to stone seems to intensify deterioration instead of affording protection. This is due to the fact that such preservatives do not penetrate deep enough into the stone to form a secure bond between the sound underlying stone and the weakened surface layer.

If objects made of sandstone or limestone are relatively porous, they will absorb soluble salts during burial in the ground, and these absorbed soluble salts constitute a potential source of deterioration when these objects are excavated and brought into the museum. Owing to fluctuations in the relative humidity, the soluble salts will tend to work their way to the surface of the stone, where they will crystallize out, sometimes as a hard deposit, but more frequently in the form of filamentous crystals which appear as if extruded from the pores (Pls. 38A and B). The growth of the crystals imposes such a strain that the surface becomes fragile and may eventually break away so that ornamental details are defaced and incised inscriptions become illegible. Preservation of stones in this condition can only be achieved if the soluble salts are extracted from the whole body of the stone.

PRESERVATIVE TREATMENTS

1. Removal of soluble salts

(a) *By immersion in water.* In cases where the salts have not yet started to crystallize on the surface, the stone object, supported if necessary on a wooden frame, is immersed completely in a tank of water. When, however, crystals have formed on the surface, these should be removed as far as possible by dusting them off gently with a small soft brush prior to immersion in the tank. The tank can be made of glass or a plastic such as PVC or polythene for small objects, but for large objects it is convenient to construct a heavy wooden tank lined with polythene sheeting. Iron or copper should never be used as these are liable to cause staining of the stone. The water used in the early stages of washing can be ordinary tap water, provided it is not too hard, but the washing should be completed by using distilled water. The progress of the washing is followed by testing the wash-water for chlorides periodically with silver nitrate (p. 201). Depending upon the size of the object and the amount of salts in the stone, the tank water must be changed periodically. Washing is continued until the silver nitrate test shows that as much as possible of the chloride has been removed.

Since heating increases the solvent action and diffusion of water, the rate of desalting can be increased if the temperature of the water is raised to about 60 °C. by incorporating an electric heating device in the tank.

It is important to note that once the stone is wet, it must not be allowed to dry out at any stage during the washing process; damage may be caused by further crystallization of salts until these have been removed. Also if the stone has a weak structure or is decorated with polychrome, consolidation of the stone will be necessary before washing is commenced, and it may be preferable to use the paper-pulp method.

(b) *By extraction with moist paper pulp*. Paper pulp is available commercially, but it can easily be prepared by boiling good quality blotting-paper with distilled water and beating it until completely disintegrated and the cellulose fibres mat together forming a pulp. When cold, the wet paper pulp is thrown against the stone so that it adheres, and a kind of papier mâché garment is gradually built up until the object is concealed completely (Pl. 39). The water in the pulp will be absorbed by the stone and the pulp will shrink slightly as it dries so that eventually the stone will be covered with a porous layer of material about 1–2 cm. thick. The water absorbed by the stone will dissolve the soluble salts, and, at first, carry them farther in; but, because salts in solution tend to move towards a surface where evaporation is taking place, they will in time change direction and eventually leave the stone, forming an incrustation in the pulp. The pulp is left in position for about three weeks, when it may easily be removed; it is then replaced with fresh pulp and if the stone is very salty a third application may be necessary.

In cases where the surface of the stone has been loosened by incrustations of crystals, or where there is painted decoration, as in Egyptian tomb paintings, consolidation is necessary *before* applying the pulp. This is done by painting the stone freely with a 2 per cent solution of soluble nylon in ethyl alcohol or industrial methylated spirit. By this means the powdery grains are held together and the paint fixed, and when quite dry the stone is ready for the pulp treatment. The film of soluble nylon does not prevent the extraction of the salts, but as the diffusion takes place more slowly it may be necessary to continue the treatment for several months, renewing the pulp coating from time to time during this period. The painted decoration will not appear shiny after treatment, because the film of soluble nylon is very matt. It is usual for the texture and appearance of the painted surface to be improved after treatment by the paper pulp method. It should be noted that although the paper pulp method can be extremely effective, it does not remove all the soluble salt from an incrusted stone; a certain residue is bound to remain, but if the work has been carried out properly this will have no material effect upon the stability of the specimen when it is preserved under museum conditons.

(c) *By transpiration through the stone.* In this process, recently introduced by Kratz,[1] the stone object is enclosed in a vacuum-tight impermeable coating of a plastic material, the base of the object being left free. The object is then placed in a small tank of distilled water which is drawn up through the body of the stone by means of vacuum induced through one or more openings in the top of the plastic coating connected to a vacuum pump. By this means the stone is flushed out until all the soluble salts have been removed. The method is simple and rapid, but it may be necessary to

[1] Kratz, A., *Museumskunde*, 1963, No. 1, p. 32.

consolidate the surface of the stone before the plastic coating is applied, and care should be taken in removing the coating after the treatment.

2. Removal of insoluble salts

Sometimes the prevailing incrustation is insoluble in water so that washing is of no avail and alternative methods must then be employed. These will depend on the chemical nature of the incrustation. If the salt is carbonate, it can be decomposed by any acid, but a warning is necessary since even sandstones may contain calcite (calcium carbonate) as an essential part of their structure; before using acid, therefore, it must be established that the rock is neither a limestone nor a sandstone containing calcium carbonate. The rock, when tested, should not itself effervesce with acid. Even when all seems well, acids should only be applied locally and sparingly, not with the object of dissolving salts wholesale, but rather with the object of loosening the crystals so that they may be dislodged mechanically. For this purpose, dilute nitric acid (5 per cent or even weaker) may be used, followed by thorough washing with water.

When the incrustation consists of selenite or gypsum (calcium sulphate dihydrate) that has been laid down in glassy crystals, it may be very disfiguring. Such incrustations have formed very slowly and are probably harder in the mass than the surface of the stone which will certainly have been weakened during their growth. It is unwise, therefore, to try any chipping or grinding process until preliminary steps have been taken to try to soften the incrustation. Unfortunately, no solvents are available that will dissolve gypsum readily. If feasible, the best treatment is to keep the stone immersed in lukewarm water for a long time, changing the water every twenty-four hours; this has been found to be more effective than immersion in either cold or hot water. Solutions of sodium thiosulphate, sodium hexametaphosphate (Calgon), or ammonium carbonate (10 per cent concentration), may be applied locally, but these chemicals act slowly and they must be washed out very thoroughly afterwards or the cure may be worse than the disease.

A novel method of treatment that at times has proved to be very effective depends on the fact that selenite is a hydrated mineral, and that it goes to powder when it is dehydrated by heating. An incrustation may sometimes be heated with an electric soldering iron, and if the temperature is strictly under control it is possible to disintegrate the gypsum so that it can be brushed away without damage to the stone. The method is obviously not without danger, but in cases where a fine object is suffering from a gross disfigurement of selenite which would otherwise be difficult to remove, it may be worthy of consideration. Needless to say, the stone must be quite dry when heat is applied, and it should be borne in mind that overheating a limestone converts it into quicklime.

Another method that may also be employed for the removal of insoluble incrustations is an ultrasonic dental tool, the so-called Cavitron. This device has been successfully used in conservation,[1] but the results achieved depend to a large extent on the skill of the operator. Hempel[2] has described its successful use for the removal of a thick black incrustation from a marble statue.

3. Consolidation

After salts have been removed from stone, it is often necessary to strengthen the surface. In the British Museum Research Laboratory hardening tests were carried out upon a number of Coptic stele of very porous limestone that had been desalted by the pulp method, using such consolidating liquids as white beeswax in turpentine, white shellac in alcohol, and solutions of cellulose nitrate and polyvinyl acetate. It was found that, under museum conditions, success was related directly to the degree of penetration of the consolidating agent. After a lapse of twenty years a further series of observations was made on the same stele after they had been exposed to damp in an unheated war-damaged building. This confirmed the earlier observations that the most satisfactory consolidating agents are those

[1] Kramer, W., in *Restaurierung und Konservierung*, Verlag Bruno Hessling, Berlin, 1964, p. 41.

[2] Hempel, K. F. B., *Studies in Conservation*, 1969, **14**, p. 126.

which can be made to penetrate well into the material and not merely remain on the surface, especially if the stones are liable to be exposed to damp and varying temperature conditions.

It is clear from the tests that it is not possible to preserve a powdery stone surface by merely giving it a coat of varnish. Porous stone contains air that will expand and contract with variations in temperature, even under museum conditions, and no thin surface film could long withstand the consequent movement without fracture. This is the reason why the most successful results have been achieved either by securing deep penetration of the consolidating agent, or by employing a form of surface treatment that leaves the stone free to 'breathe'. These treatments will now be described in detail.

(a) *Impregnation with wax*. If properly carried out, wax treatment has been shown to stand the test of time satisfactorily. Where possible the stone should be immersed in a tank of molten wax—a method of treatment that has already been described in the case of wooden objects (see p. 136). Special plant is required for such treatment, however, and the size and weight of the stone might be such as to make this method impracticable. When wax has to be applied to the surface of a large object that cannot be immersed, the only way to ensure penetration into the pores of the stone is to heat the stone for a time before applying the wax. The stone must, of course, be thoroughly dry before it is heated.

A convenient method of heating is to use an electric fire placed about three feet from the stone. By this means, a wide area can be dealt with at once. When the stone is hot, the fire is switched off and white beeswax applied in the form of a thin salve having the consistency of vaseline. This salve is prepared by stirring molten beeswax at about 85 °C. into petroleum ether (B.P. 80–100 °C.), care being taken not to do so in the presence of naked lights. When the salve is applied to the warm stone, the wax is absorbed into the pores and the inflammable solvent evaporates. After all the solvent has evaporated heating may be repeated, and further coats applied in the same manner as long as the wax is being absorbed.

Perhaps it should be mentioned, in the interests of aesthetics, that waxing invariably causes a certain dullness and lowering of tone particularly noticeable on light stones, and also that waxed stone is easily stained by dirt. This latter problem is not so serious when microcrystalline waxes are employed (see Appendix XV).

The waxing method may be used also for statuary that is kept out of doors, but it is absolutely essential that the stones should be quite dry before they are waxed and that the wax should penetrate well. Where stones are set in a wall, wax should never be used as a consolidating agent as there is always the possibility of water getting into the foundation or behind the wall and causing future trouble. An examination of many frescoes on the walls of public buildings and churches has shown, without doubt, that treatment with wax has only been successful where the fabric of the building has been kept continuously dry. Where water has had access to the walls by the chance blocking of a gutter, or perhaps through inadequate drainage on the outside, the moisture cannot escape through the waterproofed surface; it is held back by the wax barrier where it may cause deterioration at the interface, with the result that large flakes become detached, or, in some cases, even the foundation layers of the fresco.

(b) *Impregnation with resins.* In attempting to impregnate a stone with film-forming solutions of resins, one has to face the difficulty that any solvent that goes into the stone must eventually evaporate and come out again, at the same time bringing much of the resin with it to the surface, or the immediate sub-surface. This is easily demonstrated by cutting sections of a white porous stone that has been impregnated with a coloured resin solution; it will be seen that the colour has penetrated well into the stone, but that the solids remaining after the solvent has evaporated are distributed near the surface. These solutions might, therefore, seem to be of limited use, but when stones are kept indoors, they can be regarded as reasonably satisfactory. It must be emphasized, however, that this method of treatment affords no protection to stones that are exposed in the open to the undermining action of rain and frost.

Resin solutions must be applied with a brush in a series of coats, the first very dilute (about 2·5 per cent) and the succeeding ones progressively more concentrated, allowing time for each coat to dry before applying the next. Impregnating media that have proved satisfactory for indoor work are polyvinyl acetate in toluene or acetone, and Bedacryl 122 X in xylene.

(c) *Vacuum impregnation.* For small stone objects that are in a powdery condition, the best treatment is to impregnate them *in vacuo* with one or other of the above media well diluted with solvent. This is carried out in a vessel that can be made air-tight and is at the same time strong enough to withstand the strain of being evacuated.

The stone is immersed in the impregnating solution, air is sucked from the vessel, and bubbles are seen rising from the stone through the solution as the pressure falls. After most of the air has been removed and the bubbling has subsided, air may then be readmitted to the vessel. The pressure of the incoming air will force the solution into the pores of the stone. It is most important that the air should be admitted gently, as a sudden inrush might cause the stone to rupture. After impregnation, the object is allowed to drain above the solution in the atmosphere of the solvent to reduce the rate of drying. Hasty drying is liable to bring too much of the resin to the surface, leaving the stone with a shiny appearance.

(d) *Silicon ester impregnation.* For slabs of sandstone and siliceous limestone of large dimensions which are kept indoors, a possible strengthening agent is silicon ester, but it is essential that it be applied strictly in accordance with the manufacturers' directions.

There are two varieties available commercially; one is a solution of ethyl silicate in ethyl alcohol (Nubold Bonding Agent), and the other is an ethyl silicate solution to which a silicone resin has been added (Nubindex). These solutions are hydrolysed by atmospheric moisture, producing colloidal silica that is precipitated in the pores of the stone. This material is best applied by spraying, and the stone should be absolutely dry before treatment is started, since otherwise it would be immediately covered with an impenetrable film of colloidal silica.

Silicon ester is available in the form of a dilute solution in alcohol, and it is necessary to apply it with a spray or an atomizer as it is not effective when merely brushed on the stone.

The atomizer should be held at some distance from the stone, so that the liquid reaches the surface only as a fine mist. Further applications are made not oftener than once a week, thus allowing time between each operation for the ester to decompose and coat the grains of stone with silica. After about three applications the surface may be tested by rubbing lightly with the fingers, and if the dust has been fixed, this will indicate that the process is likely to prove successful. Eventually, after about three to seven applications, a trace of permanent milkiness will be observed—a sign that treatment should be discontinued, as the surface of the stone is now well consolidated without the pores being clogged. Sandstones so treated have been found to remain in good condition in the museum for many years.

The method is not so effective with fine limestones, though in some cases it seems to harden them. Disappointing results were found in the case of lavas and it would seem that the type of stone that responds best to this spray treatment is one having a gritty surface, the silicon ester reinforcing the decomposed matrix and thus consolidating the gritty constituent of the stone.

It should be added that there is a tendency for silicon ester to clog the jet of the spray, and once this happens it is difficult to clear it for use again. The spray should therefore be dismantled between operations and the jet washed with alcohol and kept, preferably, in a bottle of spirit.

Silicon ester has a comparatively short shelf life, and it should be used within a few weeks of purchase, as even dilute solutions become viscous and unfit for use after a lapse of a few months.

MARBLE

Both igneous and sedimentary rocks may be changed in form, depending on their composition and history, granitic rocks becoming gneisses, sandstones quartzites, and limestones marbles. It is the marbles that are of most interest in museum work as they have been used to such a large extent for sculpture as well as for building purposes.

Marble is a metamorphic rock arising from the action of heat or pressure, or both, on limestones. By this action the original character of the limestone is lost, and it becomes an aggregate of calcite crystals which may be pure white, coloured, veined, or black, according to the impurities present. As a result of this transformation the pore-space in the stone is reduced and is smaller than that of limestone, and marble is thus capable of taking a higher polish than limestone; but the pores are not so small as to prevent the marble from being easily stained, and special care is necessary to prevent the accumulation of dust in the hollows of white marble sculpture, as ingrained stains may be very difficult, or even impossible, to remove.

Dusting and washing. For the preservation of marble in the museum, periodic dusting is essential, and this should be done with a large feather whisk or soft brush. Cloths should never be used as they tend to rub the dust into the stone.

Washing may be necessary at times, and for this purpose it is important to use water that is free from iron, and preferably distilled. A little good-quality soap may be used, just enough to cause a slight frothing when applied with a soft brush. The solution used in the British Museum for the periodic washing of marbles consists of:

Soft soap (B.P.)	10 gm.
Distilled water	100 ml.
Ammonia (0·88)	1 ml.

This is made up as required, kept in a glass bottle, and used from a glass or pottery vessel. The mixture must not be allowed to come in contact with iron, and should not be used from an iron pail, even if galvanized, as this might lead to eventual staining. After the marble has been dusted with a feather whisk, washing operations are commenced at the bottom of the statuary. The cleansing solution is worked with a soft brush into a froth on a small area at a time, taking care to prevent dirty water from lying in the hollows or running down in rivulets over the marble. When clean, each area should be dried with a soft towel before proceeding farther. Only when all the marble has been cleaned and mopped dry is the stone washed freely with fresh water to remove the last traces of soap, which would soon collect dust again if allowed to remain.

Removal of ingrained dirt. When marble has been neglected, the greasy dirt accumulated over a period of many years becomes so deeply ingrained in the surface of the marble that it will resist removal by washing with a soap solution. In such cases it is necessary to employ a special procedure originally devised by Hempel[1] for cleaning marble statues in the Victoria and Albert Museum. The marbles are first degreased using a neutral paint stripper available commercially as Green Label Nitromors. This is harmless to marbles, but since it contains methylene dichloride, it should be used under conditions of good ventilation. The Nitromors is worked over the surface of the marble with a soft brush, using a stippling action so as to work the solvent into the crevices of the marble. This is left on the marble for about one hour and then washed off with a sponge moistened with distilled water. At this stage a considerable amount of dirt is usually removed, but grime in the depths of the surface pores will still remain and it must be removed in the next stage of the process. This involves the application to the surface of a 'mud-pack' made of Sepiolite or Attapulgite, two naturally occurring magnesium silicates that have no chemical action on the marble but merely act as a poultice to keep the surface wet without saturating the body of the stone with water. These are obtained as dry powders which should be mixed into a 'mud' with distilled water, applied to the surface by hand to form a layer about 20 mm. thick and left in position for about twenty-four hours. After this period the 'mud-pack' will have partially dried and will have many cracks across it, and is ready to be removed. The time of removal is rather critical; if it is left too long it will start to fall off the surface, and if it is removed too soon it will not come away cleanly. The 'mud-pack' should be removed a little at a time and the freshly exposed moist surface must be washed immediately with distilled water using nylon brushes and then wiped

[1] Hempel, K. F. B., *Studies in Conservation*, 1968, **13**, p. 34; 1969, **14**, p. 126.

with a sponge. A large area of the 'mud-pack' should not be removed at one time, otherwise part of the surface will dry out before it can all be washed, in which case the ingrained dirt will harden again and prove very difficult to remove. It is also important that the 'mud-pack' is not allowed to dry to such an extent that it starts to fall off the marble, as this will also cause the ingrained dirt to harden on the surface. Hence the 'mud-pack' should only be applied if it can all be removed on the following day. In very dry atmospheric conditions, drying out can be delayed sufficiently by partially covering the layer with thin polythene sheeting.

It is important to make sure that all traces of the Sepiolite or Attapulgite are washed from the surface, and also that residues are not allowed to remain in drapery folds and other crevices in the carving. Although such residues are not harmful to the marble, they give the surface a powdery appearance. This procedure is so successful in cleaning the surface that the marble is sometimes left with a hazy appearance, giving the impression that the surface is somewhat rougher than it was in its dirty state. This is due to the removal of ingrained grime which has been filling the microscopic pits and hollows in the surface, caused by natural weathering. The dirty surface was thus smoother than the clean surface and reflected the light in a different manner giving the impression that the marble has apparently undergone a major change as a result of cleaning. The appearance of the cleaned marble can if necessary be enhanced by brushing on a 10 per cent aqueous solution of a hard polyethylene glycol wax (Grade 6000). This coating provides a measure of protection against the further ingress of dirt and other harmful constituents of the atmosphere into the pores of the stone. Since it is readily soluble in water it can easily be removed from the surface and should facilitate any cleaning which may be necessary in the future.

Removal of stains. The common staining ingredients of dust are soot and traces of iron, and these give rise to grey and to rust-coloured marks respectively. White marbles easily pick up colour from contact with packing materials such as paper and straw if these are damp, and even damp clean dust-sheets have been observed to cause staining. In one such case the source of the trouble was a slight mildewing of the textile which caused the appearance on the marble of a brown line following the course of the retaining string. The susceptibility of marble, and particularly of white statuary marble, to such forms of staining makes it essential to take special precautions in packing. Where there is a possiblity of exposure to damp, white marble should not be allowed to come in contact with any organic material liable to fungal attack. This fact was brought home by the discovery of intensive polychrome staining all over a fine white marble bust of Voltaire by Houdin. The marble had been wrapped in a white silk eiderdown, boxed up, and stored in a garage where conditions were at one time so damp that the wood of the box had rotted. When the box was opened the packing was found to be concealed in a mass of mould growths, and the marble was stained brown, red, and green at all points of contact. Much of the staining was bleached by the use of an aqueous 2 per cent solution of chloramine-T, but certain areas of dark staining resisted all efforts to remove them.

Another type of staining by contact with organic material was that suffered by the Michelangelo tondo in the Royal Academy of Arts. In this case the trouble was caused by felt padding pressing against the white marble, and this resulted in the appearance of a rust-coloured smudge which was very disfiguring. Fortunately, most of the stain responded to washing and treatment with chloramine-T, but rather than take the risk of using a stronger reagent, the residual yellowing was, for aesthetic reasons, chalked over to conceal the blemish. In the course of time the yellowing became decidedly less intense. The gradual disappearance of the stain was not due in any way to the presence of the chalk but no doubt to the fading of the residual staining material.

It is not an easy matter to restore the pristine whiteness of Carrara marble that has been stained. Although it may be possible to remove coloured matter from the surface, in most cases the stain will have penetrated into the stone where it can no longer be reached by solvents, and may remain as a permanent disfigurement. The problem of removing stains from marble is further complicated by the fact that all acids disintegrate marble, and for this reason the use of specific acidic solvents for removing stains is out of the question. The common neutral organic solvents are safe to use, and slightly alkaline solvents are permissible, but when the latter are used they should not be left for long in contact with the marble and should be washed off very thoroughly afterwards as there is a possibility of their causing yellow stains by contact with colourless impurities present in the stone.

When the marble is sound and the staining is general, thorough washing, and brushing in the wet condition, may be undertaken, but when the stain is localized and highly coloured, it is usually best to determine the nature of the stain and employ selective solvents without prior washing. Thus, a freshly prepared 2 per cent aqueous solution of chloramine-T will remove stains caused by red ink and also ink stains of the blue-black type, though in the latter case a yellowish residue is likely to remain. This residual coloration may respond to treatment with hydrogen peroxide (20 vols.) to which a drop of ammonia has been added. After the stain has been removed the marble should be thoroughly washed.

A common type of staining is that due to oil paint. A thick blob of hard oil paint should be carefully softened with the Nitromors paint stripper, and any residue removed with a suitable solvent. Pyridine and morpholine are useful in dealing with bad oil stains, or staining of a bituminous character, as is also a mixture of equal volumes of toluene, ammonia (0·88), and methylated spirit. These liquids are applied locally with a stencil brush, and, after mopping with cotton-wool, the marble is washed down thoroughly with water. It should be noted, however, that the oily ingredient of the paint will certainly have been absorbed to some extent by the marble, and, even if it is possible to eradicate all of the surface pigment, the chances of extracting all the oil from the pores of the stone are very remote indeed, and a grey or brownish residue is almost certain to remain. This is not a serious matter if the area affected is in an inconspicuous part, but if the stain is a bad disfigurement it is much better

A. Plaster cast made in 1802 which shows the condition of the marble at that time

B. The marble photographed *in situ* in 1938, indicating the deterioration resulting from exposure to an industrial atmosphere

40. SCULPTURE FROM THE WEST FRIEZE OF THE PARTHENON

A. Before treatment—the tablets covered with a salt deposit making them illegible

B. After treatment—the clay stabilized, the salts removed, and legibility restored

41. A COLLECTION OF CLAY TABLETS INSCRIBED IN SUMERIAN, BABYLONIAN, AND ASSYRIAN CUNEIFORM SCRIPTS

to cover it over with chalk rather than to torture the surface of the stone with chemicals in the remote hope of improving matters.

A method that is sometimes of value in removing surface stains is to use a stripping film according to the procedure developed for recovering fossil imprints from coal. This consists in applying to the stain a viscous solution of nitrocellulose so compounded that, on drying, it leaves behind a very elastic film; when this is peeled off it may take the stain with it. The method has given good results in the case of stained marble but could be applied equally well to any other fine-grained stone. The following solvent mixtures are suggested by Duerden:[1]

(1) *Rapid drying*:	Alcohol	1 vol.
	Ether	1 vol.
	Castor oil	5 per cent by vol.
(2) *Slow drying*:	Acetone	2 vols.
	Amyl acetate	1 vol.
	Triacetin	2 per cent by vol.

A sufficient quantity of nitrocellulose must be added in each case to give a viscous solution.

A common disfigurement is the formation of organic deposits caused by the growth of lichens, algae, etc., on the surface of marble exposed in the open. These deposits may be be softened and removed by treatment with a little dilute ammonia. In cases where the algal growths are extensive, they may be arrested by spraying with formalin, and this treatment facilitates their subsequent removal.

When the surface of a finely polished marble is blemished locally by an insoluble deposit the only cure may be to wet the marble and remove the deposit by rubbing with a small chisel-shaped slip of water-of-Ayr stone or snake-stone. 'Snaking', when applied lightly, does not impair the polish of the marble.

Deterioration and consolidation. Marble consists of an aggregate of crystals of calcite, and these crystals have a different coefficient of thermal expansion in two directions. The result is that when marble

---

[1] Duerden, H., *Ann. Bot.*, 1931, **45**, p. 376.

is heated it tends to become distorted. This distortion is detectable even below 100 °C., but when the temperature is as high as 400 °C. warping may be considerable. Such deformity is sometimes noticed on old mantelpieces, and, as it is a case of the stone having taken on a permanent set, there is no way of recovering the original shape.

The second type of deterioration resulting from heat causing irregular expansion is the granulated condition sometimes observed on projecting portions of statuary. In this case, expansion at different rates in different directions causes the crystals to lose their power of cohesion and it is possible to release granules of the marble by merely rubbing such surfaces with the finger. The affected portions are a staring white, as they scatter the light more than the surrounding stone. Examples have been found in the Parthenon marbles, and in marbles from many other sources. In one case, an extended limb of a large Canova group was worn down to a shapeless mass of loosely adherent crystals having the appearance of granulated sugar.

It is possible to do something to consolidate museum marbles in this condition, but the same difficulty arises as in the consolidation of sandstones and limestones, namely that impregnating agents requiring the use of solvents that evaporate cannot be persuaded to *fill* the pores of the stone because the solvents, having gone in, must find their way out again. For some purposes the most satisfactory treatment may be to impregnate the stone with wax, even though this may seem illogical, as it involves applying heat to the stone. The aim, however, is to get the wax to penetrate well into the granular marble, and this can be achieved to a depth of two or three centimetres, if the stone is warmed by an electric radiator. The radiator should not be placed too near the stone, and sufficient time should be given for the stone to warm through gradually. Then, treat the stone with molten paraffin wax of M.P. 40–50 °C. It will penetrate the granulated marble easily, replacing the air and filling the pores so that the marble now has a more or less uniform appearance and the enfeebled stone is consolidated.

Another method of dealing with granular marble in the museum is to impregnate the porous areas with lime water, giving repeated

coats, and allowing time between each application for the marble to
dry. This is followed, if necessary, by one or two coats of a 10 per
cent aqueous solution of 'soluble casein'. By this means the granules
are consolidated by a film that consists essentially of calcium
caseinate and calcium carbonate. In cases where the original surface
of the marble remains to a large extent unimpaired, and there are only
isolated granulated patches, there may be justification for stippling
the staring white of the granulated areas with a little pastel colour to
match the surrounding unaffected marble. This masks deformities
and assists in recovering the aesthetic appeal of the work. (For repairs
to broken marble see p. 324.)

It may be of interest to reproduce laboratory notes relating to a
marble which presented several problems in one—removal of an
incrustation, removal of stains, consolidation, retouching, and repair.
The marble in question is the head regarded as that of Mithras
excavated from the Walbrook Mithraeum in London in 1955.[1]

This fine head came from a moist site where it had been in contact
with ferruginous clay, and it arrived at the laboratory damp, muddy,
and encrusted with iron compounds. The stone, particularly in the
region of the hair and peak of the Phrygian cap, was found to be
weakened by a form of sugary decomposition, which might have
resulted from the action of intense heat. There was no evidence to
show that the temple had at any time been burned down, but a
carbon residue was found in the incrustation, suggesting that the
marble may have been exposed to altar fires.

As the stone was considered to be too fragile for treatment in its damp
condition, it was allowed to dry out, and then treated as follows:

1. The bulk of the incrustation was removed with pointed match-
sticks, exposing a surface that was porous and deeply stained in parts
by iron compounds. Match-sticks were used because they are softer
than marble and could not injure the surface.

2. The iron stains were removed by sequestering reagents, applied
to the surface with cotton-wool wrapped round the end of a cocktail

[1] Grimes, W. F., *Excavations in Roman Mediaeval London*. Routledge and Kegan
Paul, London, 1968.

stick. This was a long and painstaking operation, as it was only possible to work on one small area at a time. The most effective reagent was found to be Detarol and, although this substance also sequesters calcium, it had no apparent effect on the marble in the dilute solutions employed. Care was taken not to carry this treatment too far. The discoloration resulting from the burning could not be obliterated, and it was therefore inadvisable to make the rest of the marble too white, as this would have caused it to have a patchy appearance.

3. The sugary condition of the burnt areas was dealt with by applications of lime water (calcium hydroxide), which, in time, was converted in the pores of the marble to calcium carbonate, a material of the same chemical composition as the marble itself. A small amount of crystalline efflorescence was brushed away, and, finally, two coats of a 10 per cent solution of soluble casein were applied to the areas of sugary marble to consolidate the surface, and the front of the Phrygian cap was lightly touched out for aesthetic reasons with ground pastel colour.

During the course of this work the neck of Mithras was excavated from the temple. It proved to be in a much better condition than the head and could be cleaned by ordinary washing. The neck and head were then joined together by a stout dowel of Delta metal inserted with plaster of Paris into opposing holes drilled in the fractured surfaces.

The Mithras marble was only slightly burnt and was therefore amenable to treatment, but where marbles have been exposed to temperatures sufficiently high to convert the surface into quicklime, there is nothing that can be done to restore them. Sometimes the heating may not have proceeded so far, and the surface may still be hard and intact though blackened with tarry matter. Some improvements should be possible here, but it will depend on the nature of the specimen. The use of pyridine or morpholine, made into a paste with cellulose powder, or mixed with an absorbent powder and held in intimate contact with the stone until the solvent evaporates, may help to remove such staining. Ammoniacal toluene (see p. 316) may also help, but the final treatment may have to take the form of rubbing down the surface with water-of-Ayr stone or even with fine emery powder. Such treatment would obviously be unsuitable for fine sculpture, but it might be the means of saving a good piece if the stain were restricted to the plinth, or to a small part where the modelling was suggested, rather than executed with precision. But, in general, mechanical methods of cleaning marbles involving the use of abrasives can seldom be justified in museum work, and are only used under exceptional conditions.

The use of copper chisels has been advocated as a means of cleaning marble gravestones and the like. Since copper is of the same order of hardness as fresh marble the procedure is not so drastic as it would appear to be. It is, nevertheless, quite unsuitable for museum work where surfaces are studied at close quarters and patina, an important feature of the specimen, must be preserved at all costs.

The patina of marble. The patina of marble differs from that of metals in that it is essentially of the same chemical composition as the material upon which it has been laid down, whereas, in the case of metals, the patina is non-metallic and generally consists of a variety of chemical compounds, oxides, chlorides, carbonates, etc. Marble patinas are formed in the same way as stalagmite by virtue of the fact that calcium carbonate is slightly soluble in water that contains dissolved carbon dioxide gas. When the solution (calcium bicarbonate) drips steadily from a height, the carbon dioxide gas is released, and the calcium carbonate is redeposited on the ground, where it may accumulate to form pillar-like structures or stalagmites. In the same way, when old marbles have been washed by rain for generations, there is a tendency towards solution and redeposition of calcium carbonate. Even though this be on a comparatively minute scale, a change of surface takes place and may be recognized as a variation in texture, translucency, or even colour, warm tones resulting from the presence of a little ferric iron in the solution, and cooler greenish tones from ferrous iron or copper. Plants cause staining and organic growths such as lichens or algae may also leave a greenish tinge on the marble and the patinated surface is often of such porosity that it retains coloured impurities that add interest to the stone. Where patina exists, it is an essential feature of old marble and must be retained. It will survive cleaning by the general methods described, but would be ruined by the use of abrasives, sharp tools, or acids of any kind, even lemon juice.

Examination of marble by U.V. fluorescence. It is instructive to examine a piece of ancient marble in a darkened room by ultra-violet light, and to compare the fluorescence of the patinated surface with that of a recent scratch or fracture in the same stone. Freshly exposed surfaces usually fluoresce brightly, whereas the ancient surfaces are either deep brown or unchanged in appearance. It is often possible by examining a piece of marble sculpture under ultra-violet light to determine whether it is recent or ancient and to reveal any modern cutting on an old marble, but as there can be no absolute guide as to the time required for a marble to acquire a patina recognizable as ancient, it is impossible to date marbles by the quality of their fluorescence. Discretion is required in making such examinations, and, as the fluorescence of ancient marble is low in tone, it is essential to adapt the eye to a condition of total darkness for a few minutes before making the examination, so that slight differences in fluorescence can be discriminated. The problem is much simpler in the case of a composite piece made up from fragments of marble of different origins. An example was provided by a small Greek marble figure reclining against a tree trunk. This appeared to be homogeneous but when viewed in a darkened room under ultra-violet light was found to be heterogeneous; the torso, apparently original, was of one kind of marble, while the head and limbs were cut in two others, and the tree in yet a third. Even when the position of the joints had been discovered by this means, they were still very difficult to discern in daylight.

In detecting repairs to marble and estimating their extent, an ultra-violet examination is of the greatest value, and this type of investigation is facilitated by the fact that plasters and glues fluoresce vividly. A valuable Italian marble that had been lent to an exhibition in London was alleged to have suffered damage in transit. When

examined by ultra-violet light, however, the breakages were shown
to be merely ancient repairs that had become unstuck on the journey.
It was also revealed that on one part of the marble there was a slight
abrasion (invisible in daylight) which fluoresced brightly and was
obviously of modern origin.

It is perhaps not irrelevant to add that some of the modern surface-
active agents used as detergents have a characteristic bright fluorescence in ultra-violet light, and hence it is not advisable to use them
for cleaning marble that might have to be studied under the lamp.
Detergents may have to be used for washing very dirty neglected
marbles, but traces of these materials left on or in the powdery surface of the stone would be likely to complicate fluorescence analysis
to such an extent as to vitiate this line of inquiry.

Effects of weathering. Numerous as are the problems of conservation
of stone objects indoors, they are seldom so profound or so crucial as
those presented by stones exposed outside. These have to face extremes of temperature and humidity, and the disintegrating action of
frost, to say nothing of atmospheric impurities, and adventitious
damage due to animals and plants. Sand or dust storms gradually
erode the surface, and rain causes dirt to collect in hollows of the
stone where stains are formed that can never be removed.

A most striking example of weathering is provided by comparing
photographs of the plaster casts of the West Frieze of the Parthenon
made by Lord Elgin in 1802 (which show the condition of the marbles
at that time) with photographs of the same marbles taken *in situ* in
1938, i.e. 136 years later. The photographs show (Pls. 40A and B) that,
in what may be called the industrial age, the modelling has every-
where lost its sharpness, facial expressions have changed, and whole
features have gone for ever, owing to the variety of causes that we
know collectively as 'weathering'.

Marbles of all kinds are liable to be seriously damaged by the acids
present in an industrial atmosphere. In the presence of moisture these
destroy the surface, particularly at angles and corners, and open the
joints to the disintegrating action of frost. It is not surprising, therefore, that the industrial age has already taken a heavy toll of some

of the finest marble monuments of antiquity. In the case of exposed buildings, the damage can only be arrested by the application of stringent anti-pollution laws, but where statuary is concerned, a practical alternative may be offered by the possibility of covering in the marbles or bringing them indoors, so that they may be maintained under conditions where conservation is possible.

Packing marble sculptures. The art of packing heavy stone objects can only be learnt by experience, but even the experience gained with sculptures of another kind may not suffice in the case of white marble sculpture, which is so susceptible to staining. White marbles should be packed in strong wooden boxes, made of well-seasoned timber, assembled with brass screws. As the main requirement is to dispense with all but the essential packing material, and at the same time ensure that the sculpture will not move in the case, wooden bars are screwed firmly in strategic places so that the marble is retained rigidly in position. The wooden bars must be padded with the best quality white cotton-wool covered with tissue paper. The final retaining member should be a wooden wedge similarly padded, and driven home gently with a mallet to anchor the stone in position. The wedge should be retained, if possible, with a screw and be marked as the first member to be removed when the marble is being unpacked. On no account should the use of newspaper, wood-wool, or straw be permitted. When a marble has been allowed to remain in its box over a long period it is desirable to inspect the padding and verify the tightness of the retaining wedge if removal of the box is contemplated, as the padding may have lost its resilience and the object may no longer be held securely in position.

REPAIR OF STONE OBJECTS

Adhesives that are quite satisfactory for the repair of small stone objects are inadequate where weights of 2 kg. and over have to be carried. In such cases the fractured surfaces are brought together with metal dowels or pins, and by this means the strain is no longer confined to the fractured surfaces but carried by the body of the stone.

The choice of metal for dowelling is important. Much damage has been done under the guise of conservation by dowelling stones with iron, which, on rusting, swells and opens old cracks and gives rise to new ones. Stainless steel may be used, but generally copper or one of its alloys is a better choice, one of the best and strongest for the purpose being Delta metal. As a rule the metal dowel should be of rectangular cross-section, and not so heavy that its insertion weakens the stone. The ends may be bifurcated or the edges nicked with a chisel to help the metal to key with the cementing material and form a reliable bond. In joints of this kind the dowels are made to do the work and the crack stopped afterwards with some inconspicuous filler. The procedure of fitting a metal dowel is briefly as follows.

Drill or cut a hole in one of the fractured faces of the stone at the appropriate angle, and to a depth of a little more than half the length of the dowel, and of a diameter just large enough to admit it. With the dowel temporarily in position, mark the opposite face, and sink a similar hole at the correct angle, so that the faces can be brought into correct register. (If a second dowel is required, provision is made for it in the same manner.) The dowel has now to be fixed in one-half of the joint, and this is done by wetting the stone, filling the hole to a reasonable depth with a cement such as plaster of Paris, and pushing in the dowel, and, if necessary, wedging it firmly in position. It is allowed to set overnight. Next day the two parts are brought together and any necessary adjustment made to the hole that is to accommodate the projecting dowel. It now remains to wet the stone and apply the cementing material to the second hole, and it may be desirable to coat the surfaces as well with a thin wash of plaster to help to bed the joint in position when the pieces are brought together. When the joint is permanently set, then the crack has to be made good. This is done with some form of plastic stopping which may be a cement or a mastic, i.e. adhesive plus an insert substance to act as a filler.

The following cements may be used: plaster of Paris; Keene's cement, which is a retarded plaster of a harder nature; Sirapite, a white dolomitic gypsum containing about 1 per cent of free lime;

or Portland cement, the hard strong cement obtained by heating a mixture of clay and chalk. A suitable mastic may be prepared by grinding kieselguhr in a binder such as water-glass or glue-size. For use with antiquities, the best filler is undoubtedly plaster of Paris because of the ease with which it can be applied and removed if this should ever be necessary at a future date. It is used for filling, and for repairing, and even for mounting heavy sculpture on stone plinths. When dealing with large plaster mixes the quick rate of setting becomes a problem but this may be overcome by adding a little glue to the plaster when it is made up. This has the effect of making the material workable for a longer time.

For mounting and consolidation work (see p. 330) it sometimes happens that a cement is required which is anhydrous and yet guaranteed not to shrink. This can be made from a 10 per cent solution of nitrocellulose dissolved in a solvent consisting of equal volumes of acetone and amyl acetate. If 50 gm. of fine white sand are worked up with 12 gm. of this nitrocellulose solution, the mixture will be found to be of the consistency of soft putty which can be shaped with a palette knife. As it dries it adheres very firmly. It takes about four days for a block 1 cm. thick to dry through, and then it has the appearance of light-coloured sandstone. A test block 8 cm. by 4 cm. by 1 cm. made according to this formula showed negligible contraction on drying.

CLAY

Clay is a hydrated aluminium silicate of variable composition which has the fundamental characteristic of being plastic when moist so that it can be modelled or moulded; it hardens on drying, but can be softened again by the action of water. The nature of clay is changed, however, by the action of heat, so that it becomes rigid, stony, and almost imperishable without change of form, and these qualities have been exploited by man in making bricks, terracotta objects, pottery, and porcelain. When baked above a temperature of 600 °C. the change is irreversible, but if inadequately baked the material is of uncertain hardness and not necessarily permanent.

There are thus three types of material presented for conservation—baked clay, unbaked clay, and clay that has been inadequately baked. In the latter categories are the writing tablets of clay that are too frail to handle until they have been hardened by heating in a kiln.

Clay tablets and their treatment

Clay was widely used in Sumeria, Babylonia, and Assyria in the plastic condition for writing upon, cuneiform characters being impressed in the moist surface with a stilus. The clay soon regained its solidity in the hot sun and there is evidence that, on occasion at least, it was further hardened by firing, but it is not known to what extent kiln firing was general. The hardness of the clay tablets that are excavated varies considerably and it seems likely that many were not kiln-hardened but merely sun-dried. Hundreds of thousands of clay documents have come down to us—the British Museum alone contains upwards of 100,000—and they have survived astonishingly well, on account of the dry climate of Mesopotamia.

But clay objects suffer in the same way as all porous material that has been buried in salty ground—they absorb salts which will tend to crystallize out after excavation and cause disintegration. The usual treatment for the removal of salts is washing, but with clay objects this is not possible as water would simply convert unbaked clay into mud. As it is impossible to judge by inspection what heat treatment a cuneiform tablet may have been given in antiquity, the first requirement is a controlled rebaking of the old tablet in order to convert it into brick. The tablet may then be washed, or indeed soaked for prolonged periods without being any the worse. The laboratory treatment of clay tablets thus consists in baking, washing, repairing, and cleaning the surface by mechanical methods should this be necessary to render the writing legible. Pls. 41A and B illustrate how, by this treatment, encrusted tablets can be strengthened and the writing made legible.

Baking and washing clay tablets. In the British Museum baking is carried out in an oven or furnace in which the temperature is gradually raised to 750 °C.[1] and maintained for some hours. This results in the loss of what is known as 'combined water', and the conversion of the clay into brick. The tablets are allowed to cool in the closed furnace overnight. When the baking has been properly conducted the tablets are converted to a clean hard material of a biscuit or pale ochre colour, depending on the amount of iron present in the clay. Any organic matter is, of course, burnt away, and in cases where there is saline impurity of a selenitic nature, this is dehydrated in the course of heating, leaving a white powdery residue which may be removed by brushing. When, as is generally the case, soluble salts are present, it will be necessary to immerse the baked tablets in running water for about six hours to wash away all but a negligible residue of soluble saline matter.

Unlike metal objects, where it is necessary to wash away the last trace of salt because even a small residue might cause a renewed outbreak of corrosion, stone, whether natural or artificial, is not affected by the presence of a slight amount of salt and may be considered safe as long as the bulk of the salt has been eliminated.

Rendering cuneiform writing legible. To render cuneiform inscriptions legible, the old-fashioned methods of surface cleaning such as picking with a needle or treating the baked tablets with hydrochloric acid are now out of date for routine purposes, although they may still be useful on occasion. These methods have been largely superseded by the sand-blasting technique. The sand or shot-blast method of cleaning (p. 208) is both speedy and effective; while removing debris and adherent particles from the inscription, it need not impair the surface of baked clay tablets in any way. A useful portable form of the apparatus has been devised in the British Museum Research Laboratory. This consists of a brass cylinder containing the sand or other grit. Air is blown through a tube below sand level, so that the particles form a suspension in the air stream and are ejected with the air from the nozzle which may be made from a curved glass or polythene tube. Such an apparatus may be improvised from ordi-

[1] Organ, R. M., *Brit. Mus. Quarterly*, 1961, **33**, p. 52; and Bateman, C. A., in Monograph Series 3, Colt Archaeological Institute, Bernard Quaritch Ltd., London, 1966, p. 12.

nary laboratory equipment, the air supply being obtained from a vacuum compressor at about 5 lb per sq. in. (400 gm./cm.²) pressure. The potency of the instrument will clearly depend on the nature and size of the particles, the shape of the jet, and the pressure and volume of the air.

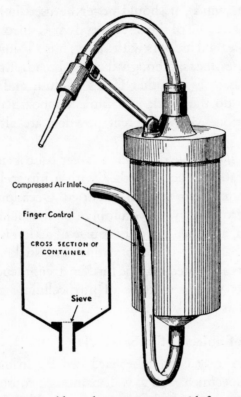

Compressed Air Inlet

Finger Control

CROSS SECTION OF CONTAINER

Sieve

FIG. 10. Portable sand-spray apparatus with finger-tip control designed for field use

The apparatus illustrated in Fig. 10 was designed for use in the field. It requires only a source of compressed air, which may be conveniently obtained either from a cylinder or from a motor-driven compressor. For cleaning tablets the jet should not be held too near the writing, nor should the pressure be allowed to become too strong; this is controlled by a movement of the finger over a hole in the feed pipe. The size of the jet must obviously be related to the coarseness of the sand, which is screened by passing it through a sieve of appropriate mesh before it is fed into the cylinder. This excludes the larger particles that would clog the jet.

It should be added that while sand may safely be used out of doors (working down wind), it should never be used indoors for health reasons, as it is the cause of the disease known as silicosis. Bauxite grit, however, may be used indoors with safety: it is an aluminium hydrate and cannot cause silicosis though it must be admitted that the grit is just as unpleasant as all other forms of dust, and the operator is well advised to do the work in a fume cupboard or where there is good ventilation. Many different powders are also sold for grit spraying.

Repairing cuneiform tablets. When a tablet is broken the fragments are baked separately, stuck together with a nitrocellulose adhesive such as Durofix, and then washed and dried. Occasionally one comes across cases where the clay is so crumbly that it would fall to powder if it were heated, and then the only course of action is to try to make good without baking, by consolidating and sticking the particles together. Tablets so treated may be further strengthened, if necessary, by filling cracks with a mixture of nitrocellulose and baked clay powder applied as a thick paste.

Consolidation of objects of unbaked clay

In cases where clay cannot be hardened by firing, as in certain ethnographical specimens and in wall-paintings, consolidation is only possible by impregnation and for this purpose dilute laquers of polyvinyl acetate, polymethacrylate, or nitrocellulose have given successful results. It is *not* advisable to use aqueous consolidating agents such as glue or casein. These might have a disintegrating effect on the clay in the first instance and, moreover, the water would be liable to affect colours adversely and to bring any soluble salts to the surface. Durofix may be used for repairs, mixed, if necessary, with fine clay. Such mixtures shrink on setting and the non-shrinking nitrocellulose/sand cement referred to on p. 326 is to be preferred.

This cement was used for the surround and backing of Sir Aurel Stein's large frescoes from Chinese Turkestan, now at the British Museum. The ground on which the frescoes were painted was mud and on arrival at the Museum the slabs were laid face downwards and the thick clay backing was cut away. About 6–12 mm. of the original ground was left and this was reinforced either by a textile covering or by a sheet of expanded aluminium, the adhesive being nitrocellulose and sand. The frescoes that were backed with textile were then framed upon a solid wooden backing, and then the surround and lacunae in the frescoes filled with the nitrocellulose cement, which had the colour and general appearance of artificial sandstone.

The pieces that were mounted on expanded aluminium frames all belonged to one large fresco and were hung on the wall by attaching them to an armature that had been prepared for their reception. It was possible to set each slab in its permanent position in relation to its neighbours by moving pairs of screws at right angles. All that remained to be done was to make good the joints, using once again the nitrocellulose/sand cement which proved invaluable.

KIMMERIDGE SHALE

The dark bituminous substance known as Kimmeridge shale is easily carved and turned, and on this account it was used for making a variety of objects—spinning whorls, weights, bowls, and even furniture in the Roman period. It has deteriorated considerably with the passage of time, however, so that artifacts of shale are usually found in fragments or in such a condition that fragmentation soon follows excavation, and this is due to the shrinkage that accompanies drying.

The form taken by the disintegrating shale depends upon how the shape and ornament are orientated relative to the bedding planes. When the two are roughly parallel, the shale splits into a series of thin distorted leaves which may break up still further; but where the carving is at an angle to the bedding planes, a series of small crescent-shaped cracks appears, and these open up in the manner of a ripened fir-cone as the shale dries. Disintegration will follow unless the object is immersed in water; if this is done in good time, however, the cracks will close up and the surface may assume its original appearance.

The only certain way of preserving all surface details is to keep an object of Kimmeridge shale continuously wet, and this can be done by sealing it in a jar of water containing about 15 per cent of glycerine, to which about 1 per cent of phenol is added to act as a preservative and prevent the growth of moulds.

In cases where it is considered desirable to dry the shale, and where a certain distortion of surface can be tolerated, the most effective procedure is to pass the object through a series of alcohols and then to impregnate in a vacuum with a consolidant such as an alcoholic solution of shellac. This, however, is not enough; the surface must be kept under continuous compression until the shellac hardens, and no further movement of the shale is possible. This is carried out as follows. The surface is first covered with absorbent paper (which can easily be removed at the end of treatment) and the object padded, if necessary, and bound tightly with polythene tape. If the shape allows, the shale is then placed in a carpenter's vice provided with thick facings of soft wood or cork and allowed to dry for several days under pressure which is so exerted as to close the cracks; additional protection may be given to any protruding portions by the application of shaped pieces of wood and the use of cramps. While such treatment prevents the loss of major fragments, it will be found, after removing the protective tape, that the surface is covered with a system of micro-cracks which have resulted from shrinkage. They are no great disfigurement as they are eventually filled with shellac during the final cleaning process. Ethyl lactate and cellosolve are recommended as effective solvents to use for the removal of any excess of shellac at the conclusion of treatment.

A better procedure that has given satisfactory results is to impregnate the shale with polyethylene glycol wax (Grade 4000) as carried out for waterlogged wood (p. 144); however, to ensure adequate impregnation the treatment must be extended over many months. When removed from the hot molten wax, the shale is very soft, but becomes quite hard on cooling.

42. PORTRAIT POTTERY VASE, MOCHICA CULTURE, FROM PERU

Flaking due to crystallization of salts on the surface

44. VENETIAN GLASS GOBLET SHOWING USE OF SILICA GEL TO KEEP DRY ATMOSPHERE IN EXHIBITION CASE

43. GLASS BEAKER (DATED 1778). CRIZZLING IS DUE TO THE EFFECT OF MOISTURE ON THE GLASS

Objects of shale differ greatly in their appearance and behaviour after excavation, and a warning should be added that the restoration of important specimens should not be lightly undertaken as the process of drying and consolidation may well extend over several weeks, and the work will require regular attention during this time if the results are to be satisfactory.

XV

CERAMICS

I⊤ has already been noted that while clay is plastic in the moist condition, it can be hardened to a stone-like mass on heating to redness. This hard condition persists on cooling, and no amount of soaking in water will soften the material again because a permanent and irreversible change has taken place. Baked clay is also highly resistant to chemical action and in this sense it is one of the most stable materials known, rivalling gold itself in permanence.

Raw clays vary in their chemical composition, and in the nature and quantity of the impurities they contain, although they are mostly basic aluminium silicates. It is only to be expected, therefore, that considerable diversity will be found in clay products. Examples of pottery of widely differing physical properties may even be made from one and the same clay, depending on the temperature and duration of firing and whether this has been carried out in the presence or absence of oxygen. Surface texture may also be varied in many ways. A common method is to dip the air-dried clay object in an aqueous suspension (slip) of an entirely different clay, prior to firing. Another method is to polish the surface before the clay is fired; this is possible because, in the normal course of air-drying, wet clay passes through a stage described by potters as being 'leather-hard' and in this condition it can be turned on the lathe and burnished, so that when eventually fired the surface is smooth and has a dull polished appearance. Or again, the fired clay or biscuit ware may be glazed.

UNGLAZED WARE

Though it may be regarded chemically as an inert material, baked clay or pottery varies considerably in its physical properties. Inadequate baking yields pottery which is soft and porous and may be

334

very frail in the wet condition. When excavated, pots are often fragmentary. The pieces require washing in order to remove earthy deposits and salts: they require strengthening, and in due course piecing together—with possibly some reconstruction of missing portions.

Pottery is often found to be damp through and through when freshly excavated,[1] and in this condition it had best be allowed to dry before much is done in the way of treatment. Pieces should be marked on the inside surface with waterproof Indian ink, and at this stage any interesting matter examined very carefully in case it should provide information that may be used in interpretation. Treatment in the field should be delayed when the pot bears evidence of food remains or imprints of seeds as these will require to be submitted to expert examination. In other cases surface dirt may be removed by washing, adding, if necessary, a small amount of a surface-active agent such as Teepol that will tend to convert the mud from its normal condition of a colloidal gel into that of a sol; it then ceases to adhere to the pottery and can be washed away. Deposits of lime and chalk may remain, and before using chemical reagents to remove them it will be necessary to determine the nature of any existing decoration and its ability to survive cleaning. Soaking in dilute hydrochloric acid might be ideal for cleaning one type of sherd but would certainly not do for all. Thus, acid would be likely to ruin any pots that had been fired at a low temperature or even coarse terracotta excavated from chalky soil where the pores of the ware are filled with calcium carbonate. In this case the acid would react with the carbonate and the resulting effervescence might cause disintegration of the pottery.

Unglazed earthenware is usually fairly porous, and will, therefore, tend to absorb soluble salts from the surroundings in which they have lain prior to excavation. When these salts crystallize out on the surface owing to variations in relative humidity under normal museum conditions (Pl. 42), the surface will be disrupted, and for this reason

[1] The excavation, recording, and repair of pottery is fully dealt with in R. J. C. Atkinson's *Field Archaeology*, Methuen, London, 2nd edn., revised 1953.

Egyptian amphorae often display a broken external surface. In these cases the salts retained in the pores must be washed out by prolonged soaking in changes of water, and, after drying, the objects may be consolidated by impregnation with a solution of a suitable synthetic resin, such as polyvinylacetate, if this should be considered necessary.

If a pot has been inadequately fired or if an object has painted decoration that is not adhering well, it is necessary to consolidate the surface before washing it. Ostraka, i.e. earthenware sherds used in Egypt for the casual recording of ephemeral writings, also belong in this category. The writing is normally carbon ink and this might be easily lost in the washing process. A material which offers many advantages as a consolidant is soluble nylon (Calaton CB) which forms a protective film having certain desirable properties; it does not exert any contractile forces on the surface as it dries, is reasonably tough and is sufficiently permeable to permit the ready elution of the salts.

The routine procedure for desalting ostraka[1] (and also similar earthenware objects) involves the following stages:

1. Soak the ostraka in ordinary tap water for a brief period to remove the crystalline deposit and expose the writing.
2. Dry the ostraka in a current of warm air.
3. Brush on a 5 per cent alcoholic solution of soluble nylon on the *written surface only*.
4. Soak the coated ostraka in tap water for about ten days, changing the water twice a day. Then transfer them to distilled water and allow them to soak with weekly changes of distilled water until a test with silver nitrate shows that the salt has been removed.
5. Dry the desalted ostraka in a current of warm air.
6. If the film of nylon appears opaque it can be rendered transparent by brushing on a fresh amount of the soluble nylon. This has the further advantage that the writing is rendered more intense.

[1] Werner, A. E. A., *Chronique d'Egypte*, 1958, **33**, No. 66, pp. 273–8.

In the case of limestone ostraka, the above procedure is slightly modified. The soluble nylon solution must be applied immediately to *both sides* before washing is commenced and the period of immersion in water must be reduced to a minimum consistent with the removal of the major quantity of the absorbed salts. Many hundreds of ostraka have already been treated by the above method and the results have been uniformly successful.

The solution of soluble nylon can be used in general for the consolidation of friable or fragile material prior to desalting. Thus it was used, for example, in the case of an Egyptian terracotta bust of a young man of the eighteenth dynasty that was found to be in a rather delicate state owing to the fact that the movement of soluble salts to the surface was rendering the surface layer friable and liable to flake off, and a salt deposit was tending to obscure surface details. It was decided to remove the salts from this object by the paper pulp method (see p. 304), but before applying the wet paper pulp the whole bust was painted with a 5 per cent solution of soluble nylon in ethyl alcohol. It was found that three coats of the solution were necessary to ensure adequate consolidation of the surface. The desalting treatment had to be continued for about eight months during which the paper pulp was renewed about forty times before the salt content had been reduced to a safe limit.

GLAZED WARE

Glazed pottery is covered by a vitreous film, but this is usually found to be incomplete or imperfect, so that soluble salts may get into the body of the ware; these will tend to crystallize and cause the glaze to flake off. Although glazes exist in infinite variety, they only seem to give serious trouble when the attachment to the body is weak.

It is usually a lengthy and difficult business to extract the salt from the body if the only means of getting it out is through cracks in the glaze. This may be facilitated by immersing the object in dilute alcohol, which, though not a very good solvent for salts, will penetrate better than water. The most effective treatment seems to be to apply the paper pulp technique.[1] This is not always possible, however, because the glaze may be loose, or fragments may be held to the ware only by the salt crystals. In such cases it is necessary to fix the glaze by applying a 5 per cent solution of soluble nylon in ethyl alcohol before washing out the salt in changes of distilled water, as described on p. 304. If the glaze requires consolidation a second coat of soluble nylon can be applied.

In common with certain kinds of enamel and glass, glaze which is subject to weathering results in a loss of translucency caused by the breakdown of the glassy structure and leaking out of one or more of its constituents. When the resulting opalescence is confined to the immediate surface, as is usually the case, translucency may be restored by rubbing the affected areas with a wet fine grade glass-paper, or by using a fine abrasive on a small polishing wheel. This treatment usually restores translucency to a certain degree, unless the opalescence goes deeper, in which case it would be unsafe to attempt further mechanical treatment. However, it may be possible that lacquering will restore translucency and for this purpose any clear lacquer of high refractive index will suffice.

A common feature of some Chinese pottery is a crackled glaze, and this might seem at first sight to be a defect, but this is very far from being the case. Crackle may arise from many accidental causes, but in the long run it is due to differences in the relative contraction and rate of cooling of the glaze and the body. The Chinese potter was able to control conditions so as to produce a definite artistic crackle and thus make capital out of an apparent deficiency.

REPAIR OF POTTERY

Pottery, earthenware, tiles, and suchlike are all porous, and if they require to be strengthened, this is done by impregnation, using dilute synthetic lacquers containing polyvinyl acetate or polymethacrylate. In some cases, vacuum impregnation may be desirable (see p. 156). Repairs may be carried out with Durofix and, if necessary,

[1] Penetration will be facilitated by the addition of one volume of Lissapol N to 200 volumes of distilled water.

a joint may be strengthened by dowelling (see p. 325), or by attaching a bandage along the back where it will be inconspicuous.

It is not possible to repair dusty joints. The first step, therefore, consists in getting rid of dust; then, if the ware is not very absorbent, the *inside* of the fractured edge is roughened in order to give a key for the adhesive. The next step consists in painting adhesive on both edges and this is allowed to become tacky. A thin film of fresh adhesive is then applied to the edges, and the joints are pressed firmly together. Pressure should be maintained for at least half an hour to ensure that satisfactory joints are formed. In this connection a sand-box is a great convenience as the repaired pieces may be stuck in the sand temporarily at any appropriate angle, so that joints will not be under strain whilst the adhesive is hardening. Small muslin bags of sand are also useful to support larger and heavier pieces of pottery in the course of reconstruction work. When dry, any excess of adhesive that has been squeezed out from the joint may be removed by rubbing with a cloth moistened with a suitable solvent, but care must be taken that there is not enough solvent present to run into any cracks and soften the joints.

The following adhesives may be used as alternatives to Durofix. For large work, a retarded plaster, e.g. 'white glue' (hot glue to which has been added plaster of Paris); for dark pottery in which repaired joints may have to be softened by heat in the course of making a complicated reconstruction, thick shellac in spirit or even solid flake shellac applied with the aid of a tiny flame.

For making permanent joints that are very strong and waterproof an epoxy resin adhesive, e.g. Araldite, can be recommended. The most convenient type of epoxy resin adhesive is one that hardens in the cold. The pieces to be joined are first degreased by wiping them with a swab moistened with acetone, and then a thin film of the resin/hardener system (prepared according to the manufacturer's instructions) is applied to both pieces which are held firmly together while the resin sets; any excess of resin exuding from the joint should be removed by wiping off lightly with acetone before the resin sets.

Another adhesive that can be specially recommended for unglazed ware is the resorcinol-formaldehyde resin known as Aerodux 185.

This is a cold-setting, gap-filling adhesive resistant to boiling water; it is mixed with a hardener before being applied to the fractured surfaces. The fact that it sets in the cold is a great convenience for many types of objects; and, since it is a gap-filling cement, it has the advantage that the joints which are being fitted together need only be lightly clamped.

In the reconstruction of pots from broken fragments, it often happens that pieces are missing, and it may be desirable to fill the lacunae with plaster that has been coloured to match the pot. The procedure is as follows. If the missing portion is triangular, clean the three sides and, if the pottery is finely grained, score the edges longitudinally in order to give the plaster a key. Soften some plasticine by warming and rolling it on a glass plate, and apply a slab, a quarter inch thick, to the inside of the pot covering the missing portion, so that, when the space is filled with soft plaster, the plasticine will form a backing and reproduce the correct curvature. With narrow-necked vessels this is not possible, and the plaster must be built up from outside, little by little, to fill the space without any backing; the repair will bulge slightly on the inside where it is not seen.

Before applying plaster it is necessary to stop the suction, i.e. to treat the pottery with a liquid in order to prevent it absorbing moisture from the plaster and thus reducing its cohesion. This could be done with water, but pottery varies so much in its condition—strength, porosity, etc., particularly when it has been broken in pieces—that water is better avoided in this kind of repair work. A dilute solution of shellac is much more effective. The joint is painted, therefore, with thin bleached shellac or french polish diluted with methylated spirit.

If a coloured plaster is required for repair work, dry powder colours are added to the plaster powder before it is made up with water. These colours should be mixed well with the plaster on a glass plate, using a steel spatula. When water is added the colour will appear much darker, but on evaporation of the water the plaster will gradually recover the original hue that was established before wetting.

To mix the plaster, put a quantity of cold water in a bowl and shake the powdered plaster on to the surface until it stands as a conical heap above the level of the water. When air bubbles cease to rise, stir with a spoon until a thick cream is obtained that shows signs of becoming thicker within half a minute, when it is ready to be applied to the break. If the plaster fails to thicken quickly in the bowl, do not stir violently, but add some more plaster powder until the correct consistency is obtained before using it to repair the pot.

When the pot has been prepared and the plaster mixed, it may be filled into the gap with the aid of a spoon. Avoid imprisoning air-bubbles and continue filling the gap until the fresh plaster is every-where slightly above the surface. After a few minutes the plaster will have set to a buttery consistency and it is then an easy matter to pare it down with a plaster scraper (a metal spatula having a comb-like edge) until it is level with the surface of the pot. After half an hour or so the surface may be finished with the appropriate grade of glass-paper—o, $1\frac{1}{2}$, or 2, as the case may be. The plasticine is then removed from the back of the repair and the exposed surface of the plaster made good as required.

If, after drying, it is found that the colour of the repaired area does not match the pot, the whole area of new plaster will have to be stopped again with a thin coating of white french polish before re-touching with fresh colour. This is essential, because, if colour is applied without previous stopping, the binding medium will be sucked from the fresh colour into the body of the repair, leaving a 'watermark' stain which is difficult to remove. To prepare a matt paint for retouching pottery, the pigments—ochres, umbers, black, white, or green—should be mixed and ground either in skimmed milk or in dilute size solution.

An alternative material that is more convenient to use for the repair of pottery than plaster has been developed in the Conserva-tion Department of the Institute of Archaeology. This is referred to as A J K Dough, because it is compounded of Alvar (polyvinyl acetal), Jute, and Kaolin. To prepare this material 100 parts by weight of Alvar 770 (alternatively Butvar B98, polyvinyl butyral can be

used) are stirred into a mixed solvent of acetone (120 parts), industrial methylated spirit (50 parts), and amyl acetate (40 parts) and left
for 24 hours in a closed container until the resin has dissolved. To this
solution 100 parts by weight of xylene are added, followed by 60
parts of water, and the whole is well stirred to form a stable emulsion.
Then a mixture of two dry measures of jute flock and one dry
measure of kaolin are stirred in with a wooden spoon until sufficient
has been added so that the mixture becomes too stiff to stir. At this
point it is turned out into a large tray and more of the jute and
kaolin mixture is kneaded in until the material is soft but no longer
sticky. The material should be stored in wide-necked bottles with
good-fitting stoppers to prevent loss of solvent; it can also be obtained
commercially under the trade name Fibrenyl Dough.

For repairing lacunae in pottery the dough is moulded into shape
and allowed to dry, when it becomes hard as the solvent evaporates.
If the piece of pottery is thick, it is convenient to build up the repair
with thin layers of the dough, allowing each to dry before applying
the next, as this procedure reduces the amount of over-all shrinkage.
An alternative procedure is to roll out the fresh dough on silicone-
coated paper, or on a board dusted with talc, to a sheet not more than
0.5 cm. in thickness; this is then scored with a spatula to form strips
about 0.75 cm. wide which can be broken apart when the sheet has
dried. For use in repair these pieces are moistened slightly with
industrial methylated spirit or warmed on a hotplate so that they
become pliable and can be filled into the lacunae or bent to the shape
of the vessel. A framework is built up, the ends of the strips being
secured to the pottery with nitrocellulose adhesive, and when this
framework has dried the lacuna can be built up by pressing in
pieces of the fresh soft dough to form the wall of the vessel, the surface being smoothed with a spatula dipped in acetone or methylated
spirit. When completely dry the surface can be finished with fine-
grade sandpaper and painted as desired. The final appearance is very
similar to that of unglazed ware.

XVI

GLASS

GLASS results from the fusion of acidic and basic oxides, the chief acidic oxides being silica and boric oxide, and the chief basic oxides soda, potash, lime, alumina, litharge, and magnesia. When selected mixtures of these oxides are fused at a high temperature, a clear liquid is obtained, which, on cooling, becomes a transparent amorphous solid. Thus, soda–lime glass is made by fusing soda, lime, and clean sand (= silica) in a refractory crucible. This is the commonest type of glass.

The physical properties of glass may be varied according to the nature and proportions of its constituent silicates. For example, potash–lime glass (crown glass) has a high fusion point. Potash–lead glass (flint glass) is softer and more easily cut and it has, moreover, a high refractive index, and is sometimes referred to as 'crystal'.

In the molten condition, glass is an excellent solvent for metallic oxides, and some, such as cobalt oxide, copper oxide, and iron oxide, are used to give the glass characteristic colours while retaining transparency; others, such as tin and antimony oxides, cause opacity and impart to the glass a white appearance. Opacity can also result from the use of larger quantities of colouring oxides.

Until the seventeenth century, almost all glass was composed of silica, lime, and soda or potash. The glass-makers themselves thought of their material as being made from only two constituents. Thus, Merret in his translation and commentary of Neri's famous book[1] defines glass as 'a concrete of salt and sand or stones'. The salt, at least in Europe, was derived from plant ashes, but plant ashes contain much besides the alkali salts; they contain lime, alumina, etc.,

[1] Neri, A., *L'Arte Vetraria*, published in Florence, 1612, translated with commentary by C. Merret in 1662.

and because of this a stable glass was produced. This early glass generally had a greenish colour owing to the presence of iron oxide, and when these early glass-makers tried to produce a colourless glass, they tended to over-purify the salts and were also tempted to add too high a proportion of salt to sand so as to lower the fusion point of the glass and make it easier to work. This was known to Merret, because in his commentary on the preface in Neri's book the following passage occurs: 'furthermore, in the finest Glasses, wherein the salt is most purified, and in a greater proportion of salt to the sand, you shall find that such Glasses standing long in subterraneous and moist places will fall to pieces, the union of the salt and sand decaying'. Unfortunately it may happen that glass objects are sometimes exposed in museums to conditions similar to those found in 'subterraneous and moist places' that can lead to their gradual deterioration.

In an interesting paper on the composition and working properties of ancient glasses, Matson[1] states that 'The eutectic mixture in the soda–lime–silica system is, approximately, silica 73 per cent, lime 5 per cent, soda 22 per cent', and he advocates using this as a yard-stick in studying analyses of ancient glasses, some of which he quotes. By studying the complete analysis, he shows that one can hazard a guess at the working properties of the glass, e.g. excess of silica makes the glass very difficult to work. But what is more important from the point of view of conservation, the analysis reflects also upon the stability of the glass. It is not only the presence of certain ingredients but the proportions in which they are present that determine the stability of the material; excess of the alkali oxides and a deficiency of the alkaline earth oxides tends to produce a glass that is especially susceptible to attack by moisture under museum conditions.

Deterioration of glass

Although glass may normally be regarded as a stable material under normal museum conditions, there are certain types of glass that are prone to lose their transparency and to become cloudy or crizzled—a phenomenon that is often referred to as 'glass disease'.

[1] Matson, F. R., *J. Chemical Education*, 1951, **28**, p. 82.

This effect can be understood in terms of the general structure of glass; this consists of an irregular three-dimensional network of negatively charged polysilicate ions within which are interdispersed positively charged ions of sodium, potassium, calcium, magnesium, and aluminium that neutralize the negative charges of the poly-silicate network. If the proportion of the calcium, magnesium, and aluminium ions is reduced below a certain limit, the mobility of the sodium and potassium is increased so that the resultant glass becomes susceptible to attack by atmospheric moisture. This means, in effect, that when a layer of moisture forms on such glass, the mobile sodium and potassium ions tend to migrate from the glass, being replaced by hydrogen ions from the water. The result is that a film of sodium and potassium hydroxide forms on the surface of the glass, which immediately reacts with atmospheric carbon dioxide to produce sodium and potassium carbonates. This film is very hygroscopic and rapidly absorbs more moisture from the air producing droplets of liquid. Glass in this condition is referred to as 'weeping' or 'sweating' glass. This is the first stage in 'glass disease', and if it is left untreated, the insidious process of disintegration will continue, until eventually the glass becomes opaque and so badly crizzled that tiny scales of glass flake off when the glass is handled (Pl. 43).

The immediate treatment for 'weeping' glass is as follows: after washing the glass thoroughly in running tap water, soak it for a short time in distilled water, then pass the glass through two baths of alcohol and allow to dry quickly. This treatment will retard the disintegration and also improve the appearance of the glass because dirt which tends to adhere to the sticky surface of 'weeping' glass will be removed. However, it does not offer any protection against the reoccurrence of 'sweating' or 'weeping', if the objects are again exposed to a moist atmosphere. Some conservators have suggested the use of organic lacquers to act as protective film, and Hedvall et al.[1] have described a special technique in which the glass object is im-pregnated under vacuum with a polymethacrylate lacquer. It may

[1] Hedvall, J. A., Jagitsch, R., and Olsen, G., *Chalmer's Tekniska Högskolas Handlingar*, 1951, No. 118.

well be that the application of a lacquer will delay the onset of further deterioration, but since the organic lacquers at present available are not completely impermeable to moisture vapour, there is always the danger that moisture will permeate the lacquer and cause deterioration of the glass. There must therefore be some doubt as to whether the application of an organic lacquer can be regarded as a permanent cure.

The safest way of dealing with potentially unstable 'weeping' glass objects is to ensure that they are kept under dry conditions. In practice this means that the relative humidity in the exhibition case or storage cupboard must be kept below 42 per cent. This figure is chosen because it represents the critical point at which potassium carbonate becomes moist owing to absorption of moisture vapour, i.e. when the glass would start to 'sweat' or 'weep'. The construction of special storage cases as used in the British Museum has been described by Organ;[1] in these the relative humidity is maintained using silica gel as a desiccant and a small fan is installed at the top of the case to ensure adequate air circulation. When it is only necessary to deal with individual glass objects on exhibition, it will be sufficient to put a supply of silica gel in the exhibition case; if the case is relatively air-tight and if an adequate amount of silica gel is used, it should only be necessary to change the silica gel about once every six months (Pl. 44).

Glass is a material that can undergo subtle physical changes in the normal process of ageing, and for this reason the reaction of ancient glass to any applied stress is difficult to predict. One such stress that must be taken into account in the treatment of glass is the effect of heat. It may be found that one glass may withstand heating up to quite a high temperature if the heating is carried out gradually, whereas another glass, which may appear to be in a sound condition, can react in a disastrous manner when heated—even under carefully controlled conditions. An example of the dangers inherent in the heating of museum glass objects arose in connection with experiments carried out in the British Museum Research Laboratory[2] some

[1] Organ, R. M., *Museums J.*, 1957, **56**, p. 265.
[2] Bimson, M., and Werner, A. E. A., *J. Glass Studies*, 1964, **6**, p. 148.

years ago to test the efficacy of a silicone preparation recommended
for applying to glass to form a water-repellent surface coating, which
involved the heating of the glass. A wheel-cut seventeenth-century
goblet cover, which appeared to the naked eye to be in a sound
condition, was treated with this silicone preparation, placed in a
hot-air oven, and heated very slowly over a period of eight hours
to 90 °C. The result of this relatively mild heat treatment was disastrous, as can be seen from Pl. 45 which shows the crizzled appearance
of the cover compared with the perfectly transparent appearance of
the broken-off knob which had been retained as a control and had
not been heated. The explanation of this unexpected behaviour
became apparent when the knob was examined under the microscope.
It was found that numerous very fine hair cracks were present showing that, although the knob appeared to the naked eye to be in a
sound condition, incipient deterioration of the glass had already
started. It may be reasonably assumed that the cover itself was also in
the same state—apparently sound, but, in reality, potentially unstable
to thermal treatment.

This warning about the possible danger of heating museum glass
objects is of some importance, because techniques have been recently
described in the literature for the treatment of glass which involve
heating at some stage. Thus Schröder and Kaufmann[1] describe a new
method for the application of an inorganic protective film to ancient
weathered glass objects which necessitates heating the objects to
250 °C., and Smith[2] says that the coloured spot, often produced
when a glass is analysed by the X-ray fluorescence technique, can
be eliminated by moderate heat. In this connection it is also interesting to consider a recent publication[3] dealing with a method for the
conservation of stained glass in which the glass is heated to a temperature of 225–35 °C. at one stage during the impregnation with a

[1] Schröder, H., and Kaufmann, R., *Beiträge zur angewandten Glasforschung*, 1959, p. 355.

[2] Smith, R. W., in *Science and Archaeology*, eds. D. Brothwell and E. Higgs, Thames &
Hudson, London, 2nd edn. 1969, p. 617.

[3] Domaslowski, W., and Kwiatkowski, E., *Annales du 2ᵉ Congrès des Journées Inter-
nationales du Verre*, Liège, 1962, pp. 137–57.

synthetic resin. The authors were aware of the fact that certain glasses might not be able to withstand this temperature. They therefore recommended that the technique of X-ray diffraction analysis should be used to determine if a particular glass was potentially unstable owing to incipient crystallization. The validity of this test seems rather doubtful. The presence of an X-ray diffraction pattern indicating crystallization might well be a sign of instability in the glass, but the real question is whether the absence of such a pattern would mean that a glass would withstand heating. To test this, a sample of glass was taken from the surface of the knob and examined by X-ray diffraction. There was no evidence of any pattern indicating incipient crystallization. It is thus clear that it is the actual physical condition of a glass, i.e. the presence of very fine cracks, which is the vital factor in determining whether or not a glass might withstand heating.

Repairing glass

Broken glass objects are difficult to repair successfully. A nitro-cellulose adhesive such as Durofix or H.M.G. is probably the most useful general-purpose adhesive, and another good one can be made by dissolving about 20 gm. of Perspex in 195 ml. of ethylene dichloride to which 5 ml. of glacial acetic acid are added. Epoxy resins have been suggested for the repair of glass, because a strong, permanent bond can be formed, but since this adhesive is immune to solvent action, and a faulty joint can only be broken by heating to soften the adhesive, its use should be confined to the repair of modern glass. The danger of heating ancient glass has already been referred to (p. 347), and Perrot[1] has drawn attention to the danger of using epoxy resins for the repair of glass objects. A seventeenth-century goblet was incorrectly repaired with an epoxy resin; when it was heated very gradually to a temperature of about 150 °C. to soften the adhesive, the originally clear glass became entirely crizzled.

When a glass object is in a fragmentary state, the pieces can be mounted on Perspex cut to appropriate sizes and fashioned into

[1] Perrot, P., *J. of Glass Studies*, 1964, **6**, p. 149.

45. LID AND KNOB OF GLASS GOBLET

Knob shows original transparency of the glass and lid shows the crizzling
produced by heating the glass

46. CONTROL EQUIPMENT FOR ELECTROLYTIC REDUCTION

This is arranged on top of fume hood from which wires for conducting the current pass
down to sink in which the reduction is carried out

shape, so that the object is suitable for exhibition. This technique requires considerable dexterity, but very pleasing results can be achieved.

Wihr[1] has described an elegant technique for the restoration and consolidation of ancient glass objects in a fragmentary condition using the polymethacrylate resin called Technovit. This material can be used as an adhesive and also for making good missing pieces, in a manner similar to that described for the repair of bronzes (p. 262). This material has also been used by Wihr for making replicas of glass objects.

Enamels

An enamel is a lead glass to which some metallic oxide has been added to colour it or make it opaque. It is applied thinly to a metal base, usually of gold or silver. When glass is melted on metal, as in the manufacture of enamels, the difference in the degree of contraction on cooling between the glass and the metal is considerable, and sometimes a state of strain is set up between the two. In order to equalize the strains, the enamel is sometimes applied all over the back of the metal as well as the front.

That the strains are not always equalized is evident from a singular occurrence that took place in the Wallace Collection in 1929.[2]

An eighteenth-century enamelled snuff-box on exhibition in the museum suddenly disintegrated, scattering glass powder throughout the case. When the powder was examined in the British Museum Research Laboratory the particles were shown to be of the same shape as those formed by the bursting of Prince Rupert drops, that is, rounded and not splintery. These drops, which have been known for centuries, are pear-shaped blobs of glass made by pouring molten glass into water. Though apparently quite stable, and so strong that they can even be hit at the thick end with a hammer without breaking, they are, in fact, under great internal strain, and have the astonishing property of flying to powder when the smallest fragment is broken

---

[1] Wihr, R., *Deutsche Kunst- und Denkmalpflege*, 1957, **2**, p. 138.
[2] Camp, S. J., *Art Work*, 1930, **21**, p. 47.

from the fine glass filament forming the stem of the pear. When made in the form of a phial it suffices to drop a tiny grain of sand inside for the glass to fall in two, and it is likely that some such simple trigger action caused the enamel in the Wallace Collection to 'explode'.

Sometimes strain causes an enamel to become fractured and detached from the base, and when this happens the only thing to do is to attempt consolidation by flooding the area with dilute lacquer so that it seeps through the cracks. When it has completely set, the excess of lacquer may be removed. In the coarser type of enamel work it is sometimes possible to execute repairs in coloured cellulose paints or varnishes that have been suitably dyed.

A curious effect occasionally to be observed is that of fungus apparently growing on one specific colour—say on a translucent crimson. On closer inspection it is found that the nutrient material is gelatine, which has been used to reinforce the weak areas of the enamelling and possibly to act as a base for retouching with pigment. The treatment in this case is to remove the gelatine carefully with a small swab of cotton-wool moistened with warm water, sterilize the area with Santobrite or Topanews (2 per cent), and after drying consolidate with lacquer tinted as required.

The opaque red glass of sealing-wax colour, often referred to as cuprous enamel, which was of universal use in the Bronze Age for the decoration of metal, is often found to be oxidized to a green colour. The earliest examples that have come to the British Museum Research Laboratory are from a glass furnace excavated at Nimrûd (650 B.C.) and are in the form of lenticular cakes from the crucible, some 20 cm. in diameter, and up to 5 cm. in their greatest thickness. These are invariably green on the surface, and are like corroded bronze in appearance. The green layer is porous and extends to a depth of almost 1·5 mm., the interior being apparently in a perfect state of preservation, rich purplish-red, opaque, and having a characteristic glassy fracture. Unfortunately, in dealing with inlays of this red glass, the only means of revealing the red colour is to grind or scrape away the superficial green layer. This treatment is by no means always practicable, but has been successfully carried out in the case of a number of Saxon hanging bowls decorated with escutcheons in which this red glass was used for enamelling. The removal of the green film enhanced the appearance of the enamel considerably.

APPENDIXES

I. STRENGTH OF SOLUTIONS

1. *Acids and alkalis*. Concentrated acids and alkalis in liquid form are sold by specific gravity as they are not necessarily of 100 per cent strength, thus:

	Sp. Gr.
Sulphuric acid	1·84
Nitric acid	1·42
Hydrochloric acid	1·18
Ammonia	0·88

The convention adopted in this book, in preparing dilute solutions, is to assume that the commercial chemical is 100 per cent and dilute accordingly. Thus,

> 10 per cent sulphuric acid is made by dissolving 100 ml. of sulphuric acid (1·84) in 1 litre of distilled water.
> 50 per cent ammonia is made by mixing equal volumes of ammonia (0·88) and distilled water.

2. *Hydrogen peroxide*. The strength of a hydrogen peroxide solution is indicated by the number of volumes representing the amount of oxygen gas produced by the decomposition of one volume of solution. It is available commercially as follows:

> '100 volumes' = approx. 30 per cent w/v hydrogen peroxide, some-times called Perhydrol.
> '20 volumes' = approx. 6 per cent w/v hydrogen peroxide.
> '10 volumes' = approx. 3 per cent w/v hydrogen peroxide.

These solutions are supplied in coloured bottles and should be stored in a cool place protected from light.

II. DANGEROUS CHEMICALS

ALTHOUGH many chemicals may be regarded as potentially dangerous, special care is needed when using the following:

(1) *Concentrated sulphuric acid*

This can cause a serious burn if brought in contact with the skin. In preparing dilute solutions of sulphuric acid the concentrated acid should always be added *slowly* to the water with continuous stirring to dissipate the large amount of heat evolved. *Never* add water to the concentrated acid.

(2) *Caustic soda*

The solid should not be allowed to come in contact with the skin. In preparing solutions of caustic soda there is a considerable evolution of heat which may cause a thick glass vessel to crack. Such solutions are therefore best made by slowly adding the solid (with care to prevent splashing) to water contained in a porcelain dish or an iron or stainless steel vessel standing in a sink.

(3) *Concentrated nitric acid*

Strongly corrosive and should not be allowed to come in contact with the skin, which it stains a deep yellow.

(4) *Concentrated hydrochloric acid*

Care should be taken when opening a bottle of this acid, as fumes are immediately evolved which will cause pain if they come in contact with the eyes.

(5) *Formic acid. Carbolic acid (Phenol)*

Powerful skin irritants.

(6) *Concentrated ammonia*

Care should be taken when opening a bottle of concentrated ammonia; the stopper may fly off due to pressure. The bottle should be kept in a cool place and must never be allowed to remain in the sun.

356

(7) *Hydrogen peroxide '100 vols.'. Perhydrol*

This must be kept in a cool place as great pressure may be set up in the bottle if left in the sun or near a source of heat.

(8) *Diethyl ether (B.P. 34·6 °C.)*

Highly volatile and inflammable. Forms explosive mixtures with air.

(9) *Carbon disulphide (B.P. 46 °C.)*

Highly volatile and inflammable. Poisonous. Forms explosive mixtures with air.

N.B. A foam fire extinguisher should be at hand in any room where diethyl ether or carbon disulphide is used.

FIRST AID

(1) *Acid burns.* Flood the affected area with water and then wash with a dilute solution of sodium bicarbonate.

(2) *Caustic soda burns.* Flood the affected area with water and then wash with very dilute acid, e.g. vinegar.

III. TOXICITY OF ORGANIC SOLVENTS

CONTINUED exposure to an atmosphere contaminated with the vapour of organic solvents may constitute a serious health hazard, so it is necessary for those using such solvents in conservation to learn to appreciate their relative toxicities, so that simple appropriate precautions can be taken. Good general ventilation is essential, and a local aspirator provided with a flexible trunking system is desirable both for safety and comfort; also cotton-wool swabs used for cleaning should not be left lying about and bottles containing solvents should be kept stoppered.

The following table lists some of the commoner organic solvents[1] used in conservation, the relative toxicity being suggested by the figures given in parts per million (p.p.m.) that are considered a lethal concentration on prolonged exposure. Any figure below 100 suggests conditions that are bad and below 25 really dangerous when fumes are inhaled for a considerable time. As the toxic ratings vary with individual susceptibility and the time of exposure they are to be taken as an indication only. It should be borne in mind that prolonged exposure to small concentrations may be as dangerous as shorter exposure to greater concentrations and that not all poisonous fumes are irritating or have a characteristic odour that would serve as a warning. It is wise, therefore, to play safe.

[1] Adapted from N. Irving Sax, *Dangerous Properties of Industrial Materials* (Reinhold N.Y.; Chapman & Hall Ltd., London), and C. Marsden, *Solvents Guide* (Cleaver Hume Ltd., London).

Solvent	Boiling point (°C.)	Flash point (°C.)	Vapour toxicity[1] (p.p.m.)
Acetone	56	—19	600
Amyl acetate	149	31	200
Benzene	80	—11	25
n-Butylamine	78	—6	5
Carbon disulphide	46	—30	20
Carbon tetrachloride	77	no inf.	10
Chloroform	61	no inf.	50
Dimethyl formamide	153	67	20
Ether (diethyl)	35	—41	400
Ethyl acetate	77	7	400
Ethyl alcohol (ethanol)	78·5	16	1000
Glycerol	290	175	—
Methyl alcohol (methanol)	65	18	200
Methyl cellosolve (ethylene glycol monomethyl ether)	125	41	slight
Methyl ethyl ketone (butanone)	80	—6	200
Morpholine	129	43	moderate
Petroleum solvents[2]	155–200	34–8	500
Pyridine	115	20	5
Toluene	110·5	4	200
Trichloroethylene	87	no inf.	100
Xylene (coml.)	138–44	75–85	200

[1] Parts of vapour per million parts of air by volume at 25° C. and 760 mm. pressure.

[2] Distillation fractions from crude oil going under various names depending on boiling range and source, e.g. Petroleum Ethers, Stoddard Solvent, Ligroin, White Spirit, etc. (See Appendix IV.)

IV. PETROLEUM AND ALCOHOL SOLVENTS

THE following notes are intended to dispel any confusion that may arise from differences in the nomenclature of these solvents in use in the United Kingdom and America.

A. *Petroleum solvents*

These are distillation fractions from crude petroleum, and consist of a mixture of aliphatic and aromatic hydrocarbons. Composition varies with the original source of the petroleum and, according to boiling range, the following categories are recognized:

1. Petroleum spirits of B.P. 40/60 °C., 60/80 °C., and 80/100 °C.
2. Petrol (U.K.) and gasoline (U.S.A.): B.P. 60/120 °C.
3. White spirit (U.K.): B.P. 155/210 °C., and Stoddard Solvent (U.S.A.): B.P. 177/210 °C. These are often referred to as 'turpentine substitutes'.
4. Kerosine and paraffin oil: B.P. 160/250 °C.
5. Odourless distillate: B.P. 190/265 °C.

The solvent action of petroleum solvents is determined not only by the boiling-point range but also by the percentage of aromatic hydrocarbons present.

B. *Alcohol solvents*

The British Pharmacopeia lists dehydrated alcohol (ethanol or absolute alcohol), alcohol 95 per cent, and alcohol 90 per cent (rectified spirit) in addition to industrial methylated spirit which contains one volume of wood naphtha in nineteen volumes of alcohol 95 per cent. All of these are suitable for use as solvents in conservation, but denatured alcohol (i.e. alcohol made unfit for human consumption by the addition of wood alcohol and pyridine plus a purple dyestuff) is not suitable.

In U.S.A. there are many formulations for denatured alcohol involving a variety of additions. Specially denatured alcohol (S.D.A.) is equivalent to industrial methylated spirit, but the completely denatured alcohol (C.D.A.) is not suitable for use as a solvent in conservation.

V. CONVERSION FACTORS FOR IMPERIAL, U.S.A., AND METRIC FLUID MEASURES

Imperial	U.S.A.	Metric
1 fluid ounce	0·96 fluid ounce	28·4 ml.
1·04 fluid ounce	1 fluid ounce	29·6 ml.
1 pint	1·20 pint	568·25 ml.
0·83 pint	1 pint	473·1 ml.
1 gallon	1·2 gallon	4·54 litre
0·83 gallon	1 gallon	3·78 litre
35·20 fluid ounce	33·81 fluid ounce	1 litre
1·76 pint	2·1 pint	1 litre
0·22 gallon	0·265 gallon	1 litre

N.B. 1 Imperial pint contains 20 fluid ounces.
    1 Pint (U.S.A.) contains 16 fluid ounces.

VI. PEARSON'S SQUARE FOR SIMPLIFYING DILUTION CALCULATIONS

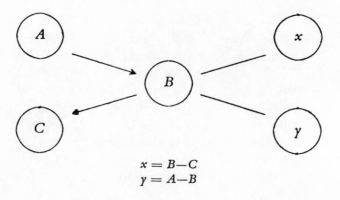

$$x = B-C$$
$$y = A-B$$

Examples:

(1) How much water has to be added to a 12 per cent solution to make a 5 per cent solution?

$$\text{Let } A = 12 \text{ per cent}$$
$$B = 5 \text{ per cent}$$
$$C = 0 \text{ per cent (water)}$$

Then $x = B{-}C = 5{-}0 = 5$ parts of the 12 per cent solution (A)
$y = A{-}B = 12{-}5 = 7$ parts of water (C)

Answer: Mix 5 parts of the 12 per cent solution with 7 parts of water

(2) How much of a 45 per cent solution has to be added to a 17 per cent solution to obtain a 30 per cent solution?

$$\text{Let } A = 45 \text{ per cent}$$
$$B = 30 \text{ per cent}$$
$$C = 17 \text{ per cent}$$

Then $x = B{-}C = 30{-}17 = 13$ parts of the 45 per cent solution (A)
$y = A{-}B = 45{-}30 = 15$ parts of the 17 per cent solution (C)

Answer: Mix 13 parts of the 45 per cent solution with 15 parts of the 17 per cent solution.

VII. THERMOMETRIC EQUIVALENTS

Centigrade	Fahrenheit	Centigrade	Fahrenheit	Centigrade	Fahrenheit
100 °C.	212 °F.	66 °C.	150·8 °F.	32 °C.	89·6 °F.
99	210·2	65	149	31	87·8
98	208·4	64	147·2	30	86
97	206·6	63	145·4	29	84·2
96	204·8	62	143·6	28	82·4
95	203	61	141·8	27	80·6
94	201·2	60	140	26	78·8
93	199·4	59	138·2	25	77
92	197·6	58	136·4	24	75·2
91	195·8	57	134·6	23	73·4
90	194	56	132·8	22	71·6
89	192·2	55	131	21	69·8
88	190·4	54	129·2	20	68
87	188·6	53	127·4	19	66·2
86	186·8	52	125·6	18	64·4
85	185	51	123·8	17	62·6
84	183·2	50	122	16	60·8
83	181·4	49	120·2	15	59
82	179·6	48	118·4	14	57·2
81	177·8	47	116·6	13	55·4
80	176	46	114·8	12	53·6
79	174·2	45	113	11	51·8
78	172·4	44	111·2	10	50
77	170·6	43	109·4	9	48·2
76	168·8	42	107·6	8	46·4
75	167	41	105·8	7	44·6
74	165·2	40	104	6	42·8
73	163·4	39	102·2	5	41
72	161·6	38	100·4	4	39·2
71	159·8	37	98·6	3	37·4
70	158	36	96·8	2	35·6
69	156·2	35	95	1	33·8
68	154·4	34	93·2	0	32
67	152·6	33	91·4		

VIII. ACIDITY, NEUTRALITY, ALKALINITY

An acid may be defined as a substance which forms hydrogen ions when dissolved in water, and an alkali as a substance which forms hydroxyl ions when dissolved in water. Acids and alkalis are capable of neutralizing one another to form salts.

When dealing with very small concentrations of acids and alkalis it is cumbersome to express the actual concentrations of hydrogen and hydroxyl ions in terms of weight per volume. A convenient method was proposed in 1909 by Sörensen who introduced the hydrogen ion exponent, commonly known as pH. The relationship between pH and hydrogen ion concentration is shown in the following nomograph:

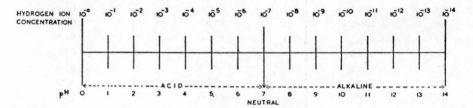

The advantage of the system is that very small concentrations of acid or alkali can be expressed as whole numbers. A solution in which the hydrogen and hydroxyl ion concentrations are equal is an exactly neutral solution and the pH = 7. In an acid solution the hydrogen ion concentration exceeds that of the hydroxyl ion and the pH is less than 7, whilst in an alkaline solution the reverse is the case and the pH is greater than 7.

Certain substances known as indicators show characteristic colour changes depending upon the pH of the solution to which they are added. Litmus, for example, is red in acid and blue in presence of alkalis. Its pH range is 5·0–8·0. A more precise estimation of the acidity or alkalinity of a solution may be made by adding to it a few drops of Universal Indicator[1]

[1] Indicators of this type are B.D.H. Universal Indicator obtainable from B.D.H. Chemicals Ltd., Poole, Dorset, and B.T.L. Universal Indicator obtainable from Messrs. Hopkin & Williams Ltd., P.O. Box 1, Romford RM1 1HA, Essex.

which shows graded colour changes from red to violet throughout the pH range as follows:

Colour of indicator	Nature of solution	pH value
Red	*Very acid*	3–4
Orange	Moderately acid	5–5·5
Yellow	Slightly acid	6–6·5
Greenish-yellow	*Neutral*	7–7·5
Green	Slightly alkaline	8
Bluish-green	Moderately alkaline	8·5
Blue	*Very alkaline*	9·5
Violet	Intensely alkaline	10–12

IX. METHODS OF RECORDING
RELATIVE HUMIDITY

TEMPERATURE and relative humidity readings are taken with a thermometer and hygrometer respectively. Several types of hygrometer are available,[1] the most convenient being the sling or whirling hygrometer or psychrometer which consists of wet- and dry-bulb thermometers fixed side by side on a frame for swinging, the wet bulb being kept damp by a wick dipping into a reservoir containing distilled water. To use the instrument it is held well away from the body and is whirled vigorously for at least a minute, readings on the wet-bulb and dry-bulb thermometers being taken immediately. Further observations should be taken till constant readings are obtained. The wet bulb will generally record a temperature lower than the dry one. This difference represents the depression in degrees resulting from evaporation of water, and from this depression, taken in conjunction with the temperature of the dry bulb, it is possible to determine the relative humidity by consulting hygrometric or psychrometric tables.[2]

The sling hygrometer has the advantage that it may be used in different parts of the room, and it will reveal the existence of any humidity gradient in the atmosphere, so that the effect of ventilation near doors and windows can be readily assessed. When daily readings are to be taken in a room, the instrument must be used in the same places, under the same conditions, and at the same time of day if results are to be comparable. When mildew is detected in a cupboard or among books, it is obvious that readings taken at the door or near a window, where the results would be influenced by ventilation, would not be a true indication of the atmospheric conditions in the danger area. Readings should be taken at the point where damp is suspected. In making a thorough assessment, conditions at night should not be neglected because in a closed room the relative humidity of the atmosphere increases with fall of temperature. The effect is most

[1] National Physical Laboratory, *Measurement of Humidity*, 1953.
[2] *Hygrometric Tables*, on Ivorine Cards, Negretti & Zambra Ltd., London; *Psychrometric Tables*, Marvin, C. F., U.S. Weather Bureau, 1941.

striking when heating appliances are of a type that become suddenly cold, such as steam radiators or electric fires.

Self-recording types of hygrometer are essential when it is necessary to obtain a continuous record. In the usual recording hygrometer an ink line is drawn by a pen on a paper cylinder which is revolved by clockwork. The up-and-down movements of the pen are controlled by the contraction and expansion of some moisture-sensitive substance, e.g. strands of hair, stretched within the instrument. By this means it is possible to obtain a record of the relative humidity as a graph on a time scale. Readings from self-recording hygrometers may be misleading, however, unless such instruments are calibrated by a periodic check with the whirling hygrometer (the more reliable instrument), and the relative humidity graph should be annotated at the time of observation. In this way it is possible to observe the amount of any slight error on the chart which may arise from slowness of response due to friction, etc., and the correction is taken into account in interpreting the records.

Dial forms of non-recording paper hygrometer[1] have the merit of compactness and are convenient for use in restricted spaces, but suffer like the self-recording types from a tendency towards slow response to rapid changes in the moisture content of the air.

[1] Obtainable from Pastorelli & Rapkin, Ltd., 287 Green Lanes, Farmers Green, London N. 13.

X. PREPARATION AND USE OF FLOUR PASTE

ADHESIVES for paper should be free from staining material, harmful preservatives and any acidic ingredients. Cheap office pastes and adhesives supplied for hanging wall-paper should be avoided as well as all preparations of doubtful or unknown composition.

For general work there is nothing to surpass freshly prepared flour paste (bookbinder's paste), as it is easy to make and to apply and has excellent adhesive properties. It is made from ordinary (not self-raising) flour and water in the following proportions:

White flour (wheat)	500 grams
Water	2·5 litres

Mix the flour with a little of the water in an aluminium or enamel pan, the lumps being broken up with the hand to form a smooth cream. Boil the remainder of the water separately and add it to the cream, stirring continuously. The paste is now heated, not directly, but by standing the pan in a container of water kept boiling (double pan). It should be stirred meantime and will soon thicken. After about ten minutes it may be decanted into a suitable vessel, and to prevent a crust forming as it cools place a sheet of paper on the surface of the paste and pour a little water above the paper. The mixture as prepared is too thick for general use: small quantities should be removed to a pasting dish and thinned with water as required. The paste keeps well for a few days in cool surroundings but should be discarded on the first sign of souring.

If it is desired to keep the paste for as long as a week, about 10 ml. of formalin may be stirred into the mixture while fresh, but for ordinary use no other form of preservative can be recommended. Alum is often present as an ingredient in formulas for paste; it hardens the adhesive so that it tends to become insoluble in water, but alum has been shown to be harmful as it makes the paper acid (see p. 56). For use in the tropics, however, the paste must contain a substance that will inhibit the growth of mould and render it unattractive to insects, and for this purpose poisonous material is introduced. Suitable formulas have been suggested containing small quantities of phenyl mercuric acetate or phenyl mercuric borate, say, about half a gram for every 2·5 litres of paste.

In applying paste it should be spread evenly and thinly so that it will dry quickly, and there should never be so much water present as to cause the paper to stretch appreciably. The paste may be applied with a brush or with an ivory or bone paper-knife. After pasting, the paper should be dried in the press or under a sheet of heavy plate glass.

XI. SILICA GEL

SILICA gel is an effective drying agent which has the considerable advantage that it does not become moist to the touch in use, nor does it cause staining; in fact the appearance of the material remains unchanged. Since it is essential to have some means of telling when it is 'spent' and no longer able to absorb moisture, it is tinted during manufacture with cobaltous salts which are deep blue in the dry condition, but become pink when silica gel has absorbed moisture. When silica gel has assumed a pink colour, it can be readily reconditioned by heating in an oven to *c.* 130 °C. until it regains its original deep-blue colour. This cycle of reheating can be repeated indefinitely.

XII. POTASSIUM LACTATE SOLUTION

POTASSIUM LACTATE is available from chemical suppliers as a 50 per cent solution. One volume of this stock solution should be added to nine volumes of water for use. Vegetable-tanned leather that is free from any sign of chemical deterioration may be protected against the deleterious action of sulphur dioxide by spraying or sponging it with this solution on both sides of the skin. This ensures, as far as possible, that freshly tanned leather will be a durable material.

The solution should be applied to the outside of leather bindings that have been washed, in order to replace protective salts that may have been washed from the surface of the leather.

Chemical decay, when once started, cannot be arrested by applying potassium lactate: the treatment is a form of protection, not a cure.

Do not store the dilute potassium lactate solution for long periods of time; it may be preserved for a limited period in a stoppered bottle by adding a little chloroform, but it is better to use the solution fresh and discard any residue.

It is unnecessary to apply lactate solution to parchment or vellum, or to alum-tawed bindings, as these are not subject to chemical deterioration by sulphur dioxide.

XIII. BRITISH MUSEUM LEATHER DRESSING

THE ingredients are:

Lanolin (anhydrous)	7 oz. or 200 gm.
Cedarwood oil	1 fluid oz. or 30 ml.
Beeswax	$\frac{1}{2}$ oz. or 15 gm.
Hexane (or petroleum ether B.P. 60–80 °C.)	11 fluid oz. or 330 ml.

These are compounded to form a yellow cream. It is highly inflammable, and no naked light must be allowed in the room during application of the preservative and for some time afterwards. It should be applied sparingly and rubbed into the leather, and two days later the surface may be polished with a soft cloth or brush.

This dressing is obtainable from Messrs. Hopkin & Williams Ltd., P.O. Box 1, Romford, RM1 1HA, Essex. A similar preparation is available under the name 'Pliantine' from Arthur Rich & Partners Ltd., 42 Mount Pleasant Drive, Belper, Derbyshire.

XIV. THE PEROXIDE TEST FOR VEGETABLE-TANNED LEATHER

THIS is an accelerated decay test, and its value lies in that it will reveal in the course of a week whether a vegetable-tanned leather is suitable for bookbinding, i.e. whether it will survive exposure to a polluted atmosphere without deterioration. It may be applied to all vegetable-tanned leathers available today, but the test would not be applicable in the case of leathers coming on the market in which the iron has been sequestered (see p. 288).

The test is carried out as follows:

A sample of leather, 15 cm. square and weighing from 2 to 6 gm., is laid on a glass plate, flesh side upwards, and evenly moistened with sulphuric acid (5 per cent) in the proportion of 1 ml. per gram of air-dried leather. The acid can conveniently be applied with a capillary pipette, and smoothed out on the leather with a glass rod. After remaining at room temperature overnight, hydrogen peroxide (10 vol. strength) is added evenly to the leather, dropwise, in the proportion of 0·6 ml. per gram of leather. It is left for twenty-four hours, and then given five further daily doses of hydrogen peroxide; this treatment will cause unsatisfactory leather to be blackened and gelatinized, but durable leather will survive, except for possible discoloration of the edges. Changes in the colour of the dye-stuffs are immaterial.

XV. MICROCRYSTALLINE POLISHING WAXES

THERE are two types, the aqueous emulsion type and the conventional solvent type, and the latter is generally preferable for application as a surface coating to antiquities and works of art.

A microcrystalline wax salve may be applied with the object of removing surface dirt, adjusting the optical quality, enhancing the appearance, or excluding moisture, and when compounded with a polythene wax as described in the following recipe it has been found to stabilize painted or varnished surfaces that are liable to bloom.

Several varieties of microcrystalline and polythene waxes are available and the gloss of the synthetic wax film can be varied by altering the grades and proportions of the waxes used.

The following basic recipe has been found to be generally satisfactory:

Cosmolloid 80 Hard (100 g.) and BASF Wax A (25 g.) are cut into small pieces and melted together, care being taken to ensure that the polythene wax is thoroughly dispersed. The molten mixture is poured quickly into white spirit (300 ml.), taking precautions against fire risk, and, while cooling, is constantly stirred so that a paste of agreeable consistency is obtained. This is stored in screw-top cosmetic jars.[1]

[It should be noted that, although the white spirit evaporates, it may have a softening action on varnish of the polycyclohexanone type. As this is not the case with petroleum ether (boiling range 80–100 °C.), the latter should be used as the diluent instead of white spirit where varnishes based on Resin AW 2 or MS 2 are to be waxed.]

The basic formula can be modified for use in the tropics as a leather dressing and it will afford protection against the attack of insects if lauryl pentachlorophenate is incorporated in a concentration of about 10 per cent.

[1] Wax made according to this recipe is available under the trade name Renaissance Wax from Picreator Enterprises Ltd., 44 Park View Gardens, London, N.W. 4.

374

XVI. SOLUBLE NYLON

THIS material is manufactured by Imperial Chemical Industries Ltd. and is available in two grades designated as DV 45 and DV 55, for which the corresponding trade names now are Calaton CA and CB.[1] The grade DV 55 (Calaton CB) is the one which is used in conservation.

Chemically, this material is N-methoxymethyl nylon and it is made by treating nylon 66 with formaldehyde. It is available as a white free-flowing granular powder containing about 25 per cent water, and it has a faint smell of formaldehyde. It is soluble in methanol and ethanol (including industrial methylated spirit and surgical spirit). Solution is best effected by pouring a weighed amount of the powder into the appropriate volume of solvent and warming gently on a water-bath with frequent stirring. The normal concentrations used are 2 per cent and 5 per cent. The solutions set to a gel when cold, and before application should be warmed to about 40 °C. until they liquify. The solutions should be kept in a tightly stoppered container to prevent loss of solvent; a bottle with a polythene stopper is the most convenient.

[1] When first used in conservation the trade name in the U.K. was Maranyl Soluble Nylon C 109/P. It should be noted also that other forms of soluble nylon are manufactured under the trade names Ultramid (Badische Anilin u-Soda Fabrik) and Zytel (Du Pont Chemical Corporation). These products are chemically different from Calaton CB, being copolymers of three different monomers, and the physical properties of the film are such that they are not suitable for purposes of conservation.

XVII. METHOD OF ADAPTING MAINS ELECTRIC SUPPLY FOR ELECTROLYTIC REDUCTION

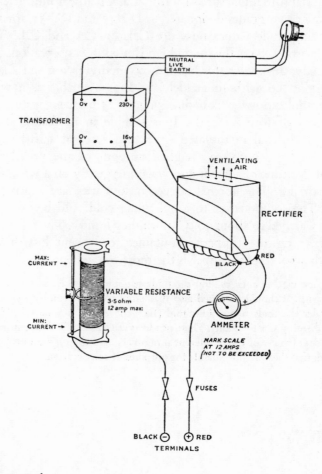

Apparatus required:

One transformer 18 v. 12 a.

One bridge-connected funnel-cooled selenium rectifier 17 v. 12 a.

One variable resistance 3·5 ohm 12 amp. max.

One ammeter 0–15 a. M.C. flush mount.

One pair of large terminals: one red, one black (Belling Lee).

One pair of Slydlock (or other) fuses.

XVIII. CIRCUIT FOR CONSOLIDATIVE
REDUCTION

CONSOLIDATIVE reduction is a slow process and may involve the treatment of many small objects, each of which requires its own supply of low current. For this reason a system has been devised so that a single source unit can supply the necessary low current simultaneously to a number of individual control units (Pl. 46). The circuits of the source unit and the control units are shown below:

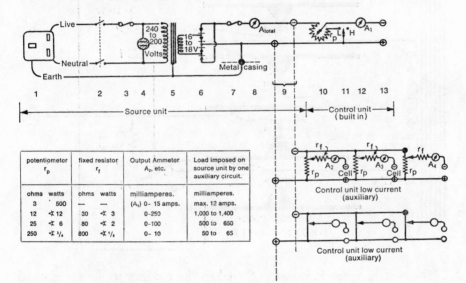

potentiometer r_p		fixed resistor r_f		Output Ammeter A_2, etc.	Load imposed on source unit by one auxiliary circuit.
ohms	watts	ohms	watts	milliamperes.	milliamperes.
3	500	—	—	(A_1) 0– 15 amps.	max. 12 amps.
12	⚡ 12	30	⚡ 3	0–250	1,000 to 1,400
25	⚡ 6	80	⚡ 2	0–100	500 to 650
250	⚡ ¾	800	⚡ ½	0– 10	50 to 65

The figures in the above diagram denote the following components:
(1) a plug-top to fit a socket-outlet; (2) a double-pole mains switch; (3) a 1 amp. fuse; (4) a neon indicator lamp; (5) double-wound step-down transformer; (6) a full-wave silicon rectifier; (7) a 15 amp. fuse; (8) ammeter reading 0–12 amp; (9) large terminals serving group of control units; (10) toroidal potentiometer, 3 ohm; (11) single-pole on-off switch, 5 amp. serving to change from low current to high current range; (12) ammeter, reading 0–12 amp. to indicate current through reduction cell

377

served by terminal 13. The values of the potentiometer r_p, the fixed resistance (resistor) r_f and the output ammeters A_2, A_3, etc., are shown in the diagram.

The source unit is basically a simple unsmoothed full-wave silicon rectifier unit designed to deliver a maximum output of 12 amps at 12 volts. The modification needed to deliver partly rectified current consists in opening two linkages in the rectifier and reconnecting these to a change-over switch associated with two small resistances, as shown below:

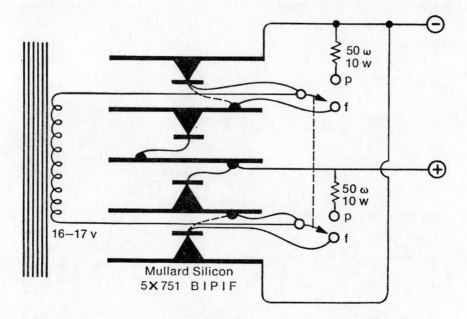

The switch, when in position f, enables the rectifier to deliver normal direct current, but, when in position p, it delivers a smaller output of partly rectified current.

Further details about sources of direct current for electrolytic treatment will be found in R. M. Organ's book (pp. 291–308), *Design for Scientific Conservation of Antiquities*, Butterworth, London, 1969.

REFERENCE MATERIAL

1. *Abstracts of the Technical Literature on Art and Archaeology*

The earliest systematic abstracts appeared in Technical Studies in the Field of Fine Arts, Fogg Art Museum, Harvard University, 1932–42 (out of print). Abstracts for the next decade are available as *Abstracts of Technical Studies in Art and Archaeology 1943–52*, compiled by R. J. Gettens and (Miss) B. M. Usilton, and published in 1955. In 1955 the International Institute for Conservation of Historic and Artistic Works began a series of *I.I.C. Abstracts*, four numbers appearing annually. This is now being published conjointly by I.I.C. and Institute of Fine Art of New York University as *Arts and Archaeology Technical Abstracts* (A.A.T.A.).

2. *Periodical Publications*

I.I.C. publishes *Studies in Conservation* from its office, 608 Grand Buildings, Trafalgar Sq., London, W.C. 2N 5HN. This journal appears quarterly. Original technical papers are also to be found in the various national museum journals and in the bulletins of scientific institutes and laboratories. The results of international studies conducted under the aegis of the International Council of Museums Conservation Committee are published in the 'Works and Publications' series of the International Centre for the Study of the Preservation and Restoration of Cultural Property, 256 Via Cavour, Rome, created in 1959 by UNESCO.

3. *Publications from Seminars and Conferences*

Special interest is attached to papers that have been contributed to seminars and conferences as these are of the nature of up-to-date monographs. Special note should be taken of all publications relating to the Conferences organized by I.I.C. which are concerned specifically with the conservation of antiquities and works of art.

SUPPLIERS OF MATERIALS

THE following list is given as a guide to sources of supply in small quantities of materials mentioned in this book. Names of the primary manufacturers will be found in the Appendix to *Conservation of Cultural Property* published by UNESCO.

Aerodux and Aerolite Araldite resins	CIBA-GEIGY (U.K.) Ltd., Duxford, Cambridge.
Arigal C.	CIBA-GEIGY Ltd., Basel, Switzerland
Alvar 770 and Butvar B98	Shawinigan Ltd., Marlow House, Lloyd's Avenue, London E.C. 3
Amberlite	B.D.H. Chemicals Ltd., Poole, Dorset
A. Wax	Bush, Beach, and Segner Bayley Ltd., 175 Tottenham Court Road, London W. 1
Attapulgite	M. W. Hardy & Co. Ltd., Gillett House, Basinghall Street, London E.C. 2
Bedacryl 122X Bedacryl L	Imperial Chemical Industries Ltd., Millbank, London S.W. 1
Bondafiller Bondaglass	Bondaglass Ltd., 158 Ravenscroft Road, Beckenham, Kent
Calaton CB (soluble nylon)	Picreator Enterprises Ltd., 44 Park View Gardens, Hendon, London N.W. 4
Carbowax	Union Carbide (U.K.) Ltd., Union Carbide House, High Street, Rickmansworth, Hertfordshire
C.D.S. (chlorine dioxide)	Lunevale Products, Low Mill, Halton, Lancashire
Cosmolloid (microcrystalline waxes)	Astor Petrochemicals Ltd., 9 Savoy Street, Strand, London W.C. 2
Crystic Resin	Scott Bader & Co. Ltd., Wollaston, Wellingborough, Northamptonshire
Delta Metal	Delta Metal Co. Ltd., 295 Tunnell Avenue, London S.E. 10

Detarol and Detarex	W. R. Grace Ltd., Elveden Road, Park Royal, London, N.W. 10
Dowicide A	Dow Chemicals Co. (U.K.) Ltd., 105 Wigmore Street, London W. 1
Ercalene and Frigilene lacquers	W. Canning & Co. Ltd., P.O. Box 288, Great Hampton Street, Birmingham 18
Fibrenyl Dough	Pelham Puppets Ltd., Marlborough, Wiltshire
Incralac	British Domolac Co. Ltd., 81 Harrow Manor Way, Abbey Wood, London S.E. 2
Jute Flock	Fibre Products (Bradford) Ltd., Castlefields, Bingley, Yorkshire
Kaolin	Hopkin & Williams Ltd., P.O. Box 1, Romford RM1 1HA, Essex
Lethane	Lennig Chemicals Ltd., Lennig House, 2 Mason's Avenue, Croydon, Surrey
Lissapol N.	Gilletts of Westminster Ltd., 590 Wandsworth Road, London S.W. 8
Modopeg	Modo Products (Chemical) Ltd., 28 Haymarket, London, S.W. 1
Mystox LP and LSE	Catomance Ltd., Bridge Road East, Welwyn Garden City, Hertfordshire
Nitromors	Wilcot (Parent) Co. Ltd., Alexandra Park, Fishponds, Bristol BS16 2BQ
Nitrocelluose adhesives	Durofix: Rawlplug Co. Ltd., Kingston upon Thames
	H.M.G.: H. Marcel Guest Ltd., Collyhurst, Manchester 9
Nubindex Nubold Bonding Agent	Nubold Development Ltd., The Mount, Crawley, Sussex
Oroglas-U.F.3	Lennig Chemicals Ltd., Lennig House, 2 Mason's Avenue, Croydon, Surrey
Plaster of Paris	British Gypsum Co. Ltd., Newark-on-Trent, Nottinghamshire
Plus Gas Fluid A.	Plus Gas Co. Ltd., Stirling Road, Acton, London W. 3

Perspex (ordinary) and Perspex VE	List of stockists from I.C.I. Plastics Division, Welwyn Garden City, Hertfordshire
Pleximon 808/809 and Primal AC-34 and C-72	Cornelius Chemical Co. Ltd., Ibex House, Minories, London E.C. 3
Santobrite	Monsanto Chemicals Ltd., Monsanto House, Victoria Street, London S.W. 1
Sepiolite	F. W. Berk & Co. Ltd., P.O. Box 56, Basing View, Basingstoke, Hampshire
Silicone rubber (Silastomer 9161)	Midland Silicones Ltd., Reading Bridge House, Reading, Berkshire
Silver Dip	S. C. Johnson & Son Ltd., Frimley Green, Camberley, Surrey
Tensol 7	G. H. Bloore, 480 Honeypot Lane, Stanmore, Middlesex
Topane	Picreator Enterprises Ltd., 44 Park View Gardens, Hendon, London N.W. 4
Technovit	Rubert & Co. Ltd., Acru Works, Cheadle, Cheshire.
Texicote VJC 555	Scott Bader & Co. Ltd., Wollaston, Wellingborough, Northamptonshire
Ultra-Violet Filter (Tube Jackets)	The Morden Co. Ltd., Harding Street, Exchange, Salford 3
Vulpex (Soap B.30)	Picreator Enterprises Ltd., 44 Park View Avenue, Hendon, London N.W. 4

Reference should also be made to the Information Sheet 'Useful Addresses for Museum Curators', obtainable from Museums Associations, 87 Charlotte Street, London WIP.2BX.

INDEX